TRADE UNION CENTURY

TRADE UNION CENTURY

Edited by
DONAL NEVIN

Published in association with
IRISH CONGRESS OF TRADE UNIONS
&
RADIO TELEFÍS ÉIREANN

MERCIER PRESS

MERCIER PRESS
PO Box 5, 5 French Church Street, Cork
16 Hume Street, Dublin 2

© The Contributors, 1994

A CIP is available for this book from the British Library

ISBN 1 85635 086 X

10 9 8 7 6 5 4 3 2 1

Printed in Ireland by Colour Books Ltd.

Contents

Introduction 7

Part I: RTE Thomas Davis Lectures

The Irish Trade Union Movement in the Nineteenth Century
Dr Fergus A. D'Arcy 9
Foundation and Early Years of the Irish TUC 1894-1912
Dr Dermot F. Keogh 19
Jim Larkin and the Risen People
James Plunkett 33
Labour and the Political Revolution
Professor Brian Farrell 42
War and Syndicalism 1914-1923
Dr Emmet O'Connor 54
The Trade Union Movement in Northern Ireland
Dr Terry Cradden 66
Decades of Dissension and Divisions 1923-1959
Donal Nevin 85
Trade Unions and the Law
Dr Mary Redmond 99
Women and Trade Unions
Professor Mary E. Daly 106
Trade Unions and Economic Development
Dr Brian Girvin 117
Industrial Relations
Professor W. K. Roche 133
Pay Bargaining: Confrontation and Consensus
Dr Niamh Hardiman 147
1894-1994: An Overview
Professor Patrick Lynch 159

Part II: Congress Centenary Miscellany

Congress Presidents' Addresses 171
Forth the Banners Go 213
Belfast in Revolt 220
'We are living in stirring times' 222
'And Nineteen Thirteen cheered from out the utter
degradation of their miseries' 225
The Gathering 225

'Christ will not be crucified any longer in Dublin
    by these men'   226
J'accuse: To the Masters of Dublin   230
Breaking the Boom of Starvation   234
The Struggle   235
September 1913   238
'Humanity long dumb has found a voice'   240
Glorious Dublin   244
Jim Larkin – his Life and Turbulent Times   247
The Lion Will Roar No More   297
Feartlaoi   298
Big Jim Crosses the City   300
Inscriptions on a Monument   303
A Literary Footnote   305
Poems, Songs and Ballads   311
Congress: An Outline History   335
Women and the Trade Union Movement   357
Trade Union Organisation   371
Profiles   376
Trade Unions and Social Policy   387
Trade Union Membership   391
Industrial Disputes 1922-1993   395
The Testimony of Josephine Soap   398
Congress Manifestoes and Documents   401
Towards a New Century   424

Appendices
Congress Membership 1894-1994   433
Congress Presidents, Treasurers and Executive Council
    Members 1894-1994   437
Northern Ireland Committee Chairpersons 1945-1994   446
Trade Union Banners   447
Bibliography: Trade Unions and Trade Unionism in Ireland   452
Main Publications of ICTU   470
Trade Union Archives and Records   472
List of Abbreviations   473

Introduction

Each year since 1953, Radio Telefís Éireann has been broadcasting series of half-hour lectures, named in honour of Thomas Davis, one of whose famous sayings, 'Educate that you may be free', inspired the series.

As part of the celebrations marking the centenary of the foundation of the Irish Trade Union Congress in 1894, RTE broadcast, between January and April 1994, a series of fourteen Thomas Davis Lectures, under the title 'Trade Union Century'.

Since then the contributors to the series have extended the texts and these revised texts constitute Part One of the centenary volume. The General Editor of the Thomas Davis Lecture Series is Michael Littleton. The consultant editor of the *Trade Union Century* series of lectures was Donal Nevin.

Part Two of this volume, Congress Centenary Miscellany, consists of writings, articles, poems and documentary and other material on trade unions and trade unionism in Ireland over the last hundred years, brought together to celebrate the Congress centenary. The Miscellany has been compiled and edited by Donal Nevin.

The publication of Part II of *Trade Union Century*, the Congress Centenary Miscellany, has been made possible through the support of the trade unions affiliated to the ICTU; the European Commission, and Power Supermarkets Ltd.

The Irish Congress of Trade Unions acknowledges with thanks and appreciation the ready co-operation of Radio Telefís Éireann in agreeing to the publication in this centenary volume, of the Thomas Davis Lecture series, *Trade Union Century*; the Director General of the Central Statistics Office for permission to include unpublished material from the 1992 Labour Force Survey; the Irish Times Ltd. for agreeing to the inclusion of extracts from reports, articles and editorials as well as poems and other material first published in *The Irish Times*.

Congress is also appreciative of the co-operation of the many publishers and authors, extracts from whose work in books, periodicals and papers have been quoted in the Congress Centenary Miscellany.

The extensive bibliography on trade unions and trade unionism in Ireland was made possible by the dedicated work over many years of Deirdre O'Connell, University College

Dublin and published in *Saothar*, the journal of the Irish Labour History Society. The contribution of *Saothar* to our knowledge of Irish trade union history will be evident from the bibliography which includes references to almost 100 articles published in the journal over the last twenty years.

The compiler and editor of the Congress Centenary Miscellany thanks the many people, friends and colleagues, who assisted in its compilation and in particular the following:

Staff of the National Library of Ireland; Hilda Breslin; Charles Callan; Peter Cassells; Tony Cerasi (Irish Times Studio); Dr Terry Cradden; R. Dardis Clarke (for permission to include Austin Clarke's poem 'Inscription for a Headstone'); Mary Clarke, Gráinne Doran and Ailish Smyth (Dublin Corporation); Mary Connolly (Public Service Executive Union); Shirley Cosgrave; Francis Devine; Oliver Donohue; Tom Dunne and Jean Kennedy (SIPTU); Donal Garvey, Deputy Director, Marie Creedon and Gerard Healy (Central Statistics Office); Des Geraghty; Tom Gillen; Dr Brian Kennedy (National Gallery of Ireland); Anthony Lennon (Irish Times Library); Professor Patrick Lynch; Máire MacDonagh; Seán MacReamoinn; Jack McGinley (Trinity College Library); Gaye Malone; Liam C. Martin; Sylvia Meehan; Teresa Moriarty; Anne Nevin; Maura Nevin; Deirdre Quinn (RDS Library); Deirdre O'Connell; Manus O'Riordan; Professor W. K. Roche; Maura Rohan (ESRI Library); John P. Swift; Muriel Todd.

Of the one hundred illustrations in the book, about three-quarters are from archival material in ICTU, SIPTU and other trade unions; the Irish Labour History Museum; trade union publications and photographs in the possession of Donal Nevin. As regards the remaining pictures, the sources are indicated in the captions with three exceptions, viz. No. 6 (from *Louie Bennett*, by R. M. Fox, 1958); No. 47 (from *Saidie Patterson, Irish Peacemaker*, by David Bleakley, 1980) and No. 53 (from *Thomas Johnson*, by J. Anthony Gaughan, 1980).

The ICTU has made its best efforts to trace any copyright holders. Some may have been inadvertently overlooked. If so, contact should be made with Congress at 19 Raglan Road, Dublin 4.

November 1994

The Irish Trade Union Movement in the Nineteenth Century

Dr Fergus A. D'Arcy

On 27 and 28 April 1894, one hundred and nineteen delegates of labour organisations assembled in the Trades Hall, Capel Street, Dublin, to found the Irish Trades Union Congress.[1] Those who did so were inheritors of a labour movement which at that time had over a hundred years of tradition behind it.

It was the eighteenth century in Ireland, as elsewhere in Europe, which saw the birth of the first trade unions.[2] It was a process in which miscarriages were frequent, deliveries difficult and the births entirely illegitimate. One can add that the mortality rates for the infant Irish trade unions of that and the next century were high, and the childhood of most unions obscure. They were not so obscure however as to leave no traces of their early days and struggles. The surviving correspondence of private individuals and public figures, the files of eighteenth and nineteenth century newspapers, and the journals of the Irish and British Houses of Parliament provide many glimpses of the illegal activities of the early Irish trade union movement and of the attempts of employers and of local and central governments to quash them.

Despite an extensive array of punitive legislation, by the time the Act of Union of 1800 had brought an end to the Irish parliament, the labour organisations of Irish workers had come to stay. Punitive legislation continued and was even intensified in the early years of the nineteenth century. The codifying legislation against trade unions passed in Britain and known as the General Combination Law of 1800 was extended to Ireland in 1803 but with stiffer penalties added. Conviction on a charge of trade union membership in Britain carried a sentence of three months imprisonment, but for Ireland this was fixed at six months.[3] This formal prohibition of trade unionism lasted until the statutes were repealed in 1824 and precisely because they were illegal organisations until then it is difficult to construct a comprehensive picture of the dimensions of labour organisations in Ireland in the early nineteenth century. Even when no longer

9

illegal, trade unions operated in an economic and political climate so hostile that for most of the century they left few formal records of their own.

For the first half of the last century most of what we know related mainly to Dublin and Cork and to a lesser extent to Limerick and Waterford, joined in the second half by Belfast. [4]

The evidence points strongly to a conclusion that for much of the century the vast majority of working people were unorganised. Labour organisation was confined almost exclusively to skilled male workers and the latter constituted not more than one-third of the male population of working age. Within that restricted category of labour only a minority in turn would have been unionised at any one time.

Nevertheless, despite these cautions the phenomenon of trade unionism was a growing one. Dublin, which in 1800 had five well-established unions, by 1825 had at least twenty and by 1859 had over forty-five. So, although only a minority of the capital's labour force was organised nevertheless there was a rapid and even impressive growth in the number of trade unions operating down to the foundation of Congress in the 1890s.

Until the middle of the 1820s these labour bodies were exclusively independent local ones. From the 1820s however British amalgamated unions began to recruit workers into Irish branches. Among the first such were the iron moulders of Dublin in 1821, and carpenters in 1827, coach makers in Cork in 1834, bookbinders in 1835, printers in Belfast in 1836 and engineers in Waterford in 1858. By the year 1870 amalgamated trade unions with British headquarters represented from a third to a half of the organised workers of Dublin. Thereafter, in Dublin, Cork and Limerick and especially in Belfast the presence of British amalgamated unions strengthened greatly until by 1894 the majority of Irish trade unionists were members of British trade unions. In 1895, for example, the affiliations to the Irish Trades Union Congress consisted of 50,000 members of British unions as against 17,000 members of Irish unions.

The growth of trade unionism in Ireland over the period 1800 to 1894 is certain enough. Whether there was a corresponding growth in their power and effectiveness is less certain. One is struck by the general improvement in conditions in some aspects of the life of certain skilled workers in the course of the century. The length of the working week for many tradesmen fell from an average seventy-two in 1800 to fifty-four by 1900 and the purchasing power of their weekly wages undoubtedly improved over the course of that time. But equally one calls to mind the several occupations that were forced close to extinction, such as the handloom weavers, the silk workers and the tanners. Nor should one forget that some of the longest and best organised of the traditional craftsmen, such as the bakers and the printers suffered major reverses in the course of the century.

Thus, the bakers, highly skilled and well-organised and with the support of many other workers as well as that of the general public and the national press, failed miserably in a six-month long campaign in the 1840s to secure the abolition of night work in the bakery trade. At the turn of this century, despite the progress of the age, the bakers of Dundalk for example were still working appallingly long hours.

Likewise the printers, those aristocrats of labour, despite their skills and organisation, failed to secure a single wage increase over the forty years from 1829 to 1869. Furthermore, despite their best efforts they failed to prevent the encroachment of women into the Belfast letterpress printing and failed to stop the employment of children by Major Knox in the production of *The Irish Times* in Dublin at the end of the 1850s.

If it is therefore difficult to establish the positive gains achieved by the infant Irish trade union movement in the nineteenth century there was one achievement that cannot be gainsaid: they survived and they grew as the century progressed. This was no negligible achievement when the economic, political and social circumstances in which they operated are borne in mind. Over the period 1800 to 1850 Ireland was not just a predominantly rural country with a small industrial base but was one which was de-industrialising. Belfast and the north-east after 1850, aside from its major towns, were in economic decline as manufacturing centres. They increasingly became towns with large pools of unemployed or under-employed poor from which a docile and dismissable labour force was easily recruited.

Both countryside and towns had a long tradition of violent protest but equally as strong was the tradition of successful government counteraction and suppression in which police surveillance was unrelenting as the century progressed. In this situation all organisation among the lower orders was suspect. Country and town constituted a society in which sectarianism threatened to divide worker from worker, and not just in Belfast and the other northern towns. At the same time Ireland was not

11

isolated from the general economic orthodoxies of the age which celebrated the virtues of individualism and deregulation and which increasingly came to reject the older protective attitudes of price control, wage regulation and arbitration.

Given these circumstances the survival of the unions was a not inconsiderable achievement. Interestingly, however, and especially so in the very difficult period from 1815 to 1850, it was not the sheer survival of unions in such a situation that attracted contemporary and historical surprise but the unrivalled vigour of the Irish trade union movement in the context of the whole United Kingdom.

In the period 1825-40 which the first trade union historians, Sidney and Beatrice Webb, described as the revolutionary period of British trade union history, the Irish unions, especially those of Dublin and Cork, achieved a unique reputation for organisational vigour, and even for violence. Over these years in particular there was an unprecedented wave of labour violence in Dublin, a gruesome catalogue of maiming, acid-throwing and murder, and in the case of one union in the late 1820s assassination as a calculated instrument of policy.[5] All unions in Ireland acquired a reputation that was inspired by the desperate excesses of the few. That violence, though inexcusable, was the perfectly explicable response of people seeing their livelihoods under severe threat and without redress.

The skilled workers of the Irish towns in the first half of the century lived under a myth or memory of unparalleled prosperity in the age of Grattan's parliament in the last two decades of the eighteenth century. With the end of the Napoleonic Wars, the onset of post-war depression and the effects of increasingly efficient British competition much of the urban prosperity of the later eighteenth century vanished.

Against the background of this depression and the loss of a parliament that had brought much business to various trades catering for the aristocracy, gentry and political establishment, the skilled male workers organised to protect their jobs. In doing so they held firmly before them three objects: firstly, to limit the number of apprentices to trades in order to prevent the substitution of adult workers by boy labour under the guise of apprenticeship; secondly, to prevent the intrusion into their trades by non-locals and by unskilled or semi-skilled workers; and thirdly, to resist the imposition of substantial wage cuts which threatened after 1815.

In the steadily deteriorating situation that obtained in the generation after 1815 it is no surprise that skilled workers organised increasingly into unions, that they offered a stout resistance to the threatened changes, and that this resistance in some cases resulted in considerable violence and even death. In the 1820s and 1830s this resistance took on the proportions of a class war in some cities not dissimilar to what was happening in the countryside. In the process the Irish unions, to an extent even greater than their British counterparts, were saddled with the responsibility for loss of trade and economic decline. It was they who chased away business and who frightened off capital. This was the recurrent theme of public meetings of outraged citizens, of indignant press editorials and of a parade of employer witnesses before parliamentary commissions of inquiry into workers' organisations in Britain and Ireland in the 1820s and 1830s.

The profound difference of view between organised skilled workers and their employers and the public came to a head in the notorious conflict between Daniel O'Connell and the trade unions in the winter of 1837–8. Its timing came at the end of a period of great deprivation which saw bread riots in the city of Dublin in the summer of 1837. While that public conflict was an extremely bruising one to both sides, one outcome of it was a new determination on the part of the Irish trade unions to seek the redress of their grievances by means that would be legal and peaceful. From about 1840 onwards the unions became seriously concerned to cultivate a new image and to secure the support of public opinion and the press in trade disputes. They sought earnestly to appear reasonable and respectable, as believers in conciliation and arbitration instead of conflict and coercion. Their leaders from the 1840s to the 1880s proclaimed their belief in the community of interest of employer and employed. Indeed, the presidential address of Thomas O'Connell to the foundation meeting of the Irish Trades Union Congress in April 1894 was the culmination of this very tradition when he spoke of the identity of interest between labour and capital. It may be argued however that appeals to reason and the recourse to public opinion brought meagre rewards in the half century that followed the major conflict of the 1830s.

In the pursuit of their aims the Irish unions did not confine themselves to the arena of trade disputes and industrial conflict whether conducted violently or peacefully. Political assumptions underlay their economic outlook, shaped their political consciousness and inspired their considerable political activity. With the exception of the skilled and mainly Protestant workers of the industrial north-east after 1850, the majority of Irish trade unionists ascribed their general condition of misfortune to the baleful effects of the Act of Union. Consequently they saw their general deliverance in the repeal of that Act and in the reconstitution of an independent Irish parliament. This held true from 1830 down to the era of Parnell and beyond. Consequently, although the unions had fierce conflict with employers and O'Connell in the 1830s over trade union rights they appear to have shared to a very great extent the political outlook of Daniel O'Connell and moderate Irish nationalism. Indeed, the unions of Dublin, Cork and Limerick pressed the cause of repeal of the Act of Union with an earnestness and independence that caused O'Connell some embarrassment during the years of his compromise alliance with the British Whig-Liberals. Throughout the 1830s and 1840s they donated money, held meetings, organised processions and passed resolutions in support of the cause.

How far the realisation of a separate legislature would have improved their lot is a moot point indeed. However, one very significant implication of their devotion to that ideal was its effect on the relations between organised labour in Ireland and the radical, democratic movement in Britain in the course of the nineteenth century. 'As zealous as O'Connell and the middle class repealers were to prevent any international action of the democracies (of Britain and Ireland) the Irish working class were as enthusiastic in their desire to consummate it,' wrote Ireland's best-known historian of labour, James Connolly.[6] In this he was hardly correct. From the 1790s to the 1880s, radicals, democrats and working-class leaders in England time and again called for a united front of the common people of both countries. John Cartwright in 1798, Henry Hunt in 1819, William Cobbett in 1834, Thomas Wakley in the 1830s, Feargus O'Connor in the 1840s, George Harney and Ernest Jones in the 1850s, Patrick Hennessy and Martin Boon in the 1860s, John Sketchley in the 1870s, Francis Soutter, Joseph Cowen and Charles Bradlaugh in the 1880s did not deny the right of the Irish masses to control of their own destiny but they argued that such control would never be conceded by a landlord-dominated parliament. They urged that English radicals and Irish workers should combine first in a joint effort to secure a democratic parliament and then, presumably, all things else would follow. This theme, constant in the

14

overtures of English radicals to Irish workers received its most forceful expression and its greatest potential realisation in the years of the Chartist movement from 1838 to 1848.[7]

However, as often as these overtures were made just as often they were spurned. O'Connell personally saw to it that emissaries would be rebuffed, and they were. Likewise, attempts by the republican element of the Chartist movement to link up with the militant Confederate Young Irelanders in 1848 came to nothing. Then in the 1860s one of the most ambitious enterprises of European radicalism came with the foundation of the International Working Men's Association, better known as the First International. Here was a body devoted to the common interests of working people across frontiers and one which developed a special interest in Ireland. It failed to secure a foothold in Dublin, never tried in Belfast and did manage to secure a branch in Cork but failed to sustain it. The most notable feature of the Irish trade union movement in relation to the First International was the entire absence of any official interest.[8]

One needs to insist that O'Connell and the leaders of Irish nationalism who came after him, from Young Irelanders to Butt, Parnell and Redmond, were not exclusively responsible for rejection of Chartist and later overtures. The Irish trade union leaders were tough-minded and independent. They preferred to see their deliverance within the fortunes of moderate Irish nationalism and the pattern of political assumptions, attitudes and responses established among the trade unionists in the period 1800 to 1850 held good for the next forty years. Can we call this an ideology? Hardly that: it was more an intuition, a prejudice or a set of assumptions rather than a systematic body of ideas.

What strikes one most forcibly is the almost complete absence of any serious critique of the society of which they were a part, and the almost total isolation of the organised Irish workers from ideas concerning the nature of poverty and wealth such as were gaining currency in Britain and the continent at the time. It is ironic that the Irishman William Thompson who laid one of the major foundation stones for radical ideology in Britain and Europe through his seminal *Enquiry into the Nature of the Distribution of Wealth* was apparently an unknown to the Irish labour movement before the 1890s. It is equally curious that that other influential Irishman, James Bronterre O'Brien, the school-master of Chartism, who laid one of the foundation stones for the theory and movement for land nationalisation in Britain was also virtually an unknown among the workers of his home country.

It is not that the Irish trade unionists of the mid-nineteenth century were completely devoid of a language of labour or of a sense of class solidarity. From the 1840s they developed a language of the rights of labour but the range of those rights was modest in the extreme: a right to a fair day's pay for a fair day's work, and a right to a fair hearing, rather than the right to the full product of their labour. They displayed a remarkable solidarity of supporting each other in strikes and in refusing to betray the names of colleagues involved in direct action in labour disputes. However, the predominant sense of political and social identity was not based on or confined to their own class, but was a sense of identity shared with the wider community.

This is evident not just in the trade union leadership's declarations of the common interests of capital and labour which dominated their public utterances from the 1840s to the 1890s and which conceivably may have been a rhetorical strategem. It is strikingly evident on a number of public occasions in the course of the century. Thus, some ten thousand organised workers marched in procession to mark the laying of the foundation stone for the Catholic University in 1862, at a time when not one of them would have the chance of even a secondary education for themselves or their children. Two years later ten thousand marched again to mark the laying of the foundation stone for a monument to Daniel O'Connell, hardly a noted friend of Irish labour and trade unionism. Clearly they identified with a vision of Ireland triumphant rather than a particular vision of labour triumphant. In short, those of them who were not Unionist in the political sense, and this was the majority, shared the political hopes and supported the political campaigns of Irish nationalism.

Those of them who were unionist in the political sense naturally identified their interests with those of the wider imperial community. Here again, as has been shown for the Unionist workers of the Belfast labour movement from 1870, they took their view from their own experience and perceptions.[9] Although it was a view shared with their own wider political community it was arrived at and maintained independently of the major political figures of their own persuasion in just the same way as Dublin, Cork, Limerick and Waterford's nationalist workers held their nationalism independently of the leading figures of the wider community from O'Connell to Parnell.

Although one notes the relative barrenness of ideas in the world of Irish labour and trade unionism in the half century after Europe had been convulsed by the revolutions of 1848, one is also compelled to acknowledge the continued survival and even growth of the trade union movement in a time of declining population in Ireland. Not only did the number of unions increase steadily but the type of skilled worker brought into the fold was also enlarged beyond the scope of the traditional trades and crafts. Skilled workers in transport, notably railway men and crane drivers joined the ranks, as did primary school teachers from 1868.

Furthermore, significant attempts were made to form inter-union structures, from the United Trades Association in Dublin in the 1860s. The first permanently successful attempts however came in Belfast and in Cork where Trades Councils were established in 1881 while the Dublin Trades Council found permanency from 1886.[10] It was from these organisational developments that the Irish Trades Union Congress came in 1894.

It is appropriate to stress however that this organisational growth, while significant in itself, was very much a case of a little more of the same again. The kind of working people who formed these working bodies was not new. The typical views they espoused had not changed in fifty years. The world they inhabited was still bound by the narrow concerns of their own trades.

It was not until the 1890s that a profound change commenced as the unskilled general workers began to be permanently organised for the first time and that marching processions began to occur for the cause of labour rather than the cause of nations. The first May Day march in Irish history was held in 1890,[11] and was symptomatic of a new age. It is ironic that the coming of this new age and climate owed nothing to the foundation of the Irish Trades Union Congress in 1894 nor to its own activities in the first decade of its existence.

1. J. W. Boyle, *The Irish Labor Movement in the Nineteenth Century*, Washington, 1988, p.149.
2. F. A. D'Arcy and K. Hannigan (eds), *Workers in Union: Documents and Commentaries on the History of Irish Labour*, Dublin, 1988, pp. 1-8.
3. J. D. Clarkson, *Labour and Nationalism in Ireland*, New York, 1925, pp. 95-97.
4. Apart from works cited already, see also E. O'Connor, *A Labour History of Waterford*, Waterford, 1989, E. O'Connor, *A Labour History of Ireland, 1824-1960,*

Dublin, 1992, A. Boyd, *The Rise of the Irish Trade Unions*, Tralee, 1972, M. Murphy, 'The working classes of nineteenth century Cork', in *Cork Historical and Archaeological Society Journal*, ixxxv, 241-2, 1980, pp. 26-51.

5. F. A. D'Arcy, 'The murder of Thomas Hanlon: an episode in nineteenth century Dublin labour history', in *Dublin Historical Record*, 29, 1974, pp. 89-100.

6. J. Connolly, *Labour in Irish History*, New Books Publications, Dublin, 1987, p.142.

7. Apart from the works of Boyle, Clarkson, D'Arcy and O'Connor cited earlier, see also R. O'Higgins, 'Irish influence in the Chartist movement', in *Past and Present*, 20, 1961, 83-96, and F. A. D'Arcy, 'Daniel O'Connell and the English Radicals', in D. McCartney, ed., *The World of Daniel O'Connell*, Dublin 1980, pp. 54-71.

8. Boyle, *op. cit.*, pp. 75-91, S. Daly, *Cork, a City in Crisis: a History of Labour Conflict and Social Misery, 1870-1872*, Cork 1978, S. Daly, *Ireland and the First International*, Cork 1984, F. A. D'Arcy, 'Marx, Engels and the Irish Question', in K. B. Nowlan, ed., *The Materialist Messiah*, Dublin and Cork 1984, pp. 23-31.

9. H. Patterson, *Class Conflict and Sectarianism: the Protestant Working Class and the Belfast Labour Movement, 1868-1920*, Belfast 1980.

10. Boyle, *op. cit.*, pp.127-143, S. Cody, J. O'Dowd and P. Rigney, *The Parliament of Labour: 100 Years of the Dublin Trades Council*, Dublin, 1986.

11. S. Cody, 'May Day in Dublin, 1890 to the present', in *Saothar* 5, 1979, pp. 73-79.

Dr Fergus A. D'Arcy
Dean, Faculty of Arts and Department of Modern History, University College Dublin. Author of *Horses, Lords and Racing Men: the Turf Club 1790-1990* (1991); Joint editor with Ken Hannigan of *Workers in Union: Documents and Commentaries on the History of Irish Labour* (1988), etc.

Foundation and Early Years of the Irish TUC 1894-1912

Dr Dermot F. Keogh

The study of modern Irish trade union and labour history has been dominated by the personalities of James Larkin and James Connolly. Biographies record their contribution to the building of modern Ireland. But who would recognise the following names? T. O'Connell, J. H. Jolly, J. D'Alton, J. McCarron, G. Leahy, W. Walker, J. Chambers, S. Dineen and John Murphy. They were among the leading Irish trade unionists of the latter part of the nineteenth and early twentieth century. They lacked the charismatic or 'star' quality of a Connolly or a Larkin. But they spent much of their lives working for their individual trade unions, playing a leading role in trades councils, and building up the Irish Trades Union Congress during its early years. All these 'unknowns' had the honour of serving as president of the ITUC, and of helping to shape Irish trade union policies in the latter part of the nineteenth and early twentieth centuries.

The ITUC held its first meeting in the Trades Hall, Capel Street, Dublin, under the auspices of the local trades council, on the 27 and 28 April, 1894. There were 119 delegates in attendance, representing 21,000 trade unionists directly, and over 39,000 indirectly through the trades councils in Dublin, Belfast, Cork, Limerick and Drogheda. There were four women delegates, two from Belfast and two from Dublin, representing small 'unskilled' unions. With the exception of its first three years, all Congress delegates were drawn from Irish craft unions and from the amalgamated, or British-based unions, such as the Typographical Association, the Amalgamated Society of Railway Servants, Amalgamated Society of Tailors etc.[1] Carpenters, tailors, printers and plumbers and the other trades dominated the workings of Congress in those early years. The arrival of James Larkin in Belfast in 1907 and his success in organising general workers throughout the country, had a radical impact on the proceedings of the ITUC.

But at its inaugural meeting in 1894, the President and Secretary of Congress were carpenters, the Treasurer was a plumber. The ITUC executive, or Parliamentary Committee as it was termed, had four printers, a cabinet-maker, a carpenter and a baker among its eight members. The new ITUC was dominated by the ideas of 'old unionism'. This was reflected in T. O'Connell's presidential address. He was cautious, reformist and moderate. O'Connell warned against the unnecessary use of the right to strike, and cautioned against the unilateral imposition of an eight-hour day. The thirty-eight resolutions brought before the conference followed the moderate tone set by the president. O'Connell, however, betrayed a streak of radicalism when he expressed a hope for the early demise of the House of Lords. He also highlighted the total absence of Irish labour representation in Westminster and at local government level. This was to remain a matter of contention until a decision was taken in 1912 to found the Irish Labour Party. Even in 1894, among representatives of 'old unionism' like T. O'Connell, there was a little new wine in the old wine skin. However, the emphasis in that inaugural year was on striking a note of respectability. The conference hospitality fund had been handsomely subscribed to by Dublin employers, including William Martin Murphy (£1) who also had free passes issued to delegates for Dublin United Tramway Company trams, of which he was the leading shareholder. Murphy, who had served as a Nationalist MP between 1885 and 1892, was a leading figure in the Irish business community. He bought three Dublin newspapers in 1904 and replaced them in 1905 with the *Irish Independent*. Murphy was a complex figure. He became a strong opponent of the 'new unionism'. But the establishment of the ITUC was not a particularly worrying development for Irish employers in the 1890s. Quite the reverse. It was positively welcomed because it might help weaken the links between Irish labour and the radicalised 'new unionism' of the British TUC. Dublin had experienced the impact of the 'new unionism' in the late 1880s and in 1890 when coal porters had gone on strike. There was also use of the 'sympathetic strike' on that occasion.[2] But it took over a decade for the grievances of general workers to surface on the floor of annual conference.

The inspiration for the establishment of the ITUC was more pragmatic than ideological. Its second president, J. H. Jolly, explained in Cork in 1895 that their object was to supplement and not to supplant the British congress. He felt that the local unions were not in a position to send adequate representation to Britain to compete with the larger amalgamated unions. Even when delegations were sent to the British TUC, Jolly said, 'the advantages accruing to the unions of Ireland have scarcely been commensurate with the expense incurred'. The British TUC usually consigned Irish motions to the final day. That was frustrating for Irish delegates. Anticipating that growing concern, the British TUC at their conference in Belfast in 1893 reserved a seat on its parliamentary committee for the Irish. But that was too little too late. The Home Rule climate of the 1880s and early 1890s was reflected in the impulse of Irish labour to set up its own TUC in 1894. (Scotland followed in 1897).

One historian, Emmet O'Connor, views this development in a negative light. He writes:

> Yet Congress was worse than useless. It was a treacherous illusion. In the vain assumption that British TUC strategy could be duplicated in Ireland, a delusion that blithely ignored the vast differences in economy, employment structure, and politics between the two countries, it split the urban from the rural labour movement, widened the breach between artisans and labourers, and denied trade unionists the political apprenticeship of a genuine labour nationalism.[3]

Alas, it is only possible to analyse history as it was and not as we might have liked it to be. There were many factors which hampered the growth of the ITUC. It was founded in the final year of a recession and the Irish economy was to experience a further cycle of recession between 1900 and 1904. Membership rose from about 40,000 to under 70,000 in 1902. The same year Scotland, which had a population similar to that of Ireland (4.5m.) but a much stronger industrial base, had 128,000 affiliated to its TUC, and the British TUC had a membership of 1.5m.

Besides a relatively low membership, the ITUC operated from hand to mouth. Its funding was derived from Congress fees and from voluntary subscriptions. Even after 1905, when funding was systematised, the net income of Congress remained much the same. Moreover, there was no single full-time Congress official. Its parliamentary committee met four times a year. Most administrative energy went into organising the annual conference. Therefore, there was no professional structure to give the ITUC a strong voice. Given such limitations, the ITUC worked relatively effectively.

But was the foundation of the ITUC, therefore, driven by 'a treacherous illusion'? This seems to me unduly harsh as is a description of delegates to annual conference allowing the years roll by as they enjoyed the occasion, 'the mock parliamentary

21

pomp and circumstance, the patronising addresses of welcome from mayors, clerics, and other dignitaries, and the hospitality of local employers'. Notwithstanding the 'pomp and circumstance', the annual conference attended to its business efficiently. After all, its proceedings had a direct bearing on the livelihoods of delegates who represented the 'labour aristocracy'. The relative blandness of the proceedings was not unrelated to the potential for division which lurked beneath the surface – there was the tension between Irish-based and the amalgamated unions; the strain between the supporters of political unionism and nationalism; nervousness over the Parnell split spilling on to the floor of Congress; and the contentiousness of the issue of direct labour representation which threatened the hegemony of the Irish Parliamentary Party.

The deliberations of Congress must also be set against the background of craft unions facing the growing challenge of cheap goods from overseas produced sometimes by non-union labour. 'Buy Irish' and 'Buy from Fair Houses' were very much the slogans of that generation of trade unionists. These preoccupations were also echoed within the trades councils. The Dublin carpenter, John Simmons, complained in 1900 that 'English ale was being palmed off on the Irish by removing the label from the bottle'. Irish brushmakers tried to prevent the sale of English, convict-made brooms. Carpenters and cabinet-makers complained about the importation of shopfronts and furniture. Printers spoke out repeatedly against the sending of lucrative contracts out of the country. It was agreed that all printing work should, without exception, be done in Ireland, on Irish paper and with fair Irish labour. The clergy regularly received complaints from Irish printers for using imported prayer books and allowing religious magazines to be produced by unfair labour. Plasterers repeatedly voiced their anger at the use of imported Italian labour to decorate churches, while marble-cutters regularly complained about the unnecessary importation of altars. Local organ makers regularly got angry with clergy over a decision to import an instrument rather than 'Buy Irish.' The list of complaints was endless.

While it was relatively easy to achieve consensus on 'Buy Irish' and 'Buy fair labour' issues, there was a general ripple of nervousness when political questions were raised. One wing of Congress was content to allow the Irish Parliamentary Party represent labour and trade union interests at Westminster. Over the years, a number of pro-trade union Irish Parliamentary Party MPs advised annual conference to avoid the perils of socialism and to maintain faith with the IPP. For example, at Athlone in 1906, the Lord Mayor of Dublin and MP, J. P. Nannetti, told annual conference that there was no necessity to set up a new party as the Irish Parliamentary Party was a labour party:

> The platform on which he was proud to stand was broad enough for any workingman. They could make the Parliamentary Party do everything they wished. They required no spur in that direction ... They were purely labour as well as nationalist and he as a worker could not be with them on the platform that day were it not that he was a nationalist.

Nanetti, a long-time member of the Dublin Typographical Provident Society, had arranged a meeting in 1902 between his leader, John Redmond and Congress's Parliamentary Committee. Redmond readily agreed to represent the interest of the ITUC and suggested regular meetings between himself and that body. The next such meeting did not in fact occur until 1909.

There had been a growing frustration among trade unionists over the failure to have direct labour political representation at local and national levels. A number of delegates continued to attempt to square the circle – that is, take a radical labour stance and at the same time support the Irish Parliamentary Party. A Derry tailor, James McCarron, had been among the most consistent advocates of a policy of support for the IPP. At the same time, he supported land nationalisation. Three times President of Congress, McCarron represented the most progressive face of 'old unionism'. In his presidential address in 1907, he said:

> It cannot be concluded that here is either equity or justice in a law which entitles a few men, who neither sow nor reap, to appropriate the wealth of creation ... by the energy and industry of the whole community. How long is this iniquitous system to continue?

While the Derry tailor could maintain his old political allegiance there were many members of Congress who sought to take a different path. Local government reform in 1898 had given a new opportunity to trade union-backed candidates to win seats in the major cities of Belfast and Dublin. There were no major Labour breakthroughs.

Neither was there any significant conversion in the ITUC to radical socialist or left-wing political ideas. The activities of the revolutionary Marxist James Connolly, who worked in Dublin

23

from 1896 until he went to America in 1903, had little impact on the local trades council or on the ITUC. While the Limerick baker, Stephen Dineen, did not share Connolly's radical socialist outlook he was nonetheless alive to the injustices of 'our present-day industrialism'. In his presidential address, he told the Athlone Congress in 1906:

> Being in business to make money, the firm or company first endeavours to find out how much of any given kind of work a man can do at his greatest capacity. That becomes the standard of production. Wages are fixed on that basis. But production largely exceeds the demand, and wages start on the down-grade until the labour of the husband cannot maintain the family. The wife helps in any way she can, and the children are eventually pressed into service. After a time the husband is squeezed out by the compelling forces of the competitive system operating upon the younger members, perhaps of his own family and he joins the dismal ranks of the unemployed.

Such views were an expression of humanitarian concern rather than a programme for radical industrial or political action. That is why, perhaps, the historian J. Dunsmore Clarkson concluded that:

> Despite the efforts of this handful of propagandists, the Irish labour movement was, in 1907, almost a generation behind the British labour movement. The 'old unionism' still held sway; the political weapon was almost neglected.[4]

But Clarkson's judgement is to underestimate certain developments which were, before the beginning of the First World War, to contribute to the development of radical Irish trade unionism and the establishment of an Irish Labour Party.

Michael O'Lehane, from Macroom, Co. Cork, was one of the trade unionists who helped bring about a change in the balance of power in Congress. He founded the Drapers' Assistants' Association on 21 August 1901 and he brought membership from 2,200 to 3,600 in 1910 and to over 20,000 at the time of his death in 1920. He confronted the inequities of the 'living in' system and challenged the morality of the fining systems operating in the large department stores. Employees lived and worked in a highly authoritarian structure. In the larger department stores many drapers' assistants 'lived in' in a premises provided by the employer. Living conditions were basic and a strict curfew was imposed. The union struggled to have minimum standards imposed by all the leading shops. O'Lehane also tackled the 'odious, illegal and pernicious system of fining'. Shop assistants were fined for minor transgressions of house discipline. There were over 200 rules in one manual. It read: 'Customers to be promptly attended to, if not fine – 3d; No toilet business or nail cleaning to be done in the shop or showrooms – fine 6d; and for unbusinesslike conduct – 6d.'

O'Lehane brought about a new militancy among shop assistants many of whom were women. That militancy was reflected in the strike action taken by O'Lehane in Dublin in 1906. The numbers involved were small but his tactics were novel. He held a series of large public meetings of over 4,000 people in order to highlight the injustice of the dispute and to uphold the right of peaceful picketing. While his members were ultimately forced back to work, O'Lehane had shown initiative and imagination in his handling of the dispute. O'Lehane and his union played a significant role in the tilting of the political balance in the ITUC towards the 'new unionism'.

Another impulse for change came around 1906 when the first determined effort since the late 1880s was made to unionise Irish general workers throughout the country. Dublin may have been a capital surrounded by golf links, but it also had one of the worst infant mortality rates in the British Isles. A third of its population lived in tenements while a majority of its 40,000 male work-force was engaged, directly or indirectly, in the distributive trade. The trade union movement had not yet penetrated that sector. Belfast was little better for the general workers as James Connolly found when he went there in 1911:

> The day's labour was unlimited. It began often before the nominal starting time and continued after the nominal knocking-off. Half the meal hour was worked in most cases and seldom was a full day's wages paid, no matter how hardly earned. The day's wages were fixed at 5s. but through stoppages and pretexts of various kinds few were the men who received five shillings even for eleven and twelve hours' work ... The man who objected to this 'jibbing' was given several weeks rest without pay or chance of employment.

James Larkin, a Liverpool docker born of Irish parents, arrived in Belfast on 20 January 1907. He was an organiser for the National Union of Dock Labourers (NUDL). Within a few months, Larkin had introduced the idea of the sympathetic strike and the blacking of goods. He believed in the tactic of confrontation. During those stormy months in Belfast, Larkin even succeeded in bringing the police out on strike. Larkin, who had visited Dublin during the Belfast strike, later moved south to set up another branch of his union in the capital. He brought his family over from Liverpool. Branches of the NUDL were established in Newry, Dundalk and Drogheda. Larkin was sent to organise the docks in Cork in July 1908. Again he was successful. But there was a strike and he was disowned by his union. Without support from headquarters there was no alternative but to found a rival organisation.

Towards the end of 1908, the idea was born to form the Irish Transport and General Workers Union (ITGWU). By January 1909 Larkin was the leader of an Irish-based general workers' union. James Connolly returned from the United States on 26 July 1910. Shortly afterwards he became a full-time official in Belfast for the ITGWU.[5] Professional organisation paid dividends for the ITGWU; it had a membership of 3,000 in 1910, and over 13,000 by 1913. Larkin's sister, Delia, set up the Irish Women Workers' Union in 1911. It had under 1,000 members in Dublin a year later. The Belfast membership was much lower.

James Larkin was supported in his efforts by a number of left-wing Dublin trade unionists. The tailor, William O'Brien – a general secretary of the ITGWU for twenty-two years – was then an admirer and helper. William O'Brien, who was made a delegate to the ITUC in 1909 where Larkin's presence had already begun to enliven proceedings, had helped strengthen support for socialism on the Dublin Trades Council. But the real impetus for direct labour representation came from Belfast. In 1908, the ITUC Presidential address, given by John Murphy of Belfast, endorsed for the first time an alliance between trade unions and socialism:

> The air is full of rumblings and threatening and disruptions, as to the alliance between the trade unions and the socialists, and dark and malignant prophecies are being uttered as to the future of British industry if this alliance should not be dissolved ... The socialist has analysed the human misery connected with our industrial conditions, and has proposed a remedy. Until a better plan is suggested we may reasonably refuse to be drawn aside from the pursuit of a scheme which, while not perfect, is at least comprehensive, and appeals to all that is best in our hearts and minds. I am not advocating anything in the nature of contentment about Irish trade unionists. We have no reasons to be contented. No doctrine which backs up the present condition of society – where the drones revel in luxury and the bees perish for want – will stand the fire of the present day criticism.

Larkin listened to that speech with approval. But he showed scant respect for the ITUC establishment. He enlivened proceedings by attacking James McCarron's progressive motion on housing for the working classes. Larkin replied that if workingmen did not get sufficient wages they were hardly likely to be able to buy out their own houses. There was a new robustness in such exchanges and the proceedings of the annual conference were enlivened as the years progressed.

Despite his attacks on the 'old orthodoxies' Larkin was elected to the ITUC parliamentary committee which was still dominated by the amalgamateds and by the Irish craft unions. In February 1909, the parliamentary committee received a complaint from the ITGWU that NUDL labourers were 'black-legging on members of the new union in Belfast'. The matter was referred to the Belfast Trades Council. It was further decided that no invitation would be sent to the ITGWU to attend Congress. The standing orders committee at Limerick in 1909 recommended by a narrow majority to admit the ITGWU. But in the debate that followed, it was decided by forty-nine votes to thirty-nine to uphold the decision of the parliamentary committee. The ITGWU was not admitted. But the 'Larkinites' did secure a decision to set up a seven-man committee to inquire into the origins of the dispute between the ITGWU and the NUDL. The committee recommended in favour of admission. In Dundalk, in 1910, annual conference voted in support of the recommendation. Because of a technicality, Larkin could not be elected to the parliamentary committee. But he had many supporters on that body. They included the Chairman, D. R. Campbell, the Treasurer, Michael O'Lehane and the Secretary, P. T. Daly. All were strong 'Larkinites'.

The ITGWU was now a member of Congress. That meant much more than the simple admission of another union; it greatly strengthened support for 'new unionism' and for the establishment of an Irish Labour Party at annual conference.[6] Unfortunately, Larkin had less than a month to savour the victory of his union's admission to the ITUC. Charged on twenty-four counts, including 'criminal conspiracy' and 'having received and misappropriated certain sums of money', he was sentenced to one year's hard labour on 18 June 1910. The chief witnesses for the Crown were a number of Cork dockers anxious to show that Larkin had 'misappropriated' union funds. Inter-union rivalry had caused great bitterness in that city. It had split the Cork Trades Council in 1909, and a breakaway Cork District Trades Council had been formed by the skilled workers. Under great

27

public pressure, the authorities released Larkin from jail after three months.

The ITUC annual conference was held in Galway in 1911. The ITGWU paid affiliation fees for 5,000 members, giving them the largest delegation. The historian, Desmond Greaves, described the conference as 'uneventful.'[7] The report in *The Irish Times* gives a very different picture. Tempers boiled over as conference debated a motion authorising the parliamentary committee to formulate a plan for the establishment of an Irish labour party. A Belfast delegate sought continued Irish support for the English Labour Party and proposed an amendment to that effect. Larkin supported the setting up of an independent Irish labour party. But he was accused of having changed his mind; a delegate from Cork accused Larkin of being a turncoat. He said that as an organiser of an English union Larkin had preached allegiance to the British Labour Party on the streets of Cork. 'That is a deliberate lie,' replied Larkin and later amid footstamping and calls for withdrawal, he shouted, 'He (Murphy) is a liar'. Another delegate from Cork named Lynch spoke in favour of the English Labour Party.

According to the colourful report by an *The Irish Times* correspondent the following ensued:

> Mr Larkin jumped to his feet, and, interrupting Mr Lynch, said he would not take such allegations from a man who burned the balance sheet of the Cork strike. Pointing at Mr Lynch, he shouted – 'You dirty cur,' adding as he buttoned his coat in a manner suggestive of possibilities – 'You are a liar.'

That remark kept some delegates on their feet, some shouting for a withdrawal and others calling for order. Above the din, Larkin was heard to shout: 'I will not withdraw for you or for this Congress either.' *The Irish Times* account continued: 'As Mr Larkin and Mr Lynch seemed desirous of speaking to each other at closer quarters, several delegates intervened and kept them apart. They continued to shout defiantly at each other, and the Chairman, with a view to restoring order, rang his bell vigorously.' But order was not easily restored as Larkin looked decidedly angry and stood, fists clenched, as a few delegates again moved between the two men to 'prevent what threatened to be a personal conflict'. Eventually apologies were exchanged with little grace shown by either side. *The Irish Times* reported on 8 June 1911 that the amendment supporting the British Labour Party was carried by thirty-two votes to twenty-nine. Belfast internationalism had scored a temporary victory over Dublin nationalism.[8]

The following year the annual conference was held in Clonmel and Michael O'Lehane was in the chair. James Connolly, who was making his debut at Conference, proposed the establishment of an Irish labour party. He was supported by James Larkin, William O'Brien and the Belfast-based Thomas Johnson who was later to become an outstanding leader of the Irish Labour Party. This was a year of Home Rule euphoria among nationalists and Connolly's motion received a majority from the eighty-seven delegates, forty-nine for, nineteen against, and nineteen unrecorded. Later that year, William O'Brien presided over the inaugural meeting. The Irish Labour Party was born.

O'Brien and his supporters also captured a majority on the ITUC Parliamentary Committee in 1911. Of the eight elected members, five were Dublin 'Larkinites' including O'Brien and Larkin himself. The hegemony of 'old unionism' had come to an end. Larkin and his group of heterodox followers were in a position to control the ITUC. That is not to argue that the ITUC had undergone a conversion to the 'fiery crusade'. But Larkinites, because of their majority on the Parliamentary Committee, had a tactical advantage over 'old unionists'. Larkin sought to make use of that political dominance.

Congress, still without funds or a full-time official, represented 100,000 workers. The structure remained the same but the philosophy which now dominated Congress was much more militant. This growing militancy took place at a time when the Liberal government had recently passed a number of pieces of progressive labour legislation. The Trade Boards Act was passed in 1909 to better wages and conditions in 'sweated' trades. Labour exchanges were opened in 1910. Health and insurance schemes were introduced the following year. Under the terms of the act, trade unions could become 'approved societies'. This accounted for a large rise in trade union membership in Ireland, particularly in the ITGWU. There was, however, one set back for British and Irish unions; the Osborne judgement of 1909 found that unions could not lawfully use their funds for political purposes. That held dangers for the new Irish Labour Party.

As the Irish trade union movement espoused wider political and industrial objectives, employers in the capital took fright. James Larkin pressed for the universal recognition of the

ITGWU. His language and methods convinced many Irish employers that Liberty Hall, the headquarters of the ITGWU, was in reality a cradle of social and political revolution. That impression was reinforced by the militant language of Larkin and his new publication; on 27 May 1911, *The Irish Worker*, was published for the first time. James Larkin was both editor and its main contributor. William Martin Murphy, the employer kind enough to contribute to the hospitality fund of the inaugural conference of the ITUC in 1894, became the target of Larkin's venom. The owner of the *Irish Independent* and the leading shareholder in the Dublin United Tramway Company, Murphy also controlled a number of other important business concerns in the capital. *The Irish Worker* depicted Murphy as 'an industrial octopus, a tramway tyrant, an importer of swell cockney shopmen, a political and social Captain Mick McQuaid, a financial mountebank, a bloodsucking vampire, a pure solid financial contortionist, a capitalist sweater, and this whited sepulchre'. In cartoon and in verse, Murphy was traduced. Take for example the following piece of verse from *The Irish Worker*:

> I went to heaven. The Jasper walls
> Towered high and wide, and the golden halls
> Shone bright beyond. But a strange new mark
> Was over the gate, viz. 'Private Park',
> What, what is the meaning of this? I cried:
> And a saint with a livery on replied,
>   'It's Murphy's'.

> I went to the only place left. 'I'll take
> A chance on the boat in the brimstone lake,
> Or perhaps I may be allowed to sit
> On the griddled floor of the bottomless pit.'
> But the jeering tout with horns on his face
> Cried as he forked me out of the place,
>   'It's Murphy's'.

Before the conflict between them was over, Larkin and Murphy were locked in a personal vendetta. In reading the excited rhetoric of *The Irish Worker*, employers had ample evidence to feed their phobias and even generate a sense of panic. The haemorrhage of strikes across the channel in 1911 had further exacerbated Irish employers' fears about the imminence of social revolution in Dublin. Railwaymen had gone out in the capital, and there had been trouble in Jacobs' biscuit factory, and on the docks. The ITGWU had begun to grow on the outskirts of Dublin and outside the capital. That was a cause of major concern to the employers in smaller Irish towns. Employers in Wexford had resorted to the draconian action of locking out their employees simply because they were members of the ITGWU. That was an attack on the very core principle of trade unionism. Whatever the cost, the strategy had to be defeated. This was a particularly ugly episode which involved over 700 workers. Much worse was to follow in 1913. Employers, tired of what they perceived as a slow decline into anarchy, organised themselves into the Dublin Employers' Federation Limited in summer 1911. They were following the example of their Cork colleagues who had taken similar action in 1909.

A number of Irish employers were deeply disillusioned with the response of the Liberal government to the growth of trade union militancy. There was wild talk at the Dublin Chamber of Commerce meeting on 3 November 1911; there was general agreement that the Irish trade union movement had 'been brought under the influence of that continental socialist plague, which had its origins in Russia and had spread into France and England'. James Shanks felt that they could no longer regard the administration with 'respect or confidence.' He demanded firmer action:

> Saintliness in rulers possessing the other qualities was not to be deprecated. For his part, he would be content with a ruler, less saint than sinner, even with a spice of the devil in his composition, if he had the capacity to govern and the wisdom and the courage to do it.

He wanted to censure the government and have the military called out. There was widespread support for the motion. But William Martin Murphy attempted to calm the meeting down. He obviously did not feel it wise to confront the government directly. But Murphy would have agreed with the employer who felt that 'a small party of agitators' had 'thought well to make Ireland the cockpit for their experiments.' The present was only the beginning of the trouble. The businessman Edward H. Andrews felt that they had wide public backing for their action:

> Gentlemen, the country and the press are at our back. All religious denominations are with us. We must not falter in our duty, nor stand at ease until full liberty throughout the length and breadth of this land (is restored), and united also with those who think with us in other lands.

It was then proposed to establish a national employers' federation. Within a year, the employers had their own 'one big union'. The stage was set for confrontation. It came in 1913 'with a spice of the devil' in its composition.

Reviewing the developments between 1894 and 1912, the Irish trade union movement had much to celebrate. The 'new unionism' had belatedly taken firm root in Ireland and its supporters controlled the ITUC. James Larkin, with the assistance of craft union leaders, had achieved what had eluded Irish trade union organisers in 1889 and 1890; the ITGWU had been established as a national organisation. An Irish Labour Party had been founded in 1912. That was not a propitious year in which to seek to unite Irish workers, north and south, into a single political movement. The Home Rule issue divided the country and divided the Irish trade union movement. The vision of Irish labour solidarity quickly faded before the 'back to the future' march of radical nationalism and northern unionism. Viewed from 1912, the message of the first president of the ITUC in 1894 appeared quite anachronistic. The interests of capital and labour were no longer complementary. The 1913 lock-out loomed.

---

1. The richest source on the origins of the Irish Trades Union Congress is John W. Boyle, *The Irish Labor Movement in the Nineteenth Century*, Catholic University of America Press, Washington DC, 1988.
2. See Dermot Keogh, 'The New Unionism' and Ireland – Dublin Coal Porters' Strike 1890: War of Attrition', *The Capuchin Annual*, 1975, pp. 64-70; Maurice Canty and Adolphus Shields were the local leaders of the British-based Gasworkers' Union.
3. Emmet O'Connor, *A Labour History of Ireland, 1824-1960*, Gill and Macmillan, Dublin, 1992, p. 60.
4. J. Dunsmore Clarkson, *Labour and Nationalism in Ireland*, Columbia University, New York, 1925, p. 214.
5. Dermot Keogh, 'A Study of the Dublin Trade Union Movement and Labour Leadership 1907-1914', MA, NUI, 1974, pp. 244 ff.
6. Emmet Larkin, *James Larkin, Irish Labour Leader 1876 – 1947*, London, 1965, p. 65.
7. C. Desmond Greaves, *The Irish Transport and General Workers' Union – The Formative Years*, Gill and Macmillan, Dublin, 1982, p. 58.
8. Arthur Mitchell, *Labour in Irish Politics 1890-1930*, Irish University Press, Dublin, 1974, p. 33.

Dr Dermot F. Keogh
Jean Monnet Professor of European Integration Studies, University College Cork. Author of *The Rise of the Irish Working Class* (1982); *Twentieth Century Ireland: Nation and State* (1994), etc.

Jim Larkin and the Risen People

James Plunkett

> And I say to my people's masters: Beware,
> Beware of the thing that is coming, beware of the risen people
> Who shall take what you would not give.

Pádraic Pearse wrote those lines in April 1916, a time when the Insurrection was imminent, yet the reference is broader than that. In the body of the poem the economic and social wrongs suffered by the poor and the destitute have their place beside the aspirations of nationalism. Back in the great Dublin lock-out of 1913, Pearse had come down strongly on the side of Jim Larkin and his ill-used followers, those outcasts referred to contemptuously by a largely antipathetic press as 'Larkin's rabble of carters and dockers'.

Ruth Dudley Edwards in her biography of Pearse quotes from his column 'From a Hermitage' in the Republican organ *Irish Freedom*, in October 1913 to establish his positive expression of support. He wrote:

> I would like to put some of our well-fed citizens in the shoes of our hungry citizens, just for an experiment ... I would ask those who know that a man can live and thrive, can house, feed and educate a large family on a pound a week, to try the experiment themselves ... I am certain they will enjoy their poverty and their hunger ... they will write books on 'How to be Happy though Hungry'; when their children cry for more food they will smile; when the landlord calls for the rent they will embrace him; when their house falls upon them they will thank God; when policemen smash in their skulls they will kiss the chastening baton ...

And so on. The sarcasm is heavy-handed, but leaves us in no doubt about his sympathies.

Pearse had made his mind clear in an earlier article. In April of 1913 he had written:

> My instinct is with the landless man against the lord of lands and with the breadless man against the master of millions. I hold it a most terrible sin that there should be breadless men in this city where great fortunes are made and enjoyed.
> I calculate that one-third of the people of Dublin are underfed; that half the children attending Irish primary schools are ill-nourished. Inspectors of the National Board will tell you that there is no

use in visiting primary schools in Ireland after one or two in the afternoon; the children are too weak and drowsy with hunger to be capable of answering intelligently.

I suppose there are 20,000 families in Dublin in whose domestic economy milk and butter are all but unknown; black tea and dry bread are their staple articles of diet. There are many thousand fireless hearth places in Dublin on the bitterest days of winter. 20,000 families live in one-room tenements. It is common to find two or three families occupying the same room – and sometimes one of the families will have a lodger! There are tenement rooms in which over a dozen persons live, eat and sleep ...

That is the voice of Pádraic Pearse. But it could be Larkin himself.

When Jim Larkin took up residence in Dublin in 1908, his reputation for making trouble had travelled before him. He was thirty-two years of age, a handsome man, tall, broad-shouldered, with a commanding appearance. He had spent the previous year in Belfast as a temporary organiser for the National Union of Dock Labourers whose headquarters was in Liverpool. His militant methods while there had alarmed not only the authorities and the employers of Belfast, but the executive of the union back in Liverpool. He had used his new-found weapon of the sympathetic strike and his doctrine of 'tainted goods' with devastating effect, closing down job after job and even persuading the Belfast police to go on strike too, by convincing them that they should claim extra payment for the extra hours they had to spend on duty trying to keep order during the unprecedented succession of strikes.

In Belfast the press had denounced Larkin as either a socialist, an anarchist, or a syndicalist. When this had no effect, they labelled him as a Papist. In Dublin the abuse was shaped to suit its different audiences. There he was declared to be an Orangeman and the rumour was circulated that he was a son of Carey, the informer.

In fact he was the second son of impoverished Irish parents who had emigrated to Liverpool. He spent most of the first five years of his life with his grandparents in Newry. At the age of nine, however, he was back in Liverpool, a breadwinner now, working forty hours a week for a wage of 2s. 6d. As a young adult he worked his passage to South America and when he returned to Liverpool he got a job on the docks as a foreman, but lost it when he came out on strike in sympathy with the men who worked under him. This led to his appointment as a temporary organiser for the National Union of Dock Labourers and so to his recruiting campaign on behalf of the trade union movement at first in Belfast and then in Dublin.

When he settled in Dublin in 1908 he found as distressing a picture as any revolutionary might look upon. The population of the city at that time was 305,000 people, a total from which Pembroke, Rathmines and Rathgar were excluded. Of these a total of 87,000 (almost one-third) were destitute. They lived in decaying tenements left behind by the rich of a vanished Georgian society which had gradually melted away in the years following the Act of Union.

When Larkin's aggressive methods of protest expanded to include an attack on the housing conditions it resulted in the setting up of a Housing Inquiry in 1913. The official report of the Inquiry divided the houses into three categories: (1) houses which appeared to be structurally sound; (2) houses so decayed as to be on the borderline of being unfit for human habitation; (3) houses unfit for human habitation and incapable of being rendered fit for human habitation.

The structurally sound houses accommodated 27,000 people. The borderline houses held 37,000 people and in the houses declared by the Commission to be absolutely unfit for habitation 23,000 lived. Witnesses summoned by the Commission testified to the living conditions in the houses. One described seeing a room sixteen feet square occupied by the two parents and their seven children. They slept on the floor on which (the witness reported) there was not enough straw to accommodate a cat, and no covering of any kind whatever. The children were poorly clad; one wrapped in a rag of some kind and his only other clothing a very dirty loin cloth. There was no furniture; a zinc bucket, a can, a few mugs or jam jars for drinking. The rent was two shillings and three pence weekly; wages over some weeks four shillings and sixpence, with a maximum of twelve shillings in the week.

A photographic survey of the tenements was commissioned by Dublin Corporation for submission to the Inquiry and these remain to add visual testimony to the grim living conditions.

However, no one who grew up in Dublin through the 1920s and 1930s and 1940s of the present century will need photographic proof because during those years many areas of the city continued in the same state of decrepitude. They will remember tottering tenements with broken or non-existent hall doors under

35

shattered fanlights; rickety stairs and foul hallways exhaling the malodorous breath of woodrot, inadequate hygiene, overcrowded human bodies, and filth which poverty had little or no means of controlling.

A spokesman for the employers admitted freely that the living conditions of the families of unskilled and casual workers were appalling but tried to excuse the part played by low wages in bringing it about. Explaining the situation as he (and, presumably, the other employers) saw it, he wrote:

> While it is impossible to withhold sympathy from classes so depressed as these slum-dwellers of Dublin are, it cannot be overlooked that the very nature of their mode of living tends to reduce their value in the labour market.
>
> One point upon which witness after witness insisted (in the course of the Inquiry) was the physical deterioration of men who found their way into these terrible hovels. Once drawn into the abyss, they speedily lose not merely their sense of self-respect but their capacity for sustained exertion. At the same time the thought of all that is implied in this vicious housing system in the way of demoralisation and decadence of physical powers should make us wary of playing the role of critic to employers who have to use this damaged material.

He speaks of 'the men who find their way into these terrible hovels' as though it was their personal choice. It was not. Inadequate wages or complete lack of employment left them with no option but life in the hovels. And, because their physical strength and health have been impaired by hunger and unhygienic living conditions he suggests it justifies paying them still lower wages, a recourse which can only leave them less able as labourers and more damaged than ever.

The society Jim Larkin came to scrutinise in angry detail was rigidly class-bound from the remote aristocratic stratum to the professional and business classes, to the traders and shopkeepers down to the aristocracy of labour which consisted of the skilled craftsmen and artisans, most of whom could cast their history back to the old guilds with their coats of arms, their mottoes, their badges of trade, their colourful medieval regalia and customs. All of these had evolved procedures for regulating wage rates and control of the internal administration of their trades.

At the bottom of all were the unskilled and casual labourers. They were looked down on by the craftsmen. The middle and upper classes were barely conscious of their existence. No trade union had succeeded in creating an effective organisation for them.

Larkin found this lowest of the classes apathetic and resigned to the hopelessness of their lot. He took on the task of instilling spirit and confidence in them through speeches which demonstrated his supreme skills as a demagogue, and impassioned exhortations in the *Irish Worker* which he began to publish in 1911. An example of the many was this:

> At present you spend your lives in sordid labour, your abode in filthy slums; your children hunger and your masters say your slavery must endure forever. If you would come out of bondage you yourself must forge the weapons and fight the grim battle.

In fact, the rapid growth of the *Irish Worker* was a measure of his impact. In June 1911 it sold 26,000 copies; in July this became 66,500; in August it grew to 74,750 and in September it was 94,994.

His style was colourful and sometimes evangelical. At a Board of Trade inquiry into the endless outbreak of industrial unrest he warned those who were the root cause of the poverty and the suffering with the words: 'Christ will not be crucified any longer in Dublin by these men.'

Daniel Corkery noted his frequent recourse to poetry when addressing his impoverished audiences. He wrote about Larkin:

> I took him to be a man of ideas, some of them wrong but most of them right – or at least right according to my lights ... I regarded him as one earnest to a fault, for I never heard him speak to the class for which he stood that he did not half offend them by dwelling on the failings which kept them powerless and timid ... By dint of experience he had slept in every workhouse from Land's End to John-o'-Groats; by dint of reading it was his custom to quote poetry as freely as I would myself if I had more courage ...

Another task confronting Larkin was to bring the artisans and the craft workers to the assistance of the unskilled and the casuals. He emphasised the element of brotherhood which should unite those who worked for the rulers of a capitalist society. It was a slow process to erode the skilled men's snobbery and sense of superiority over the unskilled and often illiterate denizens of the slums, but he moved matters slowly along the road. 'The great are not great' he told his followers time after time. 'The great only appear great because you are on your knees. Rise up.'

Another task was to arouse awareness throughout society, especially the well-to-do and the intellectuals, of the direness of the plight of the poor and the destitute. Society, by and large, seemed to be unaware of it, probably because a rigid class structure insulated them from brushing shoulders with it. Larkin's task was to implant and encourage the growth of a new social conscience. He was no mere reformer – he was a revolutionary. He described his campaign as his 'divine mission of discontent' and declared that his objective was to put on each poor family's table not only a loaf, but a vase of flowers as well.

So, from 1908 to 1913 the business life of the city staggered from crisis to crisis with thousands of unskilled workers galvanised into unprecedented acts of revolt and the employers rejecting any form of negotiation and fighting back, at first individually and then with determined solidarity through their newly-formed Employers' Federation under the leadership of William Martin Murphy. That was in 1911. Matters waited to come to a head for two years. Then, on the morning of 18 August 1913, a letter appeared in William Martin Murphy's paper, the *Irish Independent*, over the signature of C. W. Gordon, acting secretary to the Dublin United Tramway Company (which was also controlled by William Martin Murphy) which read in part:

> From the numerous applications to the company's officials by casual labourers seeking work, my directors believe there is a greater dearth of employment for this class of labour than usual. With a view to relieving to some extent the distress which is attendant on this condition of affairs, the company are about to start the relaying of some of the tramway lines they had not intended to relay until next year...

The letter went on to invite applications, but warned that since the directors believed that much of the distress could be attributed to the disruptive tactics of the Irish Transport and General Workers' Union, members of that union would not be considered for employment.

To the middle-class reader at the breakfast table or on his way to the office the letter was an admirable demonstration of the Christian concern of the Dublin employers and their solicitude for the less fortunate members of the community.

But for Jim Larkin, the thirty-seven year old agitator and trade union leader, it was a declaration that confrontation on a massive and organised scale was imminent. Twelve months before he had served demands on the Tramway Company which had still not been replied to, while a few days previously the despatch boys in the *Irish Independent* newspapers had been dismissed in a body because they had refused to leave the Transport Union.

The letter confirmed his suspicion already expressed: that William Martin Murphy, in expectation of a strike in the Tramway Company, was preparing for it by recruiting a double staff so that when the union men downed tools there would be a body of non-union employees ready to take their places.

On 21 August the employees in the Parcels Department of the Tramway Company were dismissed because they continued to be members of Larkin's Union. On 22 August the tram conductors and drivers were warned that if they went on strike for the reinstatement of their colleagues it could not last a single day, because the company had staff in readiness to take over their duties and also had guarantees of ample protection from the government and the forces of the Crown. Despite this warning the tram-men decided to do battle in defence of their colleagues and at ten o'clock on the morning of 25 August they left their cars in the street. The issue was joined.

That night Larkin addressed a massive meeting in Beresford Place. Scabs were already running the trams and feeling was growing high. Larkin spoke of the onslaught the employers had planned and of the fact that Lord Aberdeen had promised Murphy not only the police but the military as well. He advised his listeners to arm for their own protection. 'If Carson can arm his braves up in the North', he announced, 'we can too'. His resulting arrest on a charge of incitement put Dublin in a fever of protest. Riots broke out in various parts of the city and pitched battles took place with the police when the people stoned the trams and attempted at various points to dig up the tramlines. The military were called out.

Meanwhile the authorities, torn between the fury of the people at Larkin's arrest and his undoubted capacity for doing further mischief if he was let out, decided to risk releasing him on bail, probably feeling that the situation could hardly deteriorate much further. Larkin's first move was to announce that he would address a meeting in Sackville Street on the following Sunday. When the meeting was proclaimed by Magistrate Swift, Larkin assured his followers that it would be held. When Sunday came Sackville Street was packed with expectant citizens and heavily posted with Dublin Metropolitan Police and hundreds of extra police drafted in from the provinces.

There was no sign of Larkin until an elderly and apparently infirm man appeared on the balcony of the Imperial Hotel. He

39

wore a beard and was dressed in a frock coat. He surveyed the crowd below for a while, then removed the beard and began to speak. It was Jim Larkin. Within a couple of minutes he was seized and arrested by the police. Then, as he was being led away, there began a series of baton charges of such violence that reports were carried in the press all over Europe and the United States. At home and in Britain eye witnesses of eminence and importance testified to scenes of unprecedented brutality.

However, the employers remained determined on a fight to the finish. There were now 400 of them in the Employers' Federation and they united to issue a form to each of their employees with an instruction to sign it. The form declared that the signatory would leave the Irish Transport and General Workers' Union if he or she was a member or – if not a member – that he or she undertook never to become a member.

At this point Larkin's campaigning proved to have been successful. Not only did the Larkinites refuse to sign the form, but trade unionists belonging to thirty-two other trade unions took up the challenge and also refused to sign. These included the craft workers' unions. The employers stuck to their guns and shut their doors all over the city. A huge lock-out was now in progress and thousands of workers and their families faced unemployment and hunger.

In spite of attempts at mediation, the lock-out lasted for over six months. Throughout its duration Larkin made a superhuman effort to hold the workers together. James Connolly was summoned from Belfast to add his expertise to the effort and night after night meetings were held at Beresford Place, which became known among the strikers as 'the old spot by the river'. Where eloquence alone might have lost its effect Larkin's unerring instinct for the dramatic prompted him to gestures which lifted up wavering spirits and fired their determination. One of the more spectacular occurred when the workers of Britain subscribed to create a relief fund. Larkin decided to show the workers something more inspiring than a subscription list. He had the food delivered to Dublin on a food ship which was hired especially, because he knew that the sight of a food ship steaming up the river with relief supplies from their fellow workers in Britain would be a sight still to be talked about when the food itself had been eaten and forgotten.

The lock-out dragged on and gradually petered out. Men either got their jobs back without being made to sign the form, or signed it in the knowledge that it had become an empty form of words which the employers were no longer anxious to enforce.

Yet when the clamour died away, the mists lifted to reveal what had been achieved. A whole forgotten class had emerged from obscurity into a society which was conscious of a new concept of their rights and dignity. The leading voices of the liberals, the intellectuals, the patriots, the artists and the writers had spoken out almost unanimously in support of their cause. Numbered among them were: Pádraic Pearse, W. P. Ryan, Sheehy-Skeffington, Handel Booth, Tom Clarke, Ernie O'Malley, Keir Hardie, James Stephens, W. B. Yeats, G. K. Chesterton.

Maud Gonne McBride had written in their defence. Constance Markiewicz had worked in the food kitchens of Liberty Hall to cook for them and feed them. Sir William Orpen the painter and master of portraiture, was a regular visitor to Liberty Hall throughout the six months and, in his work of reminiscences, *Stories of Old Ireland and Myself* describes seeing Sheehy-Skeffington returning to the hall with his clothes in tatters after an attack on him by fanatics when he was bringing the children of strikers to the quays to be brought to homes in Britain where people would feed and look after them.

And George Russell (A. E.) wrote his letter which he headed *To the Masters of Dublin* which has become a classic of powerful and precisely moulded invective in which every sentence strikes straight into the centre of its target.

There were many many more who voiced their sympathy and compassion. In doing so they revealed that the seeds of a new concept of social responsibility had been planted in the conscience of the nation.

James Plunkett
Author of *Big Jim* (radio play broadcast by Radio Éireann in 1954); *The Risen People* (produced at Abbey Theatre in 1958); *Strumpet City* (1969); *Farewell Companions* (1977); *Collected Stories* (1977); *The Circus Animals* (1990), etc.

Labour and the Political Revolution

Professor Brian Farrell

The troubled teens of the twentieth-century were not the best of times for the birth of a new, radical political party in Ireland.

Trade unionists were divided and the imminence of Home Rule accentuated deeply-held convictions. While some in Congress clung to the idea that they should support the Irish Parliamentary Party to preserve a united Ireland, others argued that working-class unity was best secured by continuing close association with the British Labour Party. A growing group insisted that the Irish trade union movement needed to develop its own representation in any new Irish parliament. The issue became a contentious hardy annual at Congress. It was debated at the 1911 Congress, carried on Connolly's motion at the Clonmel Congress in 1912, fleshed out a little further when Congress met in Cork in 1913 but it was the twenty-first Annual Congress in Dublin in 1914 that truly marked the coming of age for Irish Labour as an organised political party. For the moment, at least, membership was confined to trade unionists.

Any optimistic expectation that the new party would transform the Irish situation was soon dampened down. Three months after its foundation the First World War broke out. Irish Labour, in common with comparable parties elsewhere in Europe, was confronted with the problem of competing loyalties challenging working-class solidarity. The First World War became another issue dividing organised Irish workers.

Even the *Irish Worker*, making a brief re-appearance during the local elections of 1915, had to acknowledge:

> the effects of the war in general, the calling up of working-class reservists, the resulting hopes for British victory, and the Labour Party's anti-war stand had damaged Labour's political appeal.[1]

In a parliamentary by-election in the Dublin College Green division the following June, Labour put in a creditable performance. There was no Labour candidate in another Dublin by-election. Indeed no official Labour candidate stood for parliamentary election until the Pact Election of 1922, seven years later.[2] The sense of drift in the newly-born Labour Party is reflected in the excuse for postponing the Congress – 'the minds of the people for the most part (were) engrossed in the progress of the European War'. In reality the trade union movement feared a split. That calculated political prudence was dramatically punctured when Connolly's potent combination of socialism and nationalism drove him into the Easter Rising and into history.

That Rising threatened the very existence of Labour. Connolly was dead. Other leaders – Foran, O'Brien, Farren, Daly, O'Shannon – were imprisoned. Liberty Hall was wrecked and files were destroyed. Labour's chosen strategy of emphasising social and economic issues and carefully avoiding the national issues of independence and self-determination was challenged by the spectacular 'propaganda of the deed' that Connolly had chosen. There is a palpable sense of embarrassment in the handling of the topic at the Annual Congress in 1916.

The international context of the 1916 Sligo Congress was critical, its local circumstances extraordinary. Across Europe a great war was already set to re-shape the political map and re-design the social and economic forces that would forge the twentieth-century. It was a moment of opportunity for the Labour movement. At home, the delegates met barely three months after the 1916 executions, at a time when thousands of Irish soldiers were fighting and dying in Flanders. It was a difficult time for any bold initiative. Its new leadership ducked.

In the vacuum created by the death of Connolly, the absence of Larkin in America and the arrest and deportation of Dublin trade-union leaders (including William O'Brien, secretary of the Dublin Trades Council, Thomas Foran, president of the ITGWU, P.T. Daly, secretary of Congress), two Belfast-based trade unionists took over temporary control: Davy Campbell, born and raised in Belfast, treasurer of Congress since 1912, and Thomas Johnson, chairman of the national executive. Johnson, so accidentally catapulted into leadership, was to have a dominant influence on the infant Irish Labour Party and remain its leader until 1927.

His leadership was dogged by disadvantage from the outset. Other Labour leaders were born in Britain but could claim Irish stock; Johnson was English and made no bones about it, claiming he was 'Liverpool English'. It was a heritage that would become increasingly problematic in the years ahead. Born in Liverpool in 1872, son of a skilled worker, he left school at the age of twelve to become an office boy and messenger. Introduced to socialism through the local branch of the Independent Labour Party, he first moved to Ireland to work for a fish merchant in Kinsale. In 1901 he moved to Belfast as commercial traveller for a fish company, but lost the job in 1918 as a result of his anti-conscription activities. In Belfast, Johnson and his wife Marie quickly became active in the Labour movement through the National Union of Shop Assistants and Clerks and the Belfast Trades Council. The Johnsons were involved in the Belfast Co-operative Society and he stood, unsuccessfully, for Labour in the Belfast Corporation elections in 1908. He was a delegate to the 1911 Congress and supported the motion for political action. By 1913 he was Vice-Chairman of the National Executive and in 1914 became Chairman.

He was a non-violent socialist in a militant and revolutionary time. He had neither the charismatic personality, nor control of a large union, to bolster his leadership. The fact that his trade unionism was a little old-fashioned, neither Marxist nor nationalist, allowed him to bridge the sectarian and political divide between Belfast and London. It fitted Tom Johnson for cautious conciliation rather than assertive leadership. Speaking to the 1916 Congress, he praised the work of Connolly, without ever endorsing his strategy or condemning his execution and contrived to knit together the horrific casualties of the First World War and Connolly's life and death:

> While laying these wreaths on the graves of our comrades who gave their lives for what they believed to be the cause of Ireland's Freedom – let us also remember those many others (some of whom had been chosen in years past to attend our Congresses) who have laid down their lives in another field, also for what they believed to be the Cause of Liberty and Democracy and for Love of their Country.

The Congress Report echoed the same carefully-balanced line of compromise. It regretted the loss of Connolly and other members, 'without for a moment pausing to consider the rightfulness or otherwise of recent events in our land'. But the delicately-phrased ambiguity masked a chronic indecision that would condemn Labour to take a seat on the sidelines in the next few critical years. At the heart of the dilemma for Labour was the need to avoid a split on Ulster.

Johnson raised the prospect of a 'bold forward move for Labour' but noted that though it was 'utterly illogical, unjust and scandalous' that unionists in arms should flaunt the will of the British parliament on Home Rule:

> there the facts are grinning! The British people are made that way, and whether we like it or not they are an important factor in the situation.

He argued that, since Labour spokesmen in the cities most affected had said they were prepared to wait fifty years for national unity, they must set about creating a strong party with a practical programme of social construction; with democracy – political and social – as an ideal and method.

But reasonable expectations and careful qualifications were soon swept aside during 1917 as a newly-organised Sinn Féin spread across Ireland. Individual Labour leaders like William O'Brien took part in the early by-election successes in North Roscommon. But in April the Dublin Trades Council declined Plunkett's invitation to join in a national assembly of various political groups. Soon after, it failed to retain a seat in a co-option contest in Dublin Corporation.

Labour's lethargy and indecision in electoral and political affairs – understandable because of the demands, successfully met, to develop trade union organisation – was in marked contrast to the energy and success of Sinn Féin, which by October 1917 had forged a new party stretching across a wide spectrum of national opinion. This broad coalition was poised to become the dominant force in an emerging new Ireland. The president of the new Sinn Féin, de Valera, invited Labour to stand aside until national freedom was attained before claiming 'its share of its patrimony'.

It was a temptation that Labour resisted. Any formal alliance or coalition posed strategically threatening questions for Labour. How could Labour join with an avowedly nationalist grouping like Sinn Féin – which included in its leadership Volunteer leaders like Eoin MacNeill and de Valera – and not lose substantial working-class support in the north? How could it be seen to accept a party whose social and economic policies had been articulated by Arthur Griffith – who had told leaders of Sinn Féin during the 1913 lock-out: 'I deny that socialism is a remedy for the existing evils or any remedy at all',[3] and not alienate its own members especially in Dublin? How could it achieve Labour's own stated objective without opposing and being seen to oppose, all bourgeois parties?

45

In Spring 1918, in the middle of the anti-conscription campaign, Congress announced its intention to nominate Labour candidates in the next parliamentary elections. This sharpened tension with Sinn Féin, which began an insidious attack on English influence in Labour. But Labour persisted with its plans. They paid particular attention to the major reform in the electoral system in the Representation of the People Bill going through parliament. It was, indeed, a radical measure that swept aside old property qualifications, introduced adult male suffrage, admitted women over thirty to the vote and trebled the size of the electorate.[4]

At the Congress held in Waterford in August 1918, chairman William O'Brien, drew attention to the great increase in the number of new voters and, in particular, of women:

> our sisters in many a good fight who have become enfranchised only as a result of many generations of great efforts ... I hope room will be made for the women voters as well as for those democratic organisations for which provision has not already been made.

Congress empowered the executive to draft a new constitution to be debated at a special Congress fixed for 2 November. The renewed political emphasis was reflected in the decision to change the name of the organisation to 'Irish Labour Party and Trade Union Congress'.

The National Executive met on 6 and 7 September and declared in favour of fielding candidates. Shortly afterwards a manifesto was issued. In an obvious effort to meet objections by nationalist-minded members, this simply committed the party 'for the moment' to a policy of abstention from Westminster. It was left open to the Special Congress to change this policy if warranted by 'altered circumstances and the interests of the workers and democracy'.

The Dublin Trades Council moved quickly to nominate candidates for four seats regarded as winnable. Elsewhere there was less enthusiasm and some confusion. In early October nominating conferences in Cork and Waterford were postponed until after the Special Congress. The Kilkenny Trades Council registered total disapproval of any contest against Sinn Féin as an 'immense disservice to Labour and the country'.

There had been suggestions throughout the year of an electoral pact between Sinn Féin and Labour. William O'Brien's private diary makes it clear that there was considerable disagreement at the highest levels of the Labour Party, both on the question of abstention and of challenging Sinn Féin. Confronted by divisions – generational, geographic, ideological and cultural – the National Executive decided to play safe.

Addressing the Special Congress, Johnson explained that much had changed in the previous six weeks. Instead of a 'War election', a 'Peace election' would now take place. 'In these circumstances,' said Johnson:

> A call comes from all parts of Ireland for a demonstration of unity on this question of self-determination, such as was witnessed on the Conscription issue. Your Executive believes that the workers of Ireland join earnestly in this desire, that they would willingly sacrifice for a brief period their aspirations towards political power. Ireland, too, demands all the rights of a free nation.[5]

Although the speech was punctuated by applause there were forceful counter arguments. But the majority was clearly relieved. Caution carried the day and Labour was not officially represented as the embryonic Irish state began to emerge through the First and Second Dáil.

There were deputies elected who could legitimately claim to carry Labour's flag, most notably, in the First Dáil, Countess Markievicz, who would become the first Irish woman minister. In the 1921 election to the Second Dáil, Richard Corish broke ranks and accepted a Sinn Féin nomination but quickly reverted to his real Labour roots. In addition there were close but official contacts between Labour and Sinn Féin. Labour organised strikes that played an important part in disrupting transport and civil authority. Union rooms were used for IRA meetings. 'The support provided by the labour movement emerged as a crucial factor'[6] in the independence struggle.

Labour was also able to influence Sinn Féin to accept, almost verbatim, its version of advanced social and democratic policy drawn up by Tom Johnson.[7] This so-called 'Democratic Programme' was adopted at the first meeting of the First Dáil on 21 January 1919. It was very far removed from the economic ideas of Griffith, but he was in jail and unable to interfere. It was resisted by a group of IRB leaders. But, after minor changes by Seán T. O'Kelly, the Democratic Programme was carried in the Dáil. It was in effect, a trade-off: it gave Sinn Féin and the Dáil legitimacy in the international socialist world and it allowed Labour, which lacked formal parliamentary representation, to claim that the Dáil was committed to a socialist programme.

The question of Labour's relations with Sinn Féin came to a head again in the long-delayed municipal and urban council elections that were called in January 1920. A special conference in Dublin adopted a programme with an emphasis on traditional Labour demands – medical treatment and meals for school children, a local housing scheme and organisation of fuel supplies. There were more radical proposals, including occupation and utilisation of lands, buildings and machinery 'unreasonably withheld from use'.

Despite problems in particular areas – most critically in Dublin – there appears to have been a reasonable working electoral alliance between Labour and Sinn Féin in most districts. The situation in Dublin was aggravated by internal feuds within the Transport Union. The attempt to foment division in Belfast by the nomination of candidates from the so-called Ulster Unionist Labour Association did not work. The overall results were impressive for Labour. It put forward 595 candidates for the 1,470 seats and a total of 341 were elected.

The political potential of Labour was again displayed in the county council and rural district elections held in June 1920. The trade union movement was barely organised in most parts of rural Ireland and most candidates chose to run as 'Labour-Republicans'. According to Sinn Féin's *Irish Bulletin* 90% of the 362 elected Labour candidates to rural district councils and 83% of the 460 elected to boards of guardians ran as 'Labour-Republicans'.

This level of participation and success contrasted with Labour's withdrawal from parliamentary elections. The party decided to abstain from the 1921 elections to both the northern and southern parliaments. As new institutions of government emerged and major issues were decided that would shape Ireland in the decades ahead, Labour remained on the side-lines. Labour played no direct part in the creation of either the Dáil or 'Stormont' regimes. It was not directly involved in the negotiation of the Treaty nor the subsequent, and divisive, debate that triggered a civil war. As partition became institutionalised, there was no attempt to persist with an all-Ireland Labour Party.

Despite all that had happened, Labour gave a remarkable performance in the Pact Election of 1922. A special conference in February 1922, held in the Abbey Theatre, recognised that there were acutely divergent views on the Treaty:

but there can be no divergence on the question of whether Labour should have its own independent representation in an Irish Parliament.

It was also pointed out that the introduction of proportional representation meant that voters could register their views, by way of transfers, on both the Treaty and their policy preferences. The election programme was reformist rather than radical and, after some difficulties, a total of eighteen Labour candidates were chosen.

Their selection showed that party managers were already adept at identifying sources of Labour support. It also showed considerable physical as well as moral courage in withstanding intimidation and a campaign that frequently fell back on abuse. Johnson was attacked not merely as English but as a 'loyal son of the Empire'; O'Shannon denounced as an atheist; O'Brien accused of trying to sabotage Sinn Féin.

The result was a success for Labour that might have been a triumph if more candidates had been selected. Securing 21.3% of the votes cast it saw seventeen of its candidates elected. The eighteenth, J.T. O'Farrell, Irish Secretary of the Railway Clerks' Association, standing in Dublin North-West (where Larkin had been originally nominated) lost by only thirteen voters. Some suggested he was cheated by anti-treaty poll workers; others that Larkin supporters did not vote for O'Farrell.[8]

There was no time to savour victory and no early opportunity for Labour to take its seats in the Dáil. Instead, like the rest of the country, the party had to cope with civil war. The Labour leaders made unsuccessful efforts to broker a peace and were abused for their pains on both sides.

As the civil war blazed, one thing after another delayed the inaugural meeting of the new Dáil. When the Dáil eventually sat, Labour began the role it would continue for the next five years because of republican abstention; it became the official opposition, pointedly critical of the government party Cumann na nGaedheal but consistently supportive of the new state. All but one of its TDs took the oath. Although Labour had consistently condemned any proposals to establish an upper chamber, five prominent members joined the Senate. Labour also assisted in drawing up the Standing Orders of the Dáil.

Labour played a vigorously critical and interventionist role as the major parliamentary opposition. It consistently attacked the Cosgrave government's draconian measures to deal with the civil war. It sought – unsuccessfully – to amend the draft IFS Constitution. It voted against the inclusion of university representation as undemocratic and attempted to have a section of the 'Democratic Programme' inserted into the preamble. Labour also urged the new government to tackle urgent issues of unemployment and taxation.

All of this was worthy and responsible. Despite considerable provocation from the government side Johnson had presented himself and his party as sober and business-like. Reduced to only fourteen deputies, Labour had a quite disproportionate impact.[9]

But much of this parliamentary activity was far removed from the everyday concerns of Labour supporters. Besides, its constructive opposition in the Dáil was overtaken by renewed internal rivalry when Jim Larkin returned from the United States. It was a dreadful backdrop to the 1923 general election. The number of Dáil seats was increased from 128 to 133. Labour nominated forty-one candidates in twenth-six of the thirty constituencies. Larkin endorsed five independent labour candidates – four in Dublin, one in Tipperary. Despite the split the party was optimistic and this rubbed off on newspaper predictions of the outcome. The actual results were most disappointing.

Labour's analysis rightly stressed the low level of organisational activity that greatly reduced Labour's turn-out:

> The results were most disappointing from a Labour point of view. The comparative smallness of the Labour vote was due in part to the want of suitable political machinery and lack of funds. But it was also due largely to the fact that Irish working-class electors have not yet fully realised the need for independent working-class representation and still allow themselves to be misled[10]

This election set the seal on the long-term trend of the Labour Party – a geographical concentration in rural Leinster and Munster associated with areas where a combination of large groups of agricultural workers and smaller sets of employees in larger towns gave the party a secure organisational base but conspicuous weakness in the large cities of Dublin, Cork and Limerick. The spread is graphically illustrated in Labour's 1923 first preference vote.[11]

The results tempted Johnson to suggest that Labour in the Fourth Dáil would restrict itself solely to social and economic issues. Such tactics would have made parliamentary democracy impossible. It would, in effect, have reduced the Dáil to the status of a single-party chamber. In fact, Johnson led his party into four years of vigorous opposition. His own contribution was heroic. With immense energy, extraordinary dedication and the range of interests of a born polymath, he produced carefully researched and argued speeches on all major and many minor issues. Indeed, it may have been a defect of his leadership that his constant interventions over-shadowed and possibly constrained his colleagues. Johnson was steady rather than spectacular, reasoned rather than rabble-rousing, persistent rather than passionate in putting Labour's case. He was, in a true sense, a founding father of modern Irish representative democracy. He must also be given much of the credit for the improvement in the party's electoral performance through the 1920s.

In the 1925 local elections the results were patchy. In the five by-elections (mainly in Dublin) contested by the party it polled above its 1923 vote but failed to win seats. These results were achieved despite the continued split between O'Brien and Larkin in the trade union movement that directly affected Labour's organisation.

In the run-up to the June 1927 election the leadership worked hard to improve the situation. There was neither the organisational nor financial backing to nominate Labour candidates in every constituency. Forty-four candidates were nominated – three less than in 1923. Most were trade union officials; there were no new outstanding national figures. The June 1927 election programme rehearsed the same reformist tone of the 1922 and 1923 manifestos. Responsibility and restraint, not revolution, were the key-words of Labour policy and strategy in the 1920s. It continued to evade the national and constitutional issues that ran, like a fault-line, through Irish public opinion.

The result for Labour was only a 2% growth in its first preference vote, but an increase to twenty-two elected deputies, largely the result of effective targeting in strongly Labour areas. The fact that the Larkinite Dublin Trades Council did not contest the election helped. But there was a warning of future trouble in County Dublin where Norton lost and party leader Johnson struggled to retain his seat. Even more ominous for Labour was the surge of support for newly-formed Fianna Fáil.

The inconclusive outcome bred a new instability. In the short-lived Dáil that followed, Johnson was again forced to avoid the contentious issue of the Oath – calling it 'a matter of subordinate interest'. But, after the assassination of O'Higgins,

51

Fianna Fáil were forced to take the Oath and their Dáil seats. That changed the whole parliamentary configuration permanently. A possible Labour-led minority government was lost on the casting vote of the Ceann Comhairle. It was Labour's last best chance to enter government; it would be more than twenty years before the first Labour ministers sat at the Irish Cabinet table. Labour's strategic displacement was signalled in the immediate new general election called for September 1927.

Labour's relative electoral success three months earlier evaporated. It could only field twenty-eight candidates. Its national vote was cut by a quarter; in Dublin it was halved. Also in Dublin, Johnson lost his seat and the party was reduced to thirteen deputies in the Dáil.

1927 marked the end of a decade of opportunity for the Labour Party. A dozen years after the party's formal foundation, it was firmly established as a permanent part of the Irish parliamentary scene. It had played an important and valuable role in ensuring the stability of the new Irish Free State and strengthening its democratic institutions. It had also allowed two emerging catch-all parties to make significant and long-lasting inroads into its basic working-class constituency. Perhaps most important of all, it had allowed others to set the political, social and economic agenda for the decades ahead.

There was, in Professor Patrick Lynch's words in a Thomas Davis lecture broadcast nearly thirty years ago, 'little use for idealism and less scope for utopianism in the Irish Free State'. Arguably, Labour had too much of both to make an effective impact on a conservative society. It had also too much internal division and too much concern for its trade union constituency, to take a stand on the Irish state. The concern to consolidate the strength of the basic trade union movement itself was paramount. Men like O'Brien were, first and foremost, trade union leaders. For a moment, under the influence of Connolly, it might have offered a combination of nationalism and socialism as an alternative political choice, even if not as a social revolution.

Connolly's execution in 1916 killed that opportunity. Labour stood on the sidelines as others defined the cleavages that shaped Irish political society. The circumstances of its birth, the weakness of its organisation, the character of its leaders and the nature of its priorities condemned it to a minority role. It is one of the reasons why political change in early twentieth-century Ireland fell so far short of being a political revolution.

1. *Irish Worker*, 30 January 1915.
2. Richard Corish broke ranks and stood for Sinn Féin in 1921.
3. 1916 Report, p. 21.
4. *Sinn Féin*, 25 October 1913. Compare Connolly's apt comment that 'a change from Toryism to Sinn Féinism would simply be a change from the devil they (the workers) do know to the devil they do not know.' James Connolly, *Socialism and Nationalism*, Three Candles Press, Dublin, 1948, p. 89.
5. On the significance of the Representation of the People Act see Brian Farrell, *The Founding of Dáil Éireann: parliament and nation-building*, Gill and Macmillan, Dublin, 1971, pp. 45-47.
6. Special Congress Report 1918, pp. 103-104.
7 Arthur Mitchell, *Labour in Irish Politics*, Barnes and Noble, New York, 1974, pp. 65-67.
8. This paragraph is based on Farrell, *op. cit.*, pp. 57-61 and appendix.
9. In an interview with the author, 6 March 1970, John T. O'Farrell said he knew little about the question of miscounts but that 'a view was taken that a Minister (his opponent, Joseph McGrath) must be protected'.
10. Of the original seventeen, Michael Bradley died without ever taking his seat, Nicholas Phelan was expelled for failure to attend and Patrick Gaffney refused to take the Oath. *Annual Report 1923*, p. 32, pp. 39-40.
11. *Special Congress Report 1924* pp. 89-90. See Map 17 in E. Rumpf and A. C. Hepburn, *Nationalism and Socialism in Twentieth-century Ireland*, Liverpool University Press, 1977, p. 66.

Professor Brian Farrell

Director-General, Institute of European Affairs, Dublin. Author of *The Founding of Dáil Éireann: Parliament and Nation-Building* (1971); *Seán Lemass* (1983), etc.

War and Syndicalism 1914-1923

Dr Emmet O'Connor

From a position of unprecedented power on the brink of the 1913 lock-out, trade unionism had become a demoralised and declining force a year later; reduced to strongholds in Dublin, Belfast, and a few other provincial towns, with a slim presence among general workers and none at all on the land.[1] The Irish Trades Union Congress was nothing more than an annual talking shop: even during the lock-out Congress had not been mobilised. It was to the British TUC that Connolly and Larkin turned for help. In theory, Congress had assumed a second function as a political party: in practice that meant very little. Initially, the outbreak of world war in August 1914 further weakened the movement. It seemed as if the industrial truce between British labour and the government would suspend militancy for the duration of the war: for despite the achievements of Larkin, labour still looked to Britain for leadership and example. Recruitment into the British army disrupted union membership, and with the army a constant source of employment the perceived need for trade unionism was diminished.

Yet, within five years, labour was stronger than ever; militant, radical, and confident of a great future. Within another five years, the wheel had turned again and, once more, trade unionism was in serious decline. How had this extraordinary change of fortunes come about? The primary factor was the war-time economic boom and subsequent slump. Secondary factors were the political unrest of 1916-23 and the climate of class struggle internationally.

The First World War had little effect on the structure of the Irish workforce. The few munitions factories located here were small and employed a mere 2,169 persons by the armistice. Yet the economic impact of the war was profound. With every passing year more sectors of industry were harnessed to the war effort. Meeting the needs of Britain's war machine brought a legendary prosperity to Irish employers. Employees were not so lucky. Food and fuel supplies deteriorated, and inflation, something most people had no previous experience of, reduced real

54

wages from 1914 to 1916, generating accusations of profiteering against farmers, businessmen, and shopkeepers.

If the first half of the war stored-up social grievances, production demands and the growing manpower shortage after 1916 provided the means of redress. Conditions for wage increases materialised in two ways: through government intervention to increase pay in war-related industries and, later through the all-round economic improvement. The government took control of the shipyards and railways in 1916 making provision for the payment of war bonuses. Aerodrome and other military construction, together with the repair of Dublin's shell-torn city centre, revived the building line in 1917-18. The major state intervention came in January 1917. To deal with an emerging crisis of food supply, compulsory tillage orders were introduced under the Corn Production Act. Tillage was labour intensive and, to keep labour on the land, an Agricultural Wages Board was appointed subsequently to set minimum wage rates for farm workers. After the war, the release of 'pent-up' consumer demand generated a brief economic boom.

The government maintained its wartime economic controls up to 1920-21. Indeed, to minimise class conflict, state intervention was extended. The British Ministry of Labour opened an Irish Department in July 1919, and fifteen new trade boards were introduced in little over a year to fix basic wage rates in the 'sweated trades'. By August 1920, there were nineteen trade boards covering 148,000 employees, the bulk of them in Ulster's textile and clothing industries, sectors of large female employment, where unions had hitherto been very weak.[2] On aggregate, wages rose faster than prices from 1916, overtaking pre-war levels by 1919-20, until the economy hit a disastrous slump in 1920-21.

Given the nature of capitalism, the money was only for those who could get it. In round figures, trade union membership rocketed from 100,000 in 1916 to 250,000 by 1920; or about 27% of the waged workforce, an impressive proportion by the standards of the time.[3] Labour became a nation-wide force. The number of trades councils for example, multiplied from six in 1914 to fifteen by 1918 and forty-six by 1921. Trade unionism was no longer confined to the craftsman or the docker, but embraced the labourer and the clerk as well. Moreover, it assimilated the class consciousness fermenting since the early months of the war, and turned it into syndicalism.

A catalyst in the making of syndicalism was the transformation of wage movements into the 'wages movement'. The 'wages movement' was not so much a co-ordinated effort as a mentality. It signified the general nature of trade unionism, and the sense of unions as incessant engines of wage militancy, geared ultimately to the triumph of the working class.

The first hint of change in the character of organised labour came with the food supply crisis. As food and fuel supplies dwindled alarmingly in the winter of 1916, Congress called a special conference in December to demand price control and a ban on exports of basic foodstuffs. It was the first time that Congress had given a lead to the movement, and it widened the agenda of labour. To combat profiteering, trade union backed consumer co-operatives were formed in many towns. Though limited in scale, and mostly of brief duration, they were important in expressing the instinctive anti-capitalist feeling welling up among the people.

With the introduction of compulsory tillage farm workers were soon exploiting their novel scarcity value, injecting life into the land and labour associations first set up in the 1890s. By 1918, they were joining trade unions in large numbers. The Irish Transport and General Workers' Union mustered 60,000 members in agriculture by 1920, chiefly in the twelve south-eastern, mostly tillage counties. Thousands of labourers in Ulster were recruited into the National Amalgamated Union of Labour and the Workers' Union. Surmounting the enormous difficulty of organising farm workers encouraged an equally remarkable rise of general unionism in the towns. As unrest spread, the rush of pay claims from so many disparate occupations turned wage movements into the 'wages movement'.

A trigger of growth among unskilled urban workers was the general strike against conscription on 23 April 1918. It was symbolic of labour's new-found ambition that it sought to play a part in the anti-conscription campaign. Though hardly a controversial action, the success of Ireland's first general strike made labour seem a power in the land.

The wages movement rolled on into the post-war years, sustained by prosperity and the continuation of government intervention in the economy, politicised by the national revolution, and facilitated by the breakdown of policing during the War of Independence.

The lion's share of growth fell to the Irish Transport and General Workers' Union.[4] Following its re-organisation after the trauma of Easter Week, the ITGWU mushroomed from 5,000 members to 120,000 by 1920. To cope with the problems posed by this massive expansion, the union turned to Larkin and Connolly for inspiration. For though Larkin was in America from 1914 to 1923, and Connolly was executed in May 1916, their syndicalist ideas had a guiding influence on tactics and strategy.

Syndicalism originated in France in the 1890s – *syndicat* is the French for trade union – in response to the failure of existing socialist politics – reformist, Marxist, and anarchist alike. Syndicalists contended that party politics created an elite, which would always betray the masses. In any case, political power simply reflected economic power. So the best means of struggle was through industrial action to establish workers' control at the point of production. This attempt to graft revolution onto trade unionism coincided with an escalation of militancy internationally, and syndicalism had an impact in most developed countries before the Bolshevik revolution made communism the world's premier revolutionary ideology.

In many places, syndicalism was more a mentality than a movement. Larkin's syndicalism was emphatically experiential and boiled down to the principle of sympathetic action, which he saw as the cutting edge of a working-class code of morality. Connolly, by contrast, learned his syndicalism from the American theorist, Daniel De Leon, and the Industrial Workers of the World – the Wobblies. The key emphasis in Connolly's approach was class unity, to be realised in industrial unions, as opposed to sectional unions, and ideally in One Big Union – the OBU.

Irish syndicalism owed much to Larkin and Connolly, but it was too the product of structural factors. With the exception of France itself, syndicalism tended to be strongest in backward pockets of advanced countries, where unskilled or marginal workers were neglected by established trade unions. In these cases, syndicalists had the scope to form their own unions. The Wobblies were most successful in the western states of America, among miners, migrant labourers and timber workers; farm labourers made up half of the Unione Sindicale Italiana's pre-1914 membership; and in Canada a clear division emerged in the post-war struggle between craft unions based in the industrial heartland of the eastern provinces, and the One Big Union, which had originated among newly-industrialised workers over

57

the Rockies in British Columbia. As a fringe area of trade unionism nominally within the remit of British labour, but in practice neglected by it; as an economically peripheral region with a heavy reliance on primary production; and as an area where effective industrial tactics had to be militant, southern Ireland was a fairly typical centre of syndicalism.

When ITGWU members spontaneously revived Larkinite sympathetic action in 1918 and after, and developed it into the more effective weapon of general action, their leaders took a leaf from Connolly's *Socialism Made Easy*. On 1 July 1918, the ITGWU issued *The Lines of Progress*, a pamphlet intended to 'advance Connolly's OBU idea' in order to develop 'a scientific solution to the Labour question'. *The Lines of Progress* argued for all workers to be in one union, organised in industrial sections. It also held out the promise that complete economic and political freedom could be achieved through the OBU:

> With this machine in their possession the workers of Ireland can break all their chains with ease and from the mere rallying cry of political parties turn Freedom into a glorious reality ...

Note the very syndicalist dismissal of political parties, and their 'mere rallying cry'. The union also revived Larkinite ideas on working-class culture. Its annual report for 1919 invited members to conceive of the union 'as a social centre, round which they can build every activity of their existence, and which, wisely used, can be made to remedy all their grievances'.

One finds a clear expression of syndicalist ideas in the ITGWU, in a rank and file tendency in the National Union of Railwaymen grouped around the journal *New Way*, and in aspects of Congress policy. Industrial unionism enjoyed a wider appeal as a model for union re-organisation. However, there was never a core of card-carrying syndicalists within the movement, and it would be a mistake to see the ideology as directed. It emerged in response to the breathless growth of membership, and the success of direct action in a climate of revolution at home and abroad. For some ITGWU leaders, notably the union's real chief, William O'Brien, syndicalism was attractive only as long as militancy was profitable.[5]

Nonetheless, for a time it appeared as if the ITGWU – or the OBU as it liked to be called – was a revolutionary force. Its members were to the fore in struggle. It was significant too that few ITGWU officials were tested bureaucrats. Having risen from the ranks in the great advance, their instincts as yet lay with the membership rather than the organisation. Despite the propaganda extolling the OBU as a finely-marshalled machine, the union grew too quickly and too spontaneously for headquarters to establish effective central control. In rural areas especially, strikes came to rely increasingly on co-ordinated violence and sabotage, tactics dependent on revolutionary conditions. In small towns the ITGWU pioneered the general local strike, of which there were eighteen during the advance of the wages movement. Workplace seizures or soviets, almost all involving the ITGWU, emerged from November 1918 onwards. Before the slump, soviets were substantially a strike tactic. In all cases, employers' property was handed back in return for wage increases. Even so, the soviets definitely indicated a political ambition. The most extensive seizure prior to the slump, that of thirteen Limerick creameries in 1920, known as the 'Knocklong soviet', was a well-planned affair directed by union officials.[6] Headquarters indulged, indeed its journals the *Voice of Labour* and the *Watchword of Labour* applauded, revolutionary methods as long as they paid dividends. That would change with the slump.

The impact of transition at the base was unmistakable at the 1918 Annual Congress. Two hundred and forty delegates attended, compared with ninety-nine the previous year. William O'Brien's Presidential address strained to strike a historic note, praising Connolly and his influence on 'the great Russian Revolution'. Equally conscious of history, the delegates passed unanimously a motion of support for the Bolsheviks, peace in Europe, and self-determination for all peoples. Congress was making progress fast. Before 1917, it had still been composed mainly of British-based unions; a drawback because one could not build a movement on trade union branches, only on trade unions. It had no secretariat, and offered no leadership. And it had no ideas beyond a few assumptions borrowed from British labourism. Now largely Irish-based, and eager to apply socialism to Irish conditions, Congress aimed to become a movement in the fullest sense. A more comprehensive policy was adopted, and the 1918 Congress took as its objective the promotion of working-class organisation socially, industrially, and politically in co-ops, trade unions, and a party. No amount of policy, however, could compensate for inexperience and lack of vision. A Congress executive accustomed since 1894 to a passive stewardship could not become a management team overnight. In three crucial areas the Congress leadership was found wanting.

The most immediate failure occurred in relation to nationalism. Congress never shook off the notion – taken from the British left – that nationalism was something to be kept at arms length. While willing to go with the flow of popular sentiment, it was not prepared to lead opinion, or bargain with the nationalists. Thus, Congress backed the anti-conscription campaign, only to withdraw from the 1918 general election rather than stand independently or conclude an electoral deal with Sinn Féin. Similarly, after the Sinn Féin landslide, Congress lent valuable assistance to the Republic without demanding concessions from Sinn Féin. The net result was an opportunity wasted. Labour got nothing out of the national revolution other than a few platitudes from republicans and the friendly neutrality of the IRA towards the wages movement. It certainly could have got more. As L. J. Duffy told the 1924 Congress:

> Sinn Féin sought, secured and acknowledged the ready co-operation of the Labour Movement during the Anglo-Irish war. But the Labour Movement entered into the compact as a vassal rather than a co-partner. Let us not blame Sinn Féin for that position. Congress is responsible entirely for the position that grew up around the struggle with England.[7]

The second policy failure was on the industrial front. In February 1919, a special Congress met to co-ordinate wage movement. Affiliates were then circulated with a document on a 'Proposed United National Wages and Hours Movement'. The objectives included a forty-four hour week, a 50 shilling weekly minimum wage, and a general 150 per cent increase on pre-war wage levels. It soon became apparent that a co-ordinated wages movement required co-ordination machinery. The Congress executive resolved on a bold and imaginative option, one obviously influenced by syndicalism. It recommended affiliates to re-group in ten industrial sectors with the intention of making Congress 'a single, all-inclusive Irish Workers' Union' which, through its political and industrial activities, would eventually realise 'the taking over control of industry by the organised working class'. Though this was agreed at the 1919 Congress in August, nothing was done to implement it. It was another opportunity wasted, for unions would never be as united again for another twenty years.

The third area of failure related to Ulster. The war years saw a growing divergence between trade unionism north and south. Whereas most southern workers joined Irish unions, most northerners joined British unions, who tended to be less involved with Congress at this time. For industrial and political reasons, northern wage movements never gelled into the wages movement. In the key engineering and shipbuilding sectors, war production brought few changes in working practices. Skill displacement or dilution, which created 'Red Clydeside' in Glasgow, was resisted successfully by the craft unions in Belfast. Government control of shipbuilding did lead to a narrowing of wage differentials between skilled and unskilled, and a big increase in membership of general unions. Craft unions went some way to restoring the differential in 1917, and the issue provoked the only major strike of the war years in Belfast.

In the uncertain aftermath of the armistice, it looked as if sectionalism might be rattled. On 25 January 1919, 30,000 Belfast engineering and shipbuilding workers struck unofficially for a forty-four hour week. Soon the trouble spread to municipal employees. Control of power supplies gave the strike committee some administrative authority and the establishment of a permit system, enforced by pickets, led journalists to refer to the 'Belfast Soviet'. Alarmed at the contagion of 'Bolshevism' and the prospect of Sinn Féin winning Protestant support through it, Dublin Castle sent in troops on 15 February to restore municipal services. The strike collapsed within a few days, and marked a deceleration of northern wage movements. In truth there was little cause for alarm. Sensitive to its fragile base, the strike committee had strained to moderate radical impulses, and ignored offers of help from Congress and the ITGWU. Although 1919-20 were paramount years for Belfast Labourism, the massive dispute carried a tentative import.

While it was certainly beyond its capacity to bring Ulster into any real industrial unity with the south, Congress can be faulted for doing nothing to foster links with the political labour groups that sprang up in Ulster after 1917, most of whom were Protestant-led, and anti-partition. When in 1920, loyalists reacted brutally against 'the labour enemy within', and expelled at least 7,400 workers from their jobs, one quarter of whom were Protestant and victimised for their labour sympathies, the Congress response was feeble.[8]

None of these failings seemed important at the time. Contemporaries were more impressed with Labour's new-found influence. Dáil Éireann had adopted, albeit in diluted form, Labour's political manifesto, the 'Democratic Programme'. On the industrial front, trade unions looked invincible. Congress itself was a revelation. In addition to the general strike against conscription, it had declared a 'general holiday' on May Day 1919 for international proletarian solidarity and self-determination for all peoples. Marking a fanfare for the 'Red Flag times', parades were held all over the country. Labour's finest hour came on 12 April 1920, when Congress called an immediate indefinite general stoppage for the release of political prisoners on hunger strike. Co-ordinated by Workers' Councils, many of which assumed a 'soviet'-style command of local government for the occasion, the strike was a spectacular demonstration of Labour discipline; Dublin Castle released the prisoners after two days. Though prompted by a national issue, the strike uncovered the social revolutionary dynamic bubbling at the base of the movement. As the *Manchester Guardian* remarked on 20 April:

> The direction of affairs passed during the strike to these (workers') councils, which were formed not on a local but on a class basis ... it is no exaggeration to trace a flavour of proletarian dictatorship about some aspects of the strike.

Whichever way the national revolution unfolded, Labour was set to be a major player in the new Ireland. Or so it seemed.

Massive expansion of the world's productive capacity during the First World War followed by a further increase in output to meet the initial demands of a peace-time market, led to a crisis of overproduction in the autumn of 1920. Food prices were the first to tumble, causing a severe depression in agriculture. During 1921, Irish manufacturing trade was almost halved. By December, over 26% of workers were idle. Rising unemployment depressed consumer demand, sending the economy tail-spinning into recession. As the British government dismantled its wartime measures to control prices and cushion wage levels, its successor regimes in Ireland showed no desire to reverse the process. Employers clamoured for the restoration of pre-war pay rates.

To avoid a death of a thousand cuts, the 1921 Congress affirmed conviction in industrial unionism as a strategic riposte to the employers' counter-attack, and pledged to 'hold the harvest' of wage gains. The plan was that a demand for wage reductions from any one sector would be met with united resistance. Lurking among the rank and file was a feeling that if employers could not survive economically, workers would take their place. In reality, inter-union solidarity soon crumbled. Irish unions, especially the ITGWU, exploited the readiness of their British-based counterparts to accept wage cuts in line with the more rapidly-falling wage rates cross-channel. During 1922, a deep and persistent anglophobia crept into the rivalry, aggravated by the inaction of British Labour in the face of northern sectarianism and its stubborn intention to remain in post-colonial Ireland. Nor was the squabbling confined to Anglo-Irish friction. Inter-union competition for a dwindling pool of membership soured industrial unionism; the OBU, the cynics said, meant 'O'Brien's Union'.

Militant action in conditions of political instability and the absence of effective policing up to the spring of 1923, enabled workers to put up a dogged fight. But labour went down, section by section, slowly but surely succumbing to the wage-cutting offensive. By December 1923 it was all over. Agricultural trade unionism was near collapse; general unions were in severe decline; craft and white-collar unions suffered too. Congress membership had fallen to 175,000 by 1924, and withered to 92,000 by 1929.

Trade unions were not just defeated; they were discredited. In many instances, workers had pressed for tougher action and then blamed the inevitable retreat on leadership betrayal. Over eighty soviets were declared in 1922 for example, but against union advice, and the ITGWU let them be crushed by the Free State army with scarcely a protest. It was naive of labour leaders to think, and reckless to promise, that they could 'hold the harvest'. Economic reality was against them. To have pledged so much and delivered so little led to disillusionment with syndicalism and all that went with the 'Red Flag times'. Ironically, the debacle was compounded by Jim Larkin. On his return to Ireland in April 1923, Larkin set about restoring his old command of the ITGWU. Neither O'Brien nor the union executive were willing to stomach his domineering ways, and with 'Big Jim' it was still a case of 'rule or ruin'. In June, as the ITGWU was steeling itself for the employers' final offensive, he criticised the executive publicly and, making little effort to rationalise his action ideologically, launched a campaign of vilification against the ITGWU and Congress leadership that would fester for ten years.[9]

Neither did the Labour Party escape from the shambles. In February 1922, Congress discussed the implications of the Anglo-Irish Treaty and decided to contest the next elections to Dáil Éireann, and, in effect, endorse the proposed Free State regime. Opposition came from a medley of communists, republicans, and those who dismissed party politics as a vain diversion from the industrial struggle. The Labour leadership, on the other hand, believed the national revolution to have run its course, and hoped that a return to normality would allow politics to focus on a social and economic agenda. Though Congress underlined its aspirations with another general strike, against pro- and anti-treaty militarism, on 24 April, the dream of a 'normal' class politics merely illustrated Labour's inability to address the visceral realities of nationalism.

Labour duly fought its first general election in June. To everyone's surprise, seventeen of its eighteen candidates were victorious. Certainly, the fact that Labour and a handful of Farmers' Party nominees offered the only alternative to continued Sinn Féin dictatorship contributed to the triumph; however, it reflected too the fighting spirit of trade unionists, most of whom were still confident of 'holding the harvest'. With the anti-treatyites rejecting Dáil Éireann, labour became the official opposition. Party leader Tom Johnson was determined to keep it that way.[10] Democracy, he believed, depended on it. This stolid constitutionalism robbed the party of the threat of abstention or a Labour-republican alliance, the one weapon which might have compelled the government to restrain the employers' attack on trade unions, an attack backed frequently by partisan use of the army. The party anticipated a good showing in the 1923 general election, oblivious to the fact that it had demonstrated its irrelevance to industrial conflict. It was reduced to fourteen TDs.

The depth of the 1921-23 catastrophe was unique in the way it turned Labour against itself, and obliterated the memory of the glory years of 1917-21; of the general strikes and the soviets, of the ambition to make One Big Union and a workers' republic. Yet, the clock had not been put back to 1914. Labour retained the structural framework developed during the post-1916 advance. Indeed, the Irish labour movement can be said to have been formed in the 'Red Flag times'. Trade unions were now largely native based, and the old dependency on Britain finally ended.

Congress had become a voice of the movement, trades councils were more numerous, and a Labour Party was in being. The principle of trade unionism for all had been established, and workers had shown that they had the capacity to apply that principle in better times.

---

1. The following account is based on Emmet O'Connor, *Syndicalism in Ireland 1917-23*, Cork, 1988, and *A Labour History of Ireland*, 1824-1960, Dublin, 1992, pp. 89-116.
2. On this neglected subject see Brendan Browne, Trade Boards in Northern Ireland, 1909-45, PhD, Queen's University, Belfast, 1989, pp. 146-57, p. 340.
3. It is difficult to be precise about membership as, up to 1919, Congress affiliation figures made no distinction between overlapping trade union and trades council membership. Also, there were trade unionists not affiliated to Congress, estimated at some 30,000 in 1920: these were located mainly in the north-east.
4. An invaluable source is C. Desmond Greaves, *The Irish Transport and General Workers' Union: the Formative Years, 1909-23*, Dublin, 1982.
5. Though the strongest man in the movement from 1918 to his retirement in 1946, O'Brien remains understudied, but see *Forth the Banners Go: Reminiscences of William O'Brien as told to Edward MacLysaght*, Dublin, 1969, and D. R. O'Connor Lysaght, 'The rake's progress of a syndicalist: the political career of William O'Brien, Irish labour leader', *Saothar* (1983), pp. 48-62.
6. The best account of the soviets is D.R. O'Connor Lysaght. 'The Munster soviet creameries', *Saotharlann Staire Éireann* (1981), pp. 36-49.
7. Irish Labour Party and Trade Union Congress, *Annual Report*, 1924, p. 120. Duffy was a member of the Congress executive.
8. See Henry Patterson, *Class Conflict and Sectarianism; the Protestant Working Class and the Belfast Labour Movement, 1869-1920*, Belfast, 1980, pp. 115-42, and Austen Morgan, *Labour and Partition: the Belfast Working Class, 1905-23*, London, 1991, pp. 250-312.
9. See Emmet Larkin, *James Larkin, 1876-1947: Irish Labour Leader*, London, 1965.
10. J. Anthony Gaughan, *Thomas Johnson*, Dublin 1980, is a very informative if apolitical biography.

Dr Emmet O'Connor
Lecturer in Politics, University of Ulster, Magee College, Derry. Author of *A Labour History of Ireland 1824-1960* (1992), *Syndicalism in Ireland 1917-1923* (1988), etc. Co-editor of *Saothar*.

The Trade Union Movement in Northern Ireland

Dr Terry Cradden

Trade unions in the North of Ireland, and especially in Northern Ireland post-partition, have often been dealt with rather harshly by writers on the labour movement.[1] Some criticism has of course been justified; but most of it has been to do with the failure of the unions to conform to the ideological predilections and political prescriptions of the people concerned. One of my purposes here, therefore, is to offer a corrective, at least, to the dismal picture of the Northern Ireland movement which has sometimes been painted.

The late Professor Charles McCarthy opened his pioneering account of trade unionism in modern Ireland by observing that:

> An understanding of the Irish trade union movement is an understanding of two cities, Dublin and Belfast ... There is a great gulf in understanding between the two cities, a radical difference in the way society is understood, and even a certain perversity of mind regarding one another ...[2]

What he was pointing us towards, of course, is a fascinating conundrum: of the persistence of all-Ireland trade union links and relationships, as against the great differences in the historical experience of trade unionism north and south over the last one hundred years. Even in the closing decade of the nineteenth century, when the Irish Trades Union Congress (ITUC) was formed, Belfast was different from Dublin in three important ways: in the level of its industrialisation; in the the more rapidly changing form of its trade unionism; and in the sectarian nature of its politics.

The rise of industry, the first difference, is the easiest to describe. By the 1890s the Lagan Valley formed part of a great northern industrial and mercantile triangle with Merseyside in the north-west of England and the Strathclyde region of Scotland. Almost half the working population in the six north-eastern counties of Ireland were employed in industrial occupations – as compared to less than a quarter in the rest of the country.[3] Belfast was the obvious leader in this development, although

Bangor, Lurgan, Portadown and even Derry were also to be affected by the extension of capitalist industrialism. Belfast's expansion was based mainly on textiles, shipbuilding, general engineering and food and tobacco products; and its population had increased almost ten-fold between 1800 and 1890, to over one-third of a million. Dublin matched Belfast in population only if some of the capital's outer suburbs were included.

The second difference – Belfast's more advanced trade union organisation – can probably be traced to this earlier growth of industry. Although historical determinism of at least one kind has gone seriously out of fashion since the collapse of eastern European state socialism, it has to be said that trade unionism all over the world appears to have followed an almost pre-determined pattern of development. To oversimplify, first comes the trade unionism of the skilled and strong; only after industrial take-off does the unskilled underclass assert itself in organisational form. And so it was in Ireland. In the late nineteenth century Irish trade unionism was still dominated by craft workers. Their unions did not make these people strong; they were rather symbolic of their existing strength – a mark, above all, of their determination to preserve the advantage which they already enjoyed in the labour market by dint of controlling the number of new entrants to their trades. But especially in Belfast what the early British labour historians, the Webbs, called the 'new unionism' – essentially a new kind of trade unionism – had already appeared, faded somewhat, and then begun to revive. Its growth was particularly associated with the demand for unskilled labour by both the developing transport network and the burgeoning factory system.

These new unions were new in philosophy, in organisation and in tactics. They catered specifically for unskilled and poorly-paid workers, and depended for their success not on careful negotiation from a position of strength, and on the provision of a range of membership benefits based on high subscription levels. They relied instead on low fees and aggressive strike action, or the threat of it, to win concessions from employers. Moreover, a radical egalitarian or socialist ideology seemed to come as part of the package.

Copying the main craft societies, the new unions generally set out to organise on a United Kingdom-wide basis. Organisations like the National Amalgamated Union of Labour, the National Union of Gasworkers, and the Amalgamated Society of

Railway Servants spread to Ireland from Britain in the late 1880s and early 1890s, usually first to Belfast and only then across the rest of the country. Their initial success in Ireland was mainly, though not exclusively, in transport operations, and together with a few small local societies using the same tactics, they scored several notable victories – though they also suffered some debilitating failures.[4]

Such was the expansion of these new unions in the north of Ireland, however, that by the mid-1890s the leaders of some craft societies were beginning to complain about the over-representation on Belfast Trades Council (BTC) of 'the labourers' – and this despite the fact that the numbers involved were still exceedingly small when set against the total of the city's unskilled workforce.[5] The craft leadership, representing predominantly Protestant members, was becoming concerned as well about the growing 'socialistic' tendency of the new unionism of their economic inferiors. Craft unionists were, in the main, content with the existing economic and social order, and regarded socialist ideas as exceedingly dangerous. What made the spread of this creed of equality even more injurious was that some of their own officials had been infected by it, and had left the service of the 'aristocrats of labour' to assist in the organisation of the new unions – to, as it were, help the labouring poor to help themselves.

Why were the working poor in need of help? Starvation wages were the obvious and paramount complaint: although the average incomes of skilled workers in Ulster were up to and sometimes exceeded those in England and Scotland, the wages of the mass of unskilled and semi-skilled workers were well below national average rates – even though better, on the whole, than in the rest of Ireland itself. Health, housing and welfare provision was also much poorer than in Britain – and hardly existed at all in rural areas. These comparisons remind us, furthermore, of something else that was different about Belfast's new unionism. Because while employers sought to defend their mean-mindedness by reference to the poorer pay and conditions which applied to labouring occupations elsewhere in Ireland, the unions preferred to contrast Belfast rates with those payable in similarly industrially developed areas 'across the water'.

In spite of the decided differences in ideology, power and approach between the craft and the new general unions there was, nonetheless, an increasing sense of shared trade union identity. The 1890 BTC Annual Report had put the point in patronising terms:

> We are proud to be in the position (which is almost unique) of having recognised the rights of the unskilled labourers to a share in our work and advantages from the very foundation of the council – all grades of worker being admitted on equal terms.[6]

As it happens, there was but a flimsy basis for this rhetoric, since the Council devoted little enough of its effort to helping the new unions off the ground. Yet, if manifest only in lip service, the concept of a shared and distinct worker – or 'labour' – interest had clearly taken hold, and it demanded expression outside the work-place as well as within it.

It is in politico-religious terms that we find the third important difference between Belfast and Dublin. For while the overwhelmingly Catholic union activists of Dublin were, in keeping with the times, increasingly nationalist in outlook, in mainly Protestant Belfast there were divided views, and there was in practice a predominantly unionist cast to the politics of trade unionism. However, differing senses of national allegiance were cut across by the growth of the solidaristic and socialistic ideas already alluded to. It was necessary, therefore, to reconcile conflicting positions on the constitutional future of Ireland with the notion of the unity of all the workers, not to mention universal proletarian brotherhood.

The strength of this imperative in Belfast may be judged, firstly, by the great 1892 solidarity march of 12,000 trade unionists of all trades and grades, and all political and religious opinions in support of linen-lappers locked out by their employers for having the temerity to join a union. Secondly, there was the ringing declaration in 1893 by one of the most unionist-minded of Belfast's craft union elite, Sam Monro, then President of BTC; he said:

> ... trade unionism is the ism ... whose mission it shall be to free our unhappy land from the incubus of religious bigotry and political intolerance.[7]

This northern vision of trade unionism as an anti-sectarian binding force was to be a recurring theme down the years. Moreover, their differences notwithstanding, the consciousness of there being an entity called the Irish working class, which required both industrial and political guidance, was one shared by Dublin and Belfast. The need for agitation on social and economic questions was of course one of the important reasons why the trades councils of the two cities came together to form the ITUC in 1894. It was in that forum, therefore, that much of the early contest for the leadership of the working class in Ireland was played out – albeit somewhat cautiously and tentatively to begin with.

The leader's mantle came to rest, for a time, on the shoulders of one William Walker, a Belfast branch official of the Amalgamated Society of Carpenters and Joiners. A radical from youth, a member of a variety of socialist organisations, and representative of the dominant view in the city's labour movement, he was ardent in pursuit of Irish working-class unity. But he also saw himself as part of the wider British working-class movement – and engaged, tantalisingly close to success on several occasions, as an election candidate on behalf of the Labour Representation Committee and its successor, the British Labour Party. For Walker and his supporters, therefore, Home Rule threatened the even more important unity of the workers of the whole of the then United Kingdom.

Whatever about politics, whether focused on economic or constitutional issues, and the role which Congress played in that arena, the fostering of inter-union co-operation on purely industrial or work-place matters remained the prerogative of local trade union institutions. It was thus to BTC that unions still looked for support and solidarity at times of dispute with employers – no more so than in 1907. It was early in that year that James Larkin arrived in the city, and subsequent events are well enough known to need only brief rehearsal here.[8] Larkin's principal mission was to revive the Belfast branch of his union, the Liverpool-based National Union of Dock Labourers (NUDL), which had faded into insignificance after a major defeat at the hands of some employers in the early 1890s. He quickly recruited more than 4,000 dockers and carters, in circumstances of growing unrest on the part of Belfast's much exploited unskilled workforce. The atmosphere of militancy increased by the day, extended well beyond Larkin's own group of members, and led to some remarkable demonstrations of Catholic and Protestant working-class unity, organised by the Trades Council.

But 1907 was also marked by violent picketing, rioting, clashes with the police (who themselves engaged in a mutiny of sorts), the introduction of troops, and their shooting dead of two bystanders. Sadly, after a range of outside interventions, the whole thing ended with no real gains for any of the workers involved. It also led Larkin to break with the NUDL, to his departure for Dublin, and to his formation there of the Irish Transport and General Workers' Union (ITGWU). Another, perhaps brighter consequence was the radicalisation of a significant group of union activists, and their turn to a more critical view both of the existing economic order and of the existing leadership of the Trades Council.

Walker's authority in the ITUC lasted for some time, but was beginning to be tested in the early years of the century. In the first place there was the growth of 'Irish separatist', as distinct from 'Home Rule' consciousness in the south, and increasing pressure from a Sinn Féin-influenced group within the unions there. The rapid development and increasing successes – everywhere but in the north – of Larkin's very obviously Irish ITGWU produced a further tide in the separatist faction's favour. Vanquishing a last minute opportunist alliance of Belfast Walkerites with Dublin Irish Party (Home Rule) supporters, it eventually came to dominate the ITUC. Secondly, the Belfast labour movement was itself moving towards a more favourable view of a separate Irish Parliament, under the sway of a coalition which included many who had been blooded in 1907, and a further group who had been persuaded to an Irish republican socialist outlook by James Connolly – who had himself arrived in Belfast in 1910 and taken on the task of building up the ITGWU in the city.

The last real victory for those who wanted the union with Britain to be maintained intact was the disaffiliation of Belfast Trades Council from the ITUC in 1912. This was provoked by a Congress declaration in favour of a separate Irish Labour Party – to be set up in anticipation of Home Rule. The background in Belfast was of massive support from Protestant workers for the Ulster unionist mobilisation. Just one consequence of this, following the passage of the offending Home Rule Bill, was the rude and rough expulsion of thousands of Catholics – together with a small group of Protestants of known socialist sympathies – from the Belfast shipyards. Yet even the Walkerites were appalled when partition was mooted in 1914, for it promised them the worst of all worlds: of being cut off from their trade union and working-class brothers both in Britain and in the rest of Ireland. BTC was thus able to declare its united opposition to

71

any partition proposal, and it immediately re-affiliated to the ITUC.

Both the Trades Council and the ITUC were now seriously out of touch with the Belfast Protestant grass roots, however, while the differences between north and south widened still further. With Home Rule set in abeyance for the duration of the Great War, with membership of British general unions growing apace, with British patriotic fervour at a peak, and with thousands of Irishmen off fighting for the Empire, Protestant workers saw the Easter Rising in Dublin in 1916 as a traitorous outrage. The efforts of the leadership of what was by then the Irish Trade Union Congress and Labour Party, to distance their organisation from the participation of Connolly and his Irish Citizen Army in the Rising did nothing to ease a nascent northern unilateralism.

In 1917, therefore, despite BTC's earlier anti-partition inclinations, it joined with a number of individual unions and the remnants of the British Independent Labour Party in the formation of an effectively separate Belfast Labour Party (BLP). Links were to be weakened in other ways: northern participation in the unions' anti-conscription agitation in 1918 was negligible, and the decision of the (again renamed) Irish Labour Party and TUC not to fight the first post-war election was also ignored. The BLP fielded four candidates in the city; all were defeated, but they did well enough to keep heart.

After a relatively quiet war on the industrial front, the 1919 'Forty-four Hour' engineering strike and BLP gains in Belfast Corporation elections suggested a change of mood. But while trade union membership passed the 100,000 mark,[9] and a couple of industrial victories were won in the early post-war years, other events stole the unions' sting. With the labour movement identified by the Unionist Party as an 'enemy within', two years of bitter inter-communal strife were opened by another expulsion of over 7,000 Catholics and 'rotten Prods' (or Protestant socialists) from the shipyards in 1920. The trade union movement came poorly out of this: there was almost unbridled sectarianism on the shop floor; equivocation in dealing with it by most executive committees; and an insistence by Congress that the problem was for the individual unions to solve.[10] Partly as a consequence, the labour leadership in Belfast was in a state of deep disillusion when the first elections for the new Northern Ireland Parliament were called in 1921, and it was left to four independents to carry the labour banner – very unsuccessfully as it transpired.

But a cooling of community passions and declining wages brought renewed local election successes for Labour as the 1920s proceeded. These were crowned in the 1925 General Election by the victory of three trade union figures standing in the new Labour Party (Northern Ireland) interest: Sam Kyle of the British Transport and General Workers' Union (known in Ireland as ATGWU), Billy McMullen of ITGWU and Jack Beattie of the Blacksmiths. As it happened – because of the nationalist policy of abstentionism – these three were to provide the only real opposition to the government in the ensuing session. They acted with vigour on a broad front, harassed the government constantly, and were particularly valuable as a parliamentary voice for the unions. Unfortunately they were unable to prevent the passage of the 1927 Trades Disputes Act, a carbon copy of the British Act introduced in the aftermath of the 1926 General Strike – by which, incidentally, Northern Ireland had hardly been touched. In an all too obvious attack on the funding of the Labour Party, the act required that members 'opt in' rather than 'opt out' of the payment of union political levies. That Labour was still seen as a serious threat to unionist control of Protestant working-class votes was confirmed when the STV proportional representation voting system was abolished – which, in a disgraceful surrender of its own responsibility, was agreed to by the British government. The change achieved its purpose: only Beattie survived in the 'first-past-the-post' election of 1929.

The early 1930s found union membership heading down to 60,000 or so, not least because there were 100,000 people jobless. In Belfast the unions, the Trades Council and what was by now called the Northern Ireland Labour Party (NILP) co-operated in a campaign of protest, but to little effect. Anger rose to a peak when a new means test applied under the Poor Law greatly increased the number of people on 'Outdoor Relief' – the most parsimonious form of assistance to the unemployed. Intervention by the communist-linked Revolutionary Workers' Groups brought matters on to the streets, and after a spate of riots and demonstrations, a victory of sorts was eventually won.[11]

But the unity in adversity of Catholics and Protestants which characterised the Outdoor Relief affair was soon followed by a clearly engineered resurgence of sectarian violence – which lasted, on and off, until 1935. The 1933 railway strike, the only sig-

73

nificant industrial action during this period, confirmed the ebb in the fortunes of organised labour. Called by the National Union of Railwaymen in protest at proposed pay cuts, it involved almost 4,000 workers, and soon began to paralyse the transport system. But after the death of two strike-breakers and the bombing by the IRA of railway property, the union capitulated and accepted conditions, including the pay cuts, which were in some respects worse than the terms originally put forward by the employers.[12] In the years running up to the start of the Second World War things began to improve a little, however. Wages for unskilled work remained below the United Kingdom's average figures, but rates generally began to rise, and union membership also recovered as unemployment slowly declined.

But the differences between the trade unionisms of Belfast and Dublin, wide as they had been some fifty years before, were by now truly vast. The syndicalism of Larkin and Connolly had largely passed Northern Ireland by; whereas ITGWU was the giant of southern trade unionism, ATGWU was the dominating influence in the north; while collective bargaining in Dublin was influenced entirely by 'internal' factors, in Belfast comparison with what was happening in the rest of the United Kingdom was the guiding principle; and although nominally an all-Ireland organisation, while the Irish Trade Union Congress was the recognised and respected trade union centre for independent Ireland, it was hardly a presence at all in British Northern Ireland.

The war was to draw the Allied north and the neutral south still further apart.[13] Unemployment was virtually eliminated in Northern Ireland, and many skilled workers from across the border were drawn in to engage in war work. Union membership more than doubled from the low of 1933, to well over 140,000 by 1945.[14] This was accompanied not only by numerous episodes of militant industrial action, but also by a surge of political mobilisation on the left. Most startling testimony to the change of temper are the raw strike figures: in Britain between 1941 and 1945 politicians were concerned about the loss of 153 days per 1,000 workers at a time of national peril; Ministers in loyal Ulster must surely have been extremely embarrassed about the equivalent provincial strike figure for the same period of 523 – some three and a half times as high.[15]

In a challenge to the authority of the conventional union leadership, an independent shop stewards' movement was also set up, and the really serious disputes took place in the key war

74

industries of shipbuilding and aircraft production. One of these lasted for well over a month and eventually involved more than 20,000 workers. In response to the resulting disruption the government was unexpectedly obliged to adopt an incorporative, consultative strategy, and to accord to the unions an unprecedented role in public affairs. Trade union representatives sat on a range of government committees for the first time, and the unions provided a major input into a review and reorganisation of the health services; key union figures even had direct access to Ministers' private offices at Stormont on occasion.

But in the middle of all this there loomed a curious paradox; for it was during this period, when there were even more reasons inclining unions in the north to look to Britain for organisational models – as well as for political and economic guidance – that the Dublin, ITUC, connection not only revived but flourished. At the start of the war the only unions operating in Northern Ireland affiliated to the ITUC were those which had members on both sides of the border. Yet by the end of the 1940s, with union membership standing at 200,000, only a tiny handful of the more than fifty unions with members in the north were outside the ITUC fold; and over twenty of these operated in Northern Ireland only. Ironically, therefore, while in the south, because of the Congress of Irish Unions (CIU) breakaway, the ITUC had come to represent just one section of a divided movement, in the north it now spoke with the authority of a fully united group of unions.

Why, then, the turn back to the ITUC? There is no evidence of a conscious or concerted policy change; rather do a number of separate factors seem to have been at work. Firstly, there undoubtedly were some northern trade union activists in the Connolly tradition who were personally committed to Irish unity, and affiliation to the ITUC was one expression of this. Secondly, for the British unions which operated on an all-Ireland basis, affiliation was essential, because the Irish TUC was a vital forum so far as the interests of their southern members were concerned. Thirdly, the departure to the CIU in early 1945 of the more nationalist-minded section of the movement in the south made the ITUC even more acceptable and – just as importantly – gave the ITUC an increasingly socialist stamp, more in keeping with the ideological inclinations of the revitalised political left in Northern Ireland.

The fourth reason for the growth of support for the link with the ITUC deserves closer attention. One of the more obvious problems thrown up during the war was the lack of a strategic and co-ordinated approach to union activity, especially as regards influencing public policy. For example, the union people actually engaged in consultation with the Unionist government were often self-selected or were 'hand-picked' by the ministries concerned, and acted, however correctly, almost entirely as free agents. The answer to that problem – following the already-established pattern in Britain and south of the border – was for the unions to have a central representative body, or trade union centre, recognised by government and entitled to act on behalf of the movement as a whole. This body would also make the nominations of union representatives to government committees, councils and boards. But there was an important choice to be made.

The Irish Trade Union Congress was the obvious port of call. Here was an existing, ready-made organisation upon which to build a Northern Ireland union federation. Moreover, the setting up of the ITUC's Northern Ireland Committee (NIC) in 1944 had been a clear if belated recognition that the interests of unions and their members north of the border had diverged so much from those in the rest of Ireland that they deserved to be separately co-ordinated. Indeed, behind the creation of the NIC was the confident expectation that it would soon become the recognised trade union centre for Northern Ireland.

However, there was an alternative way of proceeding. Why not create what in popular parlance was called an 'Ulster TUC' – a completely independent Northern Ireland trade union centre, not beholden to a superior body in another legal jurisdiction? There were indeed some few within the trade union movement itself who would have welcomed such an arrangement; but the main pressure was applied, indirectly, by the Unionist government. It should be said that for the first few years after the NIC's formation there were some noteworthy concessions to its representations by individual ministries, and indeed much sympathy on the part of civil servants for consultation with such a locally-available body. Slowly but surely, however, government resistance to giving the NIC a role grew; and when the cabinet eventually came to deal with the issue head-on, in 1952, there was an adamant refusal to recognise the Committee – on the grounds that the ITUC headquarters were in a foreign country. By the time this final blow was delivered, however, the unions were committed to the ITUC, and were resolute in resisting dictation from the government.

The preference of unionist ministers for an Ulster TUC directs us to the last important reason for the general determination to stick closely to the ITUC. Because even the most 'Unionist'-minded of union activists and officials, who might have been expected to be in favour of the north going it alone, were mostly as fearful as the rest of their colleagues of a division in the movement. There was no possibility of the ITUC fading from the picture simply because an Ulster TUC had been formed, and the danger was that the resulting breach would have taken on a sectarian colouring – with a 'Unionist/Protestant' Ulster TUC confronting a 'Nationalist/Catholic' Northern Ireland Committee of the ITUC. As well as that, the CIU breakaway was a precedent no one wished to follow; even the absence of recognition by government was a small price to pay to avoid an even worse disaster north of the border.

Turning now to the swell in political interest which accompanied the rise in trade union activity, this was to be signally marked in the immediate post-war elections. Although the combined left won in only five Stormont constituencies, its vote was massively up on previous performances – and under PR could well have delivered almost half the seats in Belfast. Strong links were soon forged between the NILP, its two MPs and the NIC of Congress, and joint action was undertaken on a range of issues much wider than the merely economic. These included many matters, it deserves to be said, which were to do with the way Northern Ireland fell short of normal liberal democratic standards – the gerrymandering of constituency boundaries, repressive legislation, job discrimination and so on. In light of all this a general confidence that the left would make further gains at the next electoral outing seemed not at all misplaced.

But that promise was never delivered. In the north's so-called 'chapel gates' election of 1948, held in the wake of the declaration of the Republic and at the peak of the all-Ireland anti-partition campaign, the results were devastating: the left attracted only just over a quarter of its 1945 vote, and two anti-partition labour candidates were the only survivors. Provoked by all this, the NILP split rather squalidly on the 'constitutional' question of whether Northern Ireland should remain forever a part of the United Kingdom. As a further result, the Northern

Ireland Committee was obliged to pull its own political horns in, withdraw from party involvements, and focus entirely on economic and trade union questions.

Surprisingly perhaps, much northern attention then turned instead to trying to heal the ITUC/CIU split. There were a couple of reasons for this. To begin with, the setting up of the CIU had had little effect in Northern Ireland, since only the relatively small numbers of ITGWU members in Belfast docks came under its purview. There were also ideological objections in some quarters to dealing with the CIU; restitution for this piece of right wing treachery, it was argued, could only be made by the total capitulation of the malefactors. But there was also, throughout the period of the division, a palpable feeling that it was a stain on the trade union movement's escutcheon. How could a body claiming devotion to the unity of the working-class be so deeply divided within itself?

Added to that, however, was a real concern that the recent split in the NILP might be echoed in the trade union movement in the north. Despite its own newly pro-'Union with Britain' posture, incidentally, the NILP made it clear that it wanted no part in a division of the unions. But the increasing attempts to effect an ITUC/CIU reconciliation from the late 1940s onwards occasionally brought hints of terms which would have been unacceptable to the mainly British-based unions in the north. A particular worry was the CIU's mounting insistence that all unions operating in Ireland must be Irish-based and Irish-controlled. Had this been fully agreed the result would clearly have been much the same as if an Ulster TUC had been created. So it was, therefore, that many activists from the north became involved in the conciliation process.

In 1959, after long negotiations, the ITUC and the CIU merged into the Irish Congress of Trade Unions (ICTU), the question of unions being Irish-controlled having been dealt with by a requirement that unions not based in Ireland should have a separate deliberative body to deal with affairs exclusive to their Irish members – a condition, incidentally, which most British-based unions already met. A further requirement that a majority of the seats on the ICTU Executive Council be reserved to Irish unions was to be dropped only a few years later. With a permanent office in Belfast by then, and a full-time Northern Ireland Officer, the Northern Ireland Committee was translated into the new Congress intact. However, having hoped that the merger might precipitate an Ulster TUC, the Unionist government was at first even less enamoured of the new arrangement than it had been of the old. A change of heart on the recognition question was going to have to await a change in political and economic circumstances.

Standards of social benefits, housing and health in the north improved steadily in the 1950s and 1960s, for the most part step-by-step with those in Britain. But old industries declined in the engineering and textile sectors, and jobs declined with them. Although even the worst unemployment figure (touching on 10% at the end of the 1950s) was low as compared to those of the 1930s, Northern Ireland was the United Kingdom's major jobs' blackspot. The government's undoubted success in attracting new industry failed to match the losses; and the concentration of incoming investment east of the River Bann left Counties Derry, Tyrone and Fermanagh with a hugely disproportionate burden of joblessness. Whether the increasing number of trades councils in these areas in the 1950s was a form of reaction to the job crisis, it is certainly fair to say that it was unemployment which led to the eventual recognition of the NIC.

How did this come about? In the Keynesian 1950s and 1960s, serious economic planning was seen to demand the full participation of what we presently call the social partners – the trade unions and employers in particular. But since there was no formally recognised voice for Northern Ireland's unions in the mid-1950s, the Unionist government set up an Industrial Development Council without them. Whether that was the reason for the Council's failure to make an impact – especially on unemployment – it was certainly how some saw it. The cross-denominational Churches Industrial Council was of this view and, together with business interests, began to lobby hard for recognition of the NIC.[16] By this time trade union membership was beginning to approach the 250,000 mark; Northern Ireland's industrial relations record in the post-war years had also been relatively good; and with a low incidence of serious disputes, the trade union movement appeared to enjoy strong public approval.[17] When the reformer, Terence O'Neill, took over as Prime Minister, therefore, the ice began to thaw. After delicate dealings, which resulted in some formal underpinning of the NIC's autonomy, O'Neill granted it recognition in 1964, and immediately appointed some NIC members to a new Northern Ireland Economic Council.

At about the same time the NIC's relations with the NILP began to be restored, especially after the party's good performance in the 1962 Stormont election. For although it retained just the four seats it had won in 1958, the NILP took over 50% of the popular vote in Belfast – and frightened the unionists quite seriously. Co-operation between the party and the NIC took place mainly on the repeal of the Trade Disputes Act (still on the statute book, in slightly modified form), unemployment and industrial development. Most significant of all, however, was a combined eleventh hour attempt in 1966 to convince the unionists to accept a programme of democratic reform. The NIC/ NILP *Joint Memorandum on Citizens' Rights in Northern Ireland* which, with remarkable prescience, included virtually all of the demands later to appear on the civil rights movement's agenda, was rejected out of hand by unionist ministers.[18] O'Neill's reforms were plainly too few, and too long delayed; soon afterwards, Northern Ireland stepped on to the slippery slope.

So what of the trade union movement since then? While much of the work of the NIC since the late 1960s has been directed at the social effects of the 'troubles', Northern Ireland's economic woes have been a major preoccupation as well. The drift of the linen industry towards disappearance was arrested slightly, but the agonising decline in engineering work continued throughout the 1970s and 1980s. Worse still, man-made fibres, the industry which brought so many new jobs in the 1960s and early 1970s – and seemed to augur more – collapsed in the face of cheaper supplies from low-wage, newly-industrialised countries. International competition, together with various economic shocks, also had their effect in other sectors: textiles, clothing, tyre manufacture and tobacco products. New 'high-tech' ventures made only a small contribution to new employment; and the encouragement of local small enterprise was effective only on the margins. Indeed, the Conservatives brought many new problems for the unions in the 1980s: privatisation of public services, compulsory competitive tendering, market testing, trust status for National Health Service hospitals, and a consequential reduction in traditionally secure, if not always particularly well-paid, public sector jobs.

Faced with such challenges, and in the virtual absence of a democratic socialist voice in elected fora in Northern Ireland, the NIC tried gamely to fill the void. During those interludes when the Northern Ireland Office was occupied by Labour ministers it was fairly influential; and even after the Conservatives came back to power in 1979 – with a mandate to clip the unions' wings – the Committee managed to preserve some of its access to the corridors of power. The effects of many of the Tory changes in labour market policy are far from worked through, however; the representations of the NIC have had little enough effect in resisting these, and further damage to union interests seems fated. Even a partial victory, in avoiding for a time much of the Conservative anti-union legislation of the 1980s, has now been overtaken by the comprehensive 1993 Industrial Relations (Northern Ireland) Order.[19]

On the other hand, despite unemployment rates of up to 17% at times during the 1980s, union membership has held up well by comparison with the position in Britain. It peaked in the early 1980s at coming on 290,000; but as well as a net loss of members since then, union density (the percentage of workers unionised) in a smaller employment pool has declined from over 55% to under 50%. Yet the equivalent figure in the rest of the United Kingdom is now below 40% – and still falling. Success is more difficult to measure as regards the effect of the unions' efforts to resist political unreason for the last quarter of a century; but if Sam Monro's prophesy that trade unionism would 'free our unhappy land from the incubus of religious bigotry and political intolerance' has not been fulfilled, the union record stands up well to closer examination.

An early effect of the troubles was a return by the Northern Ireland Committee to a policy of eschewing party and other factional involvements, but continuing to seek community reconciliation and full citizens' rights for all. Reiterating the view of the ICTU as a whole that the constitutional future is entirely a matter for decision by the people of Northern Ireland, therefore, the NIC also went on to oppose internment without trial and other erosions of democratic rights and civil liberties. Given particular attention has been job discrimination – on grounds of gender as well as on the basis of religion and political opinion. The new Fair Employment Act of 1989 was a particular achievement, for it bears the obvious marks of persistent and persuasive lobbying of the NIC and its officers.[20]

Although the Northern Ireland Committee has been much vilified – by those on both sides of the argument – for its nonpartisanship on the Irish national question, this stance has strengthened its authority, and that of the trade union movement in general, in the quest for communal harmony. It does equal service in keeping alive the historic aspiration of the left to the unity of the Protestant and Catholic working classes, and under-pins the NIC's unswerving demand for an end to the use of violence for political purposes by organisations like the IRA and the UVF. It would be wrong, of course, to suggest that the unions' efforts to keep sectarianism off the shop floor have al-ways succeeded. Yet despite some serious incidents it is import-ant to record that there has been no reversion to the mass horrors of years gone by.

Once again with the support of Congress as a whole, pub-licly crusading for peace has also been an important component of the NIC's activity for the last twenty-five years. The *Better Life for All*, the *Peace, Work and Progress* and the *Hands Off My Mate* campaigns (the last directed specifically at young workers), have been reinforced by the setting up of the Counteract anti-intimi-dation unit, and supplemented by innumerable ICTU-sponsored peace demonstrations – some with a general consciousness-raising purpose and others associated with individual terrorist atrocities.

Before offering some kind of concluding judgement on the last one hundred years of union activity in Northern Ireland, it is perhaps worth observing that only in light of the frequently unacknowledged contradiction at the heart of trade unionism is it possible fully to understand union behaviour. On the one hand there is the democratic requirement that unions respond to the demands of the dues-paying members. On the other there is the strong expectation, drawn from historical experience, that trade unions will be on the side of the oppressed, the under-privi-leged, the socially disadvantaged and the unemployed – in other words that trade unionism is about social justice, or it is about nothing. There are times, of course, when there is no discrepancy whatever between these sectional/economic and socio-political imperatives. But the pursuit of a wider social justice can some-times be in conflict with the necessity to look after the purely work-place interests of those the union in question exists to serve – and might perhaps also fly in the face of the political and social opinions of some of the members.

Yet despite the power of the latter constraint, the balance in the present case has clearly weighed in favour of the quest for justice and fairness for all. Furthermore, paradoxical though it may be, the distance between the trade unionisms of Dublin and

Belfast is arguably narrower now than it has ever been. On the side of further divergence, we need only look to the changes in ideological contexts: in the Republic the unions appear to have consolidated their place as Euro-style social partners in recent years, while in Northern Ireland the last tranche of 1980s British labour legislation has confirmed for the unions there that they belong to a very different, individualistic, kind of world.

Taking due account of that, as well as of the stresses inherent in any democratic movement and of that 'certain perversity of mind regarding one another' that Charles McCarthy referred to, there has grown an overwhelming sense of solidarity within Congress about peace in Northern Ireland – surely still the most important issue facing all the people of this island. I happily assert, therefore – though it is perhaps too early for eulogy – that the trade union movement in Northern Ireland, for all the occasional departures from grace, has been a reliable and substantial force for good during the last one hundred difficult years. And all the more so since the formation of the Northern Ireland Committee of the Irish Trade Union Congress, fifty years ago.

1. See, for example: Emmet O'Connor, *A Labour History of Ireland*, Dublin, 1992; Andrew Boyd, *Have the Unions Failed the North?*, Cork, 1984; Bill Rolston, 'The Limits of Trade Unionism', in O'Dowd, *et al*, *Northern Ireland: Between Civil Rights and Civil War*, London, 1980; and Workers' Association, *What's Wrong With Ulster Trade Unionism*, Belfast, 1975.
2. *Trade Unions in Ireland: 1894-1960*, Dublin, 1977, p. 1.
3. Henry Patterson, 'Industrial Labour and the Labour Movement, 1840-1918', in L. Kennedy and P. Ollerenshaw, *An Economic History of Ulster, 1820-1939*, Manchester, 1985, p. 159.
4. O'Connor, *op. cit.*, pp. 50-54.
5. Most of the information which follows on the years leading up to partition is drawn from Henry Patterson, *Class Conflict and Sectarianism*, Belfast, 1980; and Austen Morgan, *Labour and Partition: The Belfast Working Class 1905-1923*, London, 1991.
6. Quoted in Patterson, 1980, *op. cit.*
7. Quoted in J. W. Boyle, 'The Rise of the Irish Labour Movement, 1888-1907', PhD Thesis, TCD, 1963, p 142 – now published in revised form as *The Irish Labor Movement in the Nineteenth Century*, Washington DC, 1988.
8. For a full and colourful account of 1907, see John Gray, *City in Revolt*, Belfast, 1985.
9. Unless otherwise stated, information on union membership levels is drawn from Boyd Black, 'Against the trend: trade union growth in Northern Ireland', *Industrial Relations Journal*, Vol. 17, No. 1, Spring 1986.
10. See Morgan, *op. cit.*
11. Just one of several excellent accounts of the Outdoor Relief troubles is Paddy Devlin's *Yes We Have No Bananas*, Belfast, 1981.
12. O'Connor, *op. cit.*, pp. 178-179.

13. Unless otherwise noted, the information which follows on the labour and trade union movement in the 1940s and early 1950s is drawn from Terry Cradden, *Trade Unionism, Socialism and Partition: The Labour Movement in Northern Ireland 1939-1953*, Belfast, 1993.

14. David Bleakley, 'The Northern Ireland Trade Union Movement', *Journal of the Statistical and Social Inquiry Society of Ireland*, XVI, 1954, p. 158.

15. Cited in O'Connor, *op. cit.*, p. 187.

16. See Andrew Boyd, *The Rise of the Irish Trade Unions 1729-1970*, Tralee, 1972, Appendix II.

17. This view remained unchallenged until relatively recently – see Boyd Black, 'Collaboration or Conflict? Strike Activity in Northern Ireland', *Industrial Relations Journal*, Vol. 18, No. 1, March 1987.

18. Charles Brett, *Long Shadows Cast Before*, Edinburgh, 1978, p. 134. The Memorandum was eventually published in 1967.

19. See Terry Cradden, 'The Tories and Employment Law in Northern Ireland: Seeing Unions in a Different Light?', *Industrial Relations Journal*, Vol. 24, No. 1, March 1993.

20. Terry Cradden, 'Trade Unionism, Social Justice and Religious Discrimination in Northern Ireland', *Industrial and Labor Relations Review*, Vol. 46, No. 3, April 1993.

Dr Terry Cradden
Senior Lecturer in Resource Management, University of Ulster, Magee College, Derry. Author of *Trade Unionism, Socialism and Partition* (1993); co-editor with Paul Teague of *Labour Market Discrimination and Fair Employment in Northern Ireland* (1992), etc.

Decades of Dissension and Divisions 1923–1959

Donal Nevin

On the foundation of the Irish Free State in 1922, an observer might well have felt that the prospects were bright for the trade union movement.

The Democratic Programme adopted without dissent by the first Dáil in January 1919, which included radical aspirations for social progress and economic change, had been based on a draft prepared by the secretary of the Irish TUC, Thomas Johnson. The general election held in June 1922 had returned seventeen of the eighteen candidates nominated by the Congress and their share of the poll was a respectable twenty-one per cent. Trade union membership had risen dramatically in the preceding years, particularly in rural and provincial areas.

On the other hand, the observer would have been aware of a number of negative factors in the situation. The new state was overwhelmingly agricultural with only one-third of the people living in cities and towns. There was very little industry and that restricted to simple processing of agricultural products, drink, and a narrow range of other industries catering for the limited domestic market. With a few exceptions industry was organised in small-size enterprises. The industrialised part of the country in the north-east had remained part of the United Kingdom and even Dublin could boast of few large industrial enterprises.

As well, the trade union movement was highly fragmented with a multiplicity of unions, most of them very small, many of them competing for small groups of workers. From 1918 new unions had been set up either as replacements for branches of unions which had their chief offices in Britain – the amalgamated unions as they were called – or in competition with other Irish unions. This fragmentation was a recipe for organisational chaos.

At national level the structure of the trade union movement in Ireland was unique in Europe, another perverse ingredient in the organisational mixture. In 1917 the title of the organisation had been changed from the Irish TUC and Labour Party to Irish Labour Party and TUC, symbolising the greater importance of the political purposes of the organisation and signifying the adherence of the leadership of the ITGWU to syndicalism, the doctrine that had been espoused by James Connolly, the acting general secretary of the union who was executed in 1916, and to which its absent general secretary, James Larkin also adhered.

In its report to the International Labour and Socialist Conference held at Berne in February 1919, the National Executive of the Congress declared that it was the 'national organisation of the working class in Ireland on both the political and industrial fields' and that it combined in one body the 'joint functions of a Labour Party and a Trade Union Congress'. The report claimed that the number of members had risen from 100,000 in 1913 to 250,000 in 1918 and that there were only 40,000 members of trade unions that remained unaffiliated.

It must have seemed to some as if in the years from 1917, Congress had been 'hi-jacked' by the ITGWU and its allies in other unions and the Trade Councils which had mushroomed in the provincial areas, regarding the Congress as its political/ electoral machine while the union pursued its industrial goal of becoming the OBU. Officials of the ITGWU held the office of president of Congress in 1918, 1920, 1921, 1922, 1925 and 1928. In 1919 and 1920, the general treasurer of the union (William O'Brien) was secretary of Congress and its treasurer from 1921 to 1929 with the exception of the year he was president. All but three of the seventeen Labour deputies elected to the Dáil in 1922 were members of the ITGWU.

The combination of the political and industrial sides of the labour movement in a so-called conjoint body can be seen to have been a critical mistake and not conducive to a rational form of organisation for either wing of the movement. As a vehicle for revolution it might have made some sense but in the then circumstances of Irish society and the economy it made none. In Ireland, as Dr Emmet O'Connor has put it, 'syndicalism was more a mentality than a movement'. The aspiration to One Big Union was to be an organisational will-o'-the-wisp.

Unfortunately, the syndicalist notion continued to be taken seriously by the ITGWU leadership well into the 1920s. As late as 1924 Senator Thomas Farren, a leader of the union and a former president of Congress, rebuked Louie Bennett of the Irish Women Workers' Union who sought that greater attention be paid by Congress to trade union matters, stating that the party-congress constitution 'was based throughout on the principle advocated by Connolly that political and industrial organisation should go hand in hand'. 'Miss Bennett,' he added, 'wanted organisation on the English model.'

Incidentally the syndicalist motto, OBU (One Big Union) was to remain on ITGWU badges and banners until the union merged with the Federated Workers' Union of Ireland in 1990.

Throughout the 1920s therefore the leadership of the labour movement had to keep their eyes on two balls in play simultaneously and on separate pitches.

It was not long after the establishment of the Irish Free State that it became evident that no new dawn had broken for the labour movement. Indeed more likely, a nightmare scenario was in prospect. Early on in the Dáil when Labour sought to amend the Draft Constitution by including in it part of the 1919 Democratic Programme, the vice-president of the Executive Council and Minister for Home Affairs, Kevin O'Higgins, dismissed the amendment as 'largely poetry' and later insisted that 'it would certainly be a very unwise thing to embody in the Constitution ... what certainly looks very much like a Communistic doctrine'.[1]

In the general election of 1923 the Labour vote slumped to eleven per cent of the poll. By 1926 the membership of the Irish Transport and General Workers' Union had collapsed from a peak of over 100,000 in 1920 to 40,000. By the end of the decade it was less than 16,000. It seems certain, however, that the membership claimed by the ITGWU in the early 1920s was much exaggerated as a measure of regular dues-paying membership. A census of membership on 31 January 1920 had recorded 102,823 members.[2]

Internationally the tide of social upheaval that followed the war had ebbed and high expectations for social change had given way to reactionary regimes that in many cases suppressed trade unions. As well, the post-war boom had been followed by economic decline. Workers faced wage cuts, a reduction in living standards and high unemployment. Ireland was not insulated from these developments.

The first major industrial dispute in the new state was a clash in September 1922 between the postal workers and the government which challenged their right to strike. A couple of years later the government supported the contractors for the Shannon hydro-electrification scheme in their dispute with Congress about the wages to be paid. The unions boycotted the scheme for three months but they were unsuccessful as thousands of unemployed labourers flocked to seek work on the scheme at wages of thirty-two shillings a week.

As well as cutting old age pensions by ten per cent, the government reduced the salaries of teachers and civil servants. While refusing to concede labour's demand for lower taxes on tea and sugar, it twice cut the rate of income tax, then paid by a few wealthy people, from five shillings in the pound to three shillings.

Under the conditions prevailing it was not surprising that the membership of Congress fell from 189,000 in 1922 to 92,000 in 1929. The number of workers involved in strikes declined from 21,000 in 1923 to 4,500 in 1929. From a high of 1,200,000 days lost in 1923 there were only 101,000 days lost in 1929. The multiplicity and duplication of unions created great difficulties for the Congress whose efforts at reorganisation, feeble at best, were futile. Yet scarcely one-fifth of the workforce was organised.

Apart from the problems of the small size of unions and inter-union rivalries there were also major difficulties arising from the trade union structure with craft unions, industrial unions and general unions defending their organisational empires. Permeating the movement was what Dr Emmet O'Connor has described as 'suicidal sectionalism'. This situation was to persist throughout the 1930s.

In a sense the explanation for this situation was simple. Members were loyal to their own unions, rather than in some vague way, to a 'movement', and they were conservative in their attitude to change. There were hundreds of local and sectional power centres within the movement, officials and elected officers, who were intent on surviving as influential figures in their own small entities rather than being subsumed into larger organisations, with all that this meant for the positions of authority which they were so loath to forego. A quest for power may not have been the spur, rather was it that a minor position in a small union had for many become their life.

Under the existing dispensation all were barons, albeit very minor ones. There was, however, one notable exception, the general secretary of the ITGWU, William O'Brien. He was to dominate his union and Congress for twenty years and his were the initiatives that led later to disastrous splits in Congress and in the Labour Party.

Before turning to the events leading to that split, it is desirable to assess the outcome of wage bargaining by unions in the 1920s. Reference has been made to the economic conditions of the time and to the employer offensive against workers' wages, an offensive that a divided movement was helpless to counter. It would seem that between 1926 and 1931 average industrial earnings fell slightly.[3] Over the same period the cost-of-living index fell by fourteen per cent. No improvements of any kind were negotiated in conditions of employment such as hours of work or holidays with pay.

The dissolution of the conjoint organisation and the formation of two separate organisations, the Irish TUC and the Irish Labour Party in 1930 came at a time when trade union membership was declining and morale was low, a deepening economic recession and growing unemployment.

A major factor responsible for the weak position of the trade union movement was the split in the ITGWU in 1924 when its then general secretary, Jim Larkin, was expelled from the union he had founded. The events leading up to that split were tangled and are not capable of brief analysis. The main reason was the intense and bitter antagonism between Larkin and O'Brien, with their diametrically opposite temperaments and very different personalities, rather than conflicting views on political and trade union organisation. Professor Charles McCarthy was to describe the strife between them as 'squalid, personal, rather trivial'. It certainly was so but it was much more than that.

Larkin saw himself pursuing a 'divine mission of discontent', a man, as Seán O'Casey put it, who spoke to the workers 'not for an assignation with peace, dark obedience, or placid resignation; but trumpet-tongued of resistance to wrong, discontent with leering poverty, and defiance of any power strutting out to stand in the way of their march onward'. On the other hand, O'Casey saw O'Brien as a 'clever, sharp, shrewd mind of white heat, behind the cold, pale, mask ever boring a silent way through all opposition to the regulation and control of the Irish labour movement'.

Larkin was a working-class titan whose role in 1913 had made him a hero of the international labour movement. In 1914 he left for the United States where he was to remain for nearly nine years, caught up in some of the major events of a stormy period in American labour history and becoming a leader of the revolutionary left. In 1915 he had been the principal speaker at

the funeral of the executed Joe Hill, Labour's legendary trouba-
dour of song. In 1920 Larkin was sentenced to five to ten years
for criminal anarchy. Released after three years in Sing Sing and
other jails, pardoned by the newly-elected governor of New
York, Al Smith, he returned to Dublin in April 1923.

Larkin immediately became embroiled in a series of conflicts
with O'Brien who had been elected general treasurer of the
union in 1919, and with the executive. Out-manoeuvred –
O'Brien had the support of almost all the members of the general
executive – Larkin's supporters resorted to unorthodox actions
which further alienated the leaders of the union. Legal actions
and counteractions were taken which Larkin ultimately lost. He
was expelled from the union and O'Brien appointed general secretary in his place. Larkin left for Moscow to attend the Fifth
Congress of the Third International, the Comintern. It was during his absence, that his brother Peter Larkin – who had served
four years in Australian jails for seditious conspiracy – launched
the Workers' Union of Ireland, with head office in Marlboro
Street and of which Jim Larkin was later made general secretary.

Larkin had lost the leadership battle with O'Brien and had
lost it decisively. However, more than two-thirds of the members
of the union in Dublin followed Larkin into the WUI but only a
fraction of the provincial membership. The scene was set for a
renewal of the struggle between the two men, a struggle that was
to be pursued relentlessly, poisoning the trade union atmosphere
for two decades.

Throughout the 1930s, the question of trade union re-
organisation was to dominate discussions within the Congress.
Differing views were held as to the path to be taken in what was
a complicated and difficult situation. The establishment of industrial unions, mergers of the smaller unions with one another or
with a general union, the absorption of the amalgamated unions
by Irish unions – all these and other courses had their advocates
but none gained general support.

Apart from the inter-union disputes in Dublin generated by
conflicts between the ITGWU and the WUI, there was also a
major stand-off between the Irish Transport and the second biggest union in Congress, the Amalgamated Transport and General Workers' Union, the bulk of whose membership was in Northern Ireland. The most important direct conflict between these
unions arose in 1934 out of the efforts of the Irish Transport
Union to take the Amalgamated Union's members in the Dublin

Tramway Company. To O'Brien the resistance of the Amalga-mated Union was tantamount, as he put it, to claiming that 'Irishmen shall not be permitted to manage their own affairs'.

In 1936, a special conference held by Congress set up a Trade Union Commission to report on the amalgamation or grouping of unions within specific industries or occupations. There were then forty-nine unions affiliated to Congress with 134,000 members but only two unions had a membership of more than 10,000. The twelve members of the commission could not reach agreement, and three years later two reports were submitted for consideration at a further conference which was held in February 1939.

After much procedural wrangling and confrontations between O'Brien and the president of Congress, P. T. Daly[4] – an old antagonist – the conference decided by a narrow majority to support the report submitted by Sam Kyle, the leader of the ATGWU while O'Brien's report was deemed to have been rejected. In protest against the president's ruling, O'Brien withdrew from the conference. This was the formal beginning of the split which was to lead to two Congresses.

Significantly the Irish unions affiliated to Congress had met the day before the conference to adopt a common position and two months later a Council of Irish Unions was set up within the Congress but not as part of it.

Thus the 1930s came to a close with the map of the trade union movement in Ireland being rolled up as Congress lurched inevitably to a new division. Affiliated membership had recovered, increasing from 92,000 in 1929 to 162,000 in 1939. Trade union membership in the state still represented less than a quarter of the employed workforce.

The position regarding multiplicity of unions had worsened. The influence of some leaders of small unions had increased. Workers were apathetic about union membership and showed few signs of militancy. Except for the year 1937 when $1^3/4$ million days were lost through strikes, due mainly to the big strike of 27,000 building workers in that year, the average number of days lost each year during the 1930s was 200,000 compared with an average of 300,000 during the 1920s. The number of workers involved in strikes during the 1930s averaged less than 10,000 a year.

With the easing of the international recession and the modest success of the industrialisation policy achieved through protectionism, industrial earnings had increased slightly between 1931 and 1939 compared with an increase of 11 per cent in the cost-of-living index. Even so the earnings of men in manufacturing industries averaged only £2.19s. (45.6 hours) in 1939 and women's earnings a mere £1.11s. 6d. (44.2 hours).[5]

During the decade some progress had been made in persuading the government to introduce legislation on working conditions. A Workmen's Compensation Act was enacted in 1934. Two years later the Conditions of Employment Act was passed dealing with hours of work of industrial workers and in 1938 an act governing conditions of employment in shops. An act passed in 1939 provided for one week's annual leave for all workers. An Agricultural Wages Board was set up in 1936 which prescribed minimum wages for agricultural workers as Trade Boards which had been in existence since 1909, did for workers in low-paid employments such as clothing. Social welfare schemes were improved especially unemployment assistance, and widows' pensions introduced.

This progressive legislative programme was the result in no small measure of persistent pressure by the trade union movement, though credit for it was attributed to the Fianna Fáil government, something that had an effect in winning support for the government from sections of the trade union leadership, a factor that was to be of some significance in the following years.

During the war years, two big issues confronted the trade union movement. On the government's wage control policy, the unions were united in opposition but on the question of trade union legislation, the movement was sharply divided.

The Wages Standstill Order 1941, as it was known, froze rates of pay and prohibited industrial action to secure increases. Later there was to be a slight easing of the order and limited increases were allowed where claims were made by unions. Ironically this led to an expansion in union membership. There was strong trade union opposition to the government order because of the strictness of the wage controls, in contrast to retail prices which soared under the pressures of war-time scarcities and profiteering. Between 1939 and 1947 average industrial earnings rose by only one-third but the cost-of-living index soared by two-thirds. After the war the trade unions had to fight long and hard to recover the ground lost through the operation of the Wages Standstill Order.

When Seán MacEntee, the Minister for Industry and Commerce, introduced the Trade Union Bill in May 1941 there was a storm of protest from trade unions but notably not from the ITGWU. The most controversial feature of the bill was the proposal to set up a Trade Union Tribunal which could award sole negotiating rights for particular categories of workers to a single union if that union organised a majority of the workers. It was a proposition that threatened many unions but especially the amalgamated unions, since the tribunal could award sole rights only to an Irish union. This was the means by which rationalisation was to be imposed on the movement and the stage set for One Big Union, the syndicalist aspiration long held by William O'Brien. The legend OBU was by now popularly translated as Old Bill's Union.

O'Brien was president of Congress in 1941 – he had also been president in 1913, 1918 and 1925 – and in his address referred guardedly to the Trade Union Bill recalling how five years before, the government had warned the movement that unless it put its own house in order, the government would be forced to do so. O'Brien's defeat at the 1939 special conference on reorganisation had clearly rankled and he told the delegates that the government's interference was something for which 'we ourselves are largely responsible'. He warned that there would be the expected outcry from 'the superfluous unions which we all want to see eliminated, or,' he added menacingly, 'to use an expression in fashion in some quarters, liquidated'. Delegates had little difficulty in identifying unions that were superfluous and ripe for liquidation, at least in O'Brien's eyes.

No delegate from the ITGWU spoke in the Congress debate on the Trade Union Bill. However Jim Larkin spoke, forcefully and to considerable effect. Larkin's union, the Workers' Union of Ireland, had been prevented from affiliating to Congress through the influence of O'Brien and he was attending the conference as a delegate from the Dublin Trades Union Council which had accepted the WUI into affiliation. This was Larkin's first time attending Congress since 1914 when he had been president. It was the Dublin Trades Council under Larkin, rather than the Congress, that had led the fight against both the Wages Standstill Order and the Trade Union Bill.

Larkin told the delegates that a trade union delegation had been informed by Mr MacEntee that the bill had not come of his initiative and that what he was doing was with the approval of

93

some trade union officials whom the minister had declined to name. The cat was definitely out of the bag. The bill was now referred to as 'Bill's Bill'.

Despite the opposition of the Labour deputies, the Trade Union Bill was enacted. In the event however the controversial Part Three of the act never came into operation as the Supreme Court in 1946 declared that it was invalid as it was in its main principles repugnant to the Constitution.

Events moved inevitably towards the final break. The trade union split was preceded by dissension in the Labour Party with the ITGWU disaffiliating from the party because of the selection of Jim Larkin as an official Labour candidate in Dublin for the 1943 general election. Its disaffiliation was followed by the secession of five of the eight ITGWU deputies from among the seventeen Labour deputies elected in 1943. Within a year, the trade union movement had split.

The immediate cause of this long-threatened split was trivial indeed. At the 1944 Congress, the fiftieth, held in Drogheda, Senator Sam Kyle of the Amalgamated Transport and General Workers Union had successfully moved a motion regretting the decision of the national executive of Congress to reject an invitation from the TUC in Britain to attend a World Trade Union Conference to be held the following year in London. O'Brien warned that if the motion was passed it would be 'the first step in the break-up of Congress'.

It was no coincidence that at this Congress there was a shift in the union alignment on the national executive. The previous year six members of amalgamated unions were elected to the fifteen-member body. In 1944, nine were elected, largely due to the recent affiliation of several unions in Northern Ireland.

Alleging that the Congress was 'now controlled by British unions', fifteen Irish unions withdrew from Congress and established the Congress of Irish Unions in April 1945. The allegation was unfounded. At no time had the amalgamated unions sent sufficient delegates to the annual conference to give them a majority. In fact at the 1944 conference the amalgamated unions had fewer delegates than the Irish unions even though their affiliated membership on an all-Ireland basis was far greater.

Another complaint against the amalgamated unions was that they constituted the main obstacle to trade union reorganisation yet less than one-fifth of trade union membership in the state were in amalgamated unions and only three of these were of any significant size, the ATGWU, the Amalgamated Society of Woodworkers and the National Union of Railwaymen.

Indeed if mergers and amalgamations were to be the basis for reorganisation, it was among the large number of small Irish unions that the solution lay. For example, of four painters' unions, three were Irish. There were at least six Irish unions organising engineering workers. Of the four general unions, three were Irish. And only six of the twenty-three Irish unions affiliated to Congress had more than 2,000 members.

Undoubtedly there was a body of opinion that was opposed to the amalgamated unions organising in the state, but this was largely limited to the leadership of the ITGWU and officials of some craft unions.

For twenty years it had been obvious that the main underlying tension in the movement and the conflict arising from it arose primarily from the hostility of O'Brien to Larkin and his determination to isolate and destroy the WUI. It is evident from the voluminous O'Brien papers in the National Library that O'Brien had a pathological antipathy to Larkin which went far beyond their differences about ideology or about the role of trade unions in society. Certainly, Larkin was arrogant and intolerant of the slightest criticism. His great oratorical powers frequently led him to flights of fancy and he indulged in vitriolic vilification of his opponents, real or imagined.

As for William O'Brien, he too was arrogant. He was domineering, feared by his officials whom he controlled with an iron hand. An organisation man, apparatchik, he wielded power from behind a desk. Feared by his colleagues, he was aloof and insensitive to the feelings of others. He considered himself to be the heir of Connolly – the only true heir.

O'Brien retired from the union early in 1946. Larkin died the following January aged seventy-three.[6] As thousands of workers, men and women, trudged through the icy streets in a blizzard following Big Jim on his last journey to Glasnevin Cemetery, O'Brien's reported comment was: 'A showman to the last'. He himself, bitter to the end, died in 1968 at the age of eighty-seven.

The departure from the trade union scene of the two most important figures of the Irish trade union movement, saw that movement to which both men, in their different ways, had contributed so much, divided, with two congresses, the Irish TUC and the Congress of Irish Unions. The membership of the unions affiliated to the CIU was confined to the Republic with the great majority in the ITGWU. On the other hand, a substantial proportion of the Irish TUC's membership was in Northern Ireland though some of the largest Irish unions including the INTO, the Irish Bakers' Union, the Irish Women Workers' Union and the Post Office Workers' Union, remained with the Irish TUC and to these was soon added a new affiliation, the Workers' Union of Ireland.

One of several efforts made to reunify the movement was made by young Jim Larkin, then a Labour deputy, in a moving open letter written on the day his father was buried. With a sharp and incisive mind, his was the most formidable intellect in the labour movement, as well as being its most outstanding industrial negotiator.

The existence of two Congresses created great difficulties for trade unions, weakening their efforts, dissipating their resources and making impossible a common front against the employer organisations, now growing steadily more powerful. In practice, there was no serious ideological or organisational differences between the two Congresses nor were there now any personal differences between the leaders.

By 1956 it had become apparent that all that was required to bring about reunification was a willingness on the part of the leaders to reach agreement. Fortunately this was forthcoming in the persons of John Conroy, general president of the ITGWU and James Larkin, general secretary of the WUI, the two most respected leaders in the movement and the dominant figures in the two Congresses.

In that year a Provisional United Trade Union Organisation was set up to co-ordinate the activities of the two Congresses and to draft a constitution for a united Congress. Through the dogged persistence and determination of Conroy and Larkin and the Congress secretaries, Ruaidhri Roberts and Leo Crawford, over three years, success attended their efforts.

In February 1959 the Irish Congress of Trade Unions was formally inaugurated and in July the Irish TUC, founded in 1894, and the Congress of Irish Unions, founded in 1945 were dissolved. The ninety trade unions affiliated to the new ICTU represented a membership of well over half a million workers, three-fifths of them in the Republic.

The healing of the trade union split in 1959 came at an appropriate time. The country was on the brink of the great economic and social changes that were to mark the 1960s. After a decade of economic stagnation and decline, high unemployment, low living standards for workers generally and great poverty for a great many of them, and a falling population, the result of a flood tide of emigration, much was about to change. In particular, dramatic social changes were in train that were to effect a revolution in Irish society, changes that could scarcely have been contemplated in the repressed and illiberal Ireland of the 1950s, with its narrow horizons and dreary conformity, gross inequality and unfair distribution of the national income.

Irish society was emerging from the shadows as was the trade union movement which, reinvigorated through reunification, was to play a major part in influencing the economic and social transformation that was coming. The role of the trade union movement over the following thirty years was to be in striking contrast to the dismal experience of the previous thirty years, three decades of dissensions, discord and divisions.

In its first post-unification manifesto to the workers of Ireland in 1959, the Irish Congress of Trade Unions set out its aspirations and hopes for the coming times:

> Our movement can now take its proper place in the nation's life, concentrating its undivided endeavours towards the achievement of working-class ideals and aspirations.
> Unity is not an end in itself but a means towards a stronger and more effective trade union movement. Our movement has over the years won tremendous advances for workers. Apart from improving material standards in terms of real wages, shorter hours and better working conditions, trade unionism has been the most potent instrument for winning dignity, self-respect and freedom for the workers.
> Congress will seek the full utilisation of the resources of Ireland for the benefit of the people of Ireland and will work for such fundamental changes in the social and economic system as may be necessary for the attainment of our objectives. In particular, the efforts of Congress will be directed towards the solution of the problems of unemployment and emigration, north and south.
> Congress will seek to promote the interests of the weaker sections of the community, the aged, the unemployed, the sick and will strive to secure radical improvements in educational facilities and opportunities, and in the health services.

---

1. Dáil Debates, Vol. 1.21, 25 September 1922, Cols. 573, 707. Ironically it was the Minister for Defence in the same Executive Council, General Richard Mulcahy, who, speaking in Irish, on 21 January 1919 had asked the First Dáil to accept the Democratic Programme whole-heartedly and to put it into effect. He concluded his speech: 'Let us enshrine it in our laws'.

2. ITGWU Annual Report for 1919. The membership figure, covering 433 branches included 38,644 agricultural labourers and other land workers, 16,063 employed in food industries, 11,951 in manufacturing, 15,169 in transport, 8,527 in construction and 10,609 in public services (road workers, etc.).

3. Department of Industry and Commerce (Statistics Branch). Census of Industrial Production 1931. (Stationery Office, 1934.)

4. P.T. Daly had been elected secretary of Congress each year from 1910 to 1917. In 1918 he was defeated by William O'Brien by the slender margin of five votes (114 to 109).

5. Department of Industry and Commerce. Some Statistics of Wages and Hours of Work. (Stationery Office, 1942.)

6. Larkin's biographers, R.M. Fox and Professor Emmet Larkin, both give his year of birth as 1876. This is also the date inscribed on the Larkin Monument in O'Connell Street, Dublin. However the historian Desmond Greaves following an intensive investigation of birth, baptismal, school and other records in Liverpool revealed in an article in the *Irish Democrat*, September 1980, convincing evidence that in fact James Larkin was born on 28 January 1874.

It is a remarkable coincidence that it was also Desmond Greaves who first established the facts about James Connolly's birth in Edinburgh on 5 June 1868 (contrary to the general belief that he had been born in County Monaghan in 1870).

Donal Nevin
General Secretary, Irish Congress of Trade Unions, 1982-89; Editor, *Jim Larkin and the Dublin Lock-out* (1964); Editor, *Trade Unions and Change in Irish Society* (1980).

Trade Unions and the Law

Dr Mary Redmond

The less the law has to do with trade unions the more trade unions like it. The less trade unions have to do with law the less lawyers like it, but for entirely different reasons. Lawyers and the law are seldom involved in collective labour law, that is, the law that concerns trade unions and their affairs. Collective labour law is not the same as individual labour law which has grown out of the inadequacy of voluntary collective bargaining to protect rights and incidents relating to the individual contract of employment. In cases involving dismissal or discrimination, for example, you will find hyperactivity for the law, and hence happy lawyers.

The law's function in relation to trade unions is best illustrated by the role of the lawyer in collective labour issues. If large scale industrial action is on the horizon, a lawyer's advice is sought as to the limits of the law, the interpretation of procedures and the redress that may be available if all else fails. Whether I act for the employer or for the trade union, each side will want to know more or less the same. My advice will be of strategic value in what is an elementary power relation between labour and management.

This is because, as the late Professor Kahn-Freund put it, collective labour law facilitates and to a lesser extent regulates the industrial relations system. That system functions autonomously, outside of the law, and guards its right to do so.

When I use the world 'law' in relation to trade unions I shall distinguish between law as laid down by the legislature and as found by the courts. This is because, in collective labour law, there have been point counter-point interventions by legislature and courts. I will illustrate these by looking at areas critical for trade union power. The interventions become an even more complex focus of study when one appreciates that by and large the efforts of the legislature over the last one hundred years have been directed towards removing trade unions and their acts from regulation by the courts. This policy of voluntarism in turn affects legal consciousness. Lawyers are professionally conservative. We respect legal tradition. The fact that there is a lack of

99

public debate about the issues, which is characteristic of a framework facilitating abstentionism, is one reason why the inherited legal tradition with its bias for individual rights is carried on.

By the time our celebrated centenarian the Irish Trades Union Congress was established in 1894, statute law had moved somewhat from the philosophy of that century which viewed trade unionism as an intolerable interference with the individual right of every person to full freedom in disposing of his labour or his capital as he willed.

In fact, when the Irish Trades Union Congress was set up trade unions had been partially legalised for about twenty-three years.[1] Their purposes, as statute put it, were no longer unlawful merely because they were in restraint of trade. And a system of voluntary registration for trade unions was already well established. Apart from the political fund rules, trade unions were relatively free to draw up their own rules and structures.

But by 1894 there was already some evidence of what has been described as 'a see-saw vendetta between the courts and the legislature'.

In general, as I have said, the policy of much statute law regarding trade unions has been to keep the common law out. I would like to look at a good example of this, trade disputes law, which is much older than our centenarian. In Ireland there is a further dimension regarding trade unions since Bunreacht na hÉireann in 1937. In Irish constitutional law the judicial mould – not surprisingly – has favoured individual over collective interest and I will advert to this. When I use the terms 'individual and collective interest' I will not please the purists. When I ascribe a collective interest to trade unions, I am using a metaphorical short-hand for the individual experience of fellowship in interests.

The *raison d'être* of a trade union is to bargain collectively. Collective agreements, in general, are not hampered by legal enforceability.[2] If it is to be effective collective bargaining must carry with it the power to engage in industrial disputes.

From the beginning, the common law courts found legal wrongs at every turn in industrial action, with an innovativeness that must have surprised even the litigants. For example, we know the legislature had legitimised trade unions acting in restraint of trade. But if there was also coercion in their acts, the courts found that trade unionists were guilty of criminal conspiracy. Thereafter the legislature removed the application of criminal conspiracy from acts done by trade unions 'in contemplation or furtherance of a trade dispute'. This was the first-ever immunity for industrial action. It was enacted in 1876.[3] Immunities remain the model.

But the courts were not slow to defeat parliament's intention. They extended the wrong of civil conspiracy to render unlawful a boycott of an employer by a trade union when the employer would not dismiss non-union men. And the common law developed other torts in addition to conspiracy, such as inducing breach of contract[4] and interference with business. Most forms of industrial action were therefore unlawful.

So far in this league we have common law: 3, parliament: 2. As though to even the score, Westminster passed the Trade Disputes Act 1906. This was a landmark in the history of labour law. Imagine being present when Jim Larkin read out the short text of this act during the Belfast dock strike with the result that the military commander was obliged to stand aside and allow Larkin and a picket of workers to enter the docks.

The aim of the 1906 Act was to take the common law out of industrial relations and to allow a voluntary structure of collective bargaining to be created. It gave an expanded system of immunities in tort to trade unions, their officials and their members. The act survived in Ireland after independence although its policy was qualified by numerous court decisions, and it had to be amended once.[5]

Those who practised under the 1906 Act, management and labour, must have felt some nostalgia when this *grande dame* of labour law, her shreds and her patches, was replaced in 1990 by the Industrial Relations Act.

The 1990 Act is similarly designed to secure the courts' abstentionism. The act is a prime example of 'negative law', a phrase coined by the late Professor Otto Kahn-Freund. That means a framework of law without which the autonomous functioning of the industrial relations system – the freedom of association – would be impeded.

The new act repeats and adds to the old immunities against criminal and civil conspiracy.[6] It repeats the prohibition of actions in tort against trade unions from the 1906 Act. But this is confined to acts done 'in contemplation or furtherance of a trade dispute'.

The act provides new examples of a policy minimising the role of the law. When the act requires trade union rule books to contain a rule providing for secret ballots before industrial action (which most trade unions already have) it confines these rights to members of the trade union concerned and 'no other person'. Most importantly, the new act restricts the granting of injunctions in trade disputes. This narrows the jurisdiction of the courts, and is a response to what trade unions perceived as abuse by employers in seeking over-readily to injunct trade disputes.

A system of immunities signifies, of course, that the acts rendered immune are unlawful in the first place. Our trade disputes law with its system of immunities is based on the premise that industrial action is unlawful. Such action is immune only for the wrongs specified in the act and then, since 1941, only for unions who are the holders of negotiation licences, their officials and members.[7] There are wrongs in industrial action which, even for such trade unions and persons, are not immune. They can be injuncted whether or not other aspects of the industrial action involve immune wrongs. Our system is something of a labyrinth.

In 1985 the Minister for Labour (as the office was then styled) trawled to see what interest there might be in a principled approach, involving a right to take strike and industrial action. In the end this trawling served only to benefit Ireland's archives of what might be called 'Rejected Suggestions for Industrial Relations Change'. A rights approach was rejected in no small way because of fear as to how the courts might interpret it, particularly if there were conflicting rights. Among trade unionists' fears was undoubtedly the concern that if a right to strike were promulgated it would be regarded as belonging to individuals.

I turn now to our Constitution. Many provisions in it are relevant to collective labour law but I want to single out freedom of association. Readers will scarcely need reminding that under Irish law, constitutional rights are supreme. Irish courts can strike down legislation if it is *ultra vires* or consistent with the Constitution.

Article 40, s. 6 includes among its provisions a guarantee of liberty for the exercise, subject to public order and morality, of the right of the citizens to form associations and unions.

The text envisages the collective interest being considered. The right is to be regulated and controlled 'in the public interest'.

Freedom of association makes sense only where there is more than one person.

In interpreting this provision the Irish courts have espoused a virtual 'dogma' of individual freedom. Not that any sensible person would advocate a dogma of collective security. But the interests of labour, of management, and the interests of the individual need to be balanced.

The starting point for analysis of the courts' interpretation of freedom of association was the striking down by the Irish courts of Part III of the Trade Union Act 1941.[8] This act sought to tackle the problem of trade union proliferation in Ireland. Within the respective judgements of the High and Supreme Courts there is no evident struggle to balance individual and collective interests. There is conflict, however, between judges who are in the majority and those who are in the minority in the court's decision. Majority judges call individual freedom exclusively in aid. Minority judges view freedom of association from a collective standpoint. There is no common ground.

The same is true of another, later, decision in which the statutory immunity for picketing in the Trade Disputes Act 1906 was found to be unconstitutional.[9] Picketing to force non-union persons into joining a particular union or to force members of one union into leaving that union is no longer protected. As a result of this decision the closed shop for workers already in employment is unconstitutional.

In the picketing case, Chief Justice Maguire, who dissented, challenged the majority on the logic of their stance. If they were right and action aimed at persuading non-union men to join a union was a denial of freedom of association, then each step taken with this in view was an infringement of the Constitution. The threat of a strike and above all the strike itself were surely just as much a derogation of the right of the non-unionist.

The response to this challenge has provided a source, in some minds, for a constitutional right to strike. The Chief Justice's argument was rebutted by another member of the court, Kingsmill Moore J., who said that the claim to picket and the claim to strike seemed to involve very different considerations:

> The right to dispose of one's labour and to withdraw it seems to me a fundamentally personal right which, though not specifically mentioned in the Constitution as being guaranteed, is a right of a nature which I cannot conceive to have been adversely affected by anything within the intendment of the Constitution.[10]

A less reliable source for the constitutional right to strike could scarcely be imagined. The right to strike is not fundamentally personal as those words are normally understood. It is exercised in concert and its very exercise by an individual necessarily involves the surrender of important elements of personal freedom. The judge's language brings one back to the nineteenth century when a right described in similar terms was perceived as under serious threat from trade unionism. Later cases invoking a constitutional right to strike or to take industrial action have proved how unreliable such rights are, and have cost at least one trade union dearly.

Unfortunately the immunities are not altogether safe from a constitutional standpoint. Some years ago, a highly respected Irish judge wrote extra judicially:

> Certain immunities against suit are available [to trade unions] which are not available to other persons or bodies ... Consequently there must be a question mark over the idea that any person or body of persons can be above the law.[11]

To be outside the law is one thing. To be above it, quite another. If the immunities are not accepted by the courts as ingredients thought to be necessary in a power relation between labour and management, they are at risk of being invalidated by the courts.

One hundred years on, therefore, there is still unease about the effects of the law in relation to issues crucial to trade unions. In the neuralgic areas I have examined involving trade disputes and freedom of association, the collective versus individual clash is still there. History has had much to do with it but it is no longer true to say that lawyers and judges are hostile to trade unions as one could have said when Congress was set up.

Legislation as drafted may become a very different force when applied by the courts. The common law has a necessary bias towards the individual. But today social cohesion is weaker than it was and individualism can shade into selfishness. In the law's ardent defence of David against Goliath, its bias can be destabilising.

Add to this the fact that legislation is rarely matched by careful study. Its original intentions may become blurred as it is brought through the process first of seeking consensus between the collective parties and then of drafting.

Our legislation is rife with close meshed phrases. There would be less chance of judges intervening in a way which, to trade unions, frustrated the collective interest if we had clear statements of principle in our labour code. The directives of trade union policy are not clearly stated in the legislation. Case law proceeds on principles which are unstated, and on attitudes which are unstated. That has been so for a century.

To allay fears, we might do well to have a specialist labour division of the High Court. Or the enactment of 'health provisions' in labour legislation enjoining judges in the event of doubt or ambiguity to choose the interpretation which furthers the aim of the statute.

As this span of one hundred years enters its close, we should look at the methods and effects of the law in relation to trade unions. Has the law served the best interests of trade unions? Are there better ways?

---

1. Trade Union Act 1871, s. 2.
2. See Kerr and Whyte, *Irish Trade Union Law*, Professional Books, 1985, pp. 153-8.
3. Conspiracy and Protection of Property Act 1875, s. 3. A person is immune in law when no redress can be awarded against him for a wrong he has committed: the wrong remains a wrong but there is no redress.
4. E.g., *South Wales Miners Federation v. Glamorgan Coal Co.* [1905] A.C. 239. A 'tort' is a civil wrong for which the law gives compensation to the person whose rights have been infringed or grants an injunction to protect those rights.
5. See Kerr and Whyte fn. 2 *ante* chapter 9.
6. Industrial Relations Act 1990, s. 10.
7. Trade Union Act 1941, see now Industrial Relations Act 1990, s. 9.
8. *National Union of Railwaymen v. Sullivan* (1947) I.R. 77. Later legislative strategies to deal with trade union multiplicity have, perforce, been tame.
9. *Educational Co. of Ireland v. Fitzpatrick* [1961] I.R. 345.
10. *Ibid.*, at 397.
11. Walsh J. in his foreword to Kerr and Whyte, fn. 2 *ante*, p. vi.

Dr Mary Redmond
Solicitor. Author of *Dismissal Law in the Republic of Ireland* (1982); Joint author with James O'Reilly of *Cases and Materials on the Irish Constitution* (1980), etc.

Women and Trade Unions

Professor Mary E. Daly

The earliest involvement of Irish women in trade union activities probably occurred when wives, sisters or daughters of male trade union members acted in support of their striking relatives in protests or demonstrations. There is a long history of women participating in such activities but otherwise they were relative late-comers to the trade union movement both in Ireland and elsewhere. Early trade unions were dominated by skilled artisans who were determined to protect their status against attacks by employers and by outside workers. Women by definition were outsiders who were excluded from most apprenticeships and from the overwhelming majority of skilled trades. Not only did these pioneering trade unions represent occupations which women were not permitted to follow, but their overall ethos was utterly opposed to women working outside the home. Nineteenth-century craft unions regarded working women as synonymous with cheap labour. They argued that women only worked because their men folk were unable to support them and that by working outside the home for low wages, women further undermined male earning-power setting in motion a vicious circle of increased working-class poverty and undermining the family in the process. The solution, according to this line of reasoning lay in paying men a Family Wage and excluding women from the labour market. Such views were not unique to Ireland, in fact they were widespread throughout Europe and the United States and persisted well into the twentieth century. As a result the relationship between women and the trade union movement, in Ireland and elsewhere was a complex and occasionally an uneasy one.

Organising women workers into trade unions proved a difficult task. In late nineteenth-century Ireland the overwhelming majority of women worked in either domestic service or in agriculture.[1] Domestic servants, who worked in ones or twos in private homes under a wide variety of conditions proved virtually impossible to organise in any country. Most female agricultural labourers were in their teens, intent on earning enough money to emigrate; others worked for relatives – again, unpromising trade

106

union material. A high proportion of women in industry worked either in small workshops or within their own homes. Whether employed in workshops or in large establishments such as the Belfast linen or Derry shirt factories, women rarely worked at tasks carried out by men. Most did not serve formal apprenticeships; consequently their work was regarded as unskilled or semi-skilled. The typical female industrial worker was young and single, with a low level of political consciousness. She tended to regard work as a transient experience prior to marriage and was unlikely to make a long-term commitment towards trade union membership. With wages often less than half those of a general male labourer and perhaps only one-sixth those of a skilled worker, she was often reluctant to pay a weekly union subscription of even a few pence. Older women who worked outside the home generally did so because of difficult family circumstances: they were widows with dependent children, wives of casual labourers or chronically-ill men; if single they often supported parents or siblings. Dual burdens of work and family left them little time for attending union meetings. Such women saw work as a necessary evil: many saw the solution to their plight, not in the higher wages or improved working conditions which a trade union might offer, but in securing an adequately-paid job for a husband, son, father or other male relative which would permit them to abandon paid work for domesticity. Many of these women would have endorsed the traditional views of male trade unionists: that a woman's place was in the home and that better pay for men or adequate welfare provisions would permit them to retire there.

In most countries the organisation of women into trade unions coincided with the unionisation of unskilled labourers. In Ireland the 1890s witnessed both the first serious efforts to organise labourers and the first trade union activity among women in the Belfast linen industry. Both the women's unions and the labourers' unions proved short-lived and by the time the Irish TUC was founded in 1894 the trade union movement was firmly dominated once more by traditional skilled unions. The first sustained breakthrough in recruiting women members came in the early years of the new century when Michael O'Lehane's Drapers' Assistants' Association became the first trade union in Ireland (with the exception of the INTO) to admit both men and women. By 1914 it had 1,400 women members among a total membership of 4,000. The upsurge of trade union militancy associated with Larkin and Connolly also impinged on women. During the Belfast docks strike of 1907 women from the linen mills demonstrated against blackleg labour; other women organised door to door collections. The first, and only long-lived Irish all-women's trade union, the Irish Women Workers' Union was founded in 1911 against a backdrop of labour militancy in Dublin. Delia Larkin, its first general secretary, was a sister of Jim Larkin, the ITGWU leader who became the first president of the Irish Women Workers' Union. During its early months the Irish Women Workers' Union sheltered under the wing of the ITGWU. By 1913 they had recruited many of the women in Jacob's biscuit factory; during the 1913 Lock-Out, the right of these women workers to belong to a union was challenged by the company in a manner similar to William Martin Murphy's assault on the ITGWU and they too were locked out. The aftermath left both unions impoverished; membership had fallen and both Jim and Delia Larkin were no longer in Ireland. Helena Molony, an actress and committed nationalist and James Connolly took on the task of reorganisation. When Molony was imprisoned for her part in the 1916 Rising, Louie Bennett, a suffragist from a prosperous Dublin family and Helen Chenevix, daughter of a Church of Ireland bishop took charge.[2] Unlike the typical male trade union leaders these three women, who were to lead the IWWU for many decades, were not members of the working class who rose into leadership roles, a characteristic they shared with the first generation of British women trade union leaders. This occasionally led them to treat the union rank and file with a degree of pity, perhaps even condescension.

The establishment of a separate union for women in 1911 reflected the conventions among British and Irish unions at the time, which excluded women from membership of male unions. In Britain however the First World War brought a sharp increase in women's waged employment and the intrusion of women into traditional male jobs. As a result male unions appear to have relaxed their hostility towards women members, if only for reasons of self-interest. Although women's employment in Ireland during the First World War showed much less expansion, Irish unions appear to have followed their British counterparts in deciding by the 1920s to admit women. The decision probably reflected a belief that having won the right to vote, women's struggle for equality was almost over. However despite overtures towards amalgamation from the ITGWU, the IWWU survived as a separate union until 1984 when it was decided to merge with the Federated Workers' Union of Ireland. From the 1920s most of the growth in female trade union membership took place in mixed general unions and in clerical and white-collar unions rather than the IWWU. This suggests that women workers were giving priority to class solidarity over gender interests. However, although these mixed unions undoubtedly protected women's working conditions and sought improved wages, until the second half of the twentieth century, they rarely articulated the point of view of women workers, nor did they do anything to reduce inequalities in pay and career prospects for women workers. Women came to account for up to one-quarter of the membership of the Irish Transport and General Workers' Union. However, the first woman was not elected to the national executive until 1955 and Sheila Williams, better known as Sheila Conroy, was the only female member of the executive of the ITGWU before the 1970s. For many decades therefore, the IWWU remained the sole voice within the trade union movement which spoke for women's interests.

The 1920s proved a difficult period for Irish trade unions. After the rapid growth of membership in the aftermath of the First World War, the number of both male and female members slumped as many industries either closed down or reduced the size of their workforce. In marked contrast, the 1930s saw steady expansion both in overall trade union membership and in women's participation.[3] Women proved to be major beneficiaries of the Fianna Fáil programme of tariff protection; many of the new industries established – clothing, shoes, textiles, toiletries and a range of other consumer goods employed a majority of women workers. By 1936 women accounted for 31% of the manufacturing work-force compared with 26% ten years earlier. The numbers of women employed in the civil service also rose rapidly in the early years of the state though they tended to be concentrated in the lowest grades of writing assistant and typist; posts which were confined to women and offered few prospects for promotion.[4] Whether they were employed in factories, shops or offices, most women workers tended to be young and single – marriage bars were the norm for most white-collar jobs and many women in industry resigned voluntarily on marriage. Women's jobs offered lower pay than comparable jobs for men. Yet despite this, aggregate statistics showing rising female employment in industry and services aroused considerable disquiet among male trade unionists; disquiet which was shared by the Fianna Fáil government whose industrial policy was geared to maximising male employment. Many male trade unionists believed that women were supplanting men in industrial and service employment; in fact there was no evidence to support such beliefs, instances of men and boys taking over jobs previously done by women in laundries and factories are much more readily documented. Often this occurred because of the ban on women's night work, which was enforced both by Irish law and by the International Labour Organisation with full support from all Irish trade unions with the qualified exception of the Irish Women Workers' Union. However in an era when complaints of women taking jobs away from men were rife, women trade unionists were necessarily put on the defensive. In 1932 Louie Bennett's presidential address to the Irish TUC described the growing number of women working in industry as 'a menace to family life', and argued that 'in so far as it has blocked the employment of men it has intensified poverty among the working class'. Bennett and other trade unionists of the 1930s tended to defend women's work, not as a right but as a necessary evil. Further evidence of the vulnerable position of women trade unionists and the hostile climate in which they had to survive emerges from the INTO's acquiescence in the government's imposition of a ban on married women teachers despite having a majority female membership,[5] and the trade union response to the Conditions of Employment Act.

In many respects the 1936 Conditions of Employment Act should be regarded as a model of reforming labour legislation: it provided guaranteed holidays with pay, set down maximum working hours and imposed controls over workers' overtime. The act which was drafted by Seán Lemass, Minister for Industry and Commerce following detailed consultation with male trade union leaders, also gave the minister the power to prohibit women from working in designated industries and to set quotas for women workers in individual industries. Senator Thomas Foran, President of the ITGWU, a union containing approximately 36,000 members at that time was thoroughly supportive of the proposed legislation and roundly denounced women who opposed it. His speech in the Irish Senate asked: 'Do the feminists want here what occurs in certain industrial countries across the water where the men mind the babies and the women go to the factories? Do they want that in this holy Ireland of ours?'[6]

When confronted with such viewpoints women trade unionists were in a vulnerable position: a weak and financially vulnerable minority in a predominantly male movement. The Irish Women Workers' Union sought in vain to modify the clauses which discriminated against working women; however their opposition was tempered by a recognition that they could not afford an open dispute with the Irish trade union movement. For that reason, despite strong personal reservations concerning the clauses relating to women in the 1937 Constitution, IWWU leaders such as Louie Bennett felt themselves constrained from uniting openly with an Irish feminist movement, which was dominated by women graduates, in outright opposition to the Constitution.

However while it is important to record the existence of tensions between women's rights and the trade union movement, we should beware of presenting an unduly negative picture of women's status. If male trade unionists showed little sympathy with demands for equal rights, they were often gracious towards individual women trade unionists: both Louie Bennett and Helen Chenevix served as presidents of Congress, the former on two occasions.[7] Women trade unionists led the way in campaigns for a cleaner, safer working environment; during the Second World War the Irish Women Workers' Union campaigned for more effective food rationing and assisted in the formation of the Irish Housewives Association; in 1945, following a three month strike, they negotiated an agreement which gave Dublin laundry workers two weeks holidays with pay; this was the landmark decision which eventually made two weeks holidays with pay the norm of most industrial workers.

None of these campaigns broached on controversial issues such as disparities in pay between men and women or women's exclusion from many areas of employment. Indeed health, hygiene and consumer issues could be seen as part of a woman's traditional role. Contentious issues such as equal pay tended to be avoided, perhaps because they might split the trade union movement, or because they were not necessarily supported by the majority of women trade union members. In 1953 the Irish Women Workers' Union supported a demand for equal pay at Congress, but wished to 'debar the young married women or "the single girl" from its terms'.[8] For the overwhelming majority of women, who worked in single-sex occupations, equal pay was an irrelevance. The depressed state of the Irish economy throughout most of the 1950s resulting in a falling level of employment and record emigration, meant that workers' interests became focused on protecting their jobs and standard of living and showed little interest in apparently-unattainable goals such as equal pay. In addition Irish society was preoccupied with the low marriage rate and particularly with rural population decline; many commentators saw the employment of women in towns and cities as a factor which contributed to this crisis. Such a climate was not conducive to advancing the status of women. In addition the pioneering generation of Irish women trade union leaders was fading from the scene; a new female leadership was only beginning to emerge.

In contrast the 1960s and early 1970s were a period of optimism and economic growth, a time when the trade union movement looked anew at women workers. The number of women employed in manufacturing industry fell as many of the protected industries established in the 1930s crumpled in the face of competition from imports. Although overall employment in manufacturing industry rose, the new jobs tended to be male jobs; government policy dictated that the industrial promotion agencies give preference to creating male employment. As a result women's share of jobs in manufacturing industry in the Republic fell from 35% in 1951 to 30% in 1971 and 27% in 1981. Although no similar policy existed in Northern Ireland, the sharp decline of the traditional textile and clothing industries brought a similar trend, with women's share of manufacturing jobs falling from 43% in 1951 to 33% in 1981.[9] At the same time overall employment in the public service and in the financial sector rose significantly as did the percentage of jobs in these sectors which were held by women. Thus the profile of women workers changed; the importance of industrial workers declined, white-collar workers came to assume a greater prominence. The Irish female labour force continued to be dominated by young, single women to a greater extent than in any other western economy. However, from the early 1970s, with the disappearance of the marriage bar in both the public service and the private sector, the percentage of married women increased suddenly.

Changes in trade union membership reflected the pattern of female employment. The number of women trade unionists showed little increase during the 1950s, rising only from approximately 55,000 in 1950 to 60,000 ten years later. By 1970, however, numbers had grown to 100,000; by 1977 there were

112

over 158,000 women trade union members: approximately two-thirds of all female employees.[10] Although male trade union membership was also on the increase, growth was faster among women. By the end of the 1970s men and women were equally likely to be members of trade unions, a dramatic change from previous generations when women were significantly less likely than men to become trade union members. Many of the new women recruits joined white-collar unions, particularly those representing public service workers, a trend which reflects the expansion of women's jobs in these sectors, though many white-collar workers also became members of general unions, whose female representation also rose considerably. Although women continue to be under-represented on union executives, women delegates, shop stewards and trade union officials have become more common.[11] This was a natural outcome of the fact that a greater proportion of women have remained in the workforce after marriage in recent years – trade union activists tend to be experienced workers, though conscious moves within the trade union movement to achieve greater gender equality, have also proved significant.

From the 1960s equal pay and promotion prospects began to feature to a greater extent among the demands of women trade union members. The fact that an increasing number of women members worked in white-collar occupations, side by side with men who often had significantly better pay and promotion possibilities brought a sharper focus on inequality in the workforce than was possible for women who worked in occupations where an all-female workforce provided no basis for comparison. The gulf between male and female pay rates and levels of pay increase was highlighted by the centralised agreement of 1964 and by the succession of National Wage Agreements which began in 1970. The overall economic optimism of the 1960s and early 1970s raised workers' expectations. During the mid and late 1960s the rising marriage rate and falling age of marriage combined with the tendency for most Irish women to quit work on marriage, either voluntarily or because of the existence of a marriage bar, meant that some employers faced a shortage of experienced women workers at a time of rapid economic growth and skills shortages. As a result the National Industrial Economic Council began to express concern about shortages of women workers. The combination of economic growth and shortage of experienced workers, also resulted in a small number of women

113

being promoted into positions hitherto regarded as male pre-
serves. By the early 1970s pressure on the labour market meant
that the ban on married women being employed in many white-
collar jobs was in the process of being eroded. Thus both Irish
women and Irish society were already undergoing change before
the emergence of the modern feminist movement; in consequence demands from the women's movement for improved
opportunities at work and the removal of gender-based discrimination found a not unreceptive audience among Irish women,
the trade union movement, and even, by comparison with the
past, within Irish society as a whole.

The trade union movement proved relatively adept at responding to the changes in women's demands; whether this reflects a change of mind, or simply a pragmatic awareness that
women constituted an important growth market for trade union
recruitment cannot be known. The decision by the newly-reuni-
ted Irish Congress of Trade Unions in 1959 to appoint a Wom-
en's Advisory Committee proved particularly fortuitous. Although its initial impact was slight, the Committee's annual report to Congress provided a platform for raising issues of specific interest to women. Congress had provided women members with a voice and they were not slow to use it. The first
evidence of a new female assertiveness emerged in 1964 when
the annual motion in favour of equal pay – a long-standing token
gesture of no practical significance – gave way to protests against
the failure to award women the same minimum pay increase as
men under the centralised agreement of that year. The prominence attached to wage rounds during these years and the fact
that information on pay bargaining and wage and salary increases was readily available in the media undoubtedly made
women more conscious of inequalities. The inequality between
the minimum rates of male and female wage increases provided
women workers with a clearly-defined issue, on which Congress
could be challenged; it resurfaced in 1965 in the course of a Special Delegate Conference on Wages when pressure from women
members led Congress to establish a Committee on Equal Pay.
This may well have been a delaying tactic; the report was still
outstanding in 1968 when the committee's brief was extended to
examine the wider question of women and work. In the same
year Congress passed a resolution calling on the government to
set up a Commission on the Status of Women, a demand which
had also emerged from a number of independent women's or-

114

ganisations who were responding to a 1967 United Nations directive. The Commission's interim report on equal pay, which was published in 1971, forced trade unions seriously to confront the position of women in the labour market for the first time; its proposals for legally-enforceable equal pay, investigation of women's promotion prospects and the opening of a wider range of careers for women marked a new era for the Irish trade union movement. Both the interim report and the full report of the Commission set an agenda for Irish women; many of the recommendations such as the removal of the marriage bar, introduction of equal pay and changes in social welfare provision were of direct relevance to trade unions.

Perhaps the Commission's greatest contribution was in raising consciousness about women's issues and setting an agenda for achievement. The 1974 Anti-Discrimination (Pay) Act provided a framework for the pursuit of equal pay and anti-discrimination claims as did the work of the Employment Equality Agency, which was founded in 1977. The succession of National Wage Agreements throughout the 1970s also gave the unions scope for including equal pay provisions as part of the overall negotiations. Trade unions have also played an important role in developing women's leadership skills and have provided many women members with opportunities for further education.

The pace of change in recent years has proved breathtaking in comparison with previous generations; most remarkable is the fact that much of this has been achieved at a time of high unemployment when a backlash against working women might have been anticipated. In fact women have weathered recent decades better than men: the number of women at work has risen by over 40% in the period 1971-91, the number of men at work fell by 4.8%. The gap between male and female wage rates has narrowed considerably; it is now estimated to be approximately 20%, compared with over 40% in 1971. Despite these positive trends, progress towards equality has proved more onerous than many would have anticipated in the 1970s. The removal of measures which formally discriminated against women has not proved sufficient to attain this goal. The current generation of trade union reports on women in the labour market reflects a growing awareness of the multiple factors involved.

Finally we should note that the growing importance of women's issues has brought about a significant transformation in the trade union movement as a whole. It has largely shed its traditional patriarchal ethos in favour of a strong formal commitment to gender equality. Women trade union members have helped to redefine jobs and trade union agendas. Trade union conferences now debate child-care, job-sharing, sexism and sexual harassment. This transformation cannot have been painless; in 1984 female employees of the ITGWU were forced to take the union to the Labour Court in order to achieve equal pay; women's representation in the craft unions and in many skilled trades remains limited. However the success of the trade union movement in responding to the demands of modern working women is a tribute to its resilience; in turn the rapid growth in the number of women members reflects the trade union movement's relevance to their needs.

1. Mary E. Daly, 'Women in the Irish workforce from pre-industrial to modern times', *Saothar* 7, 1981, pp. 74-82.
2. Mary Jones, *These Obstreperous Lassies. A History of the IWWU*, Dublin, 1988, pp. 6-22.
3. Mary E. Daly, *Industrial Development and Irish National Identity*, 1922-1939, Syracuse and Dublin, 1992, pp. 120-121.
4. *National Library of Ireland, Minutes of Inquiry into the Civil Service* Ms, 953, pp. 4-6. The number of women civil servants increased from 940 in April 1922 to 2,260 in April 1932.
5. Eoin O'Leary, 'The Irish National Teachers' Organisation and the marriage ban for women national teachers, 1938-58', *Saothar*, 12, 1987.
6. *Debates Seanad Éireann*, 27 November 1935.
7. Mary E. Daly, 'Women, work and trade unionism', in Margaret MacCurtain and Donncha Ó Corráin (editors), *Women in Irish Society. The Historical Dimension*, Dublin, 1978, pp. 72-73.
8. *Report of Irish Trade Union Congress, 1953-54.*
9. Liam Kennedy, *The Modern Industrialisation of Ireland 1940-1988*, Dublin 1989, p. 45.
10. Membership figures from Registrar of Friendly Societies. See also F. O'Brien, *A Study of National Wage Agreements in Ireland* , Dublin: ESRI Paper No. 104, 1981, and *Report of Commission of Inquiry on Industrial Relations*, Dublin, 1981, pp. 21-24.
11. Irish Congress of Trade Unions, *Implementation of the Equality Report*, 'Programme for Progress'.

Professor Mary E. Daly
Department of Modern History, University College Dublin. Author of *Dublin: The Deposed Capital: A Social and Economic History 1800-1914* (1984); *The Famine in Ireland* (1986); *Industrial Development and Irish National Identity 1922-39* (1992), etc.

Trade Unions and Economic Development

Dr Brian Girvin

Economic development and social change often provide trade unions with the opportunity to influence government economic policy, to increase membership and to play an expanded role in the public life of the state. Industrialisation usually has the most profound impact on this process, providing the opportunity for organisation and influence not usually available in pre-industrial societies. Although trade unions pre-date industrialisation, they achieve their most effective organisational form when the labour force is essentially wage or salary-earning. The Irish trade union movement has shared these assumptions and has had a long and, at times, successful influence on economic policy and has contributed to economic development in a number of ways. However, its impact has not been uniform, but has been heavily dependent on the nature of the political environment and the strength and determination of the movement itself.

Traditionally, trade unions have been concerned with economic development for two reasons. Economic development has usually been associated with growth and expansion in the economy, and many recognised that the changes accompanying this process provided an opportunity for trade union organisation and expansion. Economic growth is normally associated with the transition from a primarily agrarian society to one where the main focus for development is in the industrial area. For the most part conditions for trade union members tend to improve in democratic industrial societies, whereas in agrarian or non-democratic ones conditions for expansion and influence may be quite limited. The second reason for economic development has to do with unemployment. Trade unions, by their nature, require a low level of unemployment to allow them to operate successfully. At the very least they must be able to use industrial pressure in the absence of a reserve army of the unemployed which might undermine this position. Economic growth, if accompanied by high employment, thus increases the potential of the movement to gain higher wages, but also places it in a position to maximise its influence.

This is a rather idealised version of what trade unionists might wish to achieve. In most cases in Europe these conditions only prevailed after the Second World War, and even then not universally. Since the late 1970s some of the positive features of this phenomenon have weakened in a number of states due to the growth of anti-union politics, such as Thatcherism. Irish trade unions, in contrast with those in a number of European states, have not always been in a position to realise their objectives. One major reason for this has been the absence of industrial growth itself and the failure of the Irish state to realise its economic potential. The establishment of the Irish Free State enhanced the trade union movement's concern for economic development, yet the political and social environment was not one where trade unionism had either access to power or status with the government or the new institutions in the state. One consequence of independence was that the new state was overwhelmingly dependent on agriculture for employment, exports and wealth creation. The manufacturing industry comprised less than ten per cent of the labour force which in turn was heavily concentrated in the Dublin region and in specific sectors such as drink and biscuit making. Furthermore, most of these industries were heavily dependent on exports for growth, requiring easy access to the British market.[1]

The optimism which accompanied independence was quickly dissipated by the civil war and the subsequent restoration of order. The political and economic environment remained difficult for much of the 1920s; after the rapid expansion of membership during the First World War, there was a precipitous decline following independence. This decline was accompanied by the serious divisions between the Irish Transport and General Workers' Union and the Workers' Union of Ireland, contributing further to the malaise. Within this context, it is difficult to detect a developmental strategy on the part of the trade union movement. Yet even if there had been a united movement and a coherent policy, its potential would have been difficult to achieve. Throughout the industrial world economic policy was dictated by conservative considerations at this time. Socialism and trade unions were on the defensive from a propertied centre-right electoral block which dominated policy-making in virtually every European state. In Ireland this problem was compounded by a

118

number of specific factors which weakened trade unions. The first of these was the strength of the proprietorial sector of the economy. Not only did a majority of the labour force work on the land, but a majority was also associated with property in one way or another. In Finland or Sweden, trade unions were successful in rural areas because of the extent of an agrarian labouring class, one that only existed in limited areas of the Free State. Nor could labour find allies in government. The civil service was generally opposed to trade unionism and to its influence in industrial relations, never mind on the economy. The Department of Finance maintained a strong commitment to limited state involvement and rejected any thought of 'unorthodox' economic policies. In turn, the Cumann na nGaedheal government considered agriculture to be the main avenue for economic growth and rejected any innovative economic or social policy between 1922 and 1932.

Despite this, a policy debate on the future of the economy did emerge. Traditional nationalist theory asserted that an industrial sector could only be built if the economy was protected from external competition. This was a view which received some, though not universal, support from sections of the trade union movement. When the government set up the Fiscal Inquiry Committee in 1923 to examine issues affecting the industrial economy, it provided an opportunity to promote protectionism. However, the case made for protection was weak; the majority of industrialists remained opposed to protection, as did many trade unions. Irish flour millers advocated a tariff on imports, but were opposed by the ITGWU on the grounds that the problems which faced the industry had little to do with competition and more to do with the internal organisation of the industry. In other areas trade unions feared that protection would lead to a loss of employment in industries dependent on exports, while urban opinion was often concerned for the possible increase in the cost of living which might accompany protection.[2]

There is no recognisable developmental strategy within the trade union movement at this time. Congress lobbied government on issues relating to unemployment, social welfare and state intervention, but the evidence suggests that little influence was actually exercised. The main developmental organisation, the Department of Industry and Commerce, was concerned with economic development, but paid little attention to the demands of labour. Indeed, the policy of that department was to give

119

privileged access to Irish industrialists who wished to promote industry and required tariffs to do so. Industry and Commerce at this stage does not appear to have given consideration to trade union demands on economic questions. Nor did the trade union movement take an active role in promoting or opposing protective tariffs once the Tariff Commission was established in 1926. In the course of the 1920s a weak trade union movement secured a place for itself in Irish society, but one where its influence was seriously constrained by the hostile environment in which it functioned. This was recognised by Congress with one leading member, P. T. Daly, suggesting that the position of labour was as bad under the Free State as it had been under the British. However, by the end of the 1920s the mood within Congress changed and protectionism became the focus for policy. The *Industrial Charter* presented by the National Executive in 1931 was explicitly nationalist in its objectives. Furthermore, in his presidential address to the 1931 Congress, Denis Cullen expressly called for a wide-ranging protectionist policy.[3]

The election of Fianna Fáil in 1932 changed the political conditions under which Congress had to operate. In contrast to Cumann na nGaedheal, Fianna Fáil appealed directly to working-class voters and offered economic and social policies designed to attract them. Furthermore, the Labour Party supported successive Fianna Fáil governments for much of the 1930s, arguing that on economic and foreign policy the parties shared common goals. Most importantly perhaps was the close identity between the policies promoted by Fianna Fáil in government and those adopted by the ITUC. The decision by the new government to promote the expansion of Irish industry could not but have been welcomed by the labour movement. Furthermore, the expansion of welfare provision institutionalised many demands which had been previously made by the ITUC. In addition, the conditions for trade union organisation and expansion became far more favourable as a result of the new government than heretofore. Fianna Fáil used the state as an instrument for intervention in the economy and social life along lines favoured by the labour movement. This can be seen in the positive response to government policy at annual conferences, while the economic war with Britain and the rise of the Blueshirts also drew the government and the labour movement together.

On a wide range of issues Congress influence was felt almost immediately. Seán Lemass, the Minister for Industry and Commerce, proved responsive to representations from labour. In the Dáil in 1933 Lemass recognised the importance of trade unions by accepting that where organised labour predominated in an industry, then their right of representation on industrial bodies would be recognised. He frequently appointed members of Congress to public bodies, while state action often helped individual unions. The years between 1932 and 1936 were ones of fruitful co-operation between the ITUC and the Fianna Fáil government. Congress influence can be detected in many policy areas. This is not to suggest that Congress was involved in the detail of legislation, but that most of the legislation incorporated elements which had been promoted by the labour movement. This close co-operation culminated in the introduction of the Conditions of Employment Act, 1936, which prescribed the environment in which labour would function. It responded to the fear that in a protected economy labour would be at a disadvantage in terms of wages, conditions and organisation. It was generally welcomed by the trade unions, in fact the government insisted that it had been introduced as a result of representations by the trade unions. This act also imposed restrictive conditions on women in the workplace, but one which was widely accepted by trade union leaders, Fianna Fáil and by the majority of male members of unions.[4]

While labour was successful in improving the conditions for workers during the 1930s, its influence was strongest on social policy, industrial relations and wages. In terms of economic policy Congress was generally supportive of industrial protection, but does not seem to have had a direct input into policy-making itself. This can be attributed to two factors. The first is that the government, and Lemass in particular, refused to concede any direct involvement to either business or labour. Lemass was anxious to consult with interest groups, but he did not conceive of either sector as social partners with government. Lemass' notion of the state led him to concentrate power in the state and to exercise it through the civil service and legislation. However, secondly, Congress rarely moved beyond general exhortation on macroeconomic policy. Although less dependent on the state than business for its existence, by the end of the 1930s the trade unions accepted that the limits of Irish industrial development were within the context established in the 1930s.

121

There is little in Congress discussions, or individual unions, to illustrate that an independent developmental strategy was forthcoming at this time. In so far as one existed it presupposed that the employment-generating capacity of the Irish economy had been reached and that further growth was not possible. The policy conclusion which was drawn from this was that state ownership should be promoted to protect workers from the disruption of the world and the domestic economy. Nor was this restricted to trade unions. The business community and the new industrialists were as pessimistic about development and openly rejected Lemass' suggestions for a deepening of the industrial process prior to the Second World War.

The Second World War proved to be disastrous for the Irish trade union movement. The industrial economy shrunk in the absence of essential imports and many workers migrated to Britain to work in the war economy. In sharp contrast to Britain, the United States and Scandinavia, Irish trade unionism was weaker after the war than before it. In 1945, when the labour movement elsewhere was poised to take power or significantly increase its strength and influence, the Irish labour movement split in a disastrous manner. The history of this split is not the main concern here, what is, is the failure of the trade union movement to realise its potential and shift government policy in a direction other than the one actually followed. The Trade Union Act, 1941 had a number of aspects to it, the most important being the co-ordination of trade unionism and the other to eliminate both British unions and the Workers' Union of Ireland. If the two aims had been successful, it is likely that it would have forced Irish unions to develop along lines adopted by the Scandinavian unions earlier in the century. Lemass noted in 1942 that the elimination of British unions and the creation of a centralised union structure would not necessarily have ended disputes with employers or make the unions less powerful. The contrary may well have been the outcome, with a strong and centralised union movement making increasing claims for access and participation. In the event the disruption caused by the subsequent split prevented the movement from realising even the smallest element of influence at this time.

Yet the period from 1942 to 1947 was a time when the potential for change was great; once the opportunity was lost it was difficult to recover any initiative. In 1942 Lemass authored a memorandum on Labour Policy which, though concerned with immediate problems, assumed a radical shift in industrial relations and especially in the relationship between the state and the economy. This was followed in 1945 by an elaborate and ambitious set of proposals to generate full employment after the war. The Industrial Relations Act, 1946, which established, *inter alia*, the Labour Court, was a further attempt to co-ordinate the economy and its various interest groups. Moreover, Lemass was also proposing a radical overhaul of trade policy, a change which would have increased state involvement in the exporting sector of the economy. A final measure, and the most radical, was the introduction of the Control of Prices and Promotion of Industrial Efficiency Bill, 1947, which, if implemented, would have given the government unprecedented power over the economy. In each case Lemass was defeated by the conservative forces in the society, including the trade union movement itself. The 1941 Trade Union Act was in part declared unconstitutional by the Supreme Court, while the interventionist role for the Labour Court was undermined by trade union opposition. Other radical initiatives were countered by opposition among government ministers or by the civil service, normally the Department of Finance. The industrial efficiency proposals, though welcomed by Labour, fell when the 1948 general election was called. Yet even if Fianna Fáil had won the election, it is questionable if they would have been reintroduced.

Not all of these failures can be attributed to the divisions in the trade union movement or the establishment of the Congress of Irish Unions in opposition to the ITUC. However, at the very moment when Irish politics moved in a conservative direction, the trade union and labour movement was unable to present a common front to the state or the employers. It may not be an accident that the decade after 1945 was one of weakness not only for Congress, but also for Lemass. In a political environment where Lemass was clearly the architect of the government's industrial strategy, his failure to co-opt and integrate a unified Congress into his support base weakened him within Fianna Fáil. His close identification with the labour wing of the party had secured him advantages in the past, which now worked to his disadvantage. The consequences were severe, conservative economic policy prevailed for most of that period, while wage levels remained depressed for a considerable time. It is at least arguable that alternative industrial and economic strategies would have received a better hearing if Congress had been united and if Lemass could have used his influence by reflecting the relationship. The divisions in Congress and in the Labour Party may have allowed the conservatives within Fianna Fáil to ignore the trade union movement as of little importance. Whereas after the 1943 general election Lemass defeated the conservative elements within the party on the issue of co-operation with labour, after the 1948 election he was unable to prevent conservative dominance.[5]

When Congress reunited in 1959 the political and industrial landscape of Ireland had been transformed. The previous decade had been a very difficult one, protectionism had been continued after the war and reinforced during the 1950s. The rate of growth in industrial employment continued to increase, but at a slower rate than heretofore. Unlike the 1930s it proved impossible for protected industry to provide enough employment for those coming on the labour market. One consequence of this was the accelerating emigration which was a feature of the decade. Furthermore, Irish wage rates, which had historically remained quite close to those prevailing in Britain, now fell far behind; by 1960 British workers earned at least forty per cent more than the average Irish worker. This income gap operated as a strong incentive for skilled workers to emigrate even when not threatened by unemployment. The real crisis in the 1950s related to agriculture, but precisely because agriculture was so important the crisis affected the whole economy. Put in a wider perspective, Ireland after 1945 failed to maximise its opportunities in the expanding European economy and consequently did not share in the affluence which accompanied it. It was during this decade that Ireland went into relative decline against similar states in Western Europe. Irish growth rates and national income approximated with the average states in Europe during the interwar era; but began to fall well behind thereafter, a situation which has not been reversed subsequently.[6]

There is a further contrast to be made. In Sweden during the 1950s the government's macroeconomic programme was designed by a trade union economist, Rudolf Meidner, while in Britain the TUC had considerable influence over a conservative government's economic policy. In Ireland, however, trade union influence was at best indirect, but what influence there was depended on Fianna Fáil being in office. In July 1953 de Valera and Lemass held a meeting with the ITUC and though Lemass denied that Ireland faced a recession, he used the occasion to recommend to the government the need for significantly increased public expenditure. Moreover, here and subsequently Lemass set out policy objectives in the area of employment similar to those of both Congresses. Furthermore the means of achieving this aim was similar, massive state intervention. Throughout the next four years Lemass was to retain his commitment to state-led economic expansion, though still apparently within a broadly protectionist framework, However, on his return to office in 1957 he began the gradual process of opening up the state to new foreign investment, though without as yet removing tariff obstacles. A report from the Department of Industry and Commerce at this time predicted that in the event of protection ending, a significant section of Irish industry would simply disappear.[7]

Notwithstanding these fears the pressure to change increased between 1957 and 1960. As the crisis deteriorated new policy options were promulgated. Lemass believed that a massive injection of capital into the economy was the only way to break the depressive cycle. In the Department of Finance, T K Whitaker, the new secretary, produced *Economic Development* which provided an outline for the first *Programme for Economic Expansion* in 1958. By late 1958 the mood in government was one of change and the need to seriously address the crisis in the economy. The establishment of the Irish Congress of Trade Unions in 1959 came at an opportune time; for a unified body could again provide advice if not at first influence. Even more important, in 1959 Mr de Valera retired and Lemass succeeded him as Taoiseach. While Lemass did not at first transform government, his perspective on economic development and on growth in the economy was closer to that of Congress than his predecessor who embraced a more traditional attitude to economic issues generally.

Shortly after Lemass became Taoiseach, he invited Congress to meet him to discuss the question of development and how co-operation might be generated between the various economic interests. Lemass' speeches in 1959 often paralleled the positions adopted in previous years by Congress. These included the need for planning, for state involvement in development and the expansion of the state sector. In broad policy terms Congress was adopting a consumptionist strategy, one which would increase purchasing power on the grounds that this would boost demand. Lemass seemed to recognise the importance of this approach, but appeared to believe that Ireland had up to ten

125

years to effect substantial change before having to face external competition. Congress argued that government policy, while broadly correct, would not necessarily bring about quick results in employment or export terms. Congress insisted that Ireland could not wait for an export-led expansion, but should also pump prime the domestic economy to achieve growth. At this stage, the government was pursuing a cautious fiscal policy, maintaining spending at existing levels but shifting investment from social to capital spending. The argument forwarded by Congress was that while capital investment was important and welcome, it would not suffice to expand the economy. Social spending should not be seen as non-productive, as it often injected money into the economy which had a knock-on effect elsewhere. Within a year of Lemass becoming Taoiseach he had abandoned the cautious economic policy, and budgets began to expand with increased investment in those areas identified by Congress both in policy documents and in its private research.[8]

Notwithstanding this change and its importance to Congress and the trade union movement, Lemass continued to maintain his distance from the major economic organisations. He valued consultation and discussion, but was not prepared at first to deepen the relationship between government, business and labour. Congress itself had some qualms about any close relationship, but events pushed both parties together during the following years. Lemass believed, when he became Taoiseach, that Ireland had some space to get its economic house in order prior to having to face demands to dismantle its tariff barriers. The government was willing to eliminate obstacles to inward investment, but was not at first prepared to open Irish industry to competition from the more efficient industrial might of Europe. This illusion was quickly undermined when the United Kingdom applied for membership of the Common Market in 1961. Although Ireland quickly submitted an application, it was not ready for the first application and a number of Community members were sceptical of Ireland's ability to meet its commitments. The refusal of General de Gaulle to allow the United Kingdom's application to proceed in January 1963 gave Ireland the breathing space to restructure the Irish economy to face this challenge.[9]

Prior to 1961 farming organisations were the only strong supporters for Common Market entry, appreciating the value of subsidies available under the Common Agricultural Policy.

Industry did not share this enthusiasm, nor did Congress. In Congress' first policy statement on entry it urged caution, and, while not actively opposing entry at this time, suggested that the government should pursue alternative strategies, including searching for new markets. This was an unrealistic view on the part of Congress. Events moved quickly on the tariff front and the government agreed that unilateral tariff reductions should proceed from 1963. This in turn led to the 1965 Anglo-Irish Free Trade Agreement and the second application for Community membership. By this stage however, the government had also moved to involve trade unions, and Congress especially, in the process of economic development. A new pattern of participation by Congress in government institutions emerged between 1959 and 1965. The Committee on Industrial Organisation was established in 1961, but had been preceded by the Irish National Productivity Committee in 1959. The Employer-Labour Conference also came into existence in 1962, while in 1963 the National Industrial and Economic Council was established. These new agencies paralleled the state's commitment to economic planning as contained in the first two programmes for economic expansion. To a large extent the objectives of these agencies were similar to those of Congress. Congress believed that native entrepeneurship could not generate employment at the levels required to significantly reduce unemployment in the event of free trade. The conclusion drawn was that government had to play a more vigorous role in directing the economy.

This was a view increasingly shared by Lemass. The reports of the CIO demonstrated the weakness of Irish industry, especially when it came to export potential. However, Congress influence was not to be fully realised during the expansion of the late 1960s. One reason for this was that growth was increasingly generated by multi-national companies investing in Ireland under its favourable tax legislation. The objectives of multi-national companies were invariably different from those of native industry or state companies, and were largely outside the influence of the planning mechanism. A second reason is that the decision to enter the EEC undermined the commitment to planning in any systematic sense. Once it was accepted that international competitiveness was the main aim of policy, then planning on a national basis became much more difficult. Furthermore, the NIEC, while playing an important role in developing debate, did not function as a forum for policy development. Its 1965 report on economic planning came at the moment when planning was ceasing to play a central role in economic policy. While Congress welcomed this report, it was far less enthusiastic in its response to the 1970 report on incomes and prices policy, a report which was rejected by the Annual Conference in any event. Finally Congress had torn itself apart during the maintenance strike and labour relations were in crisis as a result of the government's threat to introduce legislation to control strikes and industrial relations generally.

By 1970 Ireland was undergoing significant change. Industry was now the primary source of job creation and exports. In addition, the social structure was beginning to reflect this; a process which could be seen in education, urbanisation, politics and lifestyle. Yet in some ways the trade union movement was still trapped in the older and traditional forms of conflict and assumptions. The maintenance strike in 1969 reflected older concerns; ones dominated by proprietorial and status assumptions, whereas the new unionism of the 1960s and 1970s was increasingly concerned with industrial organisation, the expansion of the public service and the possibility of influence over policy-making in an industrial society. The resolution of this division within Congress led to the defeat of the pre-industrial section of trade unionism, and the increasing dominance of industrial unions and the public sector. The decision in 1970 to introduce two-tier picketing can be seen as a 'rubicon' for Irish trade unions; but more importantly its acceptance increased the authority of Congress itself and provided it with added influence in its dealings with government. The National Wage Agreement in 1970 did not reflect any new-found confidence on the part of Congress, but did establish the basis for growth during the following decade. The agreements which followed were more sophisticated and comprehensive, but stopped short of the radical challenge of genuine tripartite arrangements.

The institutionalisation of pay bargaining through the Employer-Labour Conference enhanced the influence of Congress and its constituent unions. In particular, Congress could normally deliver on agreements; a major reason for this was the level of democratic accountability among the unions. This allowed Congress to approach government with a mandate on issues other than pay and conditions. Entry to the European Community and the recession of 1973/74 increased the willingness of government to negotiate pay agreements with unions, while

Congress and employers were prepared to do so in recognition of the challenge posed by inflation. Increasingly, it became more difficult to separate the National Wage Agreements from other issues, such as budgetary strategy and welfare provision. This process culminated in the creation of the Department of Economic Planning and Development in 1977 after Fianna Fáil's landslide electoral victory. The incoming government was committed to a full employment strategy, while recognising that such an objective would not be achieved without considerable state intervention and a deepening of the tripartite relationship between government, labour and business. The two crucial strategy documents produced by the minister, Martin O'Donoghue, were ambitious and addressed the concerns of Congress in large part. While it is unlikely that Congress had a direct input into the formulation of the government's strategy it is evident that O'Donoghue and the Taoiseach, Jack Lynch, believed that Congress support was indispensable to the achievement of the government's aims. This ambitious project was overtaken by internal divisions within the government and by the second oil crisis of 1979 which perpetuated the recession and facilitated the introduction of monetarist policies elsewhere in Europe. This policy is often seen as a disastrous and mistaken one, yet its failure was not inevitable. True, the chances of success were small, but other states in Europe, such as Austria and Sweden, successfully navigated the second oil crisis without recourse to monetarism. Ireland was not alone in its attempts to develop sophisticated social contract mechanisms, nor was it alone in failure. Britain and Italy also experimented with similar policies and also failed, often for reasons similar to those in Ireland.[10]

With raging inflation and rising unemployment after 1979 the attempt to construct policy on a new framework within the National Understandings failed. Notwithstanding this failure, involvement by Congress in the process demonstrated the potential for such understandings. The collapse of pay bargaining and the election of the Fine Gael-Labour coalition government marginalised Congress from the decision-making process. In stark contrast to Fianna Fáil, the new government had no intention of including the 'social partners' in policy formation. It was a bleak period for Congress and labour, though in contrast to the British experience, Irish 'Thatcherism' remained weak. Most of the actions of Congress and individual trade unions between 1981 and 1987 were defensive, seeking to maintain wages and employment against the pressure from employers and the indifference of the government. Out of this difficult environment a new sense of realism emerged in Congress and among the labour movement generally. This involved developing a coherent strategy for economic development which would bring about stable prices and lower unemployment. Congress also identified closely with tax reform, a belated response to the mass mobilisation of 1979. Within the National Economic and Social Council a series of important reports since 1980 has reflected many of these concerns on job creation, the European Community, and a renewed emphasis on indigenous job creation.

Influence can be conceived as active or passive. An institution can have a negative power of veto, or can make the cost of implementing policy too high for the government. The agricultural and property lobbies have had the most negative influence on policy formation in Ireland. The orchestrated attacks on property tax in 1994 is a reminder of how strong this lobby actually is, an attack which led the Minister for Finance to describe it as a hysterical response and to highlight the relatively low levels of personal taxation in Ireland. Congress' influence has rarely been negative in this sense, though at times it has been rather passive in promoting its objectives in the light of opposition. However, since the 1970s Congress has recognised the need to influence policy in a positive fashion and has sought access to government on this basis. This has been a consequence both of social change and a learning process. The failed opportunity of the 1970s drew attention to the difficulties involved in this approach, as did the years in the wilderness after 1981. This situation changed radically after 1987. The return of Fianna Fáil to office in that year also marked a return to centralised pay bargaining in the form of first the Programme for National Recovery, and subsequently the Programme for Economic and Social Progress; a process continued in 1994 with the Programme for Competitiveness and Work. There is room for debate about the merits of these agreements, what is important about them is their very existence. In Britain, the trade union movement has been critically weakened by the recession and Thatcherism, whereas developments in Ireland reflect the institutionalisation of a quite different tradition. Ireland is now closer to the northern European model of consensus between the social partners. These new arrangements have re-established a reciprocal relationship between Congress, the government and employers on a much stronger institutional

130

footing than heretofore. Congress has been more cautious and realistic during this phase of negotiation, recognising the exposed position of labour in a recessionary environment. A further reflection of the flexibility of Congress can be appreciated in the 1993 report on 'New Forms of Work Organisation', a study which recognises the changing economic environment and attempts to shape a positive trade union response to the novel circumstances of the 1990s.

A recent NESC report, comparing Ireland with other small European states, suggested that Ireland has been part of a vicious circle of decline, whereas many other states in Western Europe have achieved the benefits of 'autocentric' development; that is sustained economic growth with real improvement in the conditions of the people. The current tripartite relationship allows Congress to influence the movement towards autocentric development. Congress policy documents have stressed the need for rapid economic development if Ireland is to reduce the massive level of unemployment in the near future. The coalition government seems intent on addressing some of these demands. However, the real measure of Congress' influence will be the extent to which unemployment can be reduced radically over the next four years. The recent tripartite agreements have demonstrated Congress' ability to maintain living standards and conditions for the majority in work, but it is the most exposed section of Irish society which is affected by unemployment. Here is the real challenge for the end of the century and arguably one to which only Congress and the trade union movement can supply an adequate answer.

1. Brian Girvin, *Between Two Worlds: Politics and Economy in Independent Ireland*, Dublin: Gill and Macmillan, 1989, pp. 11-46.
2. Fiscal Inquiry Committee, *Reports*, Dublin: Stationary Office, 1923; National Archives Department of the Taoiseach (NADT), S 3107 'Fiscal Inquiry Committee' for responses to the reports.
3. Irish Trade Union Congress, 37th *Annual Report*, Dublin: ITUC, 1931, pp. 22, 23, 68.
4. Congress openly recognised the close co-operation and the influence which this brought. See its own list of achievements in ITUC, 40th *Annual Report*, Dublin: ITUC, 1934 pp. 32-45; See the claim made in an *Irish Press* editorial 17 May, 1937, that the Conditions of Employment Act was widely supported within the labour movement.
5. The detail of Lemass' success in defeating MacEntee over how to respond to the Labour Party and the working class can be found in MacEntee Papers,

Archives Department, University College Dublin, P67/362-66 which includes correspondence concerning the 1943 General Election.

6. Joseph Lee, *Ireland 1912-1985: Politics and Society*, Cambridge: Cambridge University Press, 1989, pp. 511-21; Kieran A. Kennedy, 'The Context of Industrialisation in Ireland', in John H. Goldthorpe and Christopher T. Whelan (eds.), *The Development of Industrial Society in Ireland*, Oxford: Oxford University Press, 1992, pp. 5-29.

7. Peter Baldwin, *The Politics of Social Solidarity*, Cambridge: Cambridge University Press, 1990; NADT: S13101c/1, 'Report of meeting between ITUC, the Labour Party and the Taoiseach and Tanaiste', 4 July 1953 and memorandum to government by Lemass; S.152281, 'European Free Trade Area', 2 February, 1957, Appendix II, 'Effects on Industry of the formation of the Free Trade Area'.

8. NADT: ICTU Archive, Box 42 (part 2) Economic Policy, 4002, 'Meeting with the Taoiseach 1959'; Kieran A. Kennedy and Brendan R. Dowling, *Economic Growth in Ireland*, Dublin: Gill and Macmillan, 1979, pp. 225-30.

9. Brian Girvin, 'Economic Development and the Politics of EC Entry: Ireland 1956-63', Paper for conference *The First Attempt to Enlarge the European Community, 1961-63*, European University Institute, Florence, February 17-19, 1994.

10. Lee, *op. cit.*, pp. 487-90, accepts uncritically the monetarist view of inevitable failure; for alternative approaches to this period see Marino Regini, 'The Conditions for Political Exchange: How Concertation Emerged and Collapsed in Italy and Great Britain', in John H. Goldthorpe (ed.) *Order and Conflict in Contemporary Capitalism*, Oxford: Clarendon, 1984, pp. 124-42; Peter Gerlich, Edgar Grande and Wolfgang Muller (ed.) *Sozialpartnerschaft in der Krise*, Vienna: Bohlaus, 1985 for a discussion of the Austrian case.

Dr Brian Girvin
Department of History, University College Cork. Author of *Between Two Worlds: Politics and Economy in Independent Ireland* (1989); *The Right in Twentieth Century Europe* (1994), etc.

Industrial Relations

Professor W. K. Roche

Trade union members and activists well understand the factors that influence the growth and decline of membership and organisation. Since the early 1980s these factors have led to the most serious and sustained losses in trade union membership in Ireland since the 1920s; though in recent years there are signs that the setbacks of the 1980s have been halted and that unions have recovered momentum.

The factors influencing the waxing and waning of union membership and organisation can be divided into three distinct categories. First of all, the economic or business cycle affects the inclination and opportunity of people to join and remain members of trade unions. When the labour market is buoyant, unions benefit in various ways, some obvious, others less so. The pay rises that result from economic prosperity allow unions to point to the effectiveness of their role in wage-bargaining. By winning credit in the eyes of members and potential members for significant improvements in pay, unions become more capable of recruiting and retaining members than in times when, at best, only modest pay rises are possible. When the business cycle is in upswing, employers are also more reliant on the co-operation of employees to keep businesses in motion. Industrial disruption at such times can be particularly costly for employers in terms of production and profits foregone. Employees, for their part, are more confident of their own, and their unions', ability to defend and improve their conditions of employment. As a result, when trade is good, employers are less likely to resist attempts by unions to win recognition and employees are more likely to press confidently for trade union recognition and supports to organisation. From the interplay of these and other business-related factors, emerges those fluctuations in trade union membership and in the strength of organisation over time, which are well known to students of the trade union movement.

But the booms and slumps of the business cycle influence unionisation not exclusively but in combination with other factors. A second distinctive set of influences arises from the changing structure of the work-force. Historically, unions have found their greatest strength in particular industrial sectors and among certain sections of the work-force. The traditional industrial heartlands of trade union movements internationally have been the mining, docking and transport industries, and in areas of heavy industry, such as engineering, food and textiles. The occupational heartlands of trade unions have been among skilled craftsmen, semi-skilled and unskilled workers and workers in the public sector.

Over time, in response to economic development, the composition of the work-force gradually changes. During the early phases of industrialisation the work-force grows proportionately in industrial sectors and in occupations in which unions find a ready response to their calls for organisation. As a result, union growth accelerates. Such a broad pattern of change in the composition of the Irish work-force assisted union efforts to gain and hold members for much of this century up to the 1980s. If industrialisation and attendant sectoral and occupational changes in the work-force serve to accelerate union growth, de-industrialisation, or the rising importance of services and service workers in economic activity, tends to put the brakes on unionisation. Thus, in Ireland during the 1980s, the overall direction of change in the composition of the work-force has contributed to the deceleration of unionisation. For the first time in Irish labour history, change in the composition of the work-force seemed, in virtually every respect, to increase the obstacles faced by unions in winning and retaining members and in preserving and extending organisation. Thus, work-force growth was concentrated in private or traded service industries, where unions have always been weak. The white-collar component of the work-force continued its long-term rising trend. The proportion of the work-force employed in the public sector declined continuously for practically the first time in the history of the state. And, though much less well documented in official statistics, the numbers of people employed on part-time, short-term and on other so-called 'atypical' contracts rose significantly.

Important though structural and cyclical factors are in understanding the past course and future outlook of trade unions, I have chosen to concentrate in this lecture on a third set of influences on unionisation: that is, on the impact of the institutions and practices of industrial relations on the fortunes of unions and their members. For the manner in which industrial relations are conducted can be of profound significance for the ease with which unions can recruit, organise and represent members.

The establishment of the Labour Court in 1946 was a milestone in Irish industrial relations. The court's conciliation and investigation services soon served to underwrite a particular approach to the conduct of industrial relations at company and workplace levels. The principles of 'good industrial relations' inherent in the deliberations of the court and the activities of conciliation officers, envisaged employers and managers engaging, as a matter of routine, in ongoing compromises over pay and conditions with well-organised trade unions. The main channel through which industrial relations between employers and employees were to be conducted was seen to be collective bargaining. Because effective collective bargaining was viewed as the pivot of good industrial relations, union recognition and union organisation received encouragement. Thus, in its early years, the Labour Court played a key role in encouraging employers to concede union recognition in sectors like the insurance industry where hitherto the efforts of unions to organise had met with staunch resistance. As time wore on, the numbers of employers and employees having recourse to the services of the court rose steadily, until during the 1970s the court had become a standard, some would say a 'chronic', feature of collective bargaining and dispute settlement in industrial relations.

The particular importance of the court for the development of stable trade union organisation and expanding union membership lay in its recognition that industrial relations was an essentially adversarial process, involving the interplay of the partly common but also partly conflicting interests of employers and employees. The court's very existence, its composition, and methods of working were indeed predicated on this fundamental premise. Thus, it was accepted that the primary interest of employers was to increase profits or deliver goods and services at sustainable levels of cost; this necessitated the control of wage costs. The primary interest of trade unions and their members involved the defence and improvement of living standards at a sustainable pace of work; this imposed upward pressure on wage costs. The ongoing compromise of these interests through collective bargaining could be expected, from time to time, to result in industrial conflict; and it was good industrial relations practice to develop procedures for resolving conflict at workplaces and companies. In this understanding of what good industrial relations entailed, trade unions, collective bargaining and adversarialism were seen to be intrinsic to the process. In contrast, the options of regulating the conduct of industrial relations by legal means, through state intervention or through the unilateral exercise of managerial authority, were looked on as counter-productive.

So it was that the Labour Court, the most important public policy initiative in industrial relations since the foundation of the state, came both to exemplify in its own activities and to recommend to Irish business a model of good and enlightened industrial relations in which strong independent trade unions were of central importance.[1] Small wonder, then, that the most dramatic surge of trade union growth recorded in independent Ireland occurred during the second half of the 1940s, following the establishment of the Labour Court. Though in accounting for the dramatic expansion of unionisation during these years, one must also consider the influence of the economic recovery of the period; the advent of wage-round bargaining and the strong pressure that had built up during the war years for the restoration of pre-war living standards.[2]

It should be recognised that the principles which came increasingly to define the canons of good industrial relations in the period after 1945 were built on foundations of industrial relations practice set down amid the social upheavals of the first two decades of this century – foundations which reflect the influence of British ideas and practices. These foundations were buttressed during the 1920s and 1930s by Ireland's participation in the International Labour Organisation and the enshrinement of a right to freedom of association in the 1937 Constitution.

It should also be recognised that the political architects of the Labour Court originally conceived of that institution as part of a comprehensive programme of reforms which might foster a different understanding or model of relations between employers and employed. Here we encounter the chameleon-like figure of Seán Lemass. Lemass' pragmatism and readiness to change posture on industrial relations at least rivalled his changes of direction on economic and industrial affairs more generally. During the 1930s Lemass had broadly endorsed prevailing practices in industrial relations, showing himself ready to step into the breech as a mediator in serious industrial disputes. Lemass' experience of wartime economic intervention when, as Minister for Supplies and Industry and Commerce, he exercised unprecedented control of economic life, led him to the view that post-war reconstruction would require strong state direction of business and labour affairs. Despite his sharp dismissal of 'corporatist' ideas and ideology, as evidenced by the short shrift given to the report of the Commission on Vocational Organisation, Lemass' ideas in the 1940s on business, labour and industrial relations have been described as essentially corporatist in character. Two things are implied by such a description. First, Lemass had come to the belief that the state should control the manner in which union and employer organisations exercised their functions in the areas of organisation and collective bargaining. Second, he envisaged the establishment of joint 'development councils' charged with improving efficiency in different industries. It is testimony to the strength of established industrial relations practices that Lemass' legislative proposals on industrial efficiency came to nought and that the planned cornerstone of corporatist control of collective bargaining, the Labour Court became instead the cornerstone of so-called free collective bargaining and industrial relations adversarialism.[3]

Important though it was in legitimising the role of unions and collective bargaining, the Labour Court was but one contributor to the increasingly orthodox doctrine that good industrial relations practice should be based on strong unions, arms-length dealings between management and managed, collective bargaining and adversarialism.

Three further contributory factors also bear emphasis and will be considered in turn.

The first of these was, ironically perhaps, the professionalisation of Irish management. Professional management, based on functional specialisation in areas or departments like marketing, production, finance and personnel/industrial relations, is a relatively recent arrival in Irish business. It was during the 1960s that modern management ideas, principles and models of industrial organisation probably first became a significant force across Irish business. Professional personnel and industrial relations management, in which the job of managing people was delegated to trained specialists, was but one aspect of a more general growth in management professionalism during the 1960s and 1970s. An Irish Management Institute survey conducted in 1964 showed that personnel managers and departments were present to any significant extent only in large companies. A decade later, research revealed that professional personnel management had become a standard feature of Irish companies, particularly in the medium and large employment categories.[4] These growing numbers of personnel and industrial relations professionals were the first managers specifically accountable to senior management for the quality of industrial relations in companies. Thereby they had a strong vested interest in developing and maintaining good relations with trade union officials, both professional and lay. Personnel and industrial relations professionals gradually gained greater stature – their slow climb up the ladder of managerial authority and prestige aided by a growing body of employment legislation and rising industrial conflict. As responsibility for personnel increasingly devolved to professionals, the influence of other management specialisms, as well as that of proprietors and corporate shareholders, over the conduct of industrial relations was commensurately tempered or diluted. These groups were likely, in most instances, to be considerably less inclined towards ongoing compromise as a method of running businesses. As such, the dilution of their influence by personnel professionals contributed further to the legitimisation of industrial relations based on strong unions and adversarial collective bargaining.

The new personnel professionals also served as a *conduit* for modern techniques and wider bodies of ideas on the management of industrial relations. Thus industrial relations techniques like job evaluation, productivity bargaining and the use of formal procedures to settle union recognition and resolve disputes gradually became widespread. Company-sponsored supports to union membership and organisation, such as the automatic deduction of union dues, time off work for union duties and the use of company facilities for union business also became commonplace.

Through the application of the techniques of modern personnel administration, and through concessions to unions on supports to organisation, management by the professionals effectively drew union officials, professional and lay, into the governance of organisations to a degree never before witnessed. Union participation in corporate governance was still conducted, however, at arms length; adversarialism remained the order of the day; unions and their members influenced many core aspects of business decision-making only marginally, if at all; and if at all, then only by challenging management authority and managerial decisions. Yet the professionalisation of management

138

over the post-war period contributed significantly to union recognition, the growth of union membership and the consolidation of union organisation.

Unionisation also found support in the broad thrust of public policy on industrial relations over the period between 1946 and the 1970s. Besides the establishment of the Labour Court, the early post-war years witnessed the advent of a series of schemes for conciliation and arbitration in the public service. These schemes, the outcome of a long-standing demand for collective bargaining by public servants, brought a highly regulated and formalised version of the adversarial model to different groups of public servants. The operation of the C and A schemes again involved the kinds of supports to union organisation developing in the private sector and the commercial semi-state companies.

But the state also supported unionisation more directly. It was a principle of public policy to encourage companies to recognise trade unions and engage in collective bargaining with their staffs. The Department of Industry and Commerce and later the Department of Labour advised such a stance when ministers were asked to intervene in disputes over union recognition. Of even greater importance, given the commitment of successive governments from the late 1950s to foreign investment as the engine of economic development, was the industrial relations policy adopted by the Industrial Development Authority and SFADCO. These agencies followed a policy of advising incoming multi-nationals to concede union recognition and adapt to local traditions of industrial relations. In general this policy met with considerable success. However, notorious recognition disputes at EI Shannon in the 1960s – when bus burning allied with the nineteenth century tradition of 'collective bargaining by riot' made a fleeting reappearance, and in 1979 at the Dublin franchise of McDonalds – indicated that in an advanced manufacturing and a modern service industry, management ideology might still be stubbornly hostile to unions and collective bargaining.

For the most part, the policy of the development agencies resulted in incoming multi-nationals concluding single-union recognition deals. In these so-called 'pre-employment agreements', companies effectively undertook to sign up union members even before they had been employed. As Bill Attley was to put it, in the more taxing circumstances of the 1980s, during the

1970s trade unions had organised companies more actively than they had organised individual members.

The final force supporting unionisation and collective bargaining during the 1960s and 1970s was the growth of education in management and industrial relations. The availability to growing numbers of managers and trade union activists of education and training, both reflected and contributed to the professionalisation of industrial relations. Isolated initiatives aside, industrial relations education had been pioneered in Ireland during the 1950s by the Jesuit-run College of Industrial Relations. University College Dublin entered the field in earnest in the 1960s, to be followed by Trinity College in the 1970s. The Irish Management Institute covered industrial relations issues in programmes of training for practising managers. The Institute of Personnel Management gradually became a major force. By the 1970s the IPM was active in determining the curriculum and professional standards of those entering the field and in influencing the qualifications sought by companies seeking to recruit personnel and industrial relations managers. On the trade union front, the ICTU played an active role in educating union officials and activists, while the major unions, in particular the ITGWU, also conducted training courses for officials and shop stewards. Finally, through the Irish Productivity Centre, financial assistance for research in industrial relations was provided for the first time, enabling the publication of a brave, if short-lived, series of studies on human sciences in industry.

To be sure, caution is warranted concerning the number of people exposed to these initiatives in management and trade union education. It is also reasonable to question whether many were exposed to the field in sufficient detail or depth for the experience to become professionally formative. Yet I believe that both the direct and indirect effects of expanding education and training were significant. The activities of the colleges, professional institutes and trade unions exposed many, who were to rise to key positions, to modern international thinking on the conduct of industrial relations. In the universities, business schools helped to foster in aspiring general managers attending MBA courses a more detailed and balanced understanding of industrial relations than they might otherwise have acquired at a formative early stage of their managerial careers. Indeed, the study of industrial relations was becoming both popular and respectable – a far cry from the days when industrial relations was all a matter of hammering the table and having enough stamina to withstand protracted negotiations and the inevitable friction of industrial conflict.

Through their education and training programmes, their writings and contribution to professional and public debate during the 1960s and 1970s, universities, colleges and professional institutes underscored the prevailing model of 'good industrial relations'. The major texts of industrial relations in Irish universities and colleges during the 1970s included the celebrated report and research papers of the (British) Royal Commission on Trade Unions and Employers' Associations – the so-called 'Donovan Commission'. The Donovan report, as well as the writings of the influential academic members of the Royal Commission, received intensive study in Ireland. Irish versions of similar models of good industrial relations, such as the Fogarty Report on industrial relations in the ESB, also received close attention as exemplary practice.[5] It was a contributor to Donovan, the Oxford academic Alan Fox, who mounted the most explicit defence of collective bargaining between professional managers and strong unions as the best possible basis on which to conduct industrial relations. Fox also adopted an academic term from US industrial relations to denote this now orthodox and respectable model of industrial relations: the term was 'industrial relations pluralism'.[6] Adversarial collective bargaining was now analysed by the academics and their students more rigorously than ever before and a compelling rationale was developed in its favour, based on a synthesis of writings and research in the United Kingdom and the United States.

Students were encouraged to question whether in reality all-powerful managers or compliant employees afforded the best basis on which to run companies. The superficially appealing ideal of consensus or harmony in industrial relations was looked on critically. Did it not appear more pragmatic and sensible, in the context of modern industrial conditions, to recognise that employees would typically perceive their interests to be in conflict, in significant respects, with those of management? Would not attempts to deny or suppress such a reality, for example, by appealing for the undivided loyalty of employees, turn out to be fruitless and counter-productive. Evidence could be pointed to that productivity was higher under unionisation than under autocratic styles of management. A case could equally be made that strong adversarial unions were conducive to business success and that industrial conflict, properly managed, was a dynamic force in organisations. For students these arguments were excitingly counter-intuitive; for practitioners they seemed to find ready resonance in the hard school of professional experience. Adversarial industrial relations between professional managers and strong unions had reached their high water mark in both a theoretical and practical sense.

Thus it was in the 1970s that the three trends we have identified, the professionalisation of management, the evolution of public policy and the growth of industrial relations education, came together to underscore the model of good industrial relations inherent in the deliberations of the Labour Court since 1946. A positive stance on union recognition, the encouragement of union membership and the provision of supports to union organisation were integral to this model of industrial relations. It might be noted in passing that the otherwise profound changes which occurred during the 1970s in the conduct of pay bargaining and the role of the state in Ireland had little significant impact on the conduct of industrial relations at company or workplace level.

During the 1980s, as union membership fell precipitously from one year to another, for the first time since the 1920s, the tide began to flow against this now very orthodox model of industrial relations practice.

Challenges to the established model arose simultaneously from several directions. Unions began to face a resurgence of old-fashioned resistance to attempts to win recognition. Old familiar exercises in union suppression by employers, particularly small employers, had long ebbed and flowed in Irish industrial relations, peaking at times of highest unemployment and union weakness. But in the 1980s resistance of this kind became more common and more intense than at any time since the 1940s. By the early 1990s a catalogue of bitter recognition disputes existed as evidence of the renewed force of a very old employer stance: in Lett's Fish Processors, in Nolan Transport and in Pat the Baker.

Resistance to union recognition of a very different kind also became more common. In the 1970s incoming multi-nationals, particularly in the electronics industry, had begun to reveal a new face of union avoidance. In the 1980s increasing numbers of incoming companies sought to resist unionisation in a sophisticated manner. The broad thrust of policy in these companies

142

involved developing so-called 'human resource policies' in an effort to substitute for trade unions. Union substitution relies on such things as excellent communications, good pay and conditions, and innovative forms of work organisation to persuade employees that it was unnecessary to unionise. Some commentators have viewed this development as an exclusively US phenenomenon. While many of the exemplars of non-union HRM were indeed US companies, many other US companies were satisfied to recognise trade unions. Thus, the adoption of such a strategy can more validly be viewed as a feature of the particular sectors in which most of the companies involved operated – in particular, micro-electronics and computer software – rather than as a distinct reflection of the nationality of the parent company.[7] Whatever the origin of new-style union avoidance or substitution, it struck at the core of the post-war model of good industrial relations. Now unions were presented with a tougher prospect than the old-style anti-unionism which they had long learned to outflank. The viability of sophisticated union avoidance strategies was also supported by a change in the stance of public agencies towards union recognition. In the 1980s commentators noted that agencies like the IDA and SFADCO no longer actively encouraged incoming multi-nationals to recognise unions and adapt to local traditions of industrial relations. Moreover, the Federation of Irish Employers, now merged into the Irish Business and Employers' Confederation, itself reflected these changes by developing advisory services for companies unwilling to follow the traditional industrial relations model.

Perhaps of more long-term relevance than either of these challenges to the established model of industrial relations, was a third challenge, this time developing from within the basic features of the established model itself. From about the mid 1980s business schools, managers and then trade unionists began to debate a new model of good industrial relations which sought to fuse so-called 'human resource policies' with collective bargaining based on strong trade unions. The concept of the 'new industrial relations' or of 'new realism' in industry was born; and in the debates and controversy which the new arrival provoked, what seemed to have been settled over the period 1946 to 1980 was now back in the melting pot.

The essence of the new industrial relations can be distilled into several central claims. First, current competitive conditions and changing patterns of consumer demand warrant a major restructuring of established industrial relations practices. Second, good industrial relations must now be built upon strong bonds of commitment between employers and employees and common objectives have thus to be given greater weight. And third: collective bargaining, based on adversarialism and arms-length dealings between unions and employers, could no longer serve as the sole, or even the main, channel of industrial relations. Parallel channels were required. These were to be built upon direct employee involvement in the organisation of work and trade union co-operation in the resolution of business problems.

These claims challenge the established post-war model of industrial relations from within: trade unions and collective bargaining remain the cornerstone of good industrial relations; but unions take on new responsibilities for the operation of the business and collective bargaining is to coexist with joint union-management decision-making based on consensus. The merits of the new industrial relations have been pressed with increasing insistence since the mid 1980s. Even though developments on the ground are running well behind the rhetoric and ideology of new industrial relations – now much beloved of managers – there is nevertheless evidence that new concepts and principles have become a force for change in the practice of Irish industrial relations. In Bord na Mona, in ESB, in Shannon Aerospace, in Syntex and in many other companies, we see the practical working out of these concepts and methods.

Because new industrial relations appear to challenge, sometimes profoundly, the dominant understanding of good industrial relations developed over the past fifty years, it is small wonder that unions, in particular, have reacted cautiously and sometimes with hostility to the blandishments of the new model. For some in the trade union world these new ideas represent a siren call, luring unions towards the rocks on which they will be sundered. For others, they represent a thinly disguised recipe for intensifying work or for promoting deunionisation, gradually and by stealth. Critics have sought to link the advent of these new ideas and the human resource management phenomenon generally to the precipitous membership declines and the organisational reverses of the 1980s. They also suspect that the image of consensual industrial relations, based on involvement and maximum job security for some employees, necessarily entails a return to autocracy, exclusion and insecurity for many

144

others. They point to the evidence of growing casualisation; increased use of part-time and contract workers and the rising incidence of other 'atypical' forms of employment. Trends such as these, critics plausibly argue, are the very antithesis of the brave new world of new industrial relations.

The research evidence presently available for Ireland, though admittedly tentative, fails to bear out a direct link between the simple adoption of human resource management policies in general and attempts to withhold union recognition. Nor can compelling evidence be found that in instances where human resource policies are grafted on to collective bargaining, levels of union membership thereby decline.

The recent decision of the Irish Congress of Trade Unions to support the new model of industrial relations, provided that safeguards to organisation can be guaranteed, is a bold and reasonable response to current trends. Congress has issued a challenge to employers and shown that it will not easily be out-manoeuvred or marginalised in debates on industrial relations change.

Yet the sinking currency of adversarial industrial relations and the rising currency of the new industrial relations pose serious dilemmas for the Irish trade union movement as it approaches its second century. Of these dilemmas and uncertainties, the following seem particularly pressing. Is strong commitment to the company consistent with strong commitment to a trade union? Is union involvement in business decision-making and problem-solving consistent with the effective conduct of collective bargaining? Can unions be part and parcel of the managerial process and yet mount a challenge to management decisions? Is employee involvement in the job and in the organisation of work consistent with their protection by unions against intensifed work effort, stress and ill health? Can unions encourage employees to become partners in business enterprise and still hope to mobilise the power of their stronger members to defend the weak by appealing to ideals of social justice?

One thing alone is certain. The working out of these dilemmas in the years ahead will provide much material for the history of Irish trade unions in their second century.

1. This approach to the conduct of industrial relations and its support through public policy was also followed in the United States, the United Kingdom and a number of European countries. See Bruce E. Kaufman, *The Origins and Evolution of the Field of Industrial Relations in the United States*, New York, ILR Press, 1993; and see also Alan Fox, *History and Heritage: The Social Origins of British Industrial Relations*, London, Allen and Unwin, 1985.

2. For a detailed statistical analysis, see W. K. Roche and J. Larragy, 'Cyclical and Institutional Determinants of Annual Trade Union Growth in the Republic of Ireland: Evidence from the DUES Data Series, *European Sociological Review*, 6, 1990, 49-72.

3. For discussions of the Lemass proposals and their fate, see Brian Girvin, *Between Two Worlds: Politics and Economy in Independent Ireland*, Dublin, Gill and Macmillan, 1989, chs 5-6 and J.J. Lee, *Ireland 1912-1985: Politics and Society*, Cambridge, Cambridge University Press, ch. 4.

4. See Brefni Tomlin, *The Management of Irish Industry*, Dublin, Irish Management Institute, 1966; Liam Gorman, et al., *Managers in Ireland*, Dublin, Irish Management Institute, 1974 and Liam Gorman et al., *Irish Industry: How it's Managed*, Dublin, Irish Management Institute, 1975.

5. *Final Report of the Committee on Industrial Relations in the Electricity Supply Board* (Michael Fogarty, chair), Dublin, Stationery Office, 1969.

6. Alan Fox, *Industrial Sociology and Industrial Relations*, Royal Commission on Trade Unions and Employer Associations, Research Paper No. 3, London, HMSO, 1966.

7. See W.K. Roche and Tom Turner, 'Testing Alternative Models of Human Resource Policy Effects on Trade Union Recognition in the Republic of Ireland', in *The International Journal of Human Resource Management*, 1994.

Professor W. K. Roche

Director of Research at Graduate School of Business, University College Dublin. Author with K. Hinrichs and C. Sirianni of *Working Time in Transition* (1991); Joint editor with Tom Murphy of *The Practice of Industrial Relations in Ireland* (1994), etc.

Pay Bargaining:
Confrontation and Consensus

Dr Niamh Hardiman

To survey trends in pay bargaining in Ireland over one hundred years is a large undertaking. The social and economic structure has been transformed over this period, and the conduct of pay bargaining has correspondingly changed a great deal.

One hundred years ago collective bargaining over pay was largely confined to craft workers, but it was far from being an established feature of the industrial world. In most cases, there was no regular contact between employers and unions at workplace level. Bargaining arrangements were not formalised, and there was no agreed procedure for conducting negotiations. Bargaining was infrequent and episodic, and was often preceded by an outburst of industrial conflict. The range of issues which was subject to any negotiation was narrow. There was no expectation of a regular cycle of bargaining activity, and no expectation on either the union or the employers' side that there would be regular increases in pay. Indeed, at times pay bargaining was not about securing an increase in pay, but about resisting a pay cut.

Bargaining was also small-scale and localised: the newly-formed Irish Trades Union Congress took no role in co-ordinating pay bargaining. The significance of pay agreements for the national economy was small. Government involvement in regulating the conduct of industrial relations was at an early stage, and its role in regulating economic performance was still very limited.

Each of these features of the conduct of pay bargaining was to change significantly in the course of a hundred years. Over time, we see the development of recognised procedures for work-place collective bargaining and the institutionalisation of employer-union relations. Pay claims began to be submitted more frequently. The expectation developed that employees would be compensated for increases in the cost of living, and the range of issues covered by the pay bargaining process then came to include other issues to do with the terms and conditions of employment. Awareness of the pay structure broadened, so pay relativities across occupations and enterprises became more important in formulating claims. This meant that the scale of pay bargaining extended beyond the small-scale and local range and increasingly took on a national dimension, with a correspondingly greater significance for national economic performance. It therefore became much more central to the concerns of government. In recent times, relations between unions and employers, and between both of these and government, have become institutionalised at the national level in a variety of ways. The notion of social partnership has therefore been added on, sometimes uneasily, to the bargaining relationship. I hope to trace the main trends in the evolution of these relationships of both conflict and consensus.

For the first fifty years or so of the existence of the trade union movement, the membership was dominated by manual employees. Those who had become organised earliest and most effectively were the craft workers. With the establishment of the general unions early in this century, trade union membership among less skilled employees grew rapidly, reaching record levels immediately after the end of the First World War. The fortunes of the unions were, however, very variable. The bargaining power of employees depended on the state of the economy, and with bargaining only weakly institutionalised, trade union membership was subject to large fluctuations; the 1920s saw a sharp decline in numbers.

A home-grown industrial base began to develop under the protectionist policies of the 1930s. The enterprises were mainly small-scale and oriented towards the domestic market, and in some cases these were family enterprises with a paternalist ethos which was not very conducive to union recognition. Nevertheless, the 1930s brought gains in trade union membership and recognition, especially to the big general unions. But despite an increase in bargaining activity, living standards for most remained low. One senior trade unionist recalls that: 'workers had no reserves, living from hand to mouth, week to week, so that a rise in the price of food, bus fares or gas was a disaster; people had no margin to spare.'[1]

The Second World War, or the Emergency in Irish terms, was a watershed period for the conduct of pay bargaining. During the war years, most wages and public sector salaries were regulated by statute under wartime Emergency Powers. The cost of living rose by about two-thirds, while wages increased by only about one-third.[2] There was considerable pent-up demand for pay increases immediately after the war, and a widely-shared expectation that living standards would now improve. This expectation was strengthened by awareness of the changed mood in British society which had swept the Labour Party to power on a programme of egalitarianism and social reform.

If expectations had increased, then so too had the opportunities to pursue them. From 1946 onwards, trade union membership grew rapidly and began to extend into white-collar occupations, particularly in the public sector. Pay bargaining took place on a much more secure footing than previously, a development which was both facilitated and symbolised by the establishment of the Labour Court under the terms of the 1946 Industrial Relations Act. Before the war, as one labour historian has noted, trade unionism was 'characterised by a struggle for survival; success depended on militancy'; the 1946 Act 'made unions a part of the social furniture'.[3]

Between 1946 and the late 1960s, pay bargaining took the form of a series of pay rounds.[4] The first recognisable such round, apart from the initial scramble to catch up immediately after the wartime controls were lifted, was a centralised framework agreement negotiated in 1948 under the auspices of the Labour Court. Some of the subsequent wage rounds were also negotiated centrally between the employers and the union side. Others took the form of disaggregated employer-union wage bargaining without any national-level agreement.

Either way, several features of the wage rounds contrasted with pre-war pay bargaining. The most striking is that episodes of pay bargaining became regular and recurrent events. Initially pay agreements were open-ended and generally lasted between two and three years; in the late 1960s fixed-term agreements began to be negotiated, giving a focus for the beginning of a new claim. A second contrast with the pre-war period was the emergence of informal co-ordination of wage claims even in the absence of a centrally-negotiated framework. Bargaining groups in the strongest bargaining position assumed a role of wage leadership, that is, they established the norm for the pay round which later entrants sought to emulate. The wage leaders were generally craft groups, but clerical staff in large public sector employments, particularly the ESB, also played an important role. Thirdly, bargaining was less localised: in many of the industries which had developed since the 1930s, multi-employer and industry-wide pay agreements were increasingly common. This helped to spread the prevailing pay norm within a short time. Fourthly, as a consequence, differentials and relativities between occupational groups became more visible. The effect was to inject a new restlessness into the activities of bargaining groups, which was particularly evident in the emergence of additional catch-up pay claims in between the main rounds of bargaining activity. And finally, in contrast with the pre-war years, increased expectations meant that a 'conventional wisdom' grew in union circles that the cash value of the pay increase negotiated in one round should always exceed that of the preceding round.[5]

Not all these features of the wage rounds were apparent from the beginning. The 1950s was a period of relative stability, which owed as much to economic stagnation as to any inherent virtues of the pay bargaining system. Unemployment was high by international standards, and the rate of emigration reached new peaks during the middle years of the decade. Much of the rest of the developed world was benefiting from rapid post-war growth, but protectionist Ireland was not well positioned to do so. The 1960s opened up a new period of growth and economic confidence, and it was during this decade that the destabilising potential of post-war pay bargaining became apparent.

For the first time, wage inflation began to emerge as a major issue. No single bargaining group believed it had to pay any serious attention to the impact of its activities on the overall state of economic performance.[6] Yet the cumulative consequences of everyone's bargaining practices were proving more and more harmful to overall economic performance. The devaluation of sterling in 1967 gave an additional twist to Irish inflation rates. Wage settlements, even in real terms, were very high by the end of the decade.

A second and related problem was the very high incidence of industrial conflict. The 1960s has been called the 'decade of upheaval',[7] and those years were punctuated by a number of major industrial disputes, in construction, the ESB, and most bitterly and divisively, among maintenance craftsmen in 1969.

Divisions within the trade union movement contributed to the extent of wage inflation and the scale of industrial conflict. Sectional differences between skilled workers and the rest increased the potential for leap-frogging wage claims. Moreover, economic growth and greater security of employment had made the membership of the trade unions stronger and more independent. The shop-steward movement was never as strong in Ireland as it became in Britain, but it added to the pressure on trade union officials to accord a high priority to negotiating regular pay increases. The authority of Congress, newly reunited after some fifteen years of schism, was still not fully established, and a number of unions remained outside it. On the employers' side, many of the largest employers of craft labour conducted their own bargaining outside the context of FUE advice and support altogether.

By the end of the 1960s, there was a widely-shared recognition that the system of free-for-all bargaining was too costly in every sense and therefore unsustainable, and that something else would have to take its place. All sides heaved a sigh of relief when a new centralised pay agreement was agreed in 1970, the forerunner of what turned out to be a decade-long commitment to national-level bargaining.

Compared with later agreements, the 1970 National Wage Agreement was a rather modest affair. One key participant in the negotiations recalls that its provisions were literally sketched out on the back of an envelope. But it met the most urgent problems of the day: it rationalised the widely-dispersed terminal dates of the wage rounds, it eliminated leap-frogging, and it placed limits on recourse to industrial action. Industrial craftsmen lost their pivotal role in the pay structure. And, not least, the agreement provided the basis for both ICTU and FUE to recover their own solidarity and co-ordination after the divisions of 1969.

The first National Wage Agreement was followed by others in 1972 and 1974, and in each of the four subsequent years. Successive National Wage Agreements became more sophisticated. Low-paid employees were guaranteed a minimum flat-rate increase; provisions for above-the-norm increases were introduced to permit some flexibility in wage structures, restricted mainly to productivity gains; provision was also made for firms to pay below the norm in certain circumstances. At enterprise level, bargaining groups had to concentrate on pursuing issues that did not contravene the terms of the agreements. This contributed to a broadening of the bargaining agenda within the workplace to include matters such as maternity or holiday leave in excess of the statutory minima, and compensation for changes in work practices.

At the national level, though, the bargaining agenda was

also broadened through the greater role which government came to play in influencing the terms of the agreements. In 1975, for example, the government offered a package of price-support measures in exchange for the downward renegotiation of the pay agreement, a package which the trade union movement accepted. In 1977 and 1978, tax concessions were used for the first time to try to facilitate a moderate pay agreement. Then in 1979 and 1980, two National Understandings brought pay bargaining much closer to the centre of the political process. These involved the usual agreements on pay negotiated between the unions and the private and public sector employers, and in addition, a set of non-pay elements negotiated between the unions and government, spanning a wide range of social policy issues. They were intended to be comprehensive agreements in which the pay and non-pay elements would be negotiated in a complementary way.

The centralised pay agreements of the 1970s began life as a solution to the problems of economic growth in the 1960s. Increasingly, though, they came to be relied upon to address a new set of problems arising from the very different economic conditions of the 1970s.[8]

First, the structure of the Irish economy was changing rapidly during the 1970s. Membership of the European Community in 1973 attracted inward investment, especially from US firms, during the years that followed. But increased economic openness also exposed domestic industry to harsher competition in which relative wage costs were to become more important than before.

Secondly, the effects of the oil-price crisis hit Ireland in the mid-1970s. The centralised agreements became the vehicle through which employers and unions had to accommodate to the new realities of higher and persistent levels of inflation and unemployment.

Thirdly, governments began for the first time to engage in an active fiscal policy to stimulate growth or stabilise economic performance: there had never been a planned current budget deficit before 1972. Governments hoped that the pay agreements would keep the growth of real pay levels in line with their fiscal objectives.

Fourthly, inflation pushed more and more PAYE workers into the tax net, and tax grievances gave rise to the largest street protests in the history of the state in the late 1970s. The relevance of tax to the value of disposable income had become far more evident to both employers and unions; this is why government tried to link the two through the pay agreements.

By the end of the 1970s, the centralised agreements had moved well beyond their original fairly modest beginnings. They had acquired a macroeconomic significance that pay bargaining had never had before. They were no longer simply pay agreements but wide-ranging policy agreements. But by the time the Second National Understanding expired in 1981, both unions and employers had become disillusioned with them. What went wrong?

On the trade union side, there were divided views on the merits of the centralised agreements. At each of its Special Delegate Conferences, the Executive Council of ICTU could regularly expect to see about one-third of the delegates opposing the pay agreements. To some extent, this arose from an old-established difference of principle between unions which favoured voluntarism in industrial relations and regarded any involvement with government on matters of pay bargaining with some suspicion, and unions which supported a greater involvement of the state in many aspects of industrial relations, including pay bargaining. To some extent, though, the opposition was based on pragmatic consideration of the gains to be made from going it alone rather than abiding by the terms of the centralised agreements. The most prominent opposition came from those unions organising technicial, craft and professional workers in the most profitable industries, unions which might be assumed to be in the strongest bargaining position. Besides, while the leadership of the trade union movement might be receptive to the value of a trade-off between pay moderation and tax cuts, and between both of these and job creation, it was difficult for Congress at this time to make a persuasive case to its own members for linking pay and non-pay items in a single agreement.

It was, however, the employers' dissatisfaction, in the wake of the Second National Understanding, which brought the process of centralised bargaining to an end. They took the view that a wrong balance had been struck between the general pay agreement and local bargaining. In their view, the general increases were too large and provided too little incentive for matching improvements in efficiency and productivity within the enterprise: they 'have tended to be seen by employees and by unions at local level as an award from Heaven or Dublin ... "something for nothing"'.[9] The scope for conditional local-level bargaining,

153

they held, was correspondingly too limited: it tended to encourage wage drift in the profitable industries without giving enough flexibility to the traditional labour-intensive industries. The employers had grown suspicious of productivity claims; they held that the National Wage Agreements, by allowing them, provided an inducement for the cultivation of restrictive practices. The incidence and scale of industrial conflict had also been growing over the decade. Finally, the private sector employers were unhappy about the rate of increase of public sector pay: 'special' pay increases tended to spill outwards into the private sector. The employers came to believe that government commitment to securing pay agreements was not hard-nosed enough, and that the political value of the pay agreements meant that governments evaluated them in a rather different way than did the private sector employers.

The private sector employers therefore concluded that the pay agreements were losing their effectiveness in securing employers' own interests, whether in ensuring predictable costs, guaranteeing industrial peace, or contributing to a stable macroeconomic climate.

Over the six years which followed the expiry of the Second National Understanding, then, we see a return to the conduct of pay negotiations at plant or enterprise level. But this period of decentralised bargaining was very different from that of the 1960s. There were no clear wage leaders in the private sector, and there was no clear pattern of rounds in the pay bargaining process. There was no recurrence of the distributive conflict and industrial strife of the earlier period. After all, these were years of severe economic recession, and fears for job security held back union pressures in many sectors. The FUE issued guidelines to member companies now that they had to carry the full weight of pay bargaining themselves: they were determined to reassert control over productivity bargaining and to secure pay deals that would be appropriate to local conditions.

These years were gloomy ones for the trade union movement. In the private sector, the combination of recession and the growing personal tax burden made it more difficult to protect members' living standards. Relations between the unions and government were difficult: the former Taoiseach, Garret Fitzgerald, states in his memoirs that: 'Meetings with ICTU were formal, often tense, and on the whole unproductive throughout our term.'[10] Unemployment increased steadily, and the unions seemed unable to make any coherent collective response. Philip Flynn, general secretary of the LGPSU commented at the ICTU Annual Delegate Conference in 1985 that: 'The trade union movement can hardly now be called a movement; it is more a loose federation of organisations each dismally engaged in pursuing sectional interests.' Some union leaders began to fear the prospect of being both politically and economically weakened to the extent that was then apparent in the British trade union movement.

And yet the outcomes of decentralised bargaining were not entirely as the employers might have wished either. For many firms, the re-emergence of uncertainty in pay bargaining was far from welcome. The break with sterling in 1979 produced inflationary pressures which added to domestic costs, and this was also pushing many pay claims upwards. Strike levels were still relatively high.

In the light of this experience it is tempting to see the return to centralised bargaining since 1987 as an inevitable development, or to think that there must be some consensus-seeking magnetic needle in the political process that tends to pull things back in this direction. This would of course be too simple. But social partnership agreements had not been discarded from the Irish political agenda as they had in Britain, and a centralised approach to pay bargaining remained part of the policy repertoire. Decentralised bargaining had not proved to be a self-evidently superior way of dealing with the macroeconomic implications of pay determination.

The 1986 NESC report, *A Strategy for Development, 1986-1990*, pointed the way forward, by setting out an analysis of policy priorities, including a prescription for tough fiscal remedies, to which all the main social partners had agreed. After the general election in 1987, the new Fianna Fáil government initiated the Programme for National Recovery (PNR) which involved a moderate pay agreement built on the premises of the NESC report. The perceived successes of the PNR paved the way for two further centralised pay agreements, the Programme for Economic and Social Progress (PESP) in 1991, and the Progamme for Competitiveness and Work, in 1994.

It is fairly obvious what the unions had to gain from the return to centralised agreements: first and foremost, the pay agreements helped to restore their sense of collective purpose. The advantages of a trade-off between pay and tax were also

155

more apparent now than ever before, and the centralised agreements offered the unions an opportunity to influence policies to alleviate unemployment.

The private sector employers made their involvement conditional on a moderate pay settlement and strict control over additional pay claims. An element of local bargaining was permitted under the PESP, but there was no return to the wide-ranging supplementary local bargaining which had been so prevalent in the 1970s. Many of the changes in job practices that would have attracted cost-increasing compensation claims in the earlier period had now been accepted as a normal requirement of job flexibility.

The pay terms of the centralised agreements since 1987 have been adjudged, on the whole, to be quite moderate in the light of the growth in the overall economy. Strike levels since 1987 have been well below the levels of the preceding years. Economic performance improved on a number of indicators such as growth, inflation, and fiscal imbalances, and the centralised pay agreements undoubtedly played a part in this.

However, there are some issues which it has proved difficult to manage effectively through the framework of the centralised agreements. One is public sector pay; another is the relationship between pay bargaining and unemployment.

Public sector pay is an issue because tax levels are an issue, and this implies that public spending must be effectively controlled. Special pay increases in the public sector have added significantly to the total pay bill in recent years. Public sector employees now account for over half of the membership of the trade union movement, so it is likely that pay pressures in the public sector will continue to be strong. However, the public sector negotiating machinery makes it difficult for governments to evaluate competing claims effectively. The response has generally been to roll over payment from one year to the next; this may disguise the total payable but it does nothing to bring it under control.

The trend in unemployment has worsened steadily since 1990. The problem of persistently high unemployment is not unique to Ireland, and is shared by all the countries of the European Union, but the scale of our problem is of a different order from that of any other country apart from Spain. There are no quick-fix solutions to the jobs crisis; the relationship between pay bargaining and levels of unemployment is a complex matter. But while most people would welcome measures to improve the prospects for job creation, they do not wish their own real wage levels to be affected. As a senior trade union official once commented to me, 'If there are 16% out of work, there are still 84% in work who are not too put out by the plight of the unemployed and who want their wage increase'. These conflicting priorities may limit more creative thinking about means of bridging the gulf between those in work and those out of work. However, thinking about alternatives is not a task for the trade unions alone. The Minister for Enterprise and Employment, Ruairi Quinn, speaking in 1992, put the problem as follows:

> The trade union commitment in relation to the social dialogue ... must be and is driven by the demands of their own members, very largely members who are at work and have strong political clout. On the other hand, politicians, and particularly left-of-centre politicians, have an obligation to the entire labour force, including those out of work.[11]

Although the theme of this lecture has been conflict and consensus in pay bargaining, I have not been able to trace any simple story. At the beginning of the period I have been surveying, the unions were still struggling to gain recognition for their role in protecting their members' living standards and employment conditions. Over the hundred years since then, employers and unions have developed much closer contact with one another, and both unions and employers have also become involved in social partnership arrangements at the national level.

But there is nothing inevitable about this, and we have seen oscillation between centralised and decentralised approaches, depending on such factors as the degree of dissatisfaction with the current model of bargaining, the relative bargaining power of each side, and the economic climate. In some societies with a longer tradition of consensual policy-making than our own, centralised pay bargaining systems have been put under great strain in recent years by the pressures of adjusting to changing economic conditions. In other societies, there have been attempts to weaken the influence of the unions in pay bargaining altogether. There has been no such challenge to the unions in the Irish context. But it remains to be seen how effectively the current approach to centralised pay bargaining manages to deal with the emergent challenges of the 1990s.

1. Donal Nevin, cited in Basil Chubb ed., *Federation of Irish Employers 1942-1992*, Dublin, Gill and Macmillan, 1992, p. 130.
2. Donal Nevin, 'Industry and Labour', in K. B. Nowlan and T. D. Williams eds., *Ireland in the War Years and After, 1939-51*, Dublin: Gill and Macmillan, 1969, p. 97.
3. Emmet O'Connor, *A Labour History of Ireland, 1824-1960*, Dublin: Gill and Macmillan, 1992, p.155.
4. David O'Mahony, *Economic Aspects of Industrial Relations*, Dublin: Economic and Social Research Institute, Paper No. 24, 1965, p. 32.
5. James F. O'Brien, *A Study of National Wage Agreements in Ireland*, Dublin: Economic and Social Research Institute, Paper No. 104, 1981, p. 176.
6. W. E. J. McCarthy, J. F. O'Brien, V. G. Dowd, *Wage Inflation and Wage Leadership: A Study of Key Wage Bargains in the Irish System of Collective Bargaining*, Dublin: Economic and Social Research Institute, Paper No. 79, 1975, pp. 164-7.
7. Charles McCarthy, *The Decade of Upheaval: Irish Trade Unions in the 1960s*, Dublin: Institute of Public Administration, 1973.
8. Niamh Hardiman, *Pay, Politics, and Economic Performance in Ireland, 1970-1987*, Oxford: Clarendon Press, 1988, chs. 2, 3; also 'The State and Economic Interests: Ireland in Comparative Perspective', in J. H. Goldthorpe and C. T. Whelan editors, *The Development of Industrial Society in Ireland*, Oxford: The British Academy, 1992, pp. 347-51.
9. M. P. Fogarty, D. Egan, W. J. L. Ryan, *Pay Policy for the 1980s*, Dublin: Federated Union of Employers, 1981, p.19
10. Garret FitzGerald, *All In A Life*, Dublin: Gill and Macmillan, 1991, p. 454.
11. Ruairi Quinn, in Basil Chubb ed., *Federation of Irish Employers, 1942-1992*, Dublin: Gill and Macmillan, 1992, p. 22.

Dr Niamh Hardiman
Lecturer, Department of Politics, University College Dublin. Author of *Pay, Politics and Economic Performance in Ireland* (1988), etc.

1894-1994: An Overview

Professor Patrick Lynch

The Industrial Revolution from 1760 to 1830 created the world in which we live. To understand that world we must retrace certain historical trends. Fergus D'Arcy delineated these in the first lecture of this series: they are an essential guide in assessing the achievements of trade unions and the pioneer reformers who encouraged and supported them.

Fergus D'Arcy also reminded us that when the Irish Trades Union Congress was established in April 1894, its members inherited a labour movement with more than a century of union tradition. The early unions in that movement were illegal, but they had defied draconian laws and survived in one form or another until the legislation designed to suppress them, the Combination Acts were repealed in the 1820s. Seventy years later, with the foundation of the Irish Trades Union Congress, the majority of Irish trade unionists were members of British unions.

If today we look back on the nineteenth century we can see that the future then lay with labour movements accepting the emerging industrial society and exerting their efforts to mould it to their advantage. At the time, however, this was not so easy to see. Idealists who hated what Blake called 'the dark Satanic mills' of early Victorian England rejected this new society. As Peter Mathias wrote, there was often a quest to resurrect an imaginary 'rural utopia', what he called 'a recessive death-wish for a society without exploitation or extremes of wealth, without cotton mills, stock jobbers or paper money'.

The reality was that the money wage had already become the only economic link of the workers with society. Idealistic reformers detested that link. It aroused the Messianic indignation of Karl Marx.

In Britain and Ireland trade unions have passed through three stages – oppression, toleration and privilege. Irish men and women have participated in all three stages. William Thompson of Rosscarbery, Co. Cork was a young man when the Combination Acts still prohibited organisations of workers. This untypical landowner was to become one of the first great social reformers of the nineteenth century. Immensely influential in Britain and elsewhere in Europe through his indictment of the plight of the working class in this new industrial society, his writings sought not a rejection of that society but a reconciliation of it with human happiness.

James Connolly described him as the first Irish socialist: Thompson is now acknowledged as the only scientific precursor of Marx. Strangely, however, the organised Irish workers in the nineteenth century seem to have been quite immune from ideas about poverty and the distribution of wealth in society generally.

Local agitation by trade unions was certainly often militant, but until the end of the century, the official rhetoric of the unions intoned declarations on the common interest of labour and capital. After May Day 1890 however, a profound change appeared: unskilled workers were beginning to organise and they were speaking a new language.

James Connolly, as John W. Boyle reminded us in a Thomas Davis lecture many years ago,[1] probably made his greatest contribution to the Irish labour movement in his writing: *Labour in Irish History* is an astonishing work from a writer lacking formal training in research. He had to find time for his studies when already engaged in so many and such varied practical activities.

Connolly drew his inspiration largely from William Thompson. He accepted Thompson's rejection of utopian solutions to the human and social ills of the new industrial society. Yet, he respected those who had hoped to lighten the burdens of that society on workers by a return to the land under co-operative ownership. He understood the motives impelling Fergus O'Connor in the late 1830s to bring working men and women in many parts of England to demand a People's Charter for a full part in public affairs.

O'Connor had converted Chartism into a mass movement of industrial democracy, and Connolly sympathised with that. But he also understood that Chartism failed because its aims were reactionary, however revolutionary its tactics. Although Chartism had little in common with trade union and labour movements as these were later to develop, its spontaneous arousal of the oppressed most certainly helped to inspire them.

As a socialist, Connolly knew that utopian visions would not dispel the evils of industrial capitalism. For him, the task of trade unions was to eliminate these evils and to secure the organisation of the new industrial society to promote an increase in human happiness.

Dermot Keogh showed in his lecture the development of the 'new unionism' of general workers from the first meeting of the Irish Trades Union Congress in 1894. The pace quickened after 1906. James Larkin had organised a branch of the National Union of Dock Labourers in Belfast in 1907, another in Dublin, then in Newry, Dundalk, Drogheda and Cork. Disowned by his union during a strike in Cork, he founded a rival union.

By January 1909, he was leading an Irish-based union, the Irish Transport and General Workers' Union and in 1910 James Connolly, back from the United States, became its full-time official in Belfast. In 1911, Larkin's sister Delia, set up the Irish Women Workers' Union. Soon an alliance between Larkin and William O'Brien moved the unions nearer to socialism, but it was a partnership of tempestuous and conflicting temperaments. For a time the explosive forces of these men were contained, and mutual toleration, if not admiration, prevailed. Eventually the alliance was to lead to disaster.

In 1912, the year of Home Rule euphoria, an Irish Labour Party emerged from the annual conference of the Irish Trades Union Congress. William O'Brien presided over its inaugural meeting. In the Congress, Larkin and his mixed band of supporters were soon in control. The 'new unionism' had been firmly established. Under Larkin's domination, Liberty Hall, headquarters of his own union had become the base of social and political ferment. The stage was set for the confrontation of 1913. The gap between skilled and unskilled labour had narrowed. Declarations of the common interest of labour and capital were no longer part of the language of trade unionists. The creation of the Irish Trades Union Congress had been a wise choice for Irish labour.

In tracing the course of events from 1914 to 1923, Emmet O'Connor described the complex moods of trade unionism through the difficult months after the 1913 lockout, the painful dilemmas following the outbreak of the First World War in 1914 and the ambiguities of the unions towards the emerging nationalism in the south. For Connolly, the First World War was a struggle between two groups of capitalists. In other countries, socialists had often found themselves, as citizens of these countries, reluctantly supporting the war. As a socialist, Connolly opposed it on principle.

The contrast between the political attitudes of trade unionists in the north and south can be dangerously simplified. Emmet O'Connor's careful examination of the differing positions of Connolly and Larkin justifies his conclusion that in an Irish context syndicalism was often more a state of mind than a coherent movement. Syndicalism was suspicious of party politics and urged industrial action to secure workers' control at the source of production.

Connolly, drawing on his American experience, tended to be particularly dismissive of political parties and to see a trade union as a complete social unit in itself. His concept of the One Big Union originated in the performance of the American Wobblies, the Industrial Workers of the World. For Larkin, syndicalism was a working-class code of morality, but he too was suspicious of political parties. His Irish Transport and General Workers' Union was a practical expression of syndicalist ideas.

In 1918, *The Lines of Progress*, published by the ITGWU, argued that workers should be in one union, organised in industrial sections. With Connolly dead and Larkin in the United States, the Irish Transport and General Workers' Union was now effectively under William O'Brien's influence: its membership soared, too quickly to permit the establishment of co-ordinated central control or a premeditated sense of direction. Often, irresponsibly, it promoted isolated local strikes, ill-conceived small soviets and thoughtlessly simulated revolutionary tactics. This facade collapsed with the post-war slump.

Congress was cool on nationalism up to 1918, when it withdrew from the General Election and supported Sinn Féin without gaining any concessions in return. But it no longer looked deferentially to the British Trades Union Congress as Larkin had in 1913. A special meeting of Congress in February 1919 adopted a motion recommending a regrouping of unions on industrial lines. Obviously, syndicalist ideas were still in some minds, but as such ideas were becoming increasingly irrelevant the motion was never implemented although it had subsequently been formally adopted by Congress in 1919.

This activity revealed a real weakness: Congress, without a secretariat, lacked the means of giving effect to its decisions or maintaining continuity in its leadership. In these post-war years, the greatest failure of Congress was a widening of the fissure between north and south. In the south, most workers were in Irish unions: in the north, the majority were in British unions.

Again, Congress lost an opportunity to encourage progressive Protestant-led political labour groups in the north between 1917 and 1920. Support for these groups might have achieved little, but indifference ignored their potential in bridging the sectarian divide.

The years 1920, 1921 and 1922 were depressing for the unions. The economic slump was taking its toll. In 1921, Congress again declared its faith in industrial unionism but this act of faith had no effect on increasing unemployment, falling wages and inter-union rivalries. Between 1924 and 1929, Congress membership fell from 175,000 to 92,000. In this grim setting, syndicalism had become an idle word and trade unionism was losing its credibility.

In February 1922, Congress decided to contest the general election to the post-treaty Dáil and seventeen of Labour's eighteen candidates were elected in June: they became the official opposition party under the leadership of Thomas Johnson. In the 1923 General Election, the number of Labour TDs fell to fourteen. Yet, despite this set back, the malaise of Congress and the unions in the post-war slump, hope and promise remained: trade unions were now largely based in Ireland, though not in the north: there was a Labour Party in the Dáil and the Congress was the recognised voice of the Irish labour movement.

As Brian Farrell recalled, Thomas Johnson, the labour leader, declared in 1926 that responsibility and restraint, not revolution, were now the aims of the Congress. Johnson had been consistently practical and level-headed. He had, it is true, produced the first draft for the Democratic Programme of the First Dáil. But when his draft had been revised by Seán T. Ó Ceallaigh and adopted by the Dáil on 21 January 1919, he described it as 'rhetorical humbug'.

There were indeed surprising omissions from the Programme adopted by the Dáil. Johnson's draft had declared that 'no private right to property is good against the public right of the nation' – words ironically taken from Pádraic Pearse in the *Sovereign People* on 31 March 1916. Pearse was already being expurgated.

Well, indeed might Piaras Béaslai wonder whether the Democratic Programme read to the First Dáil, first in Irish and then in English, would have been supported by the majority of its members if there had been any immediate prospect of putting it into force. Despite the many omissions from the original

Johnson draft, the version adopted by the Dáil was verbally radical but might have been further amended if de Valera, Griffith, Collins or Blythe had been present at the Dáil meeting.

As Donal Nevin explained, the state created in 1922 was overwhelmingly agricultural. Only one-third of the population lived in cities and the trade union movement was fragmented. In 1923, James Larkin returned from the United States, Congress had changed its name to the Irish Labour Party and Trade Union Congress. This combination of the two sides of the labour movement prevented, as Donal Nevin said, an orderly and rational development of either side.

In 1922, membership of the Irish Transport and General Workers' Union was 100,000. Eight years later it had fallen calamitously to less than 16,000. Congress membership, 189,000 in 1923 was only 92,000 in 1929. Trade unionism was certainly not thriving during the first decade of the Irish Free State. In 1930, Congress formally separated from the Irish Labour Party and Trade Union Congress: at the time, few saw it as an augury of further divisions when the initiatives of William O'Brien were to lead to splits both in Congress and in the Labour Party. This decline in the fortunes of trade unionism was, no doubt, in part, a reflection of the world economic depression, but also of the personality conflict between Larkin and O'Brien which damaged Irish trade unionism throughout the 1930s.

By 1939, trade union membership was rapidly recovering, but the difficulties caused by the multiplicity of unions were becoming more acute. From 1945, the unions began a vigorous struggle to regain ground lost in frozen rates of pay during the war. In 1959, the Irish Congress of Trade Unions was formed and trade union unity restored. This appropriate timing matched the great economic and social changes of the 1960s in which the revived trade union movement played a decisive and progressive part.

Brian Girvin suggested in his lecture that in 1977 there was a possibility of close relations between Congress and the new Department of Economic Planning and Development where Martin O'Donoghue was minister. He argues that the relationship lapsed because of internal divisions in the government and by the second oil crisis in 1979 which deepened the already serious economic recession. He also maintains that the new Fine Gael-Labour coalition government marginalised Congress from the decision-making process and had no intention of including the social partners in policy formation.

The Irish labour movement has been influenced over the years by many powerful and varied personalities. Intellectually, Connolly dominated. Inspired by William Thompson, he applied his formidable intelligence to an analysis of a modern industrial society and the place of trade unions in it. William O'Brien emerges as a destructive and malign force with overweening ambition and a hatred of James Larkin. This antipathy, Donal Nevin asserts, went far beyond differences of ideology or the role of trade unions in society.

James Larkin may have been unduly sensitive to criticism and could often be wildly wrong-headed and unfair to opponents. But he was a lord of language, a speaker who raised his listeners above themselves. James Plunkett told us that Larkin found unskilled and casual workers resigned to the hopelessness of their lives in sordid labour in filthy slums. He used his remarkable skills as a demagogue to arouse their spirits and confidence. His finest hour was in the 1913 Dublin lock-out. As Plunkett saw it, Larkin led a new class out of obscurity into a society conscious of their rights and dignity and achieved for himself an international reputation for leadership and inspiration.

His eldest son, also James, was intellectually the most formidable trade unionist of his generation. He had exceptional negotiating skills and always sought to achieve his aims through moderation. Outside the trade union movement, he also earned wide respect for his remarkable qualities. He had an intense sense of social responsibility, a conspicuous capacity for leadership, for clarity in his analysis of problems and lucidity in his exposition of solutions.

By 1994, the centenary year of Congress, trade unions have evolved from suppression through decades of toleration after 1824 to a position of privilege in the Republic, though Mary Redmond writing on trade unions and the law, might prefer to have this privilege described as 'qualified'. In the Republic, Congress is one of the social partners, an integral part of the establishment and trade union leaders are perceived as supporters of social stability. Whether all the founding fathers would have approved of this comfortable relationship is a fair question.

I have to admit, however, being haunted here momentarily by the ghost of James Larkin, who died in 1947. That ghost must have smiled ironically on 3 February 1994 at the photograph in a morning newspaper of the Taoiseach, Albert Reynolds, and the General Secretary of the Irish Congress of Trade Unions, Peter Cassells, at the formal opening of the Centenary celebrations of Congress in Dublin Castle the previous afternoon. For trade unionists this was, indeed, the epitome of privilege, the unmistakable outcome of a victory for which so many had fought so hard. It was also a long way from William Martin Murphy and the ramparts of Liberty Hall.

Two weeks after the publication of that historic photograph, and once more in Dublin Castle, the Taoiseach, with members of his government were joined by trade unionists and employers to launch the Programme for Competitiveness and Work. The wording may be clumsy, but the event was significant.

In Northern Ireland the political ferment of the past twenty-five years has shown the unions there to be socially constructive institutions. Terry Cradden in his lecture has shown how the Northern Ireland Committee of Congress has grown in authority over the years in its quest for communal harmony. It has maintained the historic aspiration of socialists to seek the unity of the Protestant and Catholic working classes. Supported by Congress as a whole, the Northern Ireland Committee has been unswerving in its demand for an end to violence for political purposes and in its crusade for peace.

Dr Cradden has explained how the character of trade unions in Northern Ireland is now radically different from their position at the end of the last century. He quotes Charles McCarthy who showed that northern trade unionism was then strong because industry there was strong and that Belfast then had more affinity with the Clyde than with Dublin.

William Walker, politically a Unionist, became a dominant figure in northern trade unionism. In 1905, he almost succeeded in winning a parliamentary seat at Westminster. In 1912, however, Walker left the labour movement and died six years later. He did much in a short life: in the first decade of the century he had firmly established trade unionism in Belfast. For a time he was, perhaps, the most prominent personality in the Irish labour movement, even if today, he is almost forgotten.

Professor Mary Daly leaves us in no doubt that most trade unions, especially the craft unions, believed that a woman's place was in the home until Delia Larkin formed the Irish Women Workers' Union in 1911. She was its first General Secretary. After 1916, Louis Bennett and Helen Chenevix led it for many decades. Until its merger with the Federated Workers' Union of Ireland in 1984, it was the sole voice of women's interests in the trade union movement.

Women began to be trade unionists about the same time as unskilled labourers. This coincidence was marked in the Belfast linen industry in the 1890s but it did not last for long, and when the Irish Trades Union Congress was founded, the craft unions dominated. Michael O'Lehane set the Drapers' Assistants' Association to be the first union in Ireland (apart from the Irish National Teachers' Organisation) to admit men and women.

In tune with the general role of Congress and the unions, a decade of optimism began in the 1960s. A new view was being taken of the woman worker. This development continued through the 1970s. Women members numbered 60,000 in the 1960s; there were over 158,000 women in unions in 1977. Irish women and Irish society were in the process of change with the emergence of the modern feminist movement and the trade unions readily responded. This response in favour of women workers continued even in times when unemployment was rising and when old prejudices might have been expected to reassert themselves.

Would the founders of the Congress have been satisfied with the role of their successors today? True, their successors are still looking after the work-place interests of their members as well as generally promoting social justice. Membership, however, of a consensus with the other social partners should strengthen rather than diminish their ability to pursue their objectives.

If the militancy of old is now rarely needed to protect the rights of members, there may be new battles to fight. We have a sub-class – the unemployed – for which high levels of national economic growth seem to offer little solace. Complacently, some economists regard this sub-class of long-term unemployed as an inevitable feature of a post-industrial leisure society. The solution, they say, is to redefine unemployment.

This solution cannot be accepted in our society whose economy is still a developing one, not a Third World one perhaps but certainly a long way from a mature leisured society. There remains so much for us to do, so much that could be done by that sub-class now without work and we must not forget the dignity that work itself confers on the worker.

Every unemployed person is a threat to the integrity of trade unionism. Perhaps the movement's next role is in helping to restore that sub-class, the unemployed, to a respected place in society. It would be dramatically in the tradition of James Larkin's achievement in 1913 when he instilled hope and self-confidence in the unskilled and casual workers whom he led out of despondency and despair.

Fortunately, Peter Cassells, the General Secretary of Congress is fully aware of the new battles to be fought by modern trade unionism. In a Thomas Davis lecture in 1993, he advocated a political consensus for jobs to provide a programme for jobs over the next four years. Perhaps, this may be one of the contemporary militant roles for Congress, now a recognised part of the establishment as it enters its second centenary.

Congress now finds itself surrounded by extreme advocates of the free-market economy and it cannot entirely resist the advocacy. I would urge, however, that in accepting it, the frontiers of this free market must be clearly defined. People are motivated by more than competition for monetary or material reward. In the real world, there is a wide area where the narrow concept of profit motive has no place. Even within the free market economy, commercial socially-owned public enterprises can have an important innovative part.

Privatisation is a vogue word today. Too many economists are enthusing about the race towards an unfettered, unrestrained free market economy. This is worship of an unthinking consumerism, animated not by considerations of social responsibility but a desire for the fast buck and let tomorrow look after itself.

In this concluding lecture in this series, I have tried to show that changes in the trade union movement have usually reflected changes in the prevailing economic system. The craft unions dominated the early decades of Congress. Their decisive influence delayed the emergence of organised women workers and established the intrinsically conservative character of trade unionism.

Between the First and Second World Wars, general workers, representing mainly the unskilled, were becoming increasingly prominent in the movement. Since 1945, white-collar and professional workers have been organised. Again, this is a response to changes in society, especially the growth of service industries.

The conservative character of Irish trade unions derives, perhaps, from their craft origins stretching back to the guilds of the

168

Middle Ages. This may explain the survival of small unions, union fragmentation and the slow pace of rationalisation, even when there is an obvious need for adaptation in structures when society is being transformed far more rapidly than ever before.

A new feature of the movement emerged and developed in the 1960s. Congress was now becoming increasingly involved in tripartite organisations, including the National Industrial Economic Council and later, the National Economic and Social Council. As a member of both bodies, I can recall the freshness and vigour of trade union thinking on the desirability of a consensus on the broad economic issues such as incomes policies and economic planning and development. There was not a single instance of partisanship and I can remember many enthusiastic and original contributions directed solely towards the common good. None of this surprised me as I had for a long time been associated with trade unionists and members of Congress and its small secretariat. I was aware of their mode of thought.

The support of the unions was essential for the success of the economic planning that Kenneth Whitaker was then promoting. That support was given usually after a good deal of frank and forthright debate. The unions became an integral part of the planning process and when that process was interrupted the fault did not lie with them, but that is another story.

From the countless tripartite meetings of these bodies, trade unionism was drawn inexorably into the framing of social and economic policies. This led from the National Pay Agreements to National Understandings, the Programme for National Recovery, the Programme for Economic and Social Progress and to the Programme for Competitiveness and Work.

The exchanges between the participants at these tripartite discussions produced results which have had an enduring effect on Irish society. The full story can be found in reports of the National Industrial Economic Council and the National Economic and Social Council. These reports will be basic material for the economic history of those remarkable years. They record the agreed views of representatives of the social partners but the distinctive voice of trade unionism is unmistakable. It was often decisive in originating studies and by persuasive argument, supported by careful research, tilted the balance towards conclusions acceptable to all the social partners.

From the 1960s onwards, Congress pioneered the adoption of social policies now taken for granted. There were few other effective pressure groups though the work of Declan Costello and his colleagues in producing *Planning for a Just Society* must not be forgotten.

The tripartite programmes since the 1970s represent a radical change in trade union strategy. Confrontation has been replaced by consensus with employers and government. This change is in phase with what is happening elsewhere in Europe.

Here, the tripartite programmes are of immense significance. They are an expression of the efforts of Congress to lead our society to the next century. James Connolly, following his great mentor, William Thompson, knew that study, research and a continuing educational programme must animate all trade union activity. So animated, trade unions can influence the formation of public policy as they have been able to influence it, especially over the past thirty years.

---

1. *Leaders and Workers*, ed. J.W. Boyle, Cork, 1966.

Professor Patrick Lynch
Professor Emeritus of Political Economy, University College Dublin. Joint author with John Vaizey of *Guinness's Brewery in the Irish Economy 1759-1876*; Joint editor with James Meenan of *Essays in Memory of Alexis Fitzgerald* (1987), etc.

Congress: Presidential Addresses

1894 Thomas O'Connell

The Chairman offered all present a warm welcome on behalf of the trade unionists of Dublin in general and the Dublin Trades Council and Labour League in particular. Three years ago, a Congress of trade unions was held in this hall from which good results emanated but for reasons on which it was unnecessary for him to dwell, an interval had occurred which he trusted in the future might be avoidable. One of the objects of this Congress might be the annual convening of a similar gathering in some centre of industry in Ireland. A resolution to that effect would be submitted to them.

Although he must admit that in Dublin, trade unionism was not in as perfect a state as they would desire, nevertheless the progress it had made in recent years had been so considerable that Dublin might yet set an example as the metropolitan city which would eventually be followed by other industrial centres in Ireland.

In parliamentary, municipal or poor law affairs, labour and especially trade union labour should have a large representation. In England there were trade union town councillors, magistrates and members of the legislature. In Ireland they were practically unrepresented. One of the essentials for the reformation of this state of affairs was a greater spread of trade unionism with a concentration of its power in the proper direction. Every city and town in Ireland should have its trades council which should guide the operation of the people in its district. The organisation of unions would give to labour its proper place in the country. The man that assisted in such organisation acted the part of the good citizen.

The capabilities of trade unionists for the positions he had referred to would not, he thought, be repudiated. There was evidence that the process that would raise the status of the worker was going on: it might be slow but it nevertheless was sure.

On the question of the Shop Hours Act, they would be asked to state their belief that no voluntary system of early closing would work satisfactorily; that the present number of factory

171

inspectors was totally inadequate for a proper carrying out of the duties of the position and that the inspectors should be taken from the ranks of men and women who had a practical knowledge of the duties gained in the factory and workshop.

Another important matter which they would have before them was the question of government contracts and trade unionism which would be one of the most important they would have to discuss.

On the question of technical education, they would consider the apathy displayed by Irish local authorities. They would also consider the question of women's organisation which was an important factor in the progress of our country.

Another most important resolution would be brought before them on the establishment of a government receiving depot for the army and navy contracts for the manufactured articles used by the troops in Ireland.

He trusted they would give those and other questions which would be brought before them and in which they had so deep an interest, their most serious consideration and that the voice of the working man through this Congress would receive the consideration to which he was entitled.

Extracts from the address of Thomas O'Connell, President of the Dublin Trades Council, who presided at the first meeting of the Irish Trades Union Congress in the Trades Hall, Capel Street, Dublin, Friday, 27 April 1894. There was no official report of this first Congress. The extracts above have been taken from the report in The Irish Times, *28 April 1894.*

Thomas O'Connell, a member of the Amalgamated Society of Carpenters and Joiners, was President of the Dublin Trades Council in 1893 and 1894.

1904 William Walker

We permit ourselves to be cajoled by fair promises and smooth excuses, whilst at the same time the forces of reaction are designing the destruction of our personal and political liberty. In the face of this determined attempt to subvert the powers we possess, is it not time that we were closing up our ranks, and uniting our forces? How long are we going to perpetuate this internecine warfare that has strangled at birth every new hope and every new idea making for progress in Ireland.

Surely a mature consideration will show us, no matter what political or religious opinions we may hold, that there are some questions upon which we cannot hope to unite, but is that a reason why those other one hundred and one problems, the solving of which means so much to our country, should be indefinitely shelved; how long is Ireland going to remain divided into two hostile camps, neglecting every opportunity that our united power could seize, to cope with the perplexities of our social state. Is it not possible for us to adhere to our opinions upon those questions that so sharply divide us, whilst at the same time we determine to unite our forces for the social redemption of our country. If we care to, we can bridge the chasm that separates the North from the South.

In the alembic (old distilling equipment) of Divine mysteria, it is hard to reason the why's and wherefore's of our conflicting opinions. Generation after generation, each in their turn find progress delayed, and suffering perpetuated by hostilities that to the succeeding peoples appear incomprehensible and puerile; but this condition need not always continue. The wise men of all ages have ever spoken of a time when communities will place the true interests of their country above the vain and selfish appeals of party, 'when the swords shall be turned into ploughshares, and the spears into pruning hooks'; when the aspirations of man towards a time when all men shall feel they are brethren shall be realised; when our huge expenditure on the dragooning of a nation by an armed police force, on the drilling and equipment of great armies and navies designed for hostile action shall cease; when the producer shall feel that his is the power and the right to live as God and nature intended man to live; when we shall enforce the dictum of St Paul, that he that shall not work neither shall he eat, and when we shall be able to declare that our laws give equal opportunities to all the sons and daughters of men.

Are we making for such conditions for the future, or are we standing in the way, blocking and hindering those who are working towards this end? What part is each man taking; is he going forward or backward; is he for peace, or declaring for war? For my part I stand for peace. I declare today, in the words of Ruskin, that I am willing to tolerate everything but every other man's intolerance, and if we can only tolerate opinions from which we honestly differ, then the future of Ireland is bright indeed, and that fierce internal warfare that has all but succeeded in dethroning reason amongst us will have given place to a period of unity making for progress –

> The time is ripe, a rotten ripe for change,
> Then let it come; I have no dread of what
> Is called for by the instinct of mankind;
> Nor think I that God's world will fall apart
> Because we tear a parchment more or less.

Extracts from the Presidential Address of William Walker, TC, PLG, Belfast Trades Council, to the eleventh Irish Trades Union Congress, Town Hall, Kilkenny, 23 May 1904.

William Walker, a carpenter who worked at Harland and Wolff, was Belfast District Secretary of the Amalgamated Society of Carpenters and Joiners from 1900 to 1911 and a delegate to Belfast Trades Council from 1892. Around that time he was responsible for the organisation of unskilled workers in the shipyards in the National Amalgamated Union of Labour. He also assisted in the organisation of municipal employees and was a representative of the Textile Operatives Union. At the general election in 1906 he lost to Sir Daniel Dixon, a former Lord Mayor of Belfast, by 291 votes in a poll of 9,523.

Walker was appointed a national insurance inspector in 1911 and died in 1918 at the age of forty-eight.

A banner of the Amalgamated Society of Woodworkers made in Belfast around 1920 included a portrait of William Walker. According to John Gray, his portrait hung in the Labour Club in Waring Street in the 1960s. Gray also points out in City in Revolt: James Larkin and the Belfast Dock Strike of 1907 *(1985) that Larkin's first arrest in Belfast took place following a fracas at an election count in the City Hall when Walker was contesting an election in April 1907.*

For more about Walker, see John Gray's City in Revolt, *and John Boyle in* Leaders and Workers *(1966).*

1910 James McCarron

The most immediate and pressing of the problems that confront us is the awful and widespread evil of unemployment. From our labour platform, not only in this country but throughout the civilised world, the cry is going up for a more serious grappling of the subject. I should like it to be remembered that the right to work is the right to live. But don't forget that a right ceases to be a right if you are denied the opportunity of fully exercising that right.

We have now over a year's working of the Old Age Pensions Act and we must admit that, though meagre (10s a week), the pittance has brought a ray of hope to many aged poor; but much more remains to be done: the age limit (70 years) must be reduced and the amount per week increased. The workhouse system still remains unchanged. All finer human feelings revolt at it. By general consent it stands condemned. Then why should it remain? So far as the power and influence of the organised workers are concerned, the system must be abolished and the sooner the better.

Of all the evils with which the workers are cursed, I am convinced that 'sweating' is the worst. Now and again a great outcry arises about the sweating system when the pious and philanthropic in public and the diplomatic in government feel called upon to bestir themselves for awhile, and the public conscience rests satisfied with something attempted but very little done.

The Trades Boards Act will mitigate the evil to some extent but as there are many sweated industries to which it does not apply, I am afraid that the authors of the bill cannot lay claim to having touched more than the fringe of the sweating question. The act does not apply to the poor victims who carry the work to their homes which in many instances is bedroom, sitting-room, kitchen and workshop combined where he sweats at it all day and at night makes it serve the purpose of the blanket. These poor wretches and their families are enduring a living death in their efforts to keep body and soul together.

The housing accommodation afforded the workers in the cities and towns is a question of great urgency. What purpose can be served or what remedies adopted to stamp out the White Plague (tuberculosis) and prevent the spread of consumption while these housing conditions remain?

It is our duty to demand that the government should make adequate provision for the secular education of the children of the working classes, not alone in the elementary stages but in the higher branches also. It is the duty of the nation to give her children an equal opportunity to prepare themselves for the battle of life. Let the sceptical individuals who may doubt that the children of the poorer classes are ill-fed and poorly clad, stand at the street corners of any of our large towns or cities and observe the poor children, boys and girls, pass to and from school, barefooted, with scarcely enough clothing to cover their nakedness, their faces pinched with cold and hunger, and his scepticism will soon disappear – not only that, but he will agree with us that there is something wrong with our social system which enables the few to live in luxury while the many can hardly get the bare

175

necessaries of life. But, after all, who is responsible for this state of affairs?

Edmund Burke has written of it as follows:

> Indeed the blindness of one part of mankind, co-operating with the frenzy and villainy of the other, has been the real builder of this respectable fabric of political society, and as the blindness of mankind has caused their slavery, in return their state of slavery is made a pretence for continuing them in a state of blindness, for the politician will tell you gravely that their life of slavery disqualifies the greater part of the race of man for a search of truth and supplies them with no other than mean and insufficient ideas.

This is as true today in every respect as when Burke wrote it.

Some one has said that all lawful authority originated from the people. Power in the people is like the light in the sun – natural, original, inherent and unlimited by any human. Have we the people not allowed others to pursue a scheme for us that is detrimental to our best interests? But it is never too late to mend.

Let us save our children in their infancy from being forced into the maelstrom of wage slavery. See to it that they are not dwarfed in body or mind or brought to a premature death by early drudgery. Give them the sunshine of the school and playground instead of the factory, the mine and the workshop.

We want more schools and less jails; more books and less arsenals; more learning and less vice; more constant work and less crime; more leisure and less greed; more justice and less revenge; more of the opportunities to cultivate our better natures – to make manhood more noble, womanhood more beautiful and childhood more happy and bright. These in brief are the primary demands made by the trades unions in the name of labour. These are the demands made by Labour upon modern society, and in their consideration is involved the fate of civilisation. For:

> There is a moving of men like the sea in its might;
> The grand and resistless uprising of labour;
> The banner it carries is justice and right,
> It aims not the musket, it draws not the sabre.
> But the sound of its tread over the graves of the dead
> Shall startle the world and fill despots with dread,
> For 'tis sworn that the land of the Fathers shall be
> The home of the brave and the land of the free.

Extracts from the Presidential Address of Councillor James McCarron to the seventeenth Annual Meeting of the Irish Trades Union Congress in the Town Hall, Dundalk, 16 May 1910.

James McCarron, a delegate from the Amalgamated Society of Tailors, Derry, was three times President of Congress, in 1899, 1907 and 1910, and a member of the Parliamentary Committee from 1895 to 1910. He was drowned in the sinking of the SS Leinster in 1918 while travelling to a meeting of his union's executive in London.

1911 David Campbell

With growing unemployment in a period of rising prosperity, one asks, what is wrong? Is there a delegate here who has any doubt as to the cancer, who is still in ignorance of the simple process which results in a third of our population being continually below the level of subsistence. There is no more direct challenge to the efficiency of our organisation, no greater indictment of our apathy, no more threatening menace to our continued well-being than the unemployed.

The subject of 'sweating' loomed large in the public eye in my native city (Belfast) during the year. Arising out of the scathing condemnation of the 'low rate of wages paid to outworkers in the linen and cognate trades', contained in the report of the Public Health Officer for Belfast, Dr Bailie, the Health Committee of the Corporation inquired closely into the charges and found them fully justified. Subsequent public demonstrations organised by the workers of the city were held at which a 'sworn enquiry' into the conditions and the wages paid in the linen and allied trades was demanded. The government has now announced that an enquiry will be held.

I have inspected some of our schools and believe them to be more fit for rearing swine than for the education of our children. Protests have been made all over the country time and again, but without any practical result. This, in my opinion, will ever be so until the people demand that the control of the whole education system shall be vested in the people themselves. Then, and only then, will it be possible to impart to our children an education worthy of the name.

The act for the feeding of necessitous school children in operation in the sister isle must be made applicable in this island where, on the meagre wage earned by the majority of workers it is absolutely impossible to feed the children. The medical inspection of school children should also be made compulsory in this country.

The recently suggested revival of the eight hours' day agitation should speedily find a reflex on this side of the Channel. No object more deserving of serious attention and propaganda on the part of trade unions could be mentioned. We are, I think, fully agreed that eight hours per day is sufficient for any man or woman to work. Why, then, should we falter in our efforts to secure it?

Of the recently-introduced bill for State insurance against invalidity and unemployment, it must be conceded that no measure has been introduced in recent years so pregnant with possibilities for well-being. Trade unions, however, desiring that no curtailment of their sphere of action shall result, no encroachment on the rights which have taken generations of toil, sacrifice and suffering to establish, must keep close watch on the development of the measure.

Let our fight be carried on until we establish the rights of those who create, but enjoy not, for the purity of the sweated woman and the starved child: until the 'beauty of life' has been restored to the despoiled, responding eagerly to our comrade's call –

> Come, ye that listen, rise and gird your swords,
> Win back the fields of Ireland for the poor.
> Give roses to your children's fading cheeks,
> And to the hearts of women hope again,
> Bring back content into the lives of men.

Extracts from the Presidential Address of David R. Campbell to the eighteenth Irish Trades Union Congress, in the Town Hall, Galway, 5 June 1911.

David Campbell, a delegate from the National Union of Life Assurance Agents, Belfast, was a member of the Parliamentary Committee of Congress, 1909-1918 and Treasurer, 1912-18. He was elected President of the Belfast Trades Council in 1909.

For more about Campbell, see J. Anthony Gaughan, Thomas Johnson *(1980).*

1913 William O'Brien

This Congress is a focus of working-class opinion; but unless that opinion is given practical expression in the field of political endeavour, the opinion will count for little in the arena of practical politics. More and more it is becoming recognised that the future of the working class is a wise application of its strength upon the political and industrial fields; that the same imperative necessity which exists for the industrial organisation of our class, also calls for its political organisation.

Upon the industrial field, we, as Irish workers, must steadily press forward to the greater unification and solidifying of our forces, linking up trade with trade, industry with industry, and avoiding the pitfalls of rashness and overhaste, consistently push forward to the linking of the whole working class of this country into one great union – one bond of brotherhood based upon the realisation of the vital truth that an injury to one is an injury to all. This may seem to some a dream; but it is a dream that the industrial tendencies of the time is fast weaving into the fabric of our social life.

We, Irish workers, now at this crisis in our country's history, are facing the future with determination. We see approaching the day of the emancipation of our class when the toilers, so long ground down and exploited, will at last arise and possess the earth; and when we read of the workers elsewhere, and what they have done and attempted, surely we have the right to resolve that Ireland and the toilers of Ireland, will not lag behind in the forward march of Labour. At last we see the end of our tribulations; and setting before ourselves no smaller task than the ownership of Ireland by the people of Ireland.

Extracts from William O'Brien's Presidential Address to the twentieth Irish Trades Union Congress in the City Hall, Cork, 12 May 1913.

William O'Brien, a delegate from the Dublin Trades and Labour Council, was a member of the Congress executive for twenty-five years between 1911 and 1945, President in 1913, 1918, 1925 and 1941 and Treasurer, 1921-24 and 1926-29. An official of the ITGWU from 1918, he was General Secretary from 1924 to 1946 when he retired.

For more about O'Brien, see his reminiscences as told to Edward MacLysaght, Forth the Banners Go *(1969), J. Anthony Gaughan,* Thomas Johnson *(1980), C. Desmond Greaves,* The ITGWU. The Formative Years *(1982), Emmet O'Connor,* A Labour History of Ireland 1824-1960 *(1992), Arthur Mitchell in* Studies, *20, 1971 and D. R. O'Connor Lysaght in* Saothar *9, 1983.*

1914 Jim Larkin

Comrades – we are living in momentous times, but we who have been elected to take up and carry still further the banner which was hoisted by the pioneers twenty-one years ago in this city cannot afford to make mistakes. The knowledge gained in the bitter days of the past should strengthen us in our deliberations and work in the future.

We are now on the threshold of a newer movement, with a newer hope and new inspiration. The best thanks we can offer those who went before and who raised the Irish working class from their knees is to press forward with determination and enthusiasm towards the ultimate goal of their efforts, a 'Co-operative Commonwealth in Ireland'. In the meantime, the immediate work to hand is the establishment of a new party – the Labour Party – an industrial army; a political party, whose politics would be the assurance of bread and butter for all.

We have been told in every mood and tense, throughout the long weary past, that no common denominator could govern the actions of the workers' activities – North and South. The question of Home Rule – the question of what some people call religion – has been used to divide us in the past. Now that the Government of Ireland Bill, which is alleged to be a Home Rule Bill, is on the Statute Book, and will be law in the immediate future, that question was settled once and for all. The question of religion is a matter for each individual's conscience, and in a great many cases was the outcome of birth or residence in a certain geographical area. Claiming for ourselves liberty of conscience, liberty to worship, we shall see to it that every other individual enjoys the same right. Intolerance has been the curse of our country. It is for us to preach the gospel of toleration and comradeship for all women and men.

The day has arrived for us of the Irish working class to reconsider our position. Whatever other classes in Ireland might do, we must march forward to the complete conquest of Ireland, not as representing sections, sects or parties, but as representatives of the organised working class as a whole. There must be freedom for all to live, to think, to worship. No book, no avenue must be closed. By God's help and the intelligent use of our own strong right arms we can accomplish great things.

The Irish working class are now rising from their knees and attaining full stature. The new Irish Labour Party has come of age, entered into its inheritance, and will stand erect upon its feet from this day forward.

Looking back over the immediate past – more particularly the long months of 1913 and the early months of 1914 – we saw there the attempt of an organised, unscrupulous capitalist class composed of men of different political parties and holding different sectarian views who had combined together for the purpose of destroying organised labour in Ireland. The lock-out in 1913 was a deliberate attempt to starve us into submission, and met with well-deserved failure. The workers emerged from the failure purified and strengthened, with fierce determination and a fixed purpose. The employers' attitude was a direct attack upon the essential principles of trade unionism. The outcome of the attack had been the initiating of a new principle of solidarity inside the unions, and for the first time in the history of the world of labour, the beautiful and more human principle had received universal recognition, 'An injury to one is the concern of all'. That motto would be emblazoned on the banner of labour the world over in the future. We have established a great human principle. Once again the Dublin workers stood as pioneers in the upward and onward march of labour.

The men and women engaged in the struggle had shown magnificent courage, loyalty and endurance. The history of their bitter sufferings and fortitude had rung like a clarion call throughout all the countries of the world.

In this morning's papers I read with pain and disquietude the report of the utterances of an eminent churchman – a most learned man – a man who claims to be a great educationalist and Christian – who has been speaking foolish words on the industrial question. He would find it necessary to go back to school and learn the ABC of economics. This learned gentleman said unthinkably (we will charitably suppose) that capital must be supplied by the employers – meaning by that the present controllers of capital. That statement had only to be made, to prove its absurdity. All capital is supplied by the working class; but to our undoing and our shame it was controlled by the capitalist class. A statement such as this churchman made should open the eyes of the working class to the want of knowledge of men who claim to be guides and leaders. And as much as I respect the Church to which I belong and the views of those who are inter-

181

preters of the dogmas of the Church, and as much as I respect the opinions of members of any and every church, I make this claim – that as long as the working class allow any churchman to abuse his trust and interfere in our affairs in the industrial world so long would they have to submit to hunger, privation, and wage-slavery. In matters spiritual they would obey them, but on the economic and industrial field they would be guided by knowledge gained by long and hard servitude.

I submit that the working class have as much right as any section or class in the community to enjoy all the advantages of science, art and literature. No field of knowledge, no outlook in life, and no book should be closed against the workers. We should demand our share in the effulgence of life and all that was created for the enjoyment of mankind. And here do I appeal to those who cannot see eye to eye with us – to come with us as far as their knowledge will permit. Come at least to the bottom of the boreen, and then if we must part, the pioneers will continue on and up the mountain to meet the dawning of the new tomorrow.

The working class must be free, not only economically but intellectually. Speaking to a priest some time ago he said: 'I agree with some of your views and believe that improvement and alteration is necessary in the world; but,' said he, 'we are determined to build a wall around Ireland and keep out the advanced ideas of Western Europe.' I replied, 'As much as I respect your views, Father, there is no power on earth can build a wall to keep out thought'. The men in this movement are determined to enjoy the fullness of life and of the knowledge and power that the Creator ordained them for.

I desire to bring you back for the moment, and would speak with you on one or two points of the struggle in Dublin last year. We saw too plainly then that sectionalism carried with it defeat amongst the working class. We had thirty-seven unions engaged in the struggle, each acting upon its own line of defence and attack and according to its own methods. Those who were engaged had shown magnificent courage – women and men, aye, and little children – had proven their heroism. Hunger, the gaol, and death itself did not deter them. Let us not forget our comrades, Brady, Nolan and Byrne, who were murdered in the streets of this city by the hired hooligans of the capitalist class – the police. We found that no political party, no church, made any protest against the abuse of the laws by the capitalist class.

During that period it was shown clearly then that there was neither Unionist nor Nationalist amongst the employing class; but two camps – employers and workers. We found no Red-mondites, Carsonites, or O'Brienites then. The enemy were all employers, and every weapon they could wield – political, social and administrative – they used unsparingly. Let us not talk of wooden guns or tin guns. What the working class wanted was the gun of intelligence. Let 'solidarity' be the watchword, and a few years will broaden out the liberties curtailed by the most unscrupulous and most vindictive capitalist class that any country was ever cursed with. Police, politicians, the Press, and the judges on the bench were simply the tools of the employing class. No city in the world has a more useless or vicious capitalist class than that of Dublin.

Condemnation and calumny had been poured out upon the heads of the leaders of the working class. The agitator had been denounced by Press and pulpit, but thank God, the agitator was the salt of the earth. The employers claim a victory, but the employers did not beat back organised labour in this city. I admit we had to retreat to our base, but that was owing to the treachery of leaders in affiliated unions and betrayal in our own ranks. I will mention no names, in the interest of unity, but we must see to it that such happenings shall never take place in the future. One union is the only way out – one union of all industry. One might say when they hear this suggestion that it is the term of a madman – that it is Larkin again. It is, however, the only sound, logical method and the only way that makes for success.

The cursed lines of sectarian and political demarcation must be wiped away. They must hunt the fomenters of bigotry and intolerance out of the Trade Union Movement. No employer ever asked a man whether he was a Nationalist or a Catholic, Unionist or Protestant. If a worker entered Queen's Island ship-building yard and stated that he would not work with an Orange lathe, a Protestant pneumatic rivetter, or a Catholic anvil he would be fired out at once. We must drop these party distinctions. One union is the way out. That union should embrace all departments of industry – engineers, shipbuilders, distributive trades and transport – each of these sections looking particularly after its own work, but all of them bound up together and working for the betterment of all men and women. Those who would not assist in this one-union movement were on the side of the capitalist; they must either be with us or against us. We have no time to argue further with these men and women who stand for sectionalism; we must simply march over them to the conquest and control of industry and our own destiny.

Another side of our lives which has been too long neglected – a line of advance which had not been taken seriously into consideration – the safest line of advance I speak of now – the Co-operative Movement.

The working class of Ireland would be compelled to understand the worth of co-operation. Through its agency we could supply all that life needs by ourselves and for ourselves. It needed no further argument to favour it. Life itself was co-operation in its truest sense. Man himself was a social animal and lived by co-operation. The hard-headed Northerner had appreciated the benefits of co-operation. The Northern missed some of the advantages of the Southern atmosphere in which man lives for a day like a flower of the field. That was a beautiful and inspiring thing; yet the flowers closed up at night to preserve the dew again for the appearance of the morrow's sun. They could start right away to develop Co-operation in the shop and in the home, and eventually they would have no need for an employer as he is today; but they themselves would become their own employers; produce, distribute, and consume their own products; and then in that day they would be able to give the employers well-deserved punishment. They would give him a job and he would have to work for a living.

Thanks to the last two Congresses and the resolutions therein carried, today we see the birth of an Irish Labour Party in which there would be no room for the old lines of cleavage; no sectional politics, no disagreements, no misunderstandings; cemented by their common needs, a working-class party, that would concern themselves with seeing to it that sufficient food, clothing, and shelter were enjoyed by women, men and children. We must unite as Labourites in the three-leaved shamrock of Fellowship: have Faith in our Cause, Hope of its realisation, and Charity to all men.

I have deliberately refrained from writing anything in the shape of an address to this Congress, believing the spoken word from the heart is of more value than the written word; and all that I have said I have put my soul into. I recall that only a short time ago I was expelled by those who were opposed to the newer movement; expelled by methods which were a disgrace to the Trade Union Movement. As you all know, I have been in prison on a charge such as no man of my class would be guilty of. I was released, thanks to the efforts of my friends in the Trade Union Movement. I had the honour to sit in this Council Chamber as a member of the City Corporation. My opponents took good care to have me expelled. All of these things strengthened the organisation which I have the honour to be a member of. Some day I hope that I will have the pleasure of returning as an administrator of this Corporation.[1]

I hope we will see the day when we will take full advantage of our opportunities, cry 'finis' to our differences, and obliterate all jealousies from our ranks. Be truly Irish of the Irish. Give ear to all men who do worthy work. Ireland must no longer be Niobe but Mercury amongst the Nations. Let us be comrades in the true sense of the word, and join with our brothers the world over to advance the cause of the class to which we belong. On that day we will put upon our escutcheon a mark worthy of the trust reposed upon us twenty-one years ago. We are entering upon a new era to do work worthy of the cause to which we are attached. Cathleen Ni Houlihan calls upon us to abolish old jealousies, old intolerances that she may sit enthroned in the midst of the Western Sea. I claim we have an opportunity given us of achieving much in the future of our beloved country, to work and live for, and if needs be die, to win back, in the words of Erin's greatest living poet, for Cathleen Ni Houlihan her four beautiful fields.

Extracts from James Larkin's address to the twenty-first annual meeting of the Irish Trade Union Congress, City Hall, Dublin, 1 June 1914.

James Larkin, a delegate from the ITGWU, was a member of the Parliamentary Committee of Congress, 1908 and 1911-14. He was General Secretary of the ITGWU, 1909-1924 and General Secretary of the Workers' Union of Ireland, 1924-1947.

---

1. Twenty-two years later James Larkin did return to Dublin's City Hall. He was a member of the Dublin City Council from 1936 until his death in January 1947 and chairperson of the Housing Committee from 1943 to 1947.

As a Councillor, it was Larkin who was instrumental in the City Council deciding to confer the Freedom of Dublin on George Bernard Shaw in 1946, and in persuading Shaw to agree to become a Freeman of his native city.

Two of Larkin's sons were also members of the City Council. James Junior (Young Jim) was a member of Dublin Corporation from September 1930 to June 1933, and Denis from 1949 to 1969 when the members of the City Council were removed from office, and from 1974 to 1977. Denis Larkin was Lord Mayor of Dublin during 1955-56.

1917 Thomas MacPartlin

Now, friends, in times like these, when members of the working class are being slaughtered by the thousand every day in the interests of the greedy capitalists of all the belligerent nations, one feels it very hard to concentrate one's thoughts on any question but when and how this awful carnage can be stopped and in that connection the only 'one bright spot' on the horizon is the effort that has and is being made by the organised working class of Russia, which, let us hope, in the near future, will extend to the other belligerents, to bring about a speedy conclusion to this war, and make provision in the future for the prevention of war, which always means suffering and death for the workers and heaps up more money gains for the capitalist class.

Under the Franchise Reform Bill now passing through the British Parliament, women have got some satisfaction for their long and strenuous fight and, although limited in the present measure, their rights, once recognised, it is only a question of time until everything they asked for and fought for must be conceded.

In my opinion, alongside the question of low wages, the awful conditions under which the workers are housed, is responsible for more disease and misery among the working class than any of the other grievances by which they are oppressed. In the working class districts in any of our large cities you will be sure to come across the dingy little arch inside which there is a yard surrounded by a lot of dirty little hovels, each containing nine or ten persons, one filthy lavatory and a water-tap in the centre of the yard – common to all the residents who may number eighty or a hundred souls. You will also see the large tenement house with eight or ten families, reeking with dirt and disease, whose men, women and children use the one w.c. and the ash-bin at the bottom of the stairs to receive all the refuse, and keep the house 'perfumed' in the intervals between collections, which are usually about twice each week. They will search in vain for bath or wash-house, or any of the other things that make life pleasant; but they will find cooking, washing, eating and sleeping all in the one room; and in many of them provisions made for all the calls of nature. Is it not impossible to expect that children reared under these conditions could grow up to be healthy and moral citizens? After the big lock-out in Dublin in 1913, a Departmental

Committee was appointed to enquire and report on housing in that city; and the conclusion they came to was there was nothing so bad in Western Europe!

Even in centres where there are trade union organisations in existence there are great numbers of workers who have not yet learned that the only way they can better their own condition or emancipate themselves from their present position of slavery, is by uniting with their fellow workers through the Trade Union movement.

And what about ourselves? Is there not something we can do to bring about unity? Why are these twenty or more Unions catering for workers who should all be in one engineering trade union? And in a small country like Ireland, six or seven unions of woodworkers? Then there are what ignorant people call the 'unskilled' unions. In Dublin district alone, there are half-a-dozen of these, and throughout the country numerous others, all catering for the same class of workers.

Extracts from the Presidential Address of Thomas MacPartlin to the twenty-third Annual Meeting of Congress in the Guildhall, Derry, 6 August 1917.

Thomas MacPartlin, a delegate from the Amalgamated Society of Carpenters and Joiners, was a member of the Parliamentary Committee of Congress 1912-14 and the National Executive, 1916-21. He was elected President in 1921 but was unable to act due to illness. He died in Geneva in 1923 where he was attending the International Labour Conference as one of the Irish Worker Delegates.

For more about MacPartlin, see J. Anthony Gaughan, Thomas Johnson (1980).

1919 Thomas Cassidy

Events of interest to the Irish Labour Movement during the year have included the response of Labour to the call that May 1 should be held as Labour's festival, the great struggle in which the Belfast workers engaged for the recognition of the forty-four hour week, and which, while not fully successful, has undoubtedly brought the realisation of that ideal appreciably nearer; the protest strike of the workers of Limerick against applying for military permits to allow them to go to and return from work.

On all sides at the moment we see industrial unrest. And can we wonder at this? We have for the last four years been warning our people that as sure as morning the industrial war would follow the cessation of hostilities. Our forecast has proved but too true.

The organisation of the workers of the country has made great progress in the twelve months just past. Let the same activity prevail in the years to come. Whether the workers should be organised in one big union or not is a matter I will not now discuss. Of one thing, however I am certain: there must be greater cohesion on the part of the organised workers. I believe this can be brought about by organisation on industrial lines and the amalgamation of existing unions.

To accomplish our aims, unity is essential. Today I would ask that whatever the differences may be on other matters, we should cross hands in friendship and resolve that shoulder to shoulder we will in the future fight in that movement which has room for all sections of political thought and whose object is the uplifting of the class to which we all belong.

In preparing something to say to you this morning in an opening address, I recognised how unworthy I am to occupy the position of President of Congress at such a momentous time. To Dublin in 1914 my thoughts went back, and I longed for the fiery eloquence and determination of Larkin; to Sligo, in 1916, my thoughts wandered, and I longed for the great power of reasoning and foresight shown by Tom Johnson in his address to that Congress; to Waterford last year did my thoughts stray, and I thought of the great ability displayed by William O'Brien.

Extracts from the Presidential Address of Thomas Cassidy to the twenty-fifth Annual Meeting of Congress, Whitworth Hall, Drogheda, 4 August 1919.

Thomas Cassidy, a delegate from the Typographical Society, Derry, was a member of the National Executive of Congress, 1914-18, 1924-34 and 1936. He was the Irish Organiser of the Typographical Association from 1911 to 1937.

1921 Thomas Foran

In 1914 there were affiliated to Congress forty-eight Unions representing a total trade union membership of 110,000. Today we have forty-one trade unions affiliated, representing a membership of 300,000. That shows real progress not only numerically but in the direction of closer and more efficient organisation. The old cry of 'fewer unions and more unionists' has certainly taken effect during the past seven years.

Amongst those who have been affiliated to this Congress are a very large section of workers who in the past have been the most down-trodden, the most persecuted of the whole working classes in Ireland – the agricultural labourers. Their fights have been long and strenuous, not against a foreign enemy, but against a local enemy. The Corn Production Act provided for a minimum wage, and when there was a trade union effort the minimum wage was usually applied. I am sorry to say in a great number of cases those splendid employers, the farmers, refused even to pay the miserable wage laid down by the Agricultural Wages Board. The machinery of that Board is now scrapped, and the agricultural labourer is thrown back to the hospitality of the generous employer. These men have no hope and no redemption except from the Labour movement through trade union organisation. In that they will have the support and co-operation of the trade union organisation of the whole country. With the agricultural labourers' organisations linked up with the workers in the towns and cities there is certainly a great future for the trade union movement.

The employers in this country are combining and studying what is taking place in England where the workers went down like corn before the reapers despite the magnificent struggle put up against enormous odds by the miners. They are of opinion that a similar course of events will follow here – poor deluded employers! The course of events that will certainly follow any general attack upon the standard of living in this country will be very very different.

Congress has advised that in all industries where notice of reduction in wages or attacks on working conditions are made, all the unions in this trade or that industry should come together, form a Joint Committee, and agree that whatever may be the outcome of the negotiations, strike or lock-out, all the unions in that industry pledge themselves to stand firmly together to the bitter end.

In the shipping industry, the flour milling industry, and what other few industries we have, it has been intimated that on and after the 1 August they are going to reduce the wages of their employees. Well, this is the 1 August, and there is going to be no reduction without a fight having been put up. We will stand together in this coming attack.

Extracts from the Presidential Address of Thomas Foran to the twenty-seventh Annual Meeting of the Irish Labour Party and Trade Union Congress, in the Mansion House, Dublin, 1 August 1921.

Thomas Foran, a delegate from the ITGWU, was a member of the National Executive of Congress, 1916-17 and 1920-24. He was General President of the ITGWU from 1909 to 1939.

For more about Foran, see C. Desmond Greaves, The ITGWU The Formative Years *(1982).*

1922 Cathal O'Shannon

The Irish Labour Party and Trade Union Congress is the authoritative organ of the organised workers of Ireland, on both the industrial and political fields. I consider our organisation and struggle in the industrial field of more importance and of more benefit to our class than anything we can do in the political field until by the triumph of our economic strength we attain to political power.

In the past twelve months we have not had as many big industrial victories as in the preceding years. But, on the whole, we have not had a great deal to regret. Taking all in all, we have lost less, and therefore gained more, relatively speaking, than the workers in most other countries. That result is to be attributed almost wholly to our methods of organisation and the good fighting spirit and readiness to sacrifice which are still marked characteristics of the workers in Ireland.

If I may single out the most notable factors in the fight against wage reductions and increased hours, I am fairly entitled to give more than honourable mention to the dockers of the ITGWU, the agricultural workers, especially in the counties of Dublin and Meath, and the rank and file of the railwaymen – including the rail clerks – and not least among them that section of the shopmen who stood to their guns. I have no hesitation at all in saying that the determination of the Transport Union dockers to resist to the death saved the Irish working class from the terrible consequences that followed in England upon the desertion of the miners on Black Friday.

Sections of workers have fought bravely with a considerable measure of success. Others have stumbled and suffered grievous enough defeats, and some have taken their beating lying down. Our defeats are serious enough in all conscience, but they should not have any other effect than that of spurring us on to renewed efforts. They are due to three main causes: faulty industrial organisation, poor generalship, and, let us not hide it from ourselves, lack of fighting spirit and vision on the part of some sections of our rank and file.

On the civil war our views cannot be too often or too emphatically expressed. In a word, they are: a plague on both your houses. On both sides we find people whose minds are so narrow, so warped and twisted with party passion, that they cannot conceive of any body of people not siding with one force or the other. Well, we side with neither. Neither side serves any working class interest, and our job is to steer clear of both.

I am convinced that this civil war is unnecessary, that it could have been avoided, and that it will render to the Irish people the greatest disservice they have suffered in this generation. For these reasons we call upon the organised workers to take no part in the civil war. It is not a war of the masses against the classes. It is not a war that will make the lot of the worker easier, or his status higher, or his hopes of freedom nearer.

It will not bring that peace with prosperity that the more conservative worker wants. It will not bring nearer that Workers' Republic for which the more class-conscious worker works and would die – and many Irish workers may die for it yet. Fellow-workers, keep out of it.

Those of you who have not yet been dragged or inveigled into the hell's broth, keep out of it. Starve to death rather than shed your blood in this civil war. If you are not threatened with starvation, husband your strength and your resources, build up your organisations, and make ready for the day when you will claim and hold your own. You may have enough fighting to do then to make it wisdom on your part to do no fighting now.

Above all, remember that elections and strikes, the day to day successes and reversals of Labour, are small things in their way. They are only skirmishes, they are not the battle. The real battle is the continuous struggle of the working class to free itself from slavery and from wagery, to seize and hold power and wield it in the interests of the workers, to go forward, marching steadily and battling bravely for the establishment of the Workers' Republic.

On that march, in that struggle, let us recall to our heartening the words of an imprisoned fellow-worker of ours in another land:

Mourn not the dead that in the cool earth lie –
Dust unto dust

191

The calm, sweet earth that mothers all who die,
As all men must.

But rather mourn the apathetic throng –
The cowed and meek
Who see the world's great anguish and its wrong
And dare not speak!

Extracts from the Presidential Address of Cathal O'Shannon to twenty-eighth Annual Meeting of the Irish Labour Party and Trade Union Congress, in the Mansion House, Dublin, 7 August 1922.

Cathal O'Shannon, a delegate from the ITGWU, was a member of the National Executive of Congress, 1918-20, 1922 and 1928 and Secretary, 1942-45. He was Secretary of the Congress of Irish Unions in 1945 and in 1946 was appointed, with Thomas Johnson, one of the two Worker Members of the Labour Court.

It might be noted that the first two Worker Members of the Labour Court when it was set up in 1946, had been secretaries of Congress and that the first Chairman, R. J. P. Mortished, had been assistant secretary of Congress in the 1920s.

For more about O'Shannon, see C. Desmond Greaves, The ITGWU The Formative Years *(1982).*

1939 P.T. Daly

We have found many critics and we have found some strong reliable friends. But you can take the opinion of an old man as having some weight in dealing with a question of this sort. Your critics are always unfair, and, I make bold to say, they will always be unfair. At the first Congress of this organisation the resolutions proposed were but minor cycles in the programme of world events. Our critics condemned them then. They were 'anti-Christian', and, what was more to be condemned in the views of our critics, they were 'socialistic' and should not be tolerated. Leaders were pointed out as inclining in that direction, and the workers were taught to shun them.

With the passage of time, some of the minor demands have been conceded. We have now made legal the position of the trade union picket; we have had the trade union dispute recognised as a legal entity. We have got the terribly socialistic old age pension; we have got a national system of health insurance and unemployment insurance. All these were amongst the things which were condemned close on fifty years ago, and for advocating which some of the younger men of that period were sent

CONGRESS PRESIDENTS

1. Thomas O'Connell,
Dublin Trades Council (1894)

2. J. H. Jolley,
Cork Trades Council (1895)

3. Alexander Bowman,
Belfast Municipal Employees' Society
(1901)

4. William O'Brien,
Dublin Trades Council /ITGWU
(1913, 1918, 1925, 1941)

5. James Larkin,
ITGWU (1914)

6. Louie Bennett,
Irish Women Workers' Union (1932, 1948)

7. Helena Molony,
Irish Women Workers' Union (1937)

8. John Swift,
Irish Bakers' Union (1947)

9. James Larkin Junior,
Workers' Union of Ireland (1949, 1952, 1960)

10. Helen Chenevix,
Irish Women Workers' Union (1951)

11. Jack Macgougan,
National Union of Tailors and Garment
Workers (1958, 1963)

12. John Conroy,
ITGWU (1959, 1968)

CONGRESS PRESIDENTS

13. Fintan Kennedy,
ITGWU (1966)

14. David Wylie,
Union of Shop, Distributive and Allied
Workers (1982)

15. Congress Presidents and former General Secretary at ICTU Northern Ireland
Conference held in the Guildhall, Derry, April 1994. From left: **William Wallace** (1988),
Brendan Harkin (1977), **Stephen MacGonagle** (1973), **Andy Barr** (1975), **Donal Nevin.**

BELFAST 1907

16. and 17. Strike meeting at Queen's Square, Belfast. On platform from left: Michael McKeown (National Union of Dock Labourers), Alexander Boyd (Municipal Employees), James Larkin, W. J. Murray and James O'Connor Keesock.

18. Motor vans deliver goods under police escort.

CORK 1908

19. Striking dockers march to meeting to be addressed by Jim Larkin. (Picture: Cork Examiner).

20. Liberty Hall, Dublin, Head Office of ITGWU from 1912.

21. James Connolly,
Ulster Organiser of ITGWU in 1913.

22. August 26, 1913. Larkin's message
'Strike declared Stop at once'.

23. Speakers at Fiery Cross
meeting in Liverpool:
James Larkin, James
Connolly, Big Bill
Haywood (IWW leader),
Mrs Bamber (Liverpool
Trades Council).

24. August 31, 1913. O'Connell Street, Dublin. Police made repeated baton charges against workers gathered to hear Larkin address the banned meeting. Two men died and hundreds were injured. (Picture: Illustrated London News reproduced in International Transport Workers' Federation's Journal, January 1960).

25. Manchester: Cartloads of potatoes for loading on the relief foodship.

26. Dublin: Workers await the berthing of the SS Fraternity.

27. The relief ship that carried food supplies for the families of the locked-out workers.

28. Larkin prepares to board the relief ship.

29. The lifting crane is made ready...

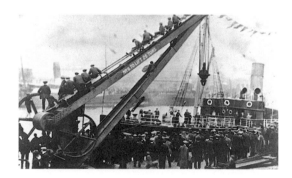

30. ...the first truck is rolled ashore.

31. and **32.**
Hungry families collect
the food 'pucks' from
the distribution shed.

33. Loaves of bread are
distributed to the
locked-out men and
women.

34. Jim Larkin,
general secretary, ITGWU.

35. Delia Larkin,
secretary, Irish Women Workers' Union.

36. Elizabeth and James Larkin at home after Larkin's release from jail in 1913 with their three sons James, Denis and Fintan. (Picture: Le Miroir, Paris).

Drawings of Larkin in Liberty Hall, Dublin, in 1913 by William Orpen.

37. From 'Stories of Old Ireland and Myself' by Sir William Orpen (1924).

38. From William Orpen Centenary Exhibition Catalogue, National Gallery of Ireland (1978).

39. Head of Jim Larkin by American artist Mina Carney (Hugh Lane Municipal Gallery of Modern Art, Dublin).

40. Drawing of Larkin by Sean Keating RHA done in 1946. (Liberty Hall, Dublin).

41. Larkin addressing meeting in O'Connell Street, Dublin in 1923 after his return from imprisonment in America. (Picture: Cashman Collection, RTE).

42. Larkin Monument, O'Connell Street, Dublin. (Picture: Tommy Clancy, Dublin).

43. Delegates to 21st annual meeting of Irish TUC held in the City Hall, Dublin, April 1914. The President, James Larkin, is seated eighth from left. The three women delegates, sitting on either side of the President, were from the Irish Women Workers' Union: Bridget Butler and Delia Larkin, Dublin and Ellen Gordon, Belfast.

44. Members of National Executive of Irish TUC, 1914. [Years indicate Presidency of Congress]. From left - standing: James Connolly, William O'Brien (1913, 1918, 1925, 1941), Michael J. Egan (1909), Thomas Cassidy (1919), W. E. Hill, Richard O'Carroll; Sitting: Thomas MacPartlin (1917), David R. Campbell (1911), Patrick T. Daly (1939), James Larkin (1914), Michael J. O'Lehane (1912). Thomas Johnson (1916), not in the picture, was also a member of the National Executive.

46. Cissy Cahalane,
Irish Union of Distributive Workers and
Clerks, Dublin.

45. Mary Galway,
Irish Textile Workers' Union, Belfast.

48. Betty Sinclair,
Belfast and District Trades Union Council.

47. Saidie Patterson,
Amalgamated Transport and General
Workers' Union, Belfast.

49. John Simmons (1894-1899)

50. Hugh McManus (1900)

51. E.L. Richardson (1901-1909)

52. P.T. Daly (1910-1918)

53. Thomas Johnson (1921-1928)

54. Cathal O'Shannon (1942-1945)

55. Ruaidhri Roberts (1945-1981)

56. Leo Crawford (1947-1966)

CONGRESS SECRETARIES

57. Donal Nevin (1982-1989)

58. Peter Cassells (1989-   )

59. Head office staff of Irish TUC in 1959.
From left: Shirley Lowe, Ruaidhri Roberts, Maire MacDonagh,
Donal Nevin, Claire O'Neill.

NORTHERN IRELAND COMMITTEE CHAIRPERSONS

60. John Freeman, Amalgamated Transport and General Workers' Union (1978-79).

61. Jim McCusker, Northern Ireland Public Service Alliance (1980-81). President of Congress 1986.

62. Inez McCormack, National Union of Public Employees (1984-85) (Picture: Irish Times).

63. A Mackle, Irish National Teachers' Organisation (1986-87).

64. Tom Douglas, GMB (1987-88). President of Congress 1993.

65. John McAteer
(1945-1953). President of
Congress 1954.

66. John Kerr
(1954-1956)

67. W. J. Leeburn
(1956-1959).

68. William J. Blease
(1960-1975).
(Picture: Irish Times).

69. Terry Carlin
(1975 -).

70. First Central Council of Congress of Irish Unions 1945. [Years indicate Presidency of Irish TUC or CIU]. Back row: Owen Hynes (1949), Michael Colgan (1942, 1950), William J. Whelan (1948), Michael Drumgoole (1936), Walter H. Beirne (1952), Thomas Kennedy (1944-45, 1947), Sean O' Moore. Front row: William O'Brien (1913, 1918, 1925, 1941), Sean P. Campbell (1933), Gerard Owens (1945, 1946), Cathal O'Shannon (1922), John O'Brien (1955), Edward Healy. Inset: Leo Crawford.

71. Presidents of Irish TUC who attended the Final Congress in Cork in 1959. [Years indicate Presidency of Irish TUC]. From left - Back row: James Larkin (1949, 1952), Jack Macgougan (1958), J. Harold Binks (1956), John Swift (1947), Norman Kennedy (1957). Front row: Sam Kyle (1940, 1950), Robert Getgood (1944), Walter Carpenter (1959), Helen Chenevix (1952), Gilbert Lynch (1945, 1946), John McAteer (1954).

72. Members of ITGWU at Croke Park, Dublin in May 1923 to welcome home from America the General Secretary of the Union, James Larkin. The General President, Thomas Foran, is in the centre with Larkin and his son James Junior on his left.

73. Final meeting of the National Executive of the Irish TUC prior to the dissolution of Congress in 1959. [Years indicate Presidency of Irish TUC]. Standing: Sean Casey Donal Nevin (Research Officer), James Larkin (1949, 1952), J. Harold Binks (1956), John McAteer (1954), Robert Smith (1955), James Tully, Andrew Faulkner. Sitting: Patrick Crowley, James Sloan, Norman Kennedy (1957), Dominick Murphy (Treasurer), Walter Carpenter (President), Ruaidhri Roberts (Secretary), Jack Macgougan (1958), W. J Leeburn (Northern Ireland Officer), Andy Barr. (Picture: The Green Studio, Dublin).

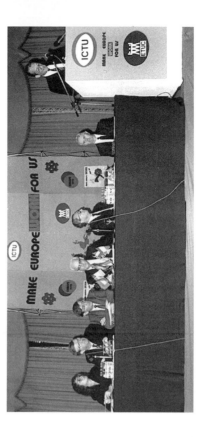

75. ICTU Conference on the European Community held in Malahide, Co. Dublin, November 1988. From left: Patricia O'Donovan (Assistant General Secretary), Chris Kirwan (Vice-President), Peter Cassells (General Secretary-Designate), Gerry Quigley (President), Jacque Delors (President, European Commission), Donal Nevin (General Secretary), Brian Lenihan TD (Minister for Foreign Affairs).

74. First annual conference of ICTU held in the Mansion House, Dublin, September 1959. From left: James Larkin, Norman Kennedy Ruaidhri Roberts (Joint Secretary), John Conroy (President), Leo Crawford (Joint Secretary), Walter Carpenter, J. Harold Binks.

76. ICTU Northern Ireland Committee's Community Rally for Peace at City Hall, Belfast, November 1993.

CONGRESS HEAD OFFICES

Drawings by Liam C. Martin (1994)

77. Trades Hall, 114 Capel Street, Dublin, where the first meeting of the Irish TUC was held in 1894. This was the Congress address from 1914 to 1920.

78. 32 Lower Abbey Street, Dublin (1920-1933).

CONGRESS HEAD OFFICES

Drawings by Liam C. Martin (1994)

79. 32 Nassau Street, Dublin
(1933-1956)

80. Merrion Building, Lower Merrion
Street, Dublin (1956-1964).

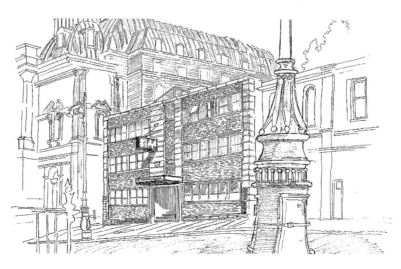

81. Congress Head Office: 19 Raglan Road, Dublin. (Drawing by Liam C. Martin).

82. Congress Northern Ireland Office: 3 Wellington Park, Belfast. (Picture: Terry Carlin).

83. Back of the banner of the Belfast District of the Amalgamated Society of Tailors (ca 1892). The front of the banner shows the insignia of the City of Belfast surrounded by floral scrollwork incorporating roses, thistles and shamrocks, (Ulster Museum, Belfast).

84. Banner of Workers' Union of Ireland. (Painted by Peter Broughal 1949).

85. Banner of the Belfast Trades Council founded 1881.

86.

87.

88. Irish TUC and ICTU: Trade Union Information (1949 -1981)

89. and **90.** A selection of ICTU publications issued since 1990.

91-94. ICTU Third World Bulletin.

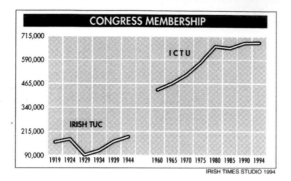

95. Congress membership 1919-1944 and 1960-1994. (Source: Congress annual reports).

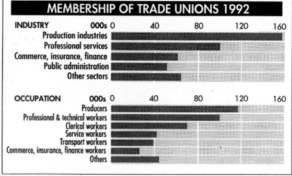

96. Membership of trade unions in the Republic 1992. (Source: Central Statistics Office Labour Force Survey).

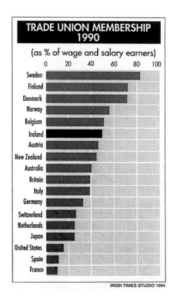

97. International comparison of trade union membership. (Source: OECD, Paris, 1994).

out into the wilderness as unclean, unfit for association with those to whom they looked for guidance. The socialist doctrine is not now condemned, but the work goes gaily on and another effort is being made to divide so that we can be the more easily defeated, and our opponents the more easily win.

Extracts from Presidential Address of P.T. Daly to the forty-fifth Annual Meeting of Irish TUC, City Hall, Waterford, 2 August 1939.
  Patrick T. Daly, a delegate from the Dublin Trades Council, was a member of the Parliamentary Committee of Congress in 1905, Secretary from 1910 to 1918 and a member of the National Executive, 1935-39. He was secretary of the Dublin Trades Council from 1919 to 1943.
  For more about Daly, see J. Anthony Gaughan, Thomas Johnson *(1980),* C. Desmond Greaves, The ITGWU The Formative Years *(1982) and Seamus Cody in* Obair, *January 1985.*

1944 Robert Getgood

It is with feelings of pride that I, a Northman, have the privilege of bidding you welcome today on this historic occasion – the Golden Jubilee of the Irish Trade Union Congress. Comrades, I would be guilty of base ingratitude if I failed to recognise your gesture of goodwill to the workers of the North and the spirit of comradeship which prompted it. In their name, I say 'thank you' for your kindly action, and as was declared on another historic occasion in the life of our country, I say 'Esto Perpetua'.

Let me, in brief outline, give you a picture of the industrial conditions of the time when our Congress started, and so enable you to see the rough and thorny path the pioneers trod ere the foundations were laid for the broad highway which greets your feet today.

The normal working week was one of fifty-five hours, and in some cases sixty hours were worked and overtime not paid for. Children of eleven years – 'half-timers' they were called – started work at 6.00 and 6.30 in the mornings. Wages afforded only the barest necessities even to craftsmen, while for the labourers and their families, for the women and children, the wolf was forever at the door. In the building trades in Dublin, Cork and Belfast, wages were 6d and 7d per hour while their labourers – the hodsman supplied his own hod – got $2^1/_2$d to 4d per hour.

So far I have spoken of the earnings of men. Now let me tell you of the earnings of women employed in the linen industry, mainly in Northern Ireland, though also at Cork, Dublin and Drogheda, and which, apart from agriculture, was Ireland's largest single industry. It then gave employment to 93,000 workers. The most highly skilled women, working 55½ hours per week in the spinning mills in 1894, received 9s per week, though many of the women got as little as 7s per week. Children between the ages of 11 and 13 years, working half-time, got from three farthings to 1d per hour. My own wage as a half-timer was 2s 9d for a fortnight. In the weaving end, piece-work earnings for the same hours ranged from 7s to 10s per week. All wages were paid fortnightly.

Emigration, low wages and industrial decline were some of the problems confronting Congress in its early days. For instance, at the Congress of 1896, reference was made to the loss to Limerick of the woollen trade, the linen trade, the glove-making trade, and later, the lace-making trade, which alone gave work to 8,500 women and girls. On the land, wages were wretched. In Northern Ireland a man got £10 and his food for the half-year and a woman got £4 and food.

The growing consciousness of their unsatisfied needs inspired the workers of Ireland to a great struggle for their emancipation from want, and during the early years of the century, and from Wexford to Belfast and Lurgan, from Dublin to Cork, the battle for trade union recognition and for improvements in wages raged against the employers. Engineering workers, dockers, carters, textile workers, railwaymen, and so-called unskilled workers each fought their own battle. One new demand which united them was that for a living wage, irrespective of current wage-rates in their particular trade.

This labour unrest had its roots in the economic conditions of the time. From the turn of the century the cost of living was rising steadily. Average prices rose 10% between 1901 and 1910. In the same years wages were being pushed down. The discontent was sharpened by the growing aggressiveness of the employing class. In such circumstances, is it surprising that the workers should demand an increased share of the wealth they produced and resorted to strike action? Thus the years 1907 to 1913 were marked by some of the bitterest struggles in our country's industrial history.

From Belfast the struggle shifted to Dublin, to Derry and then to Cork. There was a six months' strike in Wexford over the non-recognition of the ITGWU. Once again it was the turn of the North. Hitherto industrial unrest had been most in evidence among male workers, but, especially in the linen trade, women workers also had great cause for dissatisfaction. In 1911 the spinners struck for higher wages and against the fantastic rules forbidding singing, and imposing heavy fines for breaking them, or being absent.

In 1913 the Lurgan weavers struck for higher wages and won such support from the public that they returned triumphantly to work after five weeks' stoppage. The industrial struggles culminated in Dublin in 1913. There the ITGWU was determined to organise and improve the conditions of the unskilled and unorganised workers who were existing on earnings of 10s and 18s a week. Against them were ranged an arrogant employing class determined to smash the union and to resist all attempts at organisation. Dublin became the storm centre of the British Isles and throughout the year strike after strike developed. Finally after great suffering the struggle ended in a drawn battle. The union survived the attempt to smash it and the workers obtained some, but by no means all, their demands.

Those times were bitter and brutal and the workers' leaders had to fit themselves to circumstances: the occasion produces the men. The lessons were not lost on the participants. If we today have an easier path, it is because the pioneers and the unnamed thousands whom they led were prepared to sacrifice so much.

Extracts from the Presidential Address of Robert Getgood to the fiftieth Annual Meeting of Irish TUC, Whitworth Hall, Drogheda, 7 July 1944.

Robert Getgood, a delegate from the ATGWU, Belfast, was a member of the National Executive of Congress, 1940-46.

1948 Louie Bennett

In recent years it has become increasingly evident that the trade union is no longer merely an organisation to secure higher wages and defend the workers against injustice. It is now an integral part of the social fabric and as such its functions extend over a wide area of human life and activities. In its origin it was inspired by spiritual values. It drew its compelling force from the workers' revolt against the inhuman pressure of industrialism upon the mind and will of the human person. Again and again at various times and places that revolt has flared up into a passionate challenge for freedom, sometimes with success and never with complete failure. For although frustration and tragedy may have quenched the blaze, the embers have never failed to rekindle new resolves, renewed adventures.

Today, as in the past, spiritual values underlie the rough surface of trade unionism. The position of a human person in a world of applied science and rationalisation has become a serious moral problem. Today as in the past the common man's urge for a full life and the freedom that carries responsibility, springs from an innate conviction of man's spiritual destiny. Today as in the past the trade union supplies him with the instrument to satisfy that urge. That line of thought leads to a perception of the unique and valuable contribution trade unionism may make to the evolution of the new society which will emerge from the present flux and ferment.

In this country as elsewhere we are now right up against the necessity to blaze a new trail for the trade union movement. In considering the future of trade unionism we recognise that the theory of collectivism is already accepted and operating in the process of social re-organisation. Ireland's future society will be collectivist in some form. But in what form? Co-operative? State controlled? For years Irish trade unionism has upheld the ideal of a co-operative commonwealth. Now is the time to define that ideal realistically and to explore the avenues leading to its influence in the development of works committees, industrial councils, economic and social councils.

I venture to raise these questions because of my conviction that we stand today at a cross-roads in the history of trade unionism, and that trade unionism has a vital part to play in the evolution of a civilisation based on spiritual values.

Extracts from Presidential Address of Louie Bennett to the fifty-fourth Annual Meeting of the Irish TUC, Crawford Technical Institute, Cork, 7 July 1948.

Louie Bennett, a delegate from the Irish Women Workers' Union, was a member of the National Executive of Congress, 1927-32 and 1944-50 and President in 1932 and 1948. She was General Secretary of the IWWU, 1919-1955.

For more about Louie Bennett, see R. M. Fox, Louie Bennett: her Life and Times *(1958), Mary Jones,* These Obstreperous Lassies *(1988) and Ellen Hazelkorn in* Saothar 13, 1988.

1949 James Larkin

This is the fourth occasion on which the Irish Trade Union Congress has met in Belfast. Today tradition is broken in so far as I, unlike the Presidents of previous Congresses held in Belfast, am not a native of this city.

In a year when the tension between different sections of our people became, at times, exceptionally strained, it is worthy of comment that our Congress meets in Belfast, bringing together, in comradeship, men and women holding diverse opinions on many issues but yet bound together by certain fundamental beliefs and loyalties as trade unionists. No other movement has been able to overcome, or set aside, the divisions that beset our people politically, culturally, and ideologically, to the same extent as the Trade Union movement.

This city of Belfast has, from time to time, played no mean role in speaking for the common people and not merely for those of this city, but, on occasions, for the common people of our country as a whole. A century and a half ago this city was in the vanguard of the struggles for civil and religious liberty and in the effort to bury the animosities and enmities dividing Irish men and women and bring them together in a common bond of citizenship. In later years the working men and women of Belfast have not failed to belie their traducers and misleaders and, in bonds of working-class brotherhood, set aside their divisions and barriers and stood together as workers, fighting for those things so essential for common people the world over. The message of more than a century ago found its echoes in the hearts of Belfast workers in that epochal year of 1907; it quelled the raging passions of the 'twenties and gave to the idle man and woman in the hungry 'thirties renewal of spirit and hope

The basic unity and loyalty of working men and women finds its best expression in the aims and objects of the Trade Union movement, dedicated as it is to the protection of workers against economic and social injustices, and the winning for the common people of a full and rightful share of the earth's abundance.

Failure to keep these basic principles of our movement in the forefront exposes us to attempts to weaken and divide our movement by external enemies and gives rise to misunderstanding and even division in our movement. Only by an understanding of the common interests of the working class as wage earners, and by applying that understanding to the multifarious problems that beset us, is it possible to preserve the unity of our movement and reconcile within it the position of our members as workers and citizens. We have learned the lesson the hard and bitter way, that an economic system which divides society into social classes cannot create lasting and effective unity while those class divisions persist; but at least within our own class we have the possibilities, as well as the need, for unity and that unity we must preserve as our strength in the present and our hope for the future.

Fifty years ago, aye, even 20 years ago, collective effort to solve collective problems was derided and scorned. Today so much is it accepted that the argument turns not on organised, planned collective effort as against chaotic, planless individualism, but rather as to which form of planned collective effort is preferable and most likely to produce the results desired.

This change is a measure of the progress made by the common people to secure mastery over the things which determine their welfare and security. Basic economic changes are slowly and imperceptibly taking place, changes forced on us by the very economic forces of the capitalist system itself, yet an understanding and appreciation of these changes in a political and social sense tends to lag behind.

If workers are to have placed upon them responsibility for increasing production, whether through greater intensity of labour, or through co-operation in securing more efficient methods of production, then they are entitled to claim that the acceptance of such responsibility must begin at the door of the boardroom by their participation in the planning and management of industry. If employers insist that industry is their private property, to do with as they please, and workers not be permitted any participation in management, then let employers stop their hypocritical appeals to workers to produce more for the private benefit of employers. But if workers are to have placed upon them a social responsibility to the community through increased production, then industry must cease to be regarded as the private monopoly and concern of the employing class, and become a social organism in which the workers will have the right and the opportunity of discussing and determining how their labour will be applied and how the fruits of their labours will be distributed.

The year which has passed has witnessed a growth and strengthening of the Irish Trade Union Congress which is heartening. It is a source of pride that I have been honoured by holding office in that year and carrying on a tradition of service. My only hope is that this movement of Irish working men and women may continue to be, as it has been for more than fifty years, a meeting ground for Irish trade unionists, regardless of politics or religious views, that we may find ways and means of re-uniting all the trade union forces of our common country and that in the years ahead the Irish Trade Union movement will continue to serve the working class, out of whose sacrifice and struggle this great movement was born.

Extracts from the Presidential Address of James Larkin to the fifty-fifth Annual Meeting of the Irish Trade Union Congress, in the Husband Memorial Hall, Belfast, 27 July 1949.

James Larkin, a delegate from the Workers' Union of Ireland, was a member of the National Executive of the Irish TUC, 1945-59 and the Executive Council of the ICTU, 1959-69, President of the Irish TUC in 1949 and 1952 and President of the ICTU in 1960.

James Larkin Junior was General Secretary of the Workers' Union of Ireland from 1947 to 1969.

1951 Helen Chenevix

During the past two years the International Labour Organisation in Geneva have focused attention on the question of 'equal pay for equal work' as between men and women. One thing is clear. Whatever should be the basis of wage standards, it should not be the sex of the worker. If a man or a woman are doing the same type of work with equal skill and training, there is no justification for paying one of them less than the other. The whole question demands the serious consideration of both men and women workers, to both of whom the exploitation of women as cheap labour is disastrous.

The suggestion has been made that governments and public authorities should set a headline in this matter. Last month the International Labour Conference adopted both a Convention and a Recommendation on the subject of equal pay and we hope very much that our Government will put them into force. But I think that they will need a good deal of pressure from the trade union movement to do so.

It is in the field of education that the inequality between higher and lower income groups is most glaringly obvious. The rich man planning his children's education has a choice of good secondary schools with the university in the background, but with the man of small means it is far otherwise. For the great mass of our people the only education available is the primary school which the child leaves at fourteen or fifteen at most. If the child lives in a city he may very likely have been one of a class of sixty or seventy pupils, where teaching in the full sense is not possible; or, if he lives in the country, he may have had to attend school in a building no better than a tumble-down shack. How can we expect to have a mentally and physically healthy nation so long as the shadow of this disgrace remains on our national life?

There is a long road to be travelled and it must be travelled. The workers' organisations cannot afford to rest until the school-leaving age is raised to sixteen, with the necessary additional school buildings and additional teachers, with salaries befitting the importance of their work. We must also insist that special schools be provided for blind children, for crippled children, for deaf mutes, and for mental defectives. This is the bare minimum of the children's needs.

Extracts from the Presidential Address of Helen Chenevix to the fifty-seventh Annual Meeting of the Irish TUC, Town Hall, Killarney, 25 July 1951.

Helen Chenevix, a delegate from the Irish Women Workers' Union, was a member of the Executive Council of Congress, 1949-56. She was an official of the IWWU from 1917 and General Secretary, 1955-57.

For more about Helen Chenevix, see Mary Jones, These Obstreperous Lassies *(1988).*

1952 James Larkin

This is the fifth occasion in the history of the Irish trade union movement on which we have met in conference in Belfast, our first meeting here being in 1898. On the last occasion, 1949, I had the honour of presiding at the conference that year in Belfast. In the closing sentence of my Presidential Address I said:

My only hope is that this movement of Irish working men and women may continue to be, as it has been for more than fifty years, a meeting ground for Irish trade unionists, regardless of politics or religious views, that we may find ways and means of re-uniting all the trade union forces of our common country, and that in the years ahead the Irish trade union movement will continue to serve the working class out of whose sacrifice and struggle this great movement was born.

So today we meet as trade unionists from the thirty-two counties of Ireland, regardless of political or religious views, meeting in unity to serve the needs of the working class. To preside over such a conference in this city of Belfast is to me not only an honour but, even more, a hope fulfilled.

Neither time nor unity in themselves provide solutions for the problems which face the trade union movement. Time may render some existing problems less acute but simultaneously it brings forward new, and usually more complicated, problems which unity in itself does not solve. It merely allows us to concentrate our attention on the real problems rather than on side issues, and to apply more effectively our resources in tackling those real problems.

In our lifetime the trade union movement has been responsible for changes of the greatest magnitude in the lives of working people. Today we have greater power than ever before and are now confronted by the question as to what use we will put it to. Numbers, even hundreds of thousands of members, do not represent power, actual or potential, unless they are imbued with a conscious purpose and understanding, have clear, simply-defined aims, rational organisation, effective leadership and mutual confidence and loyalty.

In the main, trade unions today can effectively protect and further their members' interests insofar as wages and working conditions are concerned. Whether the rank and file trade unionist consciously realises it or not, ever-rising wages will not of themselves solve his problems or fulfil his needs. His horizon, his outlook has broadened out, his needs and demands have multiplied and taken on new forms. But it is no longer possible for trade unions, by purely trade union action, to meet the requirements of the trade unionist as a citizen, a parent, a member of society, in the second half of the twentieth century. His needs have multiplied a hundred-fold and now embrace many fields but trade unions and their members basically think and act only in relation to one sphere, the place of employment. It is this which is increasingly giving rise to a conflict between the interest of the trade union member as a producer at one moment and as a consumer at another.

In an acquisitive society such as ours, where the popular catch cry is 'I'm all right Jack', it is to be expected that workers will seek to use their potential power as trade unionists in an acquisitive manner, the same as other elements in society. But when one section of trade unionists do so as producers, other trade unionists as consumers develop a sense of antagonism. Here is fruitful ground for the enemy and traducer of trade unionism to work on. Here is the opportunity, eagerly availed of, for the reactionary to call for legal sanctions against trade unions and against striking workers. This is a trade union problem: this is our problem as the responsible, leading elements of the trade union movement. Here is a task of education for trade unions.

The tasks of trade unionists today are not just industrial. They are economic, social, cultural. Trade unions now must define their aims in relation to the satisfaction of the industrial, economic, political and cultural wants of trade unionists and of educating their members on the potential power of the trade unions to secure this satisfaction effectively. What should in broad terms be the social aim of trade unions today? Not just higher wages and shorter hours – they are limited industrial demands. What is required is a broad social aim because a trade union member is a social being and it is in relation to his social needs that today we experience the greatest frustration.

Could we say that our aim is to secure a steadily rising standard of living, based upon the intelligent use of the country's resources and in a manner which will prevent any social group or class acquiring an unequal and unjustifiable share and thereby creating or maintaining a privileged social position?

Can we convince the active members that all aspects of trade union activity must be consciously pursued to achieve that aim, not necessarily in all instances through the direct participation of the trade unions in every sphere?

Can we induce them to accept the view that, while wages and working conditions must continue to receive the main consideration of trade unions, concentration on those activities alone will not meet the requirements of the general mass of our members?

Workers, through their trade unions, have fought their way upward in society and their outlook, their whole concept of what life should and can offer, has broadened out. Trade unions must now undertake the task of applying trade union thinking to this new and higher stage in the forward struggle of the working class.

Such an approach can provide a means of removing the cynicism, indifference, even selfishness, among wide sections of trade unionists. The trade union movement has achieved great progress and won much for the workers but even greater victories await us in future years if we will but look forward rather than think of the present in the terms of the past.

Extracts from the Presidential Address of James Larkin to the fifty-eighth annual meeting of the Irish TUC, in Balmoral Exhibition Hall, Belfast, 26 July 1952.

1959 Walter Carpenter

This Congress marks the sixty-fifth year of existence of the Irish Trade Union Congress. For a man, pensionable age. If the Irish TUC were going into retirement, if it was giving up its job, we would have a very different atmosphere about this Congress, and, although it is the middle of summer, I might compare this Congress to a new year's eve party. The old year ends. The new year comes in. There is no real difference, except that we begin to look forward to the end of the dark winter days, and the beginning of spring. The Irish TUC will end, as the old year ends. The Irish Congress of Trade Unions will begin, as the new year begins. Throughout Ireland, trade unionists are looking forward to new growth, new developments, new achievements on behalf of Irish workers that will be possible now that we have achieved a united organisation.

In the sixty-five years of its existence, Congress has seen many changes. There have been changes in the political structure of the country, changes in the structure of the Congress itself, and, most important, immense changes in the conditions of work and living standards of the men and women who make up the membership of the Irish trade union movement.

I remember starting work in 1911. My wages were five shillings a week. I started work at 6.00 a.m. in the morning and worked till 6.00 p.m. at night. That was just before 1913. Like many another, 1913 spelt for me the end of my employment, such as it was, but after some time I became an apprentice joiner. The apprentice in those days was bound body and soul to his employer, but in return he got very little protection. An apprentice could not be a member of a union, but as soon as I came out of my time, I joined my union. It is often said that up to the end of the nineteenth century only the craftsmen were organised, and that the organisation of unskilled workers developed in the early years of the twentieth century. I can tell you that in the early years of this century very many of the craftsmen and skilled workers were unorganised as well.

Since 1945, Congress has not been itself. It has not been, as it had been since 1894, the single, united, central organisation of the trade union movement. Now with the formation of the Irish Congress of Trade Unions, unity has been restored. Now it is the ICTU which inherits the traditions of the united centre of 1894. It is not the name 'Irish Trade Union Congress' that represents the traditional centre; that name has been changed already no less than four times. It is not the constitution of the Irish TUC that represents the continuous tradition. Up to 1914 there were only Standing Orders for the annual meeting and no constitution. Since 1914 the constitution of this Congress was replaced by a completely new constitution in 1930, and that new constitution was the subject of many amendments. The traditions of the Irish TUC of 1894 to 1945 could only be represented by a body which represented the workers of the whole of Ireland, a body which represented all sections of workers.

The ICTU already includes sixty-eight unions with an affiliated membership of 409,000. We can say that the ICTU is now ready to carry on the proud traditions which were represented in the past by the Irish TUC. The name is changed, and may be changed again. But one thing I hope will never change again is the representation of the workers of Ireland by one trade union centre. May it go from strength to strength. The men who founded our organisation in 1894 looked forward with hope, with confidence, with enthusiasm towards the great achievements that are possible for this, the strongest trade union organisation this country has ever known.

We are now about to start a new chapter in labour history.

Extracts from the Presidential Address of Walter Carpenter to the Special (Final) Congress of the Irish TUC, School of Commerce, Cork, 22 July 1959.

Walter Carpenter, a delegate from the Amalgamated Society of Wood-workers, was a member of the National Executive of the Irish TUC, 1949-59 and the Executive Council of the ICTU in 1960.

1960 John Conroy

The task of bringing about reconciliation and unity in the trade union movement in Ireland has taken time, goodwill and prolonged, difficult negotiations. But, thank God, these have been successful and now practically all trade unions in the country are in affiliation with the Irish Congress of Trade Unions.

Having won the confidence and goodwill of the trade unionists of Ireland for unity within our ranks and for one central trade union authority, we now have the responsibility to demonstrate to the membership and to the working class, our united and progressive leadership and our ability to deliver the goods. From now on, and rightly so, the trade union movement will be judged on its achievements in winning a higher standard of living for the working class and greater job security for every worker.

In no other European country has there been such neglect of needy citizens as in Ireland. This is very apparent in so many ways but particularly in respect of unemployment, emigration, low wage levels, and the neglect of education, vocational guidance and technical training. Neglect of this kind brings with it many evils – poverty, exploitation of child labour, hardship and suffering by the unemployed and their families, by the sick and the aged, shortage of houses and schools, inadequate hospital accommodation and low living standards.

We in the trade union movement have long agitated against such a state of affairs. Now that we have united our ranks, we must unite our purpose and dedication towards the eradication of Ireland's social and economic evils.

Extracts from the Presidential Address of John Conroy to the first annual conference of the ICTU, Mansion House, Dublin, 22 September 1960.

John Conroy, a delegate from the ITGWU, was a member of the Executive Council of Congress, 1959-68, the first President of the Irish Congress of Trade Unions in 1960, President again in 1968, and Treasurer, 1961-67.

John Conroy was General President of the ITGWU, 1953-69.

1964 Charles McCarthy

Education and training must be seen in the context of our economic development generally. It must be realistic; it must take into account all our requirements, industrial and economic. This, however, is subject to an overriding truth. We must always be quite clear that we do not educate for industry; we do not educate for economic development; we educate essentially for the welfare of the individual person. Down through the years the trade union movement has stood for humanity and personal dignity. Frequently, it found ranked against it some of the most powerful forces in society. It was in those circumstances that it came to value the great importance of a free and independent educational system.

Education must not be the servant of a government; it must not be the servant of industry. At all times its ultimate purpose must be to serve the truth and there are not different kinds of truth: there is only one truth. It is only those who in their hearts doubt the validity of their own fundamental position who wish to prevent men from learning the truth and following it. This great movement of ours is based on the most fundamental of social truths: the essential dignity of man, his basic and inalienable rights, and the fundamental bonds of humanity which are frequently and so tragically distorted. If, therefore, we wish to know the truth and follow it at all times we must always protect the independence of the institutions from which we can derive it.

It is of equal importance that this education, and these institutions, should be available to all our people and no artificial barriers based on money should exclude our children or limit their opportunity for full personal development.

There are traditions in the trade union movement which humble me when I think of them. As far as philosophy is concerned, I believe that the philosophy of truth is all we require. We must serve the truth, which is no less valid and requires no less allegiance in the case of the employer and in the case of the State. The same truth that gives us the rights we so highly prize and for which so many have sacrificed so much, imposes obligations on employers and government, and indeed imposes obligations on us as well. Let us not play that damnable game which has dogged us for so long, that somehow or other, money and men of money, are entitled to operate on a different moral principle from the worker on the factory floor. The same principles govern us all, the principles of honesty, humanity and charity, the condemnation of greed and injustice no matter how they are disguised, no matter where they occur and no matter how many honours adorn them.

Extracts from the Presidential Address of Charles McCarthy to the sixth annual conference of the ICTU, Ulster Hall, Belfast, 28 July 1964.
    Charles McCarthy, a delegate from the Vocational Teachers' Association, of which he was General Secretary, was a member of the Executive Council of Congress 1960-63 and 1965-70.
    Charles McCarthy later became Professor of Industrial Relations at Trinity College Dublin and was the author, inter alia, of two major books, The Decade of Upheaval: Irish Trade Unions in the 1960s *(1973) and* Trade Unions in Ireland 1894-1960 *(1977).*

1966 Fintan Kennedy

It is fitting that in this year of commemoration of Connolly's life-work and sacrifice in death, in this year of unprecedented social and industrial upheaval, I should select as the theme of my address, an appropriate quotation from his writings. Connolly wrote in the *Workers' Republic,* a short time before the Easter Rising, fifty years ago:

> In the long run the freedom of a nation is measured by the freedom of its lowest class; every upward step of that class to the possibility of possessing higher things raises the standard of the nation in the scale of civilisation; every time that class is beaten back into the mire the whole moral tone of the nation suffers. To increase the intelligence of the slave, to so broadcast the seeds of that intelligence that they may take root and ripen into revolt, to be the interpreter of that revolt, and finally to help in guiding it to victory, is the mission we set before ourselves.

These words and these sentiments have always constituted the basic principles of the trade union movement. In some cases the recognition or acceptance of the right of all people to social justice stems from fear of the consequences of the industrial conflict that has been raging over the past twelve months or so, from fear that this trade union inspired and constitutionally conducted revolt may be translated into political action, for fear that their own status in society may be unduly affected.

In other cases, this recognition of fundamental human rights springs from the spirit of the age, from the realisation that the world is changing – and changing for the better – and that all peoples and all nations and all institutions are adapting themselves to this new world, this more equitable approach, this greater understanding and tolerance.

We can claim that while the sum total of material gain in the past year has not been as great as we would have liked, the moral victory has been a tremendous one. It has been tremendous because the trade union movement has created a situation in which government and management can no longer repudiate in public the right of workers to adequate rates of pay, to fair differentials in respect of skill, experience, service or responsibility, to pension schemes and to a high degree of uniformity in security of employment, working hours, holidays and so on.

To achieve our goals we have got to be honest with each other. We have to accept that all is not right on our side; that we have not got a monopoly of righteousness; that selfishness and greed have to be guarded against and that loyalty to each other and acceptance of truth will be more effective in our own interests than blinding ourselves by catch cries or by a philosophy which we utter on the platform but oppose in practice.

Extracts from the Presidential Address of Fintan Kennedy to the eighth annual conference of the ICTU, Seapoint Ballroom, Salthill, Galway, 19 July 1966.

Fintan Kennedy, a delegate from the ITGWU, was a member of the Executive Council of Congress, 1959-82 and Treasurer, 1968-82. He was General Secretary of the ITGWU, 1959-69 and General President, 1969-81.

1969 James Dunne

It is almost unbelievable that the two great men, John Conroy and James Larkin, present and dominant at our Conference last year, should have departed from us so soon and within one week of each other. Though the winter of their death has now given way to summer, we yet feel their absence and stand in the long shadow of their loss.

It seems to me that unless there occur great changes in our national way of doing things, we might soon be able to print in advance a copy of the President's Address and change nothing but the date. This permanent document would contain an attack upon the 'establishment', an attack on our inadequate social welfare system, an attack upon our own irresponsible elements and it would end with appeals for traditional solidarity, and be rounded off by a few apt quotations from James Connolly.

I don't mean to be sarcastic but I want to convey the feeling of frustration that I, and I believe, many others feel when we survey Irish trade unionism in practice. What does trade unionism mean today to our own members and to the people of this country? Does it project a picture of a movement possessed of zeal and enthusiasm and dedicated to reform and social change? I think not. I fear that to too many, trade union membership is, as they say, 'a licence to work' and even at this, very many of them begrudge paying for the licence. In the matter of pay increases, isn't it now our experience that much of our activities are taken for granted by those who benefit from them.

I know the answers to these unfair criticisms and unjustifiable attitudes but they are present in the minds of many trade unionists and their presence represents our failure to convey the picture of a movement that knows where it is going, why it is going there and the road it intends to travel.

Trade unionism now is judged by its strikes and their impact, and the great trade unionist today is the one who breathes fire and defiance at anybody who would dare deflect him from his strike, or draw his attention to other responsibilities. We have a 'do it yourself' brand of trade unionism which treats with contempt all the institutions, practices and procedures that our movement has created over the last sixty years.

Oh yes! we will put flowers on the graves of Connolly, Conroy and the two Larkins – but that's the end of it – don't ask us, the new and petty leaders of Irish trade unionism, to respect the organisations which these men and their colleagues built, the trade union democracy that they taught and practised and the procedures which they fashioned in the toil and sweat of their lives, experiences and deaths. That is for the fool, the conservative, the right-winger; ours is the 'instant democracy' which makes a laugh of the rights and interests of others and gives a weight to the minority far in excess of the wishes of the majority.

Bitter words – of course I'm bitter. I've come through a year in which I have seen my own union (Marine Port and General Workers' Union) smashed to the ground and bereft of everything except its fighting spirit. Smashed in a way that no employer or combination of employers could achieve in the thirty-seven years of militant trade unionism that is the history of my union. I would be a liar and a hypocrite if I came to this rostrum and left aside my feelings of hurt at the senseless and almost completely unnecessary damage done not alone to my own union, but to other affiliated organisations also. To be broken, to be smashed, this can be a proud fate and the boast of a trade union but only when such has been suffered in a just cause and in an unavoidable conflict or involvement.

Last year our President, John Conroy said:

> It may well be that there are sections and small groups of members in unions who are selfish and only concerned with securing more and more for themselves. Often they are small groups but nevertheless as key workers in an industry they use and abuse their trade union membership by using and abusing the picket line to secure for themselves alone, extra and special rates of wages and/or special conditions of employment.

Did the closeness of the grave give the gift of prophecy to Conroy or was he speaking from the sad experiences of his last years? I think it was both.

Let there be no mistake about it. In our present order, nobody in the trade union movement desires to restrict the essential right to strike or the allied weapon of the picket but for years we have warned that the irresponsible use of one or both would damage our own movement, give ammunition to our critics and present apparent justification to any government desirous of restricting hard-won trade union freedoms. Were these warnings justified? 1968/1969 give the answer.

The trade unionism of our fathers was a living, vital and dynamic force. It led them and us from the tenements and the slums to a better way of life. It curbed the power of the 'Boss', it frightened governments and, in Ireland, helped shake an Empire. But above all it attracted the young and gave a new dimension to their lives and aspirations.

Youth is still generous, idealistic, so why should it now seek new and sometimes distorted forms of expression? Is our movement tired, out of date, ill-fitted for the challenges of this day and age? I don't think so. I think that we may yet, and soon, and in our time show that the true and basic spirit of Irish trade unionism is as keen today as ever it was and though the times and methods may change, ours is still the one essential form of working-class social organisation that can achieve for all our people that way of life that is theirs by right and by nature.

It was no accident that gave us the Flag of Labour
    Gold and Silver are in the ground,
    The Stars are in the sky.

Extracts from Presidential address of James Dunne at the eleventh annual conference of ICTU, Bundoran, 1 July 1969.

James Dunne was referring in his address to the dispute of maintenance craftsmen in 1969 which directly affected only a limited number of craft union workers but which made tens of thousands of workers in the general unions unemployed. The dispute resulted in a loss of 629,000 days, over 90% of them in manufacturing industry.

James Dunne, a delegate from the Marine Port and General Workers' Union of which he was General Secretary, was a member of the Executive Council of Congress 1960, 1962-64 and 1966-71.

1974 Denis Larkin

Year after year the trade union movement has been demanding that effective action be taken to remove the injustices which continue to exist in our society, injustices which continue to debase our fellow citizens, and which result in the glaring inequalities that all of us recognise.

We see the continued high level of unemployment; the suffering, deprivation and hardship resulting from the existence over decades of an inadequate health service, an education system which still turns out from our schools, children whose education almost condemns them to a life of being hewers of wood and drawers of water.

The trade union movement has been calling particularly for action to be taken against all those who exploit the community for their own selfish purposes. Most serious of all is the situation arising from the unjust and inequitable taxation system. The failure over the years to introduce wealth and capital gains taxes and the toleration of a system under which the wage and salary earners bear the full brunt of taxation, both direct and indirect, while a significant section of our community go about scot free. The government's failure to introduce effective legislation and its evident decision to continue discriminating in favour of the wealthy, will estrange workers to an increasing extent.

Although proud to make this Presidential Address to my fellow trade unionists in our capital city, I have been disappointed because I had hoped to make this address in Belfast. The Irish

211

Congress of Trade Unions has repeatedly made its position clear on the terrible events which have cost the lives of more than a thousand fellow human beings, men, women and children. It has repeatedly expressed its opposition to the violence, the bombings, the senseless murders, and the injury and suffering inflicted on many thousands of human beings. During the last few years it has set out clearly and distinctly in many publications, the policies of Congress and its programmes on the essential issues. These publications represent our mature consideration and our determination to make a definite contribution towards healing the divisions that so tragically divide our community.

Extracts from the Presidential Address of Denis Larkin to the sixteenth annual conference of ICTU, Mansion House, Dublin, 2 July 1974.

Denis Larkin, a delegate from the Workers' Union of Ireland, was a member of the National Executive of the Irish TUC, 1956-59 and the Executive Council of the ICTU, 1969-77. He was General Secretary of the WUI from 1969-1977.

Forth the Banners Go

Oh, come cast off all fooling,
For this at least we know
That the Dawn and the Day is coming
And forth the banners go.

William Morris

'From the 1830s to the 1890s Irish trade unions paraded with extravagant splendour, decked out with sashes, rosettes and aprons, accompanied by brass bands, and having vast silken banners adorned with elaborate braid and tassels and fringes. Their greatest efforts were reserved not for labour protests or celebrations but for nationalist occasions.'

So wrote Belinda Loftus in *Marching Workers*.[1] One occasion in the last decade of the last century when the trade unions in Dublin marched with bands and banners was in celebration of the first meeting of the Irish Trades Union Congress in 1894 when a great Labour Day Demonstration was organised by the Dublin United Trades Council and Labour League on 6 May. This was probably the most extensive display of trade union banners ever in Dublin. Thirty-six unions affiliated to the Council carried their banners.[2]

These unions represented bakers, bookbinders, bottlemakers, brass founders, brush makers, butchers, cabinet makers, coach builders, coal labourers, confectioners, corkcutters, dockers, farriers, fishermen, glass cutters and glaziers, hairdressers, iron founders, labourers, letterpress printers, lithographic printers, painters, plasterers, plumbers, pork butchers, poulterers, railway workers, saddlers, sailors, silk weavers, slaters, smiths, stationary engine drivers, stone cutters, tailors, tramway men, upholsterers.

---

1. 'Marching Workers', An exhibition of Irish trade banners and regalia. Compiled by Belinda Loftus, Ulster Museum, Belfast, 2-28 May 1978 and Douglas Hyde Gallery, Dublin, 14 June-5 July 1978. The Arts Councils of Ireland Exhibition in association with the Irish Congress of Trade Unions.
2. The descriptions of the trade union banners given here have been taken from a publication issued by the Dublin United Trades Council and Labour League in connection with the holding of the first Irish Trades Union Congress in Dublin, 27 and 28 April, 1894 and the Labour Day Demonstration, 6 May, 1894. Descriptions of the thirty-six banners are given on pages 447-451. This almost certainly, is the fullest descriptive list of Dublin trade union banners extant.

Many of the banners must have been splendid indeed. The banner of the brass founders showed King Solomon receiving Cherubs from King Hiram on the completion of the Temple of Jerusalem. The fishermen carried a representation of the miraculous draught of fishes; the tailors, the arms of the trade supported by two camels; the saddlers, a shield supported by rampant horses; the brush makers, a triumphal arch supported by a wild boar and a hunter while through the arch is seen the Custom House and quays of Dublin; the tramway men, a miniature tramcar and horses.

The Stone Cutters' Union of Ireland banner must have been the most impressive. It was a representation of the Temple of Jerusalem, with a life-size figure of Hiram, the architect, bearing a scroll with a plan of the temple. Opposite Hiram was a modern stonecutter holding in his hands the implements of the trade. On the reverse of the banner was a life-size figure of Brian Boru clad in armour, leading his soldiers to victory and surmounted by the legend 'Remember the glories of Brian the Brave' while beneath was inscribed: 'Sons of Hiram, proceed and prosper.'

In contrast, less splendid but evocative, the silk weavers carried the arms of their trade: shield, fleur de lis and leopards' heads with shuttle in mouth supported by two griffins. At the top was St Patrick, the French crown and an Irish harp. (Silk weaving was introduced to Dublin by French Huguenots). The motto of the union was 'Nihil sine Labore' (Nothing without work).

Some of the banners were elaborate and detailed. Very striking was that of the bookbinders. On one side, beneath an arch supported by pillars was a shield on which was emblazoned a book containing the date 1782. (This was the year in which several members of the craft were prosecuted in London for illegal combination and sentenced to long terms of imprisonment). There was a shield supported by two journeymen with hands clasped. Above hovered a dove bearing in its bill an olive branch. In the corners were the arms of the four Provinces. The mottoes were 'Bind Right with Might' and 'United to support, but not combined to injure'.

On the reverse of the bookbinders' banner was a large oval representing a monk seated in his cell engaged in illuminating a manuscript. Completing this reverse side were oval portraits of Dean Swift, Thomas Moore, Thomas Davis, Gerald Griffin and

Oliver Goldsmith.[3]

Not to be outdone in elaboration, the lithographic printers' silk banner had a portrait of the inventor of lithography in the centre and in the top corners, representations of litho presses. At the bottom corners were figures representing Body and Soul. Two shields bore lithographic instruments supported by the figure of a youth representing the comparative youth of the art and the motto was 'Saxa loquitur' (the stone speaks).

Apart from the figures already mentioned, Solomon, Hiram, Brian Boru, St Patrick, Swift, Moore, Davis, Griffin, Goldsmith and Lenefelder, other banners had figures or medallions of Watt and Stephenson (stationary engine drivers), St Lawrence O'Toole (dockers), Daniel O'Connell (coal labourers), Caxton and Schoffer (letterpress printers), St Paul (upholsterers), Vulcan (smiths), and St Bartholomew (plasterers) as well as representations of Justice, Hope, Truth, Science, Art, Erin variously complete with Celtic Cross, round tower, wolfhound, harp, shamrock, sunburst, and pictures of Killarney and Glendalough.

Apart from the expected trade union mottoes such as Union is strength; United to protect, not combined to injure; Associated to protect our rights, not infringe on those of others; Peace, plenty, and unity; United we stand, divided we fall, other quaint and unusual mottoes adorned the banners, some of them in Latin. For example, the smiths: by hammer in hand all arts do stand; the tailors: Nundus et operuistis me (I was naked and you covered me); letterpress printers: The Light of the World, and, Behold we bring the Second Ark; saddlers: We unite for home trade; upholsterers: Uphold the truth; poulterers: All hail with joy the golden days of Erin; slaters: By love and harmony we support.

Symbolising the spirit that animated the early pioneers of the Labour movement was the bold motto of the operative bakers: May liberty for ever shine.

The reason for this display of the panoply of trade union banners in Dublin – the celebration of the founding congress of the Irish TUC and the Labour Day Demonstration – was also the occasion to participate in the international campaign in support of the demand for the 48-hour week. The *Irish Worker* described

---

3. There is a detailed description of the Bookbinders' Consolidated Union banner, by Charles Callan in *Labour History News* (Irish Labour History Society), Summer, 1993. The banner is now in the possession of the Technical Engineering and Electrical Union in Dublin.

the purpose of the May Day demonstrations throughout the world that year:

> Once again the workers are preparing to celebrate the anniversary of the day when that mighty shout of the wealth producers throughout the universe will be heard, demanding brighter conditions of existence and a more equitable share of the fruits of their labour. From the stifling mills of England, from the starved lands and attenuated workshops of Ireland, from the mines of France and Germany, from the dusty towns of the Southern hemisphere, from the mining camps of California, and from the overcrowded cities of the States the cry will come for shorter hours of labour; the cry for time to realise the beauties and wonders of nature; time to improve the mind, time for enjoyment and pleasure – in a word, time to be men, not toiling beasts or human machines.

On that May Sunday, one hundred years ago, the trade unions with their banners in colourful array, assembled in St Stephen's Green, Dublin in their allocated places, the coal labourers (Marshall, Maurice Canty) first in the procession followed by the engine and iron trades, shipping trades, labourers, clothing trades, printing trades, coach, harness, and horse trades, furnishing trades, provision trades, railway and tramway workers, and the building trades.

Headed by the Trades Council carriages (which were to be the platforms for the meetings to follow the procession), the marching thousands, in ranks of four deep, wound their way, bands playing, flags flying, banners proudly flaunting, down Grafton Street, through Westmoreland Street to O'Connell Street, turning into Britain Street (now Parnell Street) and down Capel Street. In that historic street they passed the Trades Hall where the founding meeting of the Irish TUC had been held but nine days before. Across Grattan Bridge, into Parliament Street, on to Lord Edward Street, Christchurch Place, the Corn Market to Thomas Street they marched; then on through James Street before turning into Steevens' Lane and Parkgate Street and entering the Phoenix Park.

In the Phoenix Park, the massed banners of the trade unions at the rear of the platforms formed the backdrop to the monster meeting which was to be the climax of the demonstration. At the entrance to the Phoenix Park, mounted Marshals saw the fifteen sections to the three platforms allotted to them. The Chief Marshal, James Collins, sent up a rocket and the meetings began.

Chairing the three meetings were Thomas O'Connell, President of the Dublin United Trades Council, who had presided at the founding meeting of the Irish TUC and who was to be its first President; E.L. Richardson, Vice-President of the Council, who was to be the secretary of the Irish TUC from 1901 to 1909; and P.J. Tevenan, the secretary for Ireland of the Amalgamated Society of Railway Servants, who was to be treasurer of the Irish TUC in 1898 and 1899.

Five resolutions were put to the meeting. The main resolution declared: 'This mass meeting of Dublin working men again declares that the reduction of the hours of labour is the most important and urgent reform needed', and expressed itself in favour of working hours being internationally reduced to the limit of eight per day. A second resolution impressed on workers the importance of organisation in trade unions and that 'it was absolutely necessary that the toilers of this and other countries should combine for their mutual protection and advancement'.

One hour after the first rocket, a second rocket was sent up by the Chief Marshal and the resolutions were put by the chairpersons from the three platforms. (An interesting footnote: one of the speakers at the meeting was Adolphus Shields representing the Fabian Society. He was the father of the Abbey Theatre actor, Barry Fitzgerald. A printer by trade he was the district secretary of the Gasworkers' Union led by Will Thorne, in 1890. It was then the largest union in Dublin with offices in Sandwich Street).

Thus did Dublin's trade unionists celebrate May Day 1894 and the setting up of the Irish TUC.

The last occasion on which there was to be anything comparable to the display of union banners in Dublin as in 1894 was in 1908 when many of the banners displayed in the earlier demonstration were again brought out. That year the traditional May Day demonstration was revived after a lapse of thirteen years. The Dublin Trades Council printed handbills and posters for the occasion, one of which carried the slogan, taken from the Communist Manifesto of 1848: 'Workers unite. You have nothing to lose but your chains, and a whole world to win'.

The Irish Times carried a colourful report of the demonstration on 4 May 1908:

The weather could hardly have been more favourable, and the result was that the procession through the streets prior to the meeting in the (Phoenix) Park was of very imposing dimensions. Stephen's Green was the place of muster, and there a big crowd assembled to watch the start of the procession. The first contingent to arrive was that of the Coal Labourers Society, with their fine banner and band. Shortly before the time arrived for starting, the Operative Butchers arrived making a big display, with three banners and a band.

The executive of the Trades Council led the way, the report went on, and were followed by the coal labourers, who, headed by their banner, made a very fine show. Next came the boilermakers and coach makers, both of which bodies were strongly represented. The coach makers' magnificent banner, twelve feet by nine has on its front the arms of the society surmounting a figure of Justice with the date of the society's incorporation, 31 May 1677. On the reverse side is the figure of Erin, with harp and wolfhound, and portraits of several distinguished Irishmen. The Operative Butchers were succeeded by the Drapers' Assistants who turned out in large numbers, many of them carrying cards in the shape of bannerets bearing the words, Unity and Self-reliance. Members of the Workers' Union, mineral water operatives, coffin makers, and paper cutters came along in order and were followed by the operative tailors, with their splendid banner.

> The big banner of the Stationary Engine Drivers was borne in front of the contingent of the society. After the Independent Labour Party came the bakers with their banner. The railway servants formed a large contingent, as did also the corporation and slaters, each body being well represented. The Amalgamated Society of House Painters brought several banners and passed in front of the brick and stone layers, hairdressers and brush makers who were succeeded by the united labourers, brass founders, members of the socialist party, bootmakers, iron founders and carpet planners.

Never again were so many of the old banners of the Dublin trade unions to be paraded through the streets of the capital city.[4]

Colourful Labour demonstrations were to punctuate the March of the Workers on many occasions through the succeeding years, in Belfast and in Cork as well as in Dublin. In *Drums Under the Window*, Sean O'Casey wrote of another, solemn occasion when trade union banners were seen in the streets of Dublin. It was the funeral in 1913 of John Brady who had been beaten by the police and Alice Brady who was shot by an armed blackleg on a tram:

---

4. Old trade union banners and regalia are in the National Museum, Dublin; Civic Museum, Dublin; Cork Public Museum; Ulster Museum, Belfast; Mechanics Institute, Limerick; Irish Labour History Museum, Dublin and unions in Dublin and Belfast, including SIPTU, TEEU, UCATT.

Here it comes, the Dead March in Saul, flooding the street, and flowing into the windows of (O'Connell) street's richest buildings, followed by the bannered Labour unions, colours sobered by cordons of crepe, a host of sodden grey following a murdered comrade.

In the last century, notable occasions when the banners of trade unions in other Irish cities were paraded 'in processional might in support of the cause of labour' (Belinda Loftus) were the Cork printers' strike in 1888, the Belfast linen-lappers' strike of 1892 and again in Belfast in 1893 when the British Trades Union Congress held its annual congress there.

Belfast in Revolt

On 20 January 1907, a delegate to the first annual conference of the Labour Party, successor to the Labour Representation Committee, arrived on the Belfast Steamship Company steamer from Liverpool and came down the gang-plank at the cross-channel quays near the Queen's Bridge in Belfast. He was described as distinctive in appearance, like a 'big burly docker from Liverpool or London', dressed in 'a fading great coat' and 'big rimmed hat'. When he spoke, it was in the 'approved manner of an English slum'.

As a rank-and-file delegate to the conference which was being attended by Keir Hardie, Ramsey MacDonald, Arthur Henderson and other leaders of the newly-formed party, there was no immediate reason to single him out from many others. He differed from them in that he had other work to do in Belfast.

Thus, in summary, is how John Gray in his book, *City in Revolt: James Larkin and the Belfast Dock Strike of 1907* (1985) describes the arrival in Ireland of James Larkin, for that is who the obscure delegate was. The national organiser of the Liverpool-based National Union of Dock Labourers, he had also come to organise the dockers in what was then the fastest-growing city in the United Kingdom.

Belfast in 1907 was to experience strikes and industrial disorder on an unprecedented scale, clashes between strikers and the police, rioting, something of a mutiny by the police, the introduction of the army on to the streets, mass meetings and demonstrations culminating in a huge demonstration of 100,000 workers who marched under the banner of the Belfast Trades Council on 26 July in support of the strikers. Throughout the year, over the labour scene, over the city, loomed the giant figure of Larkin who was to remain in the city for about a year. What was achieved in this turbulent year?

John Gray concludes:

> The Belfast strike movement of 1907 failed to achieve most of its immediate objectives, and the hopes of those involved who had wider aspirations were soon dashed, at least in a Belfast context. That in no way detracts from the importance of the events in the summer of 1907 as a turning point in the fortunes of the northern working class and of the Irish labour movement as a whole.

Considered purely as an industrial dispute, the Belfast dock strike, while of pioneering importance, never directly involved more than 3,500 workers. Its impact stemmed rather from the largely spontaneous and non-sectarian mobilisation associated with it, whether measured numerically, in terms of the daily attendances of 5,000-10,000 at strike meetings and the 100,000 or more who marched on the Trades Council demonstration on 26 July, or measured in terms of action on the quays and elsewhere with its cumulatively dramatic consequences.

In so far as there is a heroic and revolutionary mythology associated with the events of 1907, it quite legitimately revolves around James Larkin. His revolutionary instinct, made all the more potent because it was combined with exceptional talents as a populist orator and enthuser of men, had an immediate and profound impact and ignited tinder where others had failed for years past.

Professor Emmet Larkin in his biography of Larkin wrote about Larkin's struggle to arouse a labour revolt in Belfast:

The myth that has grown up around James Larkin claims Belfast as one of his great achievements. What happened in Belfast can, of course, be conceived in the most grandiose terms. It could include the destruction of political and religious bigotry, organising the workers for the revolutionary act, and contributing to the dignity and integrity of the working classes. The rub is that Larkin did achieve all these things, but only to a limited extent. He did blend, for example, Orange and Green on a Labour canvas, but the pigment proved soluble in the religious wash. He did explain that he was a Socialist, but his winning better wages and conditions cannot be offered as a laying of the foundations for a change in the social order. He did appeal to what was best in the Belfast workers, but how much their store of dignity and integrity was increased by him is certainly impossible to say. Still, is the attempt to count for nothing? No! – only beware of confusing it with the achievement. In the long run Larkin achieved little of a tangible nature in Belfast, not because he was something less than what he should have been, but because his enemies were too powerful and circumstances too adverse. In the short run he shook Belfast to its roots.

'We are living in stirring times'

We are living in stirring times. Those of us who during the last years have been preaching the need of organisation in the industrial field have much to be thankful for. Many times we have had to pause and consider – will anything come of our labours?

The apathy of the workers seemed to stultify all our efforts; it seemed that with the advance of education a spirit of selfishness had been imparted and self-sacrifice had died out. Men replied to your appeal for fellowship and brotherly love in the words of Cain – 'Am I my brother's keeper?' You whose lives flow on like a placid stream cannot appreciate the temperament of those who, like myself, go down amongst the exploited in the field, factory, workshop and aboard the great argosies that convey the products of fellow-workers from one area to another. We who are born with the microbe of discontent in our blood must of necessity live the strenuous life; one day down in the depths of despondency, the next day lifted up on the peak of Mount Optimism. The appeal of the fettered and harassed worker, the cry of the poor sweated exploited sister, and beyond their pain, the heartrending bitter wail of the helpless, unfed, ill-clothed, uncared for child, drives us down to the seventh Hell depicted by Dante; and then comes a moment in our lives, such a moment as we are passing through now, when we feel the very atmosphere moving in harmony, crying out in one triumphant refrain: 'Brotherhood one in spirit, oneness in action, oneness amongst the workers the world over.'

It is good to be alive in these momentous days. Reader, have you ever got up on a box or chair, physically and mentally tired, perhaps suffering from want of food; amongst strangers, say a mass of tired workers, released from their Bastilles of workshop or factory; and then suffering from lack of training, want of education, but filled with the spirit of a new gospel. You try to impart to that unthinking mass the feeling which possesses yourself. The life all round seems to stagnate, everything seems miserable and depressing. Yet you want them to realise that there is great hope for the future – that there is something worth working for, if the workers will only rouse themselves. You plead with them to cast their eyes upward to the stars, instead of grovelling in the slime of their own degradation; point out to them life's promised fullness and joy if they would only seek it. You appeal to their manhood, their love of their little ones, their race instinct, but all these appeals seem to fall on deaf ears: they turn away apparently utterly apathetic, and one tramps on to the next town or meeting, feeling it was hopeless to try and move them. You then creep into a hedgerow, pull out a cheap copy of Morris's 'News from Nowhere,' 'The Dream of John Ball, Franciscan Friar,' Dante's 'Inferno,' John Mitchel's 'Jail Journal,' or last but not least, 'Fugitive Essays' by Fintan Lalor, then forgetting the world 'and by the world forgot', one lives.

And then suddenly when things seem blackest and dark night enshrouds abroad, lo! the Sun, and lo! thereunder rises wrath and hope and wonder, and the worker comes marching on. Friends, there is great hope for the future. The worker is beginning to feel his limbs are free.

From an editorial by Jim Larkin, Irish Worker, 12 August 1911.

***

Jim Larkin was the founder-editor of *The Irish Worker and People's Advocate.* Its first issue was on 27 May 1911 and all its 189 issues were edited by Larkin over the forty-one months up to his departure to America in October 1914, except for the periods he was in jail or abroad. In addition to writing one or more editorials each week he also, according to the American scholar, Robert Lowery, contributed over 400 articles.

By the third issue of the paper, its sales were about 15,000, rising to a steady 20,000 but exceeding this figure greatly at certain times. For the time this was a huge circulation, especially as it was not sold outside Dublin to any extent.

In its first issue, Larkin declared:

Too long, aye! far too long, have we, the Irish working people been humble and inarticulate ... The Irish working class are beginning to waken. They are coming to realise the truth of the old saying 'he who would be free must strike the blow'.

The *Irish Worker* was to be the articulate voice of the workers, a clarion call to revolt against oppression.

Larkin was assisted in the editing of the paper by Jack Carney. Among the early contributors were R.J.P. Mortished (later to be Assistant Secretary of Congress from 1922 to 1930

223

and the first Chairperson of the Labour Court when it was set up in 1946), James Connolly, Desmond Ryan, Andrew P. Wilson (journalist, playwright, Abbey Theatre actor, who wrote under the pseudonym 'Euchan'), and Sean O'Casey, whose first public letters and writings appeared in the *Irish Worker*.

During the lock-out in 1913, W. B. Yeats, James Stephens, Susan Mitchell and other writers contributed to the *Irish Worker*

Professor Emmet Larkin of the University of Chicago, Larkin's biographer, wrote of the *Irish Worker:*

> Nothing like it has been seen since ... This novel production was and remains unique in the history of working class journalism. It was less a newspaper than the spirit of four glorious years. To read the *Irish Worker* of these years is to feel the quickening pulse of Dublin. Week after week the sordid tales of mischief, misery, jobbery, and injustice poured forth in a plaintive and never-ending painful dirge. Week after week, while working and waiting for the millennium, Larkin attacked with a monumental perseverance the sweating, exploiting employers and the corrupt, cynical politicians, who in his eyes were responsible for the reprehensible social conditions of Dublin. He gave no quarter and expected none as he vilified any and all, high or low, who had the misfortune to come under the notice of his pen.

Robert Lowery, in the *O'Casey Annual No. 3* (1984) described the *Irish Worker* as 'an extraordinary newspaper, a milestone in the history of working class journalism'.

To Larkin, the paper was more than simply an exposure of exploiting landlords, sweating employers and corrupt politicians. In the 29 July 1911 issue he proclaimed:

> We are not going to be beasts any longer. We are going to rouse the working classes out of their slough of despond – out of the mire of poverty and misery – and lift them a plane higher. If it is good for the employer to have clean clothing and good food, and books and music, and pictures, so it is good that the people should have these things also – and that is the claim we are making today.

'And Nineteen Thirteen cheered from out the utter degradation of their miseries'

The Gathering

> Ye who despoil the sons of toil, saw ye this sight today,
> Great stalwart trade, in long brigade, beyond a king's array;
> And know, ye soft and silken lords, won we the thing ye say,
> Your broad domains, your coffered gains, your lives, were ours
> today.

The whole forces of the Transport Union are wheeling into the battlefield, dressing their ranks, cheering with enthusiasm, deploying to their several places, looking up at the banner that shall never weaken in the grasp of those who carry it, the symbol of their hope – the banner of the Red Hand. Look over in the distance at the army of opposing Generals in their gaudy uniforms, which greed and plunder with deft hands, have decorated. Look at Marshal Murphy with his drum-head courtmartial at his back, with his manifesto on the drum-head draped with the Union Jack – swear away the Transport Workers' Union! If not, then starve!

Have a care, Marshal Murphy. Starvation is not a pleasant anticipation, it is always a difficult thing to starve thousands unwilling to suffer where food is plentiful. Hunger makes men weak; it often makes men desperate, and the ferocity of hungry men and hungry women is a dreadful thing. Other countries have experienced it. Let Murphy take care that Ireland does not furnish another dreadful example of men mad whom the capitalists would destroy.

'That ancient swelling and desire for liberty' is again stirring in our souls. The workers have lifted up their eyes unto the hills. They have no friends but themselves; but in their own strength they can conquer. Their only hope is their Union. 'Sacrifice the Union', say the employers, 'and all is gained'. Sacrifice the Union – all is lost.

What life would remain in a human body if the heart were plucked out and cast away? We know that the Transport Union is the heart of all our strength and all our hope. We are not deceived. The workers can do as much without their Union as Caesar's body when Caesar's head is off!

'Men, be men!' Who shall stop the onward march of the people? Those who oppose us we will sweep aside; those who ignore us we will ignore. The Transport Union – or –

> Then gather, gather, gather!
> While there's leaves in the forest
> And foam on the river,
> Despite them, M'Gregor shall flourish for ever!

From an article by Sean O'Casey in the Irish Worker, *27 September 1913.*
In another issue of the paper (15 November 1913), O'Casey wrote that it devolved upon the workers to 'call upon the young and hopeful to flock to the banner that waves nearest to the skies'. 'The enveloping forces of the workers are on the march', he added, concluding the article, Ecce Nunc, *with:*

> *Such a phalanx ne'er*
> *Measured firm paces to the calming sound*
> *Of Spartan flute! These on the fated day*
> *When, stung to Rage by Pity, eloquent men*
> *Have roused with pealing voice the unnumbered tribes*
> *That toil and groan and bleed, hungry and blind.*

'Christ will not be crucified any longer in Dublin by these men'

The first point I wish to make is that the employers in this City, and throughout Ireland generally, think they have a right to deal with their own as they please, and to use and exploit the workers as they please. They assume all the rights and deny any to the men who make their wealth. They deny the right of the men and women who work for them to combine and try and assist one another to improve their conditions of life.

The masters assert their right to combine. I claim that the right should be given to the workers. The employers claim that there should be rights only on one side. The employers are the dominant power in the country and they are going to dominate our lives. As Shakespeare says, 'The man who holds the means whereby I live holds and controls my life'.

For fifty years the employers have controlled the lives of the workers. Now, when the workers are trying to get some of their rights, the employers deny the right of their men to combine. Man cannot live without intercourse with his fellow beings. Man is, as has been said by an eminent authority, a social animal. But these men – these 'captains of industry' – draw a circle round themselves and say, 'No one must touch me'. But they have no right to a monopoly. The workers desire that the picture should be drawn fairly. But these able gentlemen who have drawn the picture for the employers have found that they could not do it! They have the technique, the craftsmanship but they have not got the soul. No man can paint a picture without seeing the subject for himself. I will try to assist our friends who have failed. As I say, they have the pigments and the craftsmanship, but they have not been able to paint a picture of life in the industrial world of Ireland.

Let us take the statement by Sir Charles Cameron.[1] There are, he says, 21,000 families, averaging $4^1/2$ to each family, living in single rooms in this City. Will these gentlemen opposite accept responsibility? They say they have the right to control the means by which the workers live. They must therefore accept responsibility for the conditions under which the workers live. Twenty-one thousand families living in the dirty slums of Dublin, five persons in each room, with, I suppose, less than one thousand cubic feet. Yet it was laid down that each sleeping room should at least have 300 cubic feet for each person. In Mountjoy Gaol, where I had the honour to reside on more than one occasion – criminals (but I am inclined to believe that most of the criminals are outside and innocent men inside) were allowed 400 cubic feet each. Yet men who slave and work, and their women – those beautiful women we have among the working classes – are compelled to live, many of them, five in a room, with less than 300 cubic feet each. They are taken from their mothers' breasts at an early age and are used up as material is used up in a fire. These are some of the conditions that obtain in this Catholic City of Dublin, the most church-going city, I believe, in the world.

The workers are determined that this state of affairs must cease. Christ will not be crucified any longer in Dublin by these men. I, and those who think with me, want to show the employ-

---

1. Sir Charles Cameron was the Chief Medical Officer for Dublin Corporation. His annual Public Health Reports exposed the extent of poverty and the appalling housing conditions in Dublin in the first decades of the century.

ers that the workers will have to get the same opportunity of enjoying a civilised life as they themselves have.

Mr Healy[2] has drawn a picture from the employers' viewpoint. I want to show the other side, the true side. I will use other pigments and more vivid colours. Go to some of the factories in Dublin. See some of the maimed men, maimed girls, with hands cut off, eyes punctured, bodies and souls seared, and think of the time when they are no longer useful to come up to the £1 a week or some other standard. Then they are thrown on the human scrap-heap.

See at every street corner the mass of degradation, controlled by the employers, and due to the existing system. Their only thought was the public house, and, driven to death, they made their way thither to poison their bodies and get a false stimulant to enable them for a time, to give something more back to the employers for the few paltry shillings thrown at them. These are the men whom the employers call loafers.

The employers bring up from the country poor serfs' who know nothing of Dublin or city life so that they would bring down the wages of men already here. The employers do this because their souls are steeped in grime and actuated only by the hope of profit-making, and because they have no social conscience. But this lock-out will arouse a social conscience in Dublin and Ireland generally. I am out to help to arouse that social conscience and to lift up and better the lot of those who are sweated and exploited. But I am also out to save the employers from themselves, to save them from degradation and damnation.

Mr Murphy[3] said he had had no strikes of any moment during his connection with industrial concerns, but I have proved that his life has been one continuous struggle against the working classes. I give him credit that in a great many cases he came out on top. Why? Because he has never been faced by men who were able to deal with him, because he has never been faced by a social conscience such as has now been aroused, and, according to which the working classes would combine to alter the present conditions of Labour. He had said he would drive 'Lar-

2. Tim Healy KC represented the employers at the enquiry. A leading member of the Irish Parliamentary Party for many years, he was to be the first Governor General of the Irish Free State in 1922.
3. William Martin Murphy was the President of the Dublin Chamber of Commerce. He was the proprietor of the *Irish Independent*, a large department store, and one of the leading hotels in the city, and was chairman of the Dublin United Tramway Company.

kinism' headlong into the sea – I evidently have the honour of coining a new word. But there is such a thing as human thought – and nobody has killed it yet, or driven it into the sea, or kept it from making progress.

We have seen the multifarious operations of Mr Murphy all over the world. He is an able man with the power and capacity to buy up the ablest men of the working classes, and he has used his power relentlessly. He may use that power for a while but the time always comes when such power would be smashed and deservedly smashed. There must be a break.

The Irish workmen are out to work for a living, and to get access to the means of life. They are not going to be slaves; they are not going to allow their women to be the slaves of a brutal capitalistic system which has neither a soul to be saved nor a soft place to be kicked.

I am engaged in a holy work. Of course, I cannot now get employers to see things from my point of view, but they should try to realise my work. I have worked hard from an early age. I have not had the opportunities of the men opposite, but I have made the best of my opportunities. I have been called anti-Christ. I have been called an Atheist. Well, if I were an Atheist I would not deny it. I am a Socialist. I believe in a co-operative commonwealth, but that is far ahead in Ireland.

Has there been a reason why there were not strikes long ago? Is the reason not to be found in the fact that the men have been so brutally treated that they had not the strength to raise their heads? Why, when I came to Dublin I found that the men on the quays had been paid their wages in public houses, and if they did not waste most of their money there they would not get work the next time. Every stevedore was getting ten per cent of the money taken by the publican from the worker, and the man who would not spend his money across the counter was not wanted. Men are not allowed to go to their duties on Sunday morning. After a long day's work they get home tired and half drunk. No man would work under the old conditions except he was half drunk.

I have tried to lift men up out of the state of degradation. No monetary benefit has accrued to me. I have taken up the task through intense love of my class. I have given the men a stimulus, heart and hope which they never had before. I have made men out of drunken gaol-birds. The employers may now drive them over the precipice, they may compel them, after a long and weary struggle, to recognise the document submitted to them not to belong to the Irish Transport Workers' Union, but it will only be for a time. The day will come when they will break their bonds, and give back blow for blow.

Is it any wonder a Larkin arose? Was there not a need for a Larkin? If the employers want peace they can have peace, but if they want war they will get war.

The above are extracts from the address of James Larkin as the workers' representative, to the Court of Enquiry into the Dublin dispute which opened in Dublin Castle on 29 September 1913. The enquiry was presided over by Sir George Askwith (later Lord Askwith) of the Board of Trade. Larkin's evidence was given on 5 October.

The writer John Eglinton (W. K. Magee) looked in one day and later wrote of his vivid recollection of 'the dark inchoate face of Larkin' and of his 'tall ungainly figure, craning forward as he bellowed forth his arraignment; and opposite him the calm handsome figure of Murphy, with trim white beard, speaking just above his breath and glancing occasionally at his angry foe: near him rose from time to time the robust form of his counsel, Thersites Healy, releasing effortlessly his biting speech!'

J'accuse: To the Masters of Dublin

Sirs – I address this warning to you, the aristocracy of industry in this city, because, like all aristocracies, you tend to go blind in long authority, and to be unaware that you and your class and its every action are being considered and judged day by day by those who have power to shake or overturn the whole Social Order, and whose relentlessness in poverty today is making our industrial civilisation stir like a quaking bog. You do not seem to realise that your assumption that you are answerable to your-selves alone for your actions in the industries you control is one that becomes less and less tolerable in a world so crowded with necessitous life.

Some of you have helped Irish farmers to upset a landed aristocracy in this island, an aristocracy richer and more power-ful in its sphere than you are in yours, with its roots deep in history. They, too, as a class, though not all of them, were scorn-ful or neglectful of the workers in the industry by which they profited; and to many who knew them in their pride of place and thought them all-powerful, they are already becoming a mem-ory, the good disappearing together with the bad. If they had done their duty by those from whose labour came their wealth they might have continued unquestioned in power and prestige for centuries to come.

The relation of landlord and tenant is not an ideal one, but any relations in a social order will endure if there is infused into them some of that spirit of human sympathy which qualifies life for immortality. Despotisms endure while they are benevolent and aristocracies while *noblesse oblige* is not a phrase to be referred to with a cynical smile. Even an oligarchy might be permanent if the spirit of human kindness, which harmonises all things otherwise incomparable, is present.

You do not seem to read history so as to learn its lessons. That you are an uncultivated class was obvious from recent utterances of some of you upon art. That you are incompetent men in the sphere in which you arrogate imperial powers is certain, because for many years, long before the present uprising of labour, your enterprises have been dwindling in the regard of investors, and this while you carried them on in the cheapest labour market in these islands, with a labour reserve always hungry and ready to accept any pittance. You are bad citizens, for we rarely, if ever, hear of the wealthy among you endowing your city with the munificent gifts which it is the pride of merchant princes in other cities to offer, and Irishmen not of your city who offer to supply the wants left by your lack of generosity are met with derision and abuse. Those who have economic powers have civil powers also, yet you have not used the power that was yours to right what was wrong in the evil administration of this city.

You have allowed the poor to be herded together so that one thinks of certain places in Dublin as of a pestilence. There are twenty thousand rooms, in each of which live entire families, and sometimes more, where no functions of the body can be concealed and delicacy and modesty are creatures that are stifled ere they are born. The obvious duty of you in regard to these things you might have left undone, and it be imputed to ignorance or forgetfulness; but your collective and conscious action as a class in the present labour dispute has revealed you to the world in so malign an aspect that the mirror must be held up to you, so that you may see yourself as every humane person sees you.

The conception of yourselves as altogether virtuous and wronged is, I assure you, not at all the one which onlookers hold of you. No doubt, some of you suffered without just cause. But nothing which has been done to you cries aloud to Heaven for condemnation as your own actions. Let me show you how it seems to those who have followed critically the dispute, trying to weigh in a balance the rights and wrongs. You were within the rights society allows when you locked out your men and insisted on the fixing of some principle to adjust your future relations with labour, when the policy of labour made it impossible for some of you to carry on your enterprises. Labour desired the fixing of some such principle as much as you did. But, having once decided on such a step, knowing how many thousands of men, women and children, nearly one-third of the population of this city, would be affected, you should not have let one day to have passed without unremitting endeavours to find a solution of the problem.

What did you do? The representatives of labour unions in Great Britain met you, and you made of them a preposterous, an impossible demand, and because they would not accede to it you closed the conference; you refused to meet them further; you assumed that no other guarantees than those you asked were possible, and you determined deliberately in cold anger, to starve out one-third of the population of this city, to break the manhood of the men by the sight of the suffering of their wives and the hunger of their children. We read in the Dark Ages of the rack and thumb screw. But these iniquities were hidden and concealed from the knowledge of man in dungeons and torture chambers. Even in the Dark Ages humanity could not endure the sight of such suffering, and it learnt of such misuses of power by slow degrees, through rumour, and when it was certain it razed its Bastilles to their foundations.

It remained for the twentieth century and the capital city of Ireland to see an oligarchy of four hundred masters deciding openly upon starving one hundred thousand people, and refusing to consider any solution except that fixed by their pride. You, masters, asked men to do that which masters of labour in any other city in these islands had not dared to do. You insolently demanded of those men who were members of a trade union that they should resign from that union; and from those who were not members you insisted on a vow that they would never join it.

Your insolence and ignorance of the rights conceded to workers universally in the modern world were incredible, and as great as your inhumanity. If you had between you collectively a

232

portion of human soul as large as a threepenny bit, you would have sat night and day with the representatives of labour, trying this or that solution of the trouble, mindful of the women and children, who at least were innocent of wrong against you. But no! You reminded labour you could always have your three square meals a day while it went hungry. You went into conference again with representatives of the State, because dull as you are, you know public opinion would not stand your holding out. You chose as your spokesman the bitterest tongue that ever wagged in this island, and then, when an award was made by men who have an experience in industrial matters a thousand times transcending yours, who have settled disputes in industries so great that the sum of your petty enterprises would not equal them, you withdraw again, and will not agree to accept their solution, and fall back again upon your devilish policy of starvation. Cry aloud to Heaven for new souls! The souls you have got cast upon the screen of publicity appear like the horrid and writhing creatures enlarged from the insect world, and revealed to us by the cinematograph.

You may succeed in your policy and ensure your own damnation by your victory. The men whose manhood you have broken will loathe you, and will always be brooding and scheming to strike a fresh blow. The children will be taught to curse you. The infant being moulded in the womb will have breathed into its starved body the vitality of hate. It is not they – it is you who are blind Samsons pulling down the pillars of the social order. You are sounding the death knell of autocracy in industry. There was autocracy in political life, and it was superseded by democracy. So surely will democratic power wrest from you the control of industry. The fate of you, the aristocracy of industry, will be as the fate of the aristocracy of land if you do not show that you have some humanity still among you. Humanity abhors, above all things, a vacuum in itself, and your class will be cut off from humanity as the surgeon cuts the cancer and alien growth from the body. Be warned, ere it is too late. – Yours, etc.

'A. E.'

Dublin, October 6th, 1913

Letter from George Russell (A. E.) published in The Irish Times, 7 October 1913.
George Russell (1867-1935). Poet, mystic, painter, writer, editor, 'that myriad-minded man', wrote prophetically in an editorial in the Irish Co-operative Organisation Society's paper the Irish Homestead (10 February 1912), of

which he was editor: 'we anticipate labour troubles during the next two years which will make the labour troubles of the past seem a mere murmuring of gnats'.

Jesse Dunsmore Clarkson, in his Labour and Nationalism in Ireland *(New York, 1925), records that A. E. related that one day, as he sat on the top of a Dublin tram, he felt a certain vibrancy in the air, as though he were in the presence of some vast magnetic power. He was irresistibly impelled to look up: his eyes fixed themselves on the masterful bulky figure of a man, seated at the other end of the tram. A few days later, he was introduced to that man; that man was Jim Larkin.*

In the Irish Homestead *(9 August 1913), A. E. commented on the controversy about the building of an art gallery for the Lane collection of French paintings, that the businessmen responsible for the refusal of Dublin Corporation to build the gallery had revealed themselves 'as the meanest, the most uncultured, the most materialistic and canting crowd which ever made a citizen ashamed of his fellow-countrymen'. Larkin, never short on vituperation, was more succinct. William Martin Murphy, he declared, should be condemned to keep an art gallery in Hell.*

During the lock-out, A. E. was among the writers who gathered in Liberty Hall to try to help the hungry women and men seeking food tickets. Through his support for the workers and his campaigning on their behalf in Britain as well as in Ireland, his Open Letter to the Masters of Dublin, A. E. knew that he was jeopardising his future in the cooperative movement. The influential Ancient Order of Hibernians, viciously anti-Larkin, had taken secret though unsuccessful steps to have the Irish Homestead *suppressed.*

A. E.'s Open Letter, Sir Horace Plunkett (1854-1932), the head of the cooperative movement in Ireland, referred to as a 'glorious indiscretion': 'To attack the Dublin employers, Dublin Castle, the police, the nationalist MPs, the AOH, the R. C. Church, over the condition of the Dublin slums was a magnificent exhibition of moral courage – so magnificent that I can forgive all his recklessness of consequence to my own little schemes.' (Letter, 18 December 1913 to F. S. Oliver).

Breaking the Boom of Starvation

Comrades, I left Dublin last Friday to bring back £10,000 worth of ammunition for the heroes and heroines fighting Labour's battle. Since that day I have travelled from one end of Scotland to the furthermost limits of England.

I told you before leaving I would have a steamer to bring food and would also have coal brought in. Murphy and his clique through the columns of his vicious lying press scoffed at the idea, laughed and joked and said, 'This is another of Larkin's mad ideas'. Since I left over 1,000 tons of coal have arrived. To-day, Labour's man of war *SS Hare* will break the boom of starvation loaded with £5,000 worth of food and raise the siege. In addition before Monday – I will have made good this statement that within a week I would have raised £10,000 to protect the finest army that man ever had the honour to lead.

The workers of Dublin have astonished the world again as the old race of the Gael proved that nothing can conquer them. The upper and middle class in Ireland with a few brilliant exceptions have always proved themselves to be totally selfish, and ever prepared to sacrifice the working class. We have proved to our own satisfaction and to the astonishment of the world that not only have we men who can guide us but the finest material in the world.

Steady the Old Guard. Show the Young Brigade how to fight. God bless you women and children. You are worthy of those who have gone before you. Personally, I never doubted you.

Message from Jim Larkin, in Irish Worker, *27 September 1913.*

The Struggle

The past five or six weeks in Dublin mark an epoch in the history of Ireland. The future Irish historian should devote a chapter to the fearful industrial deadlock in the autumn of 1913. He should not fail, of course, to chronicle the brutalities of the police on whom the condemnation of every fairminded man has been heaped. Then the employers' outrageous agreement; so intolerable were the provisions of that precious document that only intolerable humbugs could be responsible for its drafting.

But the old order has changed. The employers never reckoned on the great spirit of unity that has been abroad for some time now. New strength and hope have been stimulating the working class. No longer does the worker approach his 'dear, kind and indulgent' employer with cap in hand. That day is gone, and gone, I hope, for ever. No doubt he still holds a certain measure of respect for him. But when it comes to a question of gross intimidation and coercion; when the employer raises a point which tends to the trampling under foot of his workmen's rights; when in short, the employer attempts to gag and chain and stifle his employee's indisputable liberties and privileges, it was high time to stop him. Indeed, it was necessary to call a halt.

The result was the locking out of thousands of our working people within and beyond, the confines of this city.

Boss Murphy, the instigator of the lock-out, then imparted the refreshing information to his Chamber of Commerce friends, whom he has duped, that the lock-out would be over in a week by the starving-out process. As he and they were sure of three square meals a day, by inflicting the hardships, privations and tribulations consequent on the lack of food, the workers would of necessity crawl back to work. That was Murphy's wicked and murderous method of ending the trouble. So far it has worked unsuccessfully, despite the fact that six weeks almost have gone past.

Starvation! The Dublin toilers to starve. These words reached the ears of the trade unionists across the water. They at once realised that their Irish comrades were battling fiercely for the principles of Trades Unionism. The odds against them were heavy. Ammunition was wanting to sustain them in the battle-field. The sinews of war were urgently needed, and generously, indeed, did the British trade unionists respond to our appeal. Funds were immediately raised and two food ships, the SS *Hare* and the SS *Fraternity*, were sent to Dublin heavily laden with eatables for the locked-out men and their wives and families.

A sensation was created when on this day fortnight the SS *Hare*, the good food ship, steamed up the Liffey. The quays were already thronged with an eagerly expectant crowd. The appearance of the steamer was greeted with wild cheering. So help had come right enough. Larkin had promised the people that it would come, and all who know Larkin are aware that he seldom, if ever, makes vague or false promises.

That evening many willing hands were engaged in distributing the bags containing the foodstuffs to the people who had tickets, which were obtainable at Liberty Hall. At every point of the town on that Saturday night one met men, women and children trudging gaily along with their bundles on their shoulders. There was a repetition of this on the Sunday and on the following Monday. It was a cheerful sight to behold and made one strong in the knowledge that Murphy's suggested early invitation from the demon, Starvation, had met with defeat.

There were so many mouths waiting for a bit of the *Hare* that it did not take many days to finish her. However it was then announced early last week that another ship was coming. This time it was the SS *Fraternity*, the Co-operative steamer. Slowly

236

but majestically, like a trans-Atlantic liner she sped her course up the port on last Saturday morning and moored opposite the old Manchester Sheds. Here again was work for the catering staff, and right heartily they entered upon that arduous task. The system of distribution was magnificent. With mechanical precision the different foodstuffs were handed to the people as they passed in front of the temporarily-erected food stand inside the Manchester Stores.

How much we owe to our English comrades in the rank and file it would be difficult to say. At the earliest moment they gave us succour. Merely for the asking, two ships packed with victuals were sent across the Irish Sea to us, whilst funds were also raised. To all who are helping in the struggle a very deep sense of gratitude is owing.

The coming of those food ships to Dublin's shores is but another niche in the Valhalla of Ireland's history. The English working men have strengthened immensely our firing line. Their support urges us on to victory – a victory so glorious that it would be a complete triumph for Trade Unionism the world over.

Extracts from article by 'Tredagh', in the Irish Worker, *13 October 1913.*

***

Financial support for the locked-out workers and their families came from many countries. The French Confederation of Labour gave the American IWW leader, Bill Haywood, a cheque for one thousand francs, a large sum at that time, as a testimonial from France for the ITGWU. Huge sums were contributed by British trade unionists. For a time, the Miners' Federation was sending £1,000 a week (equivalent to over £50,000 today). The TUC in Britain raised over £90,000 (equivalent to £4$^{1}/_{2}$ million).

The Co-operative Movement in Britain made substantial contributions.

In London, a Dublin Distress Fund was organised by, among others, the Bishop of Oxford, the historian G.M. Trevelyan, John Masefield (later the Poet Laureate) and W.B. Yeats. The treasurer of the fund was Erskine Childers.

In all, it has been estimated that around £150,000 was subscribed to the various support and relief funds in 1913-14. This would be equivalent to about £7$^{1}/_{2}$ million at present-day values.

In an article in the *Irish Worker*, R. J. P. Mortished, who was to be the first chairperson of the Labour Court in 1946, wrote about 'the lowly upholders of the cause of freedom, the working men and women of Dublin':

> I have today seen something of these humble fighters for freedom. I have watched pale-faced thin women – mothers of seven or nine or twelve children – waiting for their rations of loaves and soup. I have seen a woman – mother of a young baby – faint from exhaustion after a day-long fast. I have seen men standing quiet and orderly, pitting their patience and fortitude against the masters' weapons of hunger and starvation. I have listened to the courageous little band of commissariat helpers singing rebel songs the while they peeled potatoes for soup.

Lord Salisbury, the former Prime Minister, wrote to Sir Horace Plunkett, wishing to subscribe to the Dublin distress fund without aiding the combatants. Plunkett replied (24 December 1913): 'The condition of the Dublin slums I always knew to be bad but had only realised one half the truth ... My feeling is that the poverty and destitution which has been revealed owing to Larkin's agitation are so awful that temporary amelioration, can be provided without any appearance of taking sides in the Dublin labour dispute.'

September 1913

Yeats' poem, 'September 1913', (page 319) was first published in *The Irish Times*, 8 September 1913 with the title 'Romance in Ireland (On reading much of the correspondence against the Art Gallery)'. It was written during the controversy about the proposal to build an art gallery designed by Sir Edward Lutyens on a bridge site across the Liffey to house the collection of French paintings that Sir Hugh Lane wished to present to the city.

On 28 July 1913, the Dublin Trades Council passed a resolution, moved by Jim Larkin, in support of the bridge site. The proposal had been strongly opposed by William Martin Murphy. In a letter to his own newspaper, the *Irish Independent* (19 July) replying to what he termed 'an insolent letter' from Sir Hugh Lane, W. M. Murphy wrote: 'There has been much eloquence wasted on this subject over the last few days and all the old platitudes have been trotted out about the "priceless collection", the "envy of Europe", the "resort of pilgrims", the educational effect on the taste of the citizens, the answer to which may be summed up in the word – Fudge.'

Doubtless, Yeats also had in mind when he wrote 'September 1913', the lock-out in Dublin which had commenced the previous month. In November, Yeats wrote in the *Irish Worker* about Dublin fanaticism in reference to the incidents that had taken place in the city when attempts were made to send hungry children from the city slums to England to be looked after there while the lock-out was on. The scheme was strongly opposed by the Archbishop of Dublin in a letter read in all the Churches in the Archdiocese. There was turmoil at the railway stations, at the North Wall and at Kingstown Pier.

Yeats wrote in the *Irish Worker* an impassioned protest which read in part:

> I do not complain of Dublin's capacity for fanaticism whether in priest or layman, for you cannot have strong feeling without that capacity, but neither those who directed the police nor the editors of our newspapers can plead fanaticism. They are supposed to watch over our civil liberties, and I charge the Dublin Nationalist newspapers with deliberately arousing religious passion to break up the organisation of the working man with appealing to mob law day after day and I charge the Unionist Press of Dublin and those who directed the police, with conniving at this conspiracy and I ask *The Irish Times* why a few sentences at the end of an article, too late in the week to be of any service, has been the measure of its love for civil liberty?
>
> There have been tumults every night at every Dublin railway station and I can only assume that the police authorities wished those tumults to continue.
>
> I want to know why the mob at the North Wall and elsewhere were permitted to drag children from their parents' arms ... I want to know by what right the police have refused to accept charges against rioters; I want to know who has ordered the abrogation of the most elementary rights of the citizen, and why the authorities who are bound to protect every man in doing that which he has a right to do have permitted the Ancient Order of Hibernians to besiege Dublin, taking possession of the railway stations like a foreign army.

A.E. (George Russell) who had not corresponded with Yeats for nine years, wrote congratulating him on his article in the *Irish Worker:* 'I have differed from you in many things but I felt all my old friendship and affection surging up as I read what you said,' he wrote, 'and I am glad to see that you, (Stephen) Gwynn, Seamus O'Sullivan, (James) Stephens are all on the same side in life.'

In a poem composed on 16 September 1913, 'To a Friend whose Work has come to Nothing', Yeats, addressing Lady Gregory, asks

> For how can you compete,
> Born honour bred, with one
> Who, were it proved he lies,
> Were neither shamed in his own
> Nor in his neighbour's eyes?

The 'he' referred to in the third line is William Martin Murphy.

In the poem composed on 29 September 1913, 'To a Shade' (Parnell), Yeats refers to Murphy as 'an old foul mouth':

> Your enemy, an old foul mouth had set
> The pack upon him.

The reference in the last line is to Sir Hugh Lane, the nephew of Lady Gregory.

'Humanity long dumb has found a voice, it has its prophet and its martyrs'

I stand for the first time on a public platform in this country. The great generosity of English to Irish workers has obliterated the memory of many an ancient tale of wrong. I come from Dublin, where most extraordinary things have been happening. Humanity long dumb has found a voice, it has its prophet and its martyrs. We no longer know people by the old signs and the old shams. People are to us either human or sub-human. They are either on the side of those who are fighting for human conditions in labour or they are with those who are trying to degrade it and thrust it into the abyss.

Ah! but I forgot; there has sprung up a third party, who are super-human beings, they have so little concern for the body at all, that they assert it is better for children to be starved than to be moved from the Christian atmosphere of the Dublin slums. Dublin is the most Christian city in these islands. Its tottering tenements are holy. The spiritual atmosphere which pervades them is ample compensation for the diseases which are there and the food which is not there. If any poor parents think otherwise, and would send their children for a little from that earthly paradise, they will find the docks and railway stations barred by these superhuman beings and by the police, and they are pitched headlong out of the station, set upon and beaten, and their children snatched from them. A Dublin labourer has no rights in his own children. You see if these children were even for a little out of the slums, they would get discontented with their poor homes, so a very holy man has said. Once getting full meals, they might be so inconsiderate as to ask for them all their lives. They might destroy the interesting experiments carried on in Dublin for generations to find out how closely human beings can be packed together, on how little a human being can live, and what is the minimum wage his employer need pay him. James Larkin interrupted these interesting experiments towards the evolution of the underman and he is in gaol.

You have no idea what the slums in Dublin are like. There are more than 20,000 families each living in one room. Many of these dens are so horrible, so unsanitary, so overrun with vermin that doctors tell me that the only condition on which a man can purchase sleep is that he is drugged with drink. The Psalmist says the Lord gives sleep to his beloved, but in these Dublin dens men and women must pay the devil his price for a little of that peace of God. It maddens one to think that man the immortal, man the divine, should exist in such degradation, that his heirship of the ages should be the life of a brute.

I beseech you not to forsake these men who are out on strike. They may have been to blame for many an action. The masters may perhaps justifiably complain of things done and undone. But if the masters have rights by the light of reason and for the moment, the men are right by the light of spirit and for eternity. This labour uprising in Ireland is the despairing effort of humanity to raise itself out of a dismal swamp of disease and poverty. James Larkin may have been an indiscreet leader. He may have committed blunders, but I believe in the sight of heaven the crimes are all on the other side. If our Courts of Justice were courts of humanity, the masters of Dublin would be in the dock charged with criminal conspiracy, their crime that they tried to starve out one-third of the people in Dublin, to break their hearts and degrade their manhood, for the greatest crime against humanity is its own degradation.

The men have always been willing to submit their case to arbitration, but the masters refuse to meet them. They refused to consult with your trade union leaders. They would not abide by the Askwith report. They refused to hear of prominent Irishmen acting as arbitrators. They said scornfully of the Peace Committee that it was only interfering. They say they are not fighting trades unionism, but they refuse point blank to meet the Trades Council in Dublin. They want their own way absolutely. These Shylocks of industry want their pound of flesh starved from off the bones of the workers. They think their employees have no rights as human beings, no spirit whose dignity can be abased.

You have no idea what labour in Ireland, which fights for the bare means of human support, is up against. The autocrats of industry can let loose upon them the wild beasts that kill in the name of the State. They can let loose upon them a horde of wild fanatics who will rend them in the name of God. The men have been deserted by those who were their natural leaders. For ten weeks the miserable creatures who misrepresent them in Parliament kept silent. When they were up for the first time in their lives against anything real, they scurried back like rats to their hole. These cacklers about self-government had no word to say on the politics of their own city, but after ten weeks of silence they came out with six lines of a letter signed by all the six poltroons. They disclaimed all responsibility for what is happening in the city and country they represent. It was no concern of theirs; but they would agree to anything the Archbishop might say. Are they not heroic prodigies! Dublin is looking on these men with alien eyes. It was thought they were democrats, we have found out they are only democratic blathers.

We are entering from today on a long battle in Ireland. The masters have flung down a challenge to the workers. The Irish aristocracy were equally scornful of the workers on the land, and the landlords of land are going or have gone. The landlords of industry will have disappeared from Ireland when the battle begun this year is ended. Democratic control of industry will replace the autocracy which exists today. We are working for the co-operative commonwealth to make it the Irish policy of the future, and I ask you to stand by the men who are beginning the struggle. There is good human material there.

I have often despaired over Dublin, which John Mitchel called a city of genteel dastards and bellowing slaves, but a man has arisen who has lifted the curtain which veiled from us the real manhood in the City of Dublin. Nearly all the manhood is found among the obscure myriads who are paid from five to twenty-five shillings per week. The men who will sacrifice anything for a principle get rarer and rarer above that limit of

242

wealth. I am a literary man, a lover of ideas, but I have found few people in my life who would sacrifice anything for a principle. Yet in Dublin, when the masters issued that humiliating document, asking men – on penalty of dismissal – to swear never to join a trade union, thousands of men who had no connection with the Irish Transport Workers – many among them personally hostile to that organisation – refused to obey. They would not sign away their freedom, their right to choose their own heroes and their own ideas. Most of these men had no strike funds to fall back on. They had wives and children depending on them. Quietly and grimly they took through hunger the path to the Heavenly City. They stand silently about the streets. God alone knows what is passing in the hearts of these men. Nobody in the press in Dublin has said a word about it. Nobody has praised them, no one has put a crown upon their brows.

Yet these men are the true heroes of Ireland today, they are the descendants of Oscar, Cuculain, the heroes of our ancient stories. For all their tattered garments, I recognise in these obscure men a majesty of spirit. It is in the workers in the towns and in the men in the cabins in the country that the hope of Ireland lies. The poor have always helped each other, and it is they who listen eagerly to the preachers of a social order based on brotherhood and co-operation.

I am a literary man and not a manual worker. I am but a voice, while they are the deed and the being, but I would be ashamed ever in my life again to speak of an ideal if I did not stand by these men and say of them what I hold to be true. If you back them up today they will be able to fight their own battles tomorrow, and perhaps to give you an example. I beseech you not to forsake these men.

Address by AE (George Russell) at Albert Hall, London, 1 November 1913.
Other speakers at the meeting included George Bernard Shaw, Charlotte Despard, Sylvia Pankhurst, James Connolly and Delia Larkin.

Glorious Dublin

Baton charges, prison cells, untimely death and acute starvation – all were faced without a murmer and in face of them all, the brave Dublin workers never lost faith in their ultimate triumph, never doubted but that their organisation would emerge victorious from the struggle. This is the great fact that many of our critics amongst the British Labour leaders seem to lose sight of. The Dublin fight is more than a trade union fight; it is a great class struggle, and recognised as such by all sides. We in Ireland feel that to doubt our victory would be to lose faith in the destiny of our class.

I heard of one case where a labourer was asked to sign the agreement forswearing the Irish Transport and General Workers' Union, and he told his employer, a small capitalist builder, that he refused to sign. The employer, knowing the man's circumstances, reminded him that he had a wife and six children who would be starving within a week. The reply of this humble labourer rose to the heights of sublimity. 'It is true, sir,' he said, 'they will starve; but I would rather see them go out one by one in their coffins than I should disgrace them by signing that.' And with head erect he walked out to share hunger and privation with his loved ones. Hunger and privation – and honour. Defeat, bah! How can such a people be defeated? His case is typical of thousands more.

Or think of the heroic women and girls. Did they care to evade the issue, they might have remained at work, for the first part of the agreement asks them to merely repudiate the Irish Transport and General Workers' Union, and as women, they are members of the Irish Women Workers' Union, not of the Irish Transport and General Workers' Union. But the second part pledges them to refuse to 'help' the Irish Transport and General Workers' Union – and in every shop, factory and sweating hellhole in Dublin, as the agreement is presented, they march out with pinched faces, threadbare clothes and miserable footwear, with high hopes, undaunted spirit, and glorious resolve shining out of their eyes. Happy the men who will secure such wives; thrice blessed the nation which has such girls as the future mothers of the race! Ah, comrades, it is good to have lived in Dublin in these days!

From an article by James Connolly in Forward *(Glasgow), 4 October 1913.*

In the Irish Worker, *18 November 1914 James Connolly wrote a long review of a recently-published book,* Disturbed Dublin, *by an English journalist, Arnold Wright, which had been commissioned by the Federated Dublin Employers.*

Connolly contrasted the treatment of the dispute by Wright with how another writer might have described the struggle:

Told by a labour writer, or even told by one of those literary men who, although not of the manual labour ranks stood so grandly by the workers during that titanic struggle, the story would indeed read like an epic, but it would be an epic of which the heroes and heroines were the humble men and women who went out in the street to suffer and starve rather than surrender their right to combine as they chose.

It will tell of how the general labourers, the men upon whose crushed lives is built the fair fabric of civilisation, from whose squalid tenements the sweet-smelling flowers of capitalist culture derive their aroma, by whose horny hands and mangled bodies are bought the ease and safety of a class that hates and despises them, by whose ignorance their masters purchase their knowledge – it will tell how these labourers dared to straighten their bent backs, and looking in the faces of their rulers and employers dared to express the will to be free. And it will tell how that spectacle of the slave of the underworld looking his masters in the face without terror, and fearlessly proclaiming the kinship and unity of all with each and each with all, how that spectacle caught the imagination of all unselfish souls so that the artisan took his place also in the place of conflict and danger, and the men and women of genius, the artistic and the literati, hastened to honour and serve those humble workers whom all had hitherto despised and scorned.

The battle was a drawn battle. The employers, despite their Napoleonic plan of campaign, and their more than Napoleonic ruthlessness and unscrupulous use of foul means, were unable to carry on their business without men and women who remained loyal to their union. The workers were unable to force the employers to a formal recognition of the union, and to give preference to organised labour. From the effects of this drawn battle both sides are still bearing scars. How deep those scars are none will ever reveal.

But the working class has lost none of its aggressiveness, none of its confidence, none of its hope in the ultimate triumph. No traitor amongst the ranks of that class has permanently gained, even materially, by his or her treachery. The flag of the Irish Transport and General Workers' Union still flies proudly in the van of the Irish working class, and that working class still marches proudly and defiantly at the head of the gathering hosts who stand for a regenerated nation, resting upon a people industrially free.

Ah, yes, that story of the Dublin dispute of 1913-1914 is meet subject for an epic poem with which some Irish genius of the future can win an immortality as great as did the humble fighters who in it fought the battle of labour.

From an article by James Connolly in the Irish Worker, *18 November 1914.*

Jim Larkin: His Life and Turbulent Times

Lord Askwith

A tall, thin man, with long dark hair and blue-grey mobile eyes, at that time (1907) wearing a very heavy black and drooping moustache, a large black sombrero hat, and a kind of black toga. He was an interesting man. 'I don't know how you can talk to that fellow Larkin,' said a Dublin employer at a later date. 'You can't argue with the prophet Isaiah.' It was not an inapt description of a man who came to believe he had a mission upon earth; and when one reflects, Isaiah must have been rather a difficult person and liable to go off at a tangent.

Larkin was adored in Dublin, as he had been in Belfast in 1907 and had about 10,000 members of his Union behind him, and at least 20,000 other supporters of both sexes and all ages. In a brief time the whole number was estimated at 80,000. It required but small observation to see that the conditions of Dublin were the chief source of its power.

Industrial Problems and Disputes (*London, 1920*)

Fred Bower

In my youth at school, there were two exciting periods each year, when lessons were forgotten in a creed feud. Liverpool then, not so much now, was divided into two camps, Orangemen (perfervid Protestants) and Catholics. It was a common sight on St Patrick's Day, or Orangeman's Day, 12 July, to see real gory battles between the sects. And we school children had our battles. Near my school was a Catholic school, and their leader, at that time, was a tall raw-boned Liverpool-born son of an Irishman. After school hours we would charge each other with sticks and stones. Sometimes we gave way, sometimes they. What with dodging the public, and the neighbours whose windows we were breaking, it was a great time. But, let that tall leader catch me by my-

247

self and I went through it. Two marks I will carry to the grave, where he cut my head open, or rather the skin that covers it.

Later Fred Bower and Jim Larkin – for he was the 'tall raw-boned Liverpool-born son of an Irishman' – both joined the local Socialist Party and were the best of comrades. Together they got a piece of tin and compressed a copy each of the *Clarion* and the *Labour Leader* of 24 June 1904 with a note written by Fred Bower, 'To the Finders, Hail!' and placed it in the foundations of Liverpool Anglican Cathedral at the point where the foundation stone was to be laid by King Edward VII on 19 July, 1904.

In 1907, Larkin invited me over to give a talk to his members in Belfast. There I saw a band composed of Orangemen and Catholics marching together, units all in one workers' army. As Jim and I lay abed together, that week, we had many things to talk of. In the boarding-house one day, the white-haired, motherly landlady said to me: 'Are you a Protestant'. 'Yes', I said, 'I was brought up so.' 'Well, do you know,' she went on, 'a month ago, I would have cut your throat before I would have let you enter my house. But Mr Larkin has changed all that.'

In 1911, Jim came over to Liverpool to bury his mother. Never had a mother such a worshipping son. As we came from the cemetery we sat together. Not a word was spoken, but I sensed his hurt.

Then in 1914 I had a visit from my old colleague, Jim Larkin. He was to sail to America and stayed his last night in Britain with me.

Rolling Stonemason *(London, 1936)*

The note that Bowers and Larkin buried in the foundations of the Cathedral read in part:

> We the wage slaves employed on the erection of this cathedral, to be dedicated to the worship of the unemployed Jewish carpenter, hail ye! Within a stone's throw from here, human beings are housed in slums not fit for swine ... Yours will indeed, compared to ours of today be a happier existence. See to it, therefore, that ye, too, work for the betterment of all, and so justify your existence by leaving the world the better for your having lived in it.

John W. Boyle

James Larkin is a figure from the heroic age of trade unionism. From 1907 to 1914, he dominated and transformed the Irish labour movement, infusing it with some of his own gospel of divine discontent. A close examination of his work shows that he organised skilfully, gathering members steadily and negotiating with considerable ability. But when he felt that a crisis was reached he would not give way.

Larkin was determined to establish the right of the labourer to join a union, and was prepared, if it was not conceded, to invoke his doctrine of 'tainted goods' and use the weapon of the sympathetic strike. These tactics called forth his superb gifts as an agitator and incidentally created in the minds of his enemies the image of Larkin as a destructive force. It is true that the organisation proper suffered in these struggles and that the work of his successors consisted of consolidation before expansion, but without Larkin's initial efforts there would have been nothing to build on.

His desire for a socialist society was strong, even if he saw it in less precise detail than his fellow-unionist Connolly. Unlike him he left no body of doctrine – he had not Connolly's powers of detachment or analysis – but what he wrote is still worth reading for his telling phrases, its hatred of cruelty and oppression and its passionate desire for justice, as the files of his paper, the *Irish Worker*, bear witness.

Leaders and Workers *(Cork, 1963)*

John Boyle is the author of The Irish Labor Movement in the Nineteenth Century *(Washington, 1988).*

Jack Carney

We were sitting together in Jim's Chicago flat when the word came through that Tom Mooney had been sentenced to death.[1] The American edition of the *Irish Worker* was about to go to press. Jim rushed to the telephone and ordered the printers to hold up the paper. Then he asked me to get to the typewriter and there and then he dictated one of the most powerful editorials it

---

1. Tom Mooney (1882-1942), a Californian labour leader, was convicted and sentenced to death for alleged responsibility for a bomb explosion during a 'Preparedness Day' parade in San Francisco on 16 July 1916 in which nine people were killed. The sentence was commuted but he served twenty years in jail before being pardoned in 1936.

has been my privilege to read and in my life I have both read and written quite a few. I remember the title: 'Irish Worker'.

Jim did not rest. He telephoned to all the delegates he knew in the Chicago Federation of Labour. He held a meeting of them in his flat and in the afternoon he went to the weekly meeting of the CFL and through the support of John Fitzpatrick, its President, a blacksmith from Athlone, a Tom Mooney Release Committee was organised. I was elected Secretary. Within a week the members of the Committee had addressed more than a hundred union meetings. In addition, Jim telegraphed to every city where the Irish were strong and inside a week the United States was covered with Tom Mooney Release Committees. Jim's actions in the case of Tom Mooney did not improve his relations with official labour in America, but the son of an Irish mother was in grave peril of his life and what else mattered, said Jim.

Without fear of contradiction I make bold to say that more than any other man, Jim Larkin was responsible for the release of Tom Mooney.

Jim could not remain long in Chicago. He toured the United States addressing mass meetings and giving striking workers the benefit of his advice. Gunmen followed him from town to town but Jim knew no fear. In Butte, Montana, the Irish lads organised a guard for him. Each night they would maintain guard outside the place where he was sleeping. One night they were surprised to find him coming in at 3 a.m. He had been for a walk around the town. The miners of Butte worshipped him. They had never known such courage and fearlessness. Butte is no seaside resort. In those days the Anaconda Mining Co., the only firm in Butte, employed an army of gunmen more than a thousand strong. They thought nothing of taking a leader of the workers out and hanging him to a railroad trestle so that in the morning the workers would see the hanging body of their leader as they went to work in the mines.[2]

***

2. One such IWW leader who was taken out and hanged was Frank Little. Jim Larkin had been with him in Butte in the days before the lynching. Elizabeth Gurley Flynn describes Little as 'tall and dark, with black hair and black eyes, a slender, gentle and soft-spoken man'. He was half-Cherokee Indian, one-eyed, one-legged (by the time he came to Butte) and 'all Wobbly'. On 1 August 1917 masked gunmen took the crippled Frank Little from his bed, tied a rope round his neck and dragged him to the outskirts of Butte where they strung him up from a railroad trestle.

Jack Carney worked with Jim Larkin in Liberty Hall, the head-quarters of the ITGWU and helped him edit the *Irish Worker*. He was born in Liverpool as was Larkin and had been converted to Socialism by him in Widnes, near Liverpool in 1906. He went to America in 1916 and helped Larkin to get out an American edition of the *Irish Worker* in Chicago.

In December 1919, Jack Carney, then editing a labour paper, *The Truth*, in Duluth, Minnesota was arrested and charged with 'wilfully attempting to obstruct the recruiting and enlistment service of the U.S. by publishing a certain weekly paper known as *Truth* containing an article entitled 'Hands off Russia'. The campaign for Carney's release was led by Eugene Debs who wrote of Carney:

> There is not a truer spirit, a more uncompromising soul in the labor movement than Jack Carney. I know him and love him. He never falters, never wavers, never turns his face from the enemy. He is true to the core of his great heart to the working class. He has never weakened, never whimpered, and never for one moment dipped his colors to the enemy. He has stood like the warrior he is, through the thickest of the battle, and there he stands today.

Eugene V. Debs (1855-1926) – the greatest of American labour leaders – had been the perennial Socialist Party candidate for President, polling 900,000 votes (6 per cent) in 1912. Both Jim Larkin and Jack Carney spoke with Debs in his birthplace, Terre Haute, Indiana, during his campaign for election to Congress in 1916.

In the Preface to his biography of Larkin, Professor Emmet Larkin, acknowledges the contribution made by Jack Carney:

> Jack Carney more than anyone else, gave me an understanding of what Jim Larkin was all about. No one, perhaps, knew Larkin better than he did, and though a warm and passionate admirer, he was never blind to the faults and defects in that great man. Jack Carney, then, saw Larkin whole and best.

At Professor Larkin's request, Carney wrote a nineteen-page Memoir of Larkin in May 1953. This memoir has not been published.

When Larkin was deported from America in April 1923, Carney signed on as a French chef on the *S.S. Majestic* on which Larkin was sailing. In the Memoir he recalled that they did not mind his not being French, but when they found out that he was not even a chef, they put him to work stoking the boilers.

Back in Dublin, Carney remained a colleague of Larkin, working with him in the Workers' Union of Ireland from 1924 and helping to edit a new series of the *Irish Worker* in 1925-26 and 1930-32. He accompanied Larkin on his second visit to the Soviet Union to attend a meeting of the Executive Committee of the Comintern. In the Memoir, Carney recalled Larkin speaking at a meeting of the Moscow Soviet of which he was a member, and how he held the 2,000 people present, very few of them understanding English, 'in the hollow of his hand'. He also recalled a discussion between Bukharin, the leader of the Comintern (he was executed in Stalin's purge of the old Bolsheviks in 1937) and Larkin when Larkin insisted, to Bukharin's surprise, that he had Faith that there was a God and that he would hold to such a Faith until he had been proved to be wrong.

During the Spanish Civil War, the Executive Committee of the Workers' Union of Ireland, of which Carney was an official, passed a resolution forbidding officials of the union from appearing on any but a trade union platform. (Carney had spoken at meetings in support of the Spanish Republicans). This decision of the union must be seen in the context of the atmosphere of the time and the hysterical support for Franco's rebellion against the legitimate government in Spain, by the Catholic Church and elements in the Fine Gael opposition, the isolation of the WUI in the trade union movement and the fierce antagonism to it of some of the most powerful figures in the movement.

Carney resigned his position in the union and went to London where he became a freelance journalist. Some 150 or so letters from Sean O'Casey to Jack Carney are included in David Krause's *Letters from Sean O'Casey*. (Letters written after 1942 are in Volume II and letters written before 1942 in Volume III.)

Jack Carney died in 1956 at the age of sixty-eight.

***

Mina Carney, Jack Carney's wife, an American artist, was a leader of the Larkin Defense Committee, who towards the end of 1922 after Larkin had served over two years, was collecting signatures of leading people for a petition to Governor Miller of New York for a free pardon for Larkin. One of the signatories she secured was that of the famous Father Duffy, the chaplain of the 'Fighting 69th'.

A bust of Jim Larkin by Mina Carney is in the Lane Municipal Art Gallery, Dublin. She died in 1974 in her early eighties.

Charles Chaplin

The last day in New York, I visited Sing-Sing with Frank Harris. Jim Larkin, the Irish rebel and labour union organiser, was serving five years in Sing-Sing, and Frank wanted to see him. Larkin was a brilliant orator who had been sentenced by a prejudiced judge and jury on false charges of attempting to overthrow the Government, so Frank claimed, and this was proved later when Governor Al Smith quashed the sentence, though Larkin had already served years of it.

Prisons have a strange atmosphere, as if the human spirit were suspended. At Sing-Sing the old cell blocks were grimly medieval: small, narrow stone chambers crowded with four to six inmates sleeping in each cell. What fiendish brain could conceive of building such horrors!

Frank inquired about Jim Larkin and the warder agreed that we could see him; although it was against the rules, he would make an exception. Larkin was in the shoe factory, and here he greeted us, a tall handsome man, about six foot four, with piercing blue eyes but a gentle smile.

Although happy to see Frank, he was nervous and disturbed and was anxious to get back to his bench. Even the warder's assurance would not allay his uneasiness. 'It's bad morally for the other prisoners if I'm privileged to see visitors during working hours,' said Larkin. Frank asked him how he was treated and if there was anything he could do for him. He said he was treated reasonably well, but he was worried about his wife and family in Ireland, whom he had not heard from since his confinement. Frank promised to help him. After we left, Frank said it depressed him to see a courageous, flamboyant character like Jim Larkin reduced to prison discipline.

My Autobiography (*London, 1964*)

Charles Chaplin (1889-1977) The greatest comedian of all time. His films such as City Lights, The Great Dictator *and* Limelight *are among the classics of world cinema.*

Ralph Chaplin

It was at 817½ North Clark Street, in the Radical Book Shop, that Bill Haywood during his first year in Chicago, used to spend evenings with a small group of friends and kindred spirits around an old round-bellied stove back of the book counter in the rear of the store. Jim Larkin came here to meet Bill for interminable arguments about class-struggle philosophy and strategy. Carl Sandburg (who had recently moved to Chicago from Milwaukee, where he had worked on Victor Berger's Socialist *Leader*), would drop in now and then for bits of labour news for the *Day Book*. The Radical Book Shop was a hangout for radicals of all shades of red and black, as well as for the Near North Side intelligentsia.

I recall one evening when Professor Hoxie of the University of Chicago (a social scientist) brought his class in economics to the Wobbly hall for first hand information about itinerant harvest workers. There were plenty of questions, not a few from Professor Hoxie himself. On the whole, I believe the college crowd, student body and faculty members alike, learned more from the stiffs than the stiffs ever learned from them. Even Professor Robert Morss Lovett, who always made a point of frequenting I.W.W. meetings, admitted that Jim Larkin, the Irish longshore leader, could always attract a larger crowd to our educational meetings than any professor in town. We put on a big entertainment one Saturday night, Larkin telling funny stories before and after his short speech. He got much applause.

Wobbly The Rough-and-Tumble Story of an American Radical (*Chicago, 1948*)

Ralph Chaplin was the author of Solidarity Forever (*see page 324*).

Jesse D. Clarkson

Larkin was ever able at a moment's notice to mingle blistering epithets with literary and classical allusions, knit together with a thoroughly Irish native humour. His outstanding characteristics throughout his life were his quick sympathy for all the downtrodden and his flaming resentment for all forms of injustice. The magnetism and courage that poured from him and the independent life and vigour that surged up among the apparently hopeless casual labourers of Dublin, Belfast, Cork and other Irish towns are well-known phenomena.

From its meagre beginnings (its original assets were a table, a couple of chairs, two empty bottles, and a candle – the Larkin family furniture on occasion was sold to eke out strike pay), the ITGWU rose swiftly to dominate the Irish Trades Union Congress and become the backbone of the nascent Irish Labour Party.

Larkin has sometimes been characterised as a revolutionary syndicalist. Certainly he brought to Ireland the 'new unionism' with all its syndicalist implications. Certainly his methods and his intent were revolutionary, both in Ireland and in America. Yet he regarded himself not as a syndicalist, but as a socialist. He was widely read in socialist literature, but he had an instinctive distrust of any nicely worked-out philosophy. His own activities were ever concerned with trade unions, though not in the old bowler-hatted sense. No mere apostle of divine discontent, he had ever in mind practical existing conditions – and the desire to remedy them in the here and now.

Larkin's nationalism was innate and intense.

Big Jim rose above all 'isms'. He was simply an outstanding human being – a man of universal stature, physically and spiritually – who acted in accord with no jelled body of doctrines, who acted intuitively, sometimes blunderingly but always honestly and fearlessly, in tune with the warmth and breadth of his own nature.

Big Jim Larkin – Footnote to Nationalism, in Nationalism and Internationalism, *edited by Edward Mead Earle (New York, 1950)*

J. Dunsmore Clarkson was the author of Labour and Nationalism in Ireland *(New York, 1925).*

James Connolly

As I am writing, the workers of Dublin are rejoicing over the fact that Larkin has withdrawn his resignation which he handed in during the past week. Instantly it became known, a general

255

meeting was called at the Croydon Park to consider the situation. The feeling of the meeting, and the general interpretation of the real nature of the crisis is, I think, best summed up in the following quotation from my own speech on that occasion.

James Connolly asked them to remember that, for seven years, working for the Union, Jim Larkin had every day done ten men's work. He had carried on his own shoulders not only his own responsibilities, but with his intense desire to see everything well done, had taken on himself, with his overflowing fund of energy, manual work and petty detail work that should have been done by others. That could not last.

He knew the working class of Dublin before Larkin came. He knew them as slaves, most slavish industrially when they were most truculent politically. Contrast that with the heroism they displayed in the recent fight. Jim Larkin had put courage into them, lifted them to their feet, taught them not only their rights, but their duty (which the English Labour leaders were afraid to teach them) to stand by one another.

If there was any friction it meant that the men to whom Larkin had given new power and dignity were taking an active interest in every detail of the Union's work instead of leaving Jim to carry it all on his shoulders. The price Jim had paid was that he had broken down physically, run down mentally, and almost worn out. Overstrained by anxiety, he, perhaps, saw opposition where there was only an anxious desire to help him.

Let them not only tell him they wanted him back, but that they were more worthy of him than when he came. Let them not – 'We'll be beaten if you go', but let them tell him: 'We were slaves; you made men of us. You trained us to fight but without you we could never carry on so magnificent, so successful a fight.'

They would not accept his resignation, but they were prepared to give him a rest. If he were to go to America and raise funds for the new Irish Labour Party it would recuperate him, and he would be back in seven days, if needed. They had amongst them a man of genius, of splendid vitality, great in his conceptions, magnificent in his courage. Were they to waste this great force in a few months or years? ('No') Let them give him every possibility of recuperating his strength. They would not part with Jim, but would always co-operate with him in the spirit of loyal comrades.

Another general meeting was held in the Antient Concert Rooms, when, with his own consent, and to the intense gratification of the members, the letter of resignation was burnt on the platform.

Forward (*Glasgow*), 27 June 1914

After spending seven years in the United States, James Connolly returned to Ireland in 1910 and the following year was appointed the Belfast organiser and Ulster district secretary of the ITGWU. On his departure for Amercia in October 1914, Larkin nominated Connolly as the acting general secretary of the Union. He was elected to the National Executive of Congress in 1914.

Daniel Corkery

I took him to be a man of ideas, some of them wrong but most of them right, or at least right according to my lights. I saw in him a powerful advocate of temperance and an apostle of nationality. I regarded him as one earnest to a fault, for I never heard him speak to the class for which he stood that he did not half offend them by dwelling on the failings which kept them powerless and timid. And in my estimate was much of pity, because I saw that the man stood alone and guideless; by dint of experience, he had slept in every workhouse from Land's End to John-O-Groats; by dint of reading it was his custom to quote poetry as freely as I would myself if I had more courage; by brooding and thinking on problems that for his companions must practically have had no existence – he had raised himself so much above his fellows that he deceived himself if he believed he could find lieutenants in their ranks. Here is a drama for any Ibsen that cares to write it – the failure of a leader of the democracy to find lieutenants.

The Leader (*Dublin*), 1 July 1910

Daniel Corkery (1878-1964) was the author of The Labour Leader *(1920) and other plays,* The Threshold of Quiet *(1915) and, most famously,* The Hidden Ireland *(1925).*

Dr Clancy, Bishop of Achonry

I avail myself of this opportunity to state that his (Larkin's) public utterances since he assumed to himself a prominent position in the direction of Irish affairs have been distinctly of a socialistic tendency; that in consequence he is distrusted by the members of the Irish Parliamentary Party, and that his name is associated in many minds with incidents which render it highly undesirable that the good people of Sligo should allow themselves to be allured into a false position by his pretended sympathy with the poor. I therefore expect and hope that no respectable citizen of our town or country and no faithful member of the Church will take part in the meeting at which this man is advertised to speak.

Extract from letter from the Bishop of Achonry read at all Masses in Churches in Sligo in March 1912, quoted in W. P. Ryan, The Irish Labour Movement *(Dublin and London, 1919).*
Jim Larkin was in the congregation when the letter was read.

Rev. M. J. Curran

The disorder here has grown very seriously since Saturday. It is no longer a question of a tram strike. It is simply the scum of our slums versus the police. Unfortunately the mob have the sympathy of the working classes and nobody helps the police. I think it is a scandal that the military have not yet been utilised. It would free the hands of the police immensely if the soldiers were stationed on the principal thoroughfares.

It is really surprising to see how much support Larkin commands among the artisans. Even the printers who refused to come out on strike at his command are very largely (loyal) to him. The workmen have gone mad over Larkin and will do almost anything for him, even respectable carpenters and bricklayers.

Rev. M. J. Curran was the Secretary to the Archbishop of Dublin, Dr William Walsh.

George Dangerfield

Larkin had begun to make his living, at the age of eleven, in one of the most viciously slum-ridden and criminal cities in Europe (Liverpool). Bellicose and imaginative, vindictive and compassionate, Larkin was a marvellous extrusion from that dreadful environment, above which he rose by sheer force of character, and which he longed to dispel.

He was a tall, ungainly man, with blue-black hair and burning eyes. He had a quick wit, an immense voice, a marvellous rhetoric, all uttered in a harsh Liverpool accent. 'You cannot argue with the prophet Isaiah,' said one Dublin employer, after an unprofitable exchange of words with Larkin: but if ever a social Isaiah was needed, surely he was needed here.

Nearly 26,000 families out of a city of 300,000 were huddled together in the Dublin slums, the verminous haunts of drunkenness, immorality, disease and crime. It is no wonder that the Dublin death rate was a horrible 24.8 per thousand, chiefly due to infant mortality and tuberculosis, both higher than anything that could be found in Great Britain, itself no sanitary paradise. And at the root of all this lay unemployment, casual employment, sweated labour, social indifference, and the Dublin Corporation, one of the most corrupt city governments in all Europe.

It is not hard to imagine how inconvenient, to say the least, was the proletarian voice of James Larkin, echoing and re-echoing in such an environment. Larkin was a virtuoso in the use of sympathetic strikes, to which Dublin as a trading city was especially vulnerable. It was for his deployment of such strikes and for his belief in one big union that Larkin was labelled a Syndicalist – a heady word in those days.

Whether he really was one is another matter. Since it meant 'Trade Unionism' and implied a belief in class warfare as a fact of life, in the primacy of production, and in the crying need for economic activism, then in these terms Larkin was a Syndicalist indeed. One thing, at any rate, is certain: his importance to the history of Irish insurrection is that he brought revolution into Dublin and this revolution had a distinctly nationalist tendency.

The Damnable Question: A Study in Anglo-Irish Relations (*London*, *1976*)

Gabriel Fallon

Came a trouble maker called James Larkin, a rabble-rouser if ever there was one, a man with a mission and one armed with the vituperative power of a Leon Bloy. Like Bloy he was on the side of the poor, the downtrodden, the oppressed.

He began to organise the workers, to instil into them the knowledge that they were men and not slaves: he was determined that they should walk erect and not on all fours like beasts of burden. He wanted to give them back their place in society and their dignity as creatures formed in the image of God.

Well-to-do Dublin organised itself against him. Pulpits thundered against his socialism. It was considered that the sacred rights of private property were in danger. No one seemingly knew enough of Aquinas to proclaim the fact that the possession of property carried with it duties as well as rights.

But Larkin raged on, declaring that he spoke and acted in the spirit of the Beatitudes. He was immediately dubbed 'Anti-Christ'.

A paper calling itself Catholic asked if the rats that infested the Dublin tenements were to be allowed to dictate to the respectable citizens of Dublin. Trade unionism took on the scarlet of a newly-discovered deadly sin. Then came the great Lock-Out and thanks to Larkin the hungry children of Dublin's workers were fed by the trade unionists of England.

This in itself was bad enough but the move to send the children to England set the devil's seal on this man's work. Now the Faith was in danger.

The pulpits thundered anew. With the honourable exception of a handful of priests – all of them regulars – the voice of every cleric in the diocese was set against the Red Hand of Larkin and his Union. Hymn-singing bands of Confraternity men marched down the quays determined to snatch from eternal perdition those children whom this Anti-Christ was attempting to deport.

Hibernia *(Dublin), August 1963*

Gabriel Fallon (1898-1983) had parts in the first productions of the early plays of Sean O'Casey at the Abbey Theatre in the 1920s. Director of the Abbey Theatre 1959-74. Drama critic and author of Sean O'Casey: the Man I Knew *(1965).*

James T. Farrell

Larkin was emotional, impetuous, violent, extravagant. In his speeches and in his actions, he was an improviser. He did not stop to reason or to plan. He spoke with a rapid flow, with sweeping gestures. His speeches were filled with hyperbole, with castigation, with acidity, with sentimentality, and with rousing appeals. In one speech he declaimed that it was his divine mission to preach subversion and discontent to the working classes. This more than suggests his style. He was brave to the point of foolhardiness, and he was self-sacrificing. Again and again, he was ready and willing to give up his life and be a martyr of the working class. In his great days as an organiser and agitator, he lived a life of danger. He gave his services to the struggle for the emancipation of the working class of the world: at the same time, he refused to appear on the same platform with an American Socialist of international repute because this man was divorced!

In a period when the most depressed sections of the Irish working class were militant, he was peculiarly fitted to play the role of agitator. His ability to lash their enemies, and to rouse and stir them, enabled him to appeal to their manhood, to the will to freedom which slept within their hearts. He added his own daring example to the appeal of his words. And when he led these workers in strikes he was adamant, uncompromising, and in the forefront when danger lurked. His bravery and daring were as extravagant as his foibles. But in a period of letdown, of retreat, of the sodden rule of the middle classes and the clergymen in Ireland, he was like a lost child. In the slums of Dublin after 'the Troubles', he could not repeat what he had done in this same area in the early days of this century. This was apparent when I saw him in Dublin in 1938. He was embittered.

Now this man is no more. He was a brave soldier of the working class. He was a great agitator. He gave his spirit, and the best years of his life in their service. Karl Marx spoke of the great heart of the proletariat in his pamphlet on the Civil War in France. Jim Larkin came from this great heart. One bows one's head in memory of this brave Irish labour leader.

The essay, from which the above was extracted, appeared in New International 13 *(March 1947) as 'Jim Larkin, Irish Revolutionist: Fighter for Freedom and Socialism'. In revised form it was included as 'Lest we Forget: Jim Larkin, Irish Labour Leader' in* James T Farrell: On Irish *Themes, edited by Dennis Flynn (University of Pennsylvania Press, Philadelphia, 1982).*

James T. Farrell (1904-1979) was the major Chicago writer, author of 'Studs Lonigan', and other notable novels. He met Larkin on his visit to Dublin in 1938 and after his return to America wrote at length about him in a letter to Leon Trotsky. In the letter (13 December 1938), he wrote:

261

This summer I was in Ireland and I saw Jim Larkin. All men have weaknesses, but all men are not the victims of their weaknesses. Jim Larkin is a victim of his own weaknesses, and his own temperament. He is untheoretical and unstable intellectually. He is always a direct actionist, and his direct actionism takes whatever turn that his impulses lead him toward. He is very garrulous, human and humane, witty, vindictive, vituperative, and he is Irish. At times, he is almost like an embittered version of the stage Irishman. Larkin was a great and courageous agitator, but not a leader of a defeated army, and he could not work with anyone. Gradually, he lost influence, and now he is old and embittered.

Farrell was a leader of the Fourth International.

Chris Ferguson

So Larkin looks to Dublin. Instinctively he knows that this is the road to Golgatha – one that requires supreme moral courage. The need for unusual physical courage merely makes him smile. He realises the difficulty of organising in a city where only small numbers of craftsmen were organised. The large mass of working people in Dublin were regarded as unskilled labourers. The overwhelming majority of men earned 12s a week and lived with their families in one-roomed tenements in unparalleled squalor. They were spiritless, lacking in character and self-respect.

It seemed that when Larkin first came to Dublin he was faced with an impossible task. Larkin, the rebel incarnate, was confronted with a dumb, driven and inarticulate working class. He would be impatient, unsympathetic. How could he understand their needs and their attitude to the world? Strangely enough the critics of Larkin often overlook his first spectacular battle. His first appeal to the working class was so effective that at once, with one tremendous gesture, he brought out everything that was fine not only in the workers but also in their wives. Larkin's first demand was that certain workers should be paid on the job and not in the public house.

Everybody knows the history of 1913. We have learned of that sudden resurgence of the working class and the unanimity of employers in their endeavours to crush Larkin and root out Larkinism. The man was violating justice and charity! He was guilty of proselytism because the working people of Britain offered to take Irish children and feed them while the lock-out was in progress! The kids, by the way, were lustily singing 'I

262

want to join Jim Larkin's Union,' and a less printable song about Boss Murphy's cat. This indeed was a genius. He could mobilise not only the men, but their wives and children.

Truly Larkin taught the working people of Dublin to rise from their knees and stand upon their feet.

Impact (Dublin), April 1951

The editorial board of Impact *included Liam Carlin, Chris Ferguson, David Greene, Sheila Greene, Brian Inglis, Donal Nevin, John O'Donovan, Ruaidhri Roberts and Patricia Rushton. The journal was published by Freeman Publications Ltd., the shares of which were held by the Irish TUC.*

Chris Ferguson was the National Organiser of the Workers' Union of Ireland from 1948 until his death in 1957.

Elizabeth Gurley Flynn

One day in 1914, a knock came on our door at 511 East 134th Street, in the Bronx. We lived up three flights of stairs and the bell was usually out of order. There stood a gaunt man, with a rough-hewn face and a shock of greying hair, who spoke with an Irish accent. He asked for Mrs Flynn. When my mother went to the door, he said simply: 'I'm Jim Larkin. James Connolly sent me.'

Larkin was a magnificent orator and an agitator without equal. He spoke at anti-war meetings, where he thundered against British imperialism's attempt to drag us into it. My mother gave him the green banner of the Irish Socialist Federation and he spoke under it innumerable times, especially on the New York waterfront.

I Speak My Own Piece (New York, 1955)

Elizabeth Gurley Flynn was The Rebel Girl about whom Joe Hill wrote his famous song (see page 317).

R. M. Fox

Into this underworld of Dublin came Jim Larkin, restless, eager, militant – a vital force expressing a burning indignation against social injustice and calling for revolt. To the conservative-minded employers he came as a dreaded, lurid 'strike organiser'.

His methods were crude – as crude as the evils he attacked. Whether Larkin roused hatred or enthusiasm none could deny that he was a force, and that with his coming the whole of the submerged element of Irish Labour stirred. He was a crater through which the rumble of social discontents poured out. The feeling of hopeless stagnation gave place to agitation and unrest.

Always Larkin relied upon defiance, upon individuality, upon a sense of justice and indignation which enabled him to triumph over wrong and to enthuse his followers. Looking at Larkin and listening to him they came to believe in their own strength and they developed a feeling of self-reliance which they never possessed before. It was to the human will and the human spirit that Larkin made his direct appeal.

He was a man of passionate sincerity and rugged poetic eloquence. I often listened to him, framed in the big window of Liberty Hall, one foot up on the sill, his arms holding each side, while a blur of white faces in Beresford Place shone through the gloom. Sometimes a train would thunder across the bridge and passengers, leaning out, would cry 'Up Larkin' as it rumbled by. He would acknowledge this by a wave of the hand and sweep away a stray lock of grey hair which tumbled over one eye.

R. M. Fox (1899-1969) was the author of The History of the Irish Citizen Army *(1943),* Connolly the Forerunner *(1947),* Jim Larkin: The Rise of the Underman *(1957), and* Louie Bennett: Her Life and Times *(1958).*

William Gallacher

Few are the workers anywhere who haven't heard or read of the name of Jim Larkin. But only those who actually lived through the period prior to the war of 1914 can truly appreciate the courage, determination and incorruptibility of this great son of the Irish working class.

Big he was in physique, Big Jim Larkin, but bigger still in his mighty desire to free the Irish working class from the terrible bondage of poverty and degradation, which was forced upon it by the ruthless exploiters of Ireland.

His battle for the right to organise, the great strikes and mass demonstrations, all inspired by his lion-hearted courage, represent an epic in Irish history.

I remember well when he came over to Britain how he elec-
trified not only the Irish workers driven from their native land,
but all workers who had the opportunity of hearing him.

Review *(Dublin), March 1947*

*William Gallacher was a Communist MP in the House of Commons from 1935
to 1950.*

David Garnett

Jim Larkin was an Irish labourer of magnificent physique, considerably over six feet in height. Soon after he began to speak
there was a noise outside (the Albert Hall, London), one of the
doors was burst open and three Royal School of Mines students
flung themselves into the hall ... The interruptions had roused
Jim Larkin to fury. He walked up and down the platform like a
caged tiger and his tremendous voice roared out angrily. Once
the sound of fighting somewhere outside the hall penetrated, but
Larkin roared a little louder, telling us of the infamies of the
Dublin employers and the corruption of the city fathers.

Golden Echo *(London, 1970)*

Elsewhere, David Garnett, author of Lady into Fox *(1923) and three
volumes of autobiography has written of Larkin:*

> Larkin was the finest orator I have ever heard, just as Chaliapin was
> the finest singer – and for the same physical reasons. Larkin was, I
> believe, actually taller than Chaliapin and could have out-roared
> the Russian. There was no fat on him. He was absolutely unselfcon-
> scious and seemed to care nothing for his audience. He was deadly
> in earnest and, walking up and down like an infuriated tiger, he
> roared out his message of defiance to the capitalist system and of
> death to Murphy. There striding about the platform one beheld the
> whole of the sweated, starved, exploited working class suddenly
> incarnate in the shape of a gigantic Tarzan of all the slum jungles of
> the West.

Keir Hardie

Why is Larkin so much feared by the employing classes in
Dublin? I shall tell you. It is because he has got down to the
foundation and the whole superstructure rises with the found-

ation. Yes, and the employers know it. The one man and the one movement which has shown how to get better pay for the down-trodden is Jim Larkin and his policy. They say they don't like Larkin's methods, very likely not. When you go down to a dentist with a bad tooth his methods are not very agreeable but you get the tooth out and then comes relief.

Jim Larkin's methods are not those of the rose leaf or the kid glove. He is a man with more heart than head as any good man the world has ever seen, has been. He doesn't sit down and calculate and weigh up chances. He sees a wrong to be righted and by God, Jim Larkin is going to do it.

From a speech in Liberty Hall, 3 September 1913, following the funeral of James Nolan who had been killed by the police in a baton charge.

Keir Hardie was the first independent Labour MP in the House of Commons and the first leader of the Parliamentary Labour Party in Britain.

Frank Harris

It is difficult to meet Larkin, even casually, without becoming interested in him. He is very tall, well over six feet, loose built, with the figure of a youth. His hair is greying and there are lines abut the eyes and mouth that tell of middle-age. The large grey eyes, however, are still laughing and boyish and the mobile lips humorous, persuasive; the features are all well-cut, Greek rather than Celtic; a very quiet, unassuming, rather handsome fellow, with sympathetic, conciliatory manners. He spoke admirable, quiet English, the English of a well-read man with a gift of fluent expression.

His choice of words reminded me of Galsworthy, his facility of Bernard Shaw. And the marvel was that what he said was as good as his easy way of saying it. He understood labour con-ditions in Ireland and England and the United States better than anyone with whom I have ever talked – a singularly wise, fair, fine mind, the equal of the best politicians I have met in Wash-ington or in France or even in England, where the politician is sometimes almost a statesman. I say, deliberately, there is no company of the most distinguished in the world where Jim Lar-kin would not hold his own and have his place.

One morning, quite unexpectedly, I was called to the 'phone by Charlie Chaplin's friend and secretary, Tom Harrington:

'Charlie wants to know would you go with him to visit Sing-Sing?' 'Come, of course, I'll go.'

At the prison I spoke to Mr Henzel, the head teacher. 'You know I have to examine all prisoners to find out how they are educated,' Mr Henzel said, 'so I asked Larkin where he had been educated and how many years he had gone to school. He replied casually: "Oh my school days were very short, you can take it that I am unlettered." That "unlettered" told me a great deal, and I soon found out that, wherever he had got his education, he had got a good deal of it.'

'He is one of God's spies,' I cried warmly. 'A wonderful man. He has got the manners of a great gentleman; you have no idea how perfectly he bore himself at the trial, though there were insulting interruptions from the judge at every moment – uncalled for and malevolent when they were not stupid. Not only has he manners and reading, but wisdom and kindness to boot – an extraordinary man, a great man. He and Debs both in prison. Could any criticism of American government be more damning!'

'They were afraid at first,' said Henzel, 'that he might use radical propaganda on the prisoners. If they only knew, this is a worse place for radical propaganda than even Wall Street. The prisoners all think Larkin a damned fool for having come here just because he would stand up for others. "What have the workmen ever done for him", they say, "the poor boob!" They all think him rather a fool. And you call him one of the noblest.'

'Yes' I said. 'We are told pretty early in life to let well alone. It is a good proverb, but no one tells us that it is still more dangerous not to leave ill alone. That's Jim Larkin's fault. He couldn't sit still and see the wrong triumph.'

We went into the boot place. Mr Joyce (the superintendent of the industries) was explaining in advance to Charlie Chaplin all about the making of boots; I with eyes for only one man, for one figure. Suddenly on the other side of the room I caught sight of him. I went across, and our hands met.

'Jim', I cried, 'I have done my best again and again, but our Government is brutally indifferent!'

'You never sent me your books,' he said.

'I sent them, Jim,' I cried, 'but you shall have them again.'

'I know,' said Jim, 'I know!'

'How are you in health?' I asked.

'Fine,' he said, carelessly raising himself to his full six feet two and throwing out his great chest.

267

'But you broke your leg?' I questioned again.

'It's first-rate now, they patched it up; I'm all right; but (this in a whisper) is there any chance they might deport us? I want to get back to my people.'

'I'll see what can be done', I said, 'you may be sure. We'll all do what we can.'

'I know, I know.'

'I want you meet Charlie Chaplin,' I said, so I brought Charlie across the room and they shook hands. Jim at once excused himself.

'I had better go off,' he said. He didn't want to take up the time of the great visitor; he is the most courteous of gentlemen, with the best of manners – heart manners.

Contemporary Portraits, Fourth Series (London, 1924)

Frank Harris (1855-1931) was born in Galway. Writer and editor. First biographer of Oscar Wilde (1920) and George Bernard Shaw (1931), he also wrote a biography of Shakespeare. Notoriously (at the time) he was the author of My Life and Loves *(1925 seq.).*

Bill Haywood

I had been in Paris not more than a week when I got a telegram from the *Daily Herald* in London asking me to come and speak on behalf of Jim Larkin, who was then in Mountjoy Prison. I went to see the officials of the Confederation of Labour and told them I was going to England on behalf of Jim Larkin and the Dublin Transport Workers' strike, and that I would like a testimonial from France to the Dublin strikers – something that the strikers could use. They gave me a check for a thousand francs, a large contribution considering the condition of the workers of France at that time.

When I arrived in London a meeting was arranged in the Albert Hall. Larkin was released from prison in time to speak at what proved to be a wonderful meeting. Twenty-five or thirty thousand people, more than could get in the hall, had gathered. Some students attempted to disrupt the meeting but the stewards or ushers were well organised and ejected the noisy bunch in quick order. A son of George Lansbury came over the railing of the first balcony and dropped into a struggling group which was fighting to get into the aisle.

The speakers were Lansbury, Cunningham-Graham, Dyson, Larkin, myself and others. Jim Larkin is a big bony man with a shock of iron-grey hair and marked features such as are appreciated by the sculptor or cartoonist. He is a vigorous speaker and this meeting was the beginning of a crusade that he called the 'Fiery Cross'. I have never spoken in any meeting with more satisfaction than in this auditorium.

Connolly asked me to go to Belfast where he said a big meeting could be arranged. Peter Larkin, a brother of Jim, was there at the time. But I was already billed for Liverpool and returned there to speak to an enthusiastic crowd. The next day on the train Jim spent much of his time reading Rabelais. At Manchester we had a fine meeting in Free Trade Hall.

Bill Haywood's Book: The Autobiography of William D. Haywood,
(London, 1929)

Bill Haywood (1869-1928) was one of the founders of the Industrial Workers of the World (Wobblies) and became its General Secretary in 1914.

Tommy Healy

I was in Liberty Hall one night and a woman came in with a child in her arms, and enquired for Mr Larkin. She was shown upstairs to room Number Seven. She reported to Larkin that her husband was in a public house drinking and she had nothing for the children. Mr Larkin came down the stairs like a lion. I was standing on the steps of Liberty Hall, and he caught me by the arm and brought me along with him. He brought me down the South Quays and we came to Pat Butler's Public House. He went in there. There were about seventy men drinking there. He cleared the public house in less than five minutes. These men were dockers and they used to be paid in Pat Butler's public house when their day's work was over. Mr Larkin stopped the payment in public houses and no docker has ever been paid in a public house since.

Tommy Healy was working in Liverpool in 1892 when he first heard Jim Larkin speak at a meeting. Returning to Ireland, he went to work in the Dublin Port and Docks Board. In 1910 he again heard Larkin speak, this time in Beresford Place, Dublin, and joining the ITGWU, became a follower of Larkin.

Irish Independent (Dublin)

It is necessarily incident to the 'sympathetic strike' ordered by the Transport Union despot that skilled workmen may be peremptorily bidden to leave their work. Was ever grosser tyranny attempted to be set up in the name of freedom of combination? Yet this is what Larkinism means and stands for. It is this attempted tyranny that Independent Newspapers and others are now out to overturn and destroy. If the employers of Dublin join forces to complete the work it can be done in a comparatively short time. Sooner or later it must be done. It is infinitely better for Dublin that whatever suffering and loss may be involved should be endured for a few weeks at most than that the city should be left helpless in the toils of Larkinism for an indefinite term of years.

The employers of Dublin must lead the way in emancipating the city from the thraldom of the international Socialist disguised as a Labour leader. In fighting their cause the employers will be battling for the real liberty of labour. This will never be until the pernicious influence of Larkinism has not merely been scotched, but killed.

2 September 1913

The Irish Times (Dublin)

No Irish radical leader of this century – perhaps no Irish radical leader of any period – had so overpowering a personality, or embedded himself so deeply in the current consciousness and the folk memory of his people.

In retrospect, the many faults of this towering figure may loom larger than his virtues. His failures appear spectacular, his political attitudes inconsistent, his quarrels with his colleagues wrong-headed and vindictive. Intellectually, Connolly was incomparably his superior. But if Larkin failed, he failed gloriously; if he was inconsistent in the matter of political theory, he was consistent in courage, in compassion and in a sort of great-hearted puritanism that sprang from knowledge of the degradation that can come from despairing self-indulgence; if he was quarrelsome, he was quarrelsome from conviction. His paradoxical mission was to bully the Dublin workers into the dignity in which he believed with such passion, and no one can say that he failed in that mission. Among the working people of the city his memory is, and deserves to be, evergreen.

26 January 1976

Emmet Larkin

Syndicalist theory developed out of the pressing need to make Socialist thought harmonise with proletarian practice. The roots of Syndicalist theory were actually first struck in the pioneer efforts to organise the unskilled worker into industrial unions. This attempt not only produced a dynamic new rationale in Socialist thought, but it resulted in the emergence of a remarkably vital new leadership. The old Socialist leadership had been made up almost entirely of converts from the intellectual middle classes. The new men, however, were almost all strictly proletarian in their origins, and could hardly be called intellectuals. They were self-educated, pragmatic, class-conscious, articulate, and individualistic to the point of being anarchic. Since they had come up through the ranks, they were as confidant, as dogmatic, and often as arrogant as only self-made men can be. They were full of the truth of their mission and determined to awaken the working classes by preaching their 'divine gospel of discontent'. Their faith was Socialism, their work was industrial unionism, and their vocation was Syndicalism.

The English-speaking world proved very receptive to these prophets of the new order. In America Eugene Debs and 'Big Bill' Haywood, in Britain Tom Mann and Ben Tillet, and in Ireland James Connolly were the outstanding personalities in this broad movement to organise the workers of the world. The most remarkable man, however, among this remarkable generation of proletarian leaders was the Liverpool Irishman – James Larkin. His accomplishment was unique and representative – unique because it was representative. His rich and complex personality allowed him to harmonise the three most dissonant themes of his day. For he claimed to be at one and the same time a Socialist, a Nationalist, and a Roman Catholic.

By 1929 Larkin's power in Dublin was the merest shadow of what it had been, and his influence in the world of Labour was

271

negligible. The Great Depression all but buried him in an unmerciful oblivion. When Larkin died nearly twenty years later in 1947 most people outside Ireland were surprised, for they had assumed he had been dead for a long time. His last years are a sad testimonial to a man whose way of life was action.

Why the fire should have gone out of so vital a man is a question that is as historically important as it is artistically awkward. The answer to that question is also complex. In the early 1930s the world in which Larkin believed was disintegrating. The collapse of the old order in the Great Depression did not surprise him because he had been predicting it all his life. The result, however, was not his prophesied Social Revolution, but the rise of a new order, more menacing and more inhumane than the old – Fascism. The European convulsion and its attendant evils were magnified in Ireland by problems implicit in the attempt to consolidate the Revolution recently made against the British. The consequence was that there was little room in Ireland for men or movements intent on perpetuating the Revolution rather than consolidating it. By 1936 Larkin also realised that at sixty he was too old to begin again. Circumstances had deprived him of his role, and time would not allow for the creation of another. To a man whose way of life was action, such a sentence was death.

James Larkin: Irish Labour Leader (London, 1965)

Emmet Larkin, Professor of History at the University of Chicago, is the author of four major works on the Catholic Church in Ireland in the nineteenth century, as well as the authoritative biography of James Larkin from the Prologue to which the above extract has been taken.

F. S. L. Lyons

Larkin read widely and used his reading to fortify a vivid imagination and a natural gift, or rather genius for flamboyant oratory. Larkin's speeches were larger than life because Larkin himself was larger than life. Physically a very powerful man, he had a big presence and an even bigger voice which allowed him to dominate vast meetings even in the open air. He himself asked little enough of existence – he was simple in his taste, simple in his religion (he may have remained a Catholic though he castigated the Church for its attitude to social problems), simple in his vision of a society that would bring beauty as well as security to the working-class home. 'Here,' as Sean O'Casey summed him up, 'was a man who would put a flower in a vase on a table as well as a loaf on a plate!' But his emotions, too, seemed more intense than those of ordinary men. He was driven by a deep compassion and tenderness for the poor to preach 'the divine gospel of discontent'. The other side of that gospel was a *saeva indignatio* against employers who exploited their workers, or against trade union officials who failed to protect their members. Larkin, once enraged, respected neither laws nor conventions nor individuals and his creative years were passed in a frenzy of passionate involvement and controversy. He was the archetypal bull in a china shop and it was a moot point whether irate industrialists or staid trade unionists were more alarmed by his eruption onto the Irish scene.

Ireland Since the Famine (*London 1973*)

Professor F. S. L. Lyons was Provost of Trinity College, Dublin from 1974 to 1981.

Francis MacManus

Towards the end of his life, Dublin, which he once ruled, seemed like a cage for the tall, handsome figure of Jim Larkin. Somehow we had met, and on trams and in the street he used to talk to me, in a paternal way, in that deep, purring growl of his that could break out into a roar from the platform. With the broad-brimmed black slouch hat and the dark clothes and the fine face, marked by suffering as by impish humour, he looked more like a poet than the noble raging lion who had transformed, as by magic, the dirty, prostituted biddy of a capital city into an honourable queen. Now the city accepted his presence as if he had always been tame and old and caged.

The 1913 Lock-out was the climax of Jim Larkin's career as leader. He had become the Chief. For this monstrous confrontation of force he, it seems, had been created. Through it he entered the folklore of a city.

In a few months in 1913, Dublin became a world city. Larkin grew in stature until he was a colossus. These were his days of glory and they were given to him, freely, by starving men, women and children who, in the end, would have to taste the defeat of stalemate.

Irish Press, 24-27 February 1965

Francis MacManus (1909-65) was Director of Talks and Features in Radio Éireann from 1947, and the creator in 1953 of the Thomas Davis Lecture series. He was the author of many novels including Stand and Give Challenge *(1935),* The Greatest of These *(1943),* Statue for a Square *(1945), short stories, biographies, and history.*

Constance Markievicz

Sitting there listening to Larkin I realised that I was in the presence of something that I had never come across before, some great primeval force rather than a man. A tornado, a storm-driven wave, the rush into life of Spring, and the lasting breath of Autumn, all seemed to emanate from the power that spoke. It seemed as if his personality caught up, assimilated, and threw back to that vast crowd that surrounded him every emotion that swayed them, every pain and joy that they had ever felt made articulate and sanctified. Only the great elemental force that is in all crowds had passed into his nature for ever.

Taller than most men, every line of him was in harmony with his personality. Not so much working man as primeval man. Man without the trickeries and finickiness of modern civilisation, a Titan who might have been moulded by Michelangelo or Rodin, such is Jim Larkin, and this force of his magically changed the whole life of the workers in Dublin and the whole outlook of trade unionism in Ireland. He forced his own self-reliance and self-respect on them; forced them to be sober and made them class conscious and conscious of their nationality.

Éire (Dublin), 16 June 1923

Constance Gore-Booth, Countess Markievicz (1868-1926) was active in support of the locked-out workers in 1913 and with Hanna Sheehy-Skeffington, Delia Larkin, Marie Johnson and Louie Bennett, set up food kitchens in Liberty Hall to feed the hungry children and women. She was elected Honorary President of the Irish Women Workers' Union in February 1917.

Robert Monteith

If ever a man suffered the full penalty of leadership Larkin is that man. This writer watched his dogged struggle from 1910 to 1913 in organising and holding together the Irish Transport and General Workers' Union. Despite the demoralising barrage of mud and filth from the Dublin Press, regardless of the thunders from platform and pulpit, he kept on with the good work. Industrial unionism was on the march. Larkin being no superman made some mistakes, 'even as you and I', but these mattered little in the great measure of success he achieved in asserting the right not only of Dublin workers but of the workers of all Ireland to live in decency and comfort. His few errors may be likened to the dust kicked up by a troop of cavalry, it does not impede the march but it does give the enemy a denser target to aim at. When Ireland comes into her own he will have a chapter in her history.

The establishment of the *Irish Worker* was an important incident in the march of the Irish workers to industrial unionism. Only those who were on the ground at the moment can fully appreciate the tremendous influence of that labour sheet. It brought about those much to be desired discussion groups of people who either through fear, or a feeling of that dear Irish respectability, did not attend Larkinite meetings. There was real progress here. Many 'settled' people began to have their doubts about the righteousness of continuing a drab existence 'in that state of life to which God had been pleased to call them'. Through the medium of the *Irish Worker* much seed was sown. Some of it, of course, fell by the wayside, some among thorns, but much fell upon good ground.

In the United States, Jim continued his work. There were few vacant seats at meetings where he was billed to speak. One naturally looked for fireworks and was seldom disappointed. His outspoken words and direct approach to the problem at issue assured him the support of wingers left and right.

Larkin's speech at his trial in New York where he was committed to Sing Sing, was a classic. His opening words held the attention of everyone. As far as memory serves they were: 'I am a man unused to four walls, the forum or debating chamber. My way has been the way of the worker, the factory, the workshop and the broad high road.' Then the story of the struggle. But

275

what was the use? He was speaking to an audience which did not understand a working man's language. He went to gaol.

I visited him in Sing Sing. He was the same old Jim, a little thinner perhaps, the silver in his hair a little more apparent. But the same old gallant spirit. The flood of memories and the few flying minutes. From Ringsend to the Park, from Liberty Hall to the Howth Road, the rising sun in the east and the warder's tap on Jim's shoulder. 'Time's up, Jim!' Then the grey cell and the bars. They still think they can lock up ideas.

Review (*Dublin*), April 1947

Captain Robert Monteith (1878-1956) accompanied Roger Casement on his journey to Banna Strand, Co. Kerry, in April 1916. He was the author of Casement's Last Adventure *(Dublin, 1953).*

J.T. Murphy

The struggle of the poorest of Dublin's workers against the combined forces of all the Dublin employers, led by Martin Murphy, stirred all sections of the working class movement as never before since the days of Chartism. Jim Larkin had launched the ITGWU and, with a dynamic power of energy such as few men possess, had succeeded in rousing and organising the almost incoherent workers of the slums of Dublin.

A great demonstration, urging sympathetic action, was organised in Sheffield at which Jim Larkin and George Lansbury were the speakers. What a contrast! Six-foot Jim Larkin and his powerful, torrentially passionate eloquence swept the audience off its feet. He finished his speech with a rendering of William Morris's *The Day is Coming*.

I had never heard an orator of his calibre before, nor seen an audience so roused to demonstrative enthusiasm. It was not the kind which greatly appealed to me at that time. I preferred the colder analytical speeches and was sceptical of emotionalism. But it was impossible to be unimpressed by this man. Here was the fighting leader, bearing in his person all the marks of battle, who would storm hell itself.

New Horizons (*London 1941*)

J. T. Murphy was a leader of the Communist Party of Great Britain and the Comintern in the 1920s.

In his book, Murphy refers to Jim Larkin's brother, Peter: 'Was there ever a man with more stentorian tones than Peter? He was not so big a man as Jim, but nevertheless powerful, a rugged, swarthy dock worker and seaman, who had knocked about the ports of the world.'

In 1913, Peter Larkin was active in Dublin and Belfast, and in campaigning in Britain. Later he went to Australia where he was jailed for four years for seditious conspiracy. Returning to Ireland in 1922, he went briefly to America, perhaps with a plan to 'spring' Jim Larkin from jail. Back in Ireland he was instrumental in setting up the Workers' Union of Ireland in 1924 when Jim Larkin was in the Soviet Union. On Sunday, 15 June 1924, at a meeting in Beresford Place, Peter Larkin formally launched the WUI. He became the first National Organiser of the Union and died in 1931.

William Martin Murphy

I want you to clearly understand that the directors of this Company (Dublin United Tramway Company) have not the slightest objection to the men forming a legitimate Union. And I would think there is talent enough amongst the men in the service to form a Union of their own, without allying themselves to a disreputable organisation, and placing themselves under the feet of an unscrupulous man who claims the right to give you the word of command and issue his orders to you and to use you as tools to make him the labour dictator of Dublin. I am here to tell you that this word of command will never be given, and if it is, that it will be the Waterloo of Mr Larkin.

A strike in the tramway would, no doubt, produce turmoil and disorder created by the roughs and looters, but what chance could the men without funds have in a contest with the Company who could, and would, spend £100,000 or more. You must recollect when dealing with a company of this kind that every one of the shareholders, to the number of five, six or seven thousands, will have three meals a day whether the men succeed or not. I don't know if the men who go out can count on this.

***

The question I have fought in connection with the Tramway Company was not one of wages, or the treatment of those employed in the tramway service. The whole issue was the supremacy of Mr Larkin and whether he was going to rule the trade of Dublin, and whether men could carry on their business and in fact be able to call their bodies and souls their own, unless they went cap in hand to him. The position was becoming intolerable. It was time to stop this man and I think I have stopped him.

The fight against Larkin was not, after all so difficult: it was easier than it appeared. The prospect of a strike and the anticipation of it had much more terror for the employer, than the actual strike when it took place. When the strike actually took place the employer had to get his back to the wall, and the workman has fired his last cartridge. The employer all the time managed to get his three meals a day, but the unfortunate workman and his family had no resources whatever except submission, and that was what occurred in ninety-nine cases out of one hundred. The difficulty of teaching that lesson to the workman was extraordinary.

The first of the two extracts is from an address by William Martin Murphy (1845-1919), chairman of the Dublin United Tramway Company to seven hundred of the company's employees, in the Antient Concert Rooms, Brunswick Street (now Pearse Street), Dublin on 19 July 1913. At the end of his address, Murphy asked the meeting to sing 'God Save Ireland'.

The second extract is from an address by W. M. Murphy to the Dublin Chamber of Commerce, of which he was President, on 1 September 1913. At the end of this meeting of tribute to the President, a resolution was passed unanimously thanking William Martin Murphy for 'the energetic manner in which he had dealt with the present labour unrest in the city'.

New Statesman (London)

(Larkin) is one of those born revolutionaries who know not diplomacy, but who believe that the Kingdom of Heaven must be taken by violence today and tomorrow and the day after. His utopia, we feel, would be a world where a general strike was going on all the time. Big and black and fierce, he is a Syndicalist of the street corners. He calls to the surface the very depth of unrest. His theory seems to be that a city should never be allowed a moment's peace so long as there remains a single poor man whose wrongs have not been righted. His genius is inflammatory. He preaches turmoil.

From article, 'Anarchism in Dublin' in New Statesman, *6 September 1913, quoted in David Howell,* A Lost Left: Three Studies in Socialism and Nationalism *(Manchester, 1986).*

George O'Brien

We occasionally had visitors and I remember one evening we had Jim Larkin who impressed me very favourably. He had a much greater knowledge of literature than I would have expected, having lived in London in the 1890s. He and Yeats exchanged recollections of the Yellow book circle. Larkin also pleased me by his generosity towards his opponents. He said that he admired W.M. Murphy because he was a hard but clean fighter for his own side.

James Meenan, George O'Brien: A Biographical Memoir (Dublin, 1980)

George O'Brien (1892-1973) was Professor of Economics in University College Dublin from 1926 to 1961. The author of many books, notably The Economic History of Ireland (three volumes, London and Dublin, 1918-21) and Labour Organisation (1921).
The reference in the extract is to a dining club which met in the Moira Restaurant in Trinity Street, Dublin in the 1920s. The members included W. B. Yeats, Lennox Robinson, Desmond FitzGerald, Thomas McGreevy, Brinsley MacNamara, P. S. O'Hegarty, and were known as the Twelve Apostles.

Sean O'Casey

Through the streets he strode, shouting into every dark and evil-smelling hallway. The great day of change has come; Circe's swine had a better time than you have; come from your vomit; out into the sun. Larkin is calling you all!

Following afar off for a while, Sean had come at last to hear Larkin speak, to stand under a red flag rather than the green banner.

From a window in the building, leaning well forth, he talked to the workers, spoke as only Jim Larkin could speak, not for an assignation with peace, dark obedience, or placid resignation; but trumpet-tongued of resistance to wrong, discontent with leering poverty, and defiance of any power strutting out to stand in the way of their march onward. His was a handsome tense face, the forehead swept by deep black hair, the upper lip of the generous, mobile mouth hardened into fierceness by a thick moustache, the voice, deep, dark, and husky, carrying to the extreme corners of the square, and reaching, Sean thought, to the outermost ends of the earth. In this voice was the march of Wat Tyler's men, the yells and grunts of those who took the Bastille, the sigh of the famine-stricken, the loud shout from those, all bloodied over, who fell in 1798 on the corn slopes of Royal Meath; here were nursery rhyme and battle song, the silvery pleasing of a lute with the trumpet-call to come out and carry their ragged banners through the gayer streets of the city, so that unskilled labour might become the vanguard, the cavaliers and cannoniers of labour's thought and purpose.

'Who will stand, who will fight, for the right of men to live and die like men?' he called out, the large, strong hand stretched out of the window gesturing over the head of the crowd.

'Gifts of the Almighty,' went on the voice, 'labour – a gift, not a curse –, poetry, dancing and principles'; and Sean could see that here was a man who would put a flower in a vase on a table as well as a loaf on a plate. Here, Sean thought, is the beginning of the broad and busy day, the leisurely evening, the calmer night; an evening full of poetry, dancing and the linnet's wings; these on their way to the music of the accordion, those to that of a philharmonic orchestra; and after all, to sleep, perchance to dream; but never to be conscious of a doubt about tomorrow's bread, certain that, while the earth remaineth, summer and winter should not cease, seed time and harvest never fail.

Drums Under the Window (*London, 1945*)

***

From that day on, I was close to Jim Larkin. From that day on, the prime battle for me was the workers' battle for a better life. There were no conversions in the common meaning of the term among the crowd that day. There was emotion, but no emotionalism. It was only that these eloquent and fiery sentences flashed upon vague and incoherent hopes in the simple minds of the workers, and gave them a clearer vision of how they were, what they were, and what they might – what they must become.

Here in the square was the vanguard of the Irish Workers' Army. The stalwarts Barney Conway, Paddy Mooney; the two Pooles, Chris and Vincent; Sean Shelly, Tom Healy and hundreds of others whose faces I see, whose forms I see still, but whose names I have forgotten. An ill-fed, ill-clad, largely inarticulate army.

So I went into 10 Beresford Place – Liberty Hall had not yet become the headquarters of the union – and, taking out a card, formally declared myself a member of Jim Larkin's Union.

Jim Larkin was a man interested in everything that embraced the full life of man. Last summer when he stayed with me, he commented on past and present politics and on his own union; on the theatre; the vagaries of an apple tree; and on how fine a spray of snowy hawthorn looked, draping itself over the wall of the back garden.

Irish Democrat (London), March 1947

***

Another Irish Chieftain has gone from us. One of the greatest of them all: a Chief of the people – Jim Larkin is his name. The banner and beacon-fire of the Irish Labour Movement. The banner is now furled. The beacon-fire is out – a little heap of ashes only.

But what ashes! Out of it will spring another flame, firing itself from that which Larkin kindled, flaming in Ireland, and flaming everywhere. It is not only that Jim Larkin will never be forgotten (to forget him would be to forget ourselves), it is that he can never be dead.

In the great things he did for the Irish workers is everlasting life. Not life that will remain as it is now; but life growing into a fuller consciousness of its own worth, of its own power, its own right to the ownership of all things.

I heard men, turning aside in moments of quiet from Irish-Ireland work murmur: 'A man has come among the Irish workers'.

Then I heard this man speak to dockers, coalheavers and drivers in Beresford Place. There he was, larger than the life we knew, standing above the Dublin workers, telling them of the story the workers must write themselves. In this man's burning words were the want, the desire, the resolution of the world's workers. Here before me was the symbol of the revolting proletariat. The personal manifestation of 'Each for all, and all for each'. The symbol of a march forward; not in twos and threes; not this union today, that one tomorrow; but a march forward en masse for what the workers never had, but for what they will have and hold for ever.

The Irish Times, 1 February 1947

We shall be told that Jim Larkin is dead. Don't believe it. He still speaks to you and me; to every man and woman who toils for a living in office, factory, field and workshop, and to all who go down to the sea in ships.

He speaks still from a platform in Pearse Street, O'Connell Street and Cathal Brugha Street. His fine head is till framed in the old window of Liberty Hall, and the voice echoes throughout Beresford Place and whirls down on the waters of the Liffey.

Irish Democrat *(London)*, *March 1947*

Sean O'Faoláin

Larkin had come out of the dark netherworld with the eyes and face of a poet. He burned with a fiery simplicity of belief in his fellow-man and his speech to them was like a lava. He had mild but wide, clear eyes, questioning almost staring; a long nose; sensuous lips; a sombre lock of hair across his forehead; the hollowed cheeks and high cheekbone of an ascetic.

Constance Markievicz *(London, 1934)*

Sean O'Faoláin (1900-1993). Writer of short stories, novels, biographies, travel books and autobiography (Vive Moi!). *Editor of* The Bell, *1940-46.*

Liam O'Flaherty

The dock workers idolised Larkin. Somebody has said of him that he 'seized the Dublin workers by the scruff of the neck' and made them stand erect.

In October 1913, a Board of Trade Inquiry was set up to examine the causes of the Labour troubles in the city. In this inquiry Tim Healy represented the employers; Larkin represented the workers. In the struggle of wits, Healy was easily defeated. Larkin's cross-examination of William Martin Murphy was masterly, and were it not for Healy's help the great employer would have cut a very sorry figure indeed.

The Life of Tim Healy *(London, 1927)*

Liam O'Flaherty (1897-1984). Novelist, including The Informer *(1925),* Famine *(1937), and short story writer. He was involved with Roddy Connolly, Walter Carpenter and Sean McLoughlin in taking control of the Socialist Party of Ireland in November 1921 and expelling William O'Brien and Cathal Ó Shannon. He led the occupation of the Rotunda Buildings, Dublin in 1922.*

Liam O'Flaherty's brother, Thomas O'Flaherty, was a colleague of Larkin in America, active in the Irish American Labor League in New York. He and Jack Carney were elected alternates to the first central executive committee of the Workers' Party of America at its founding conference in December 1921.

Deasún Ó Riain

Ní tuigtear fós i gceart, dar ndóigh, an méid maitheasa a rinne Ó Lorcáin ar son fear oibre na tíre lena linn, agus an méid a rinne sé ar a bhealach féin chun reábhlóid na hÉireann do chur ar siúl. Dúirt an tOllamh Liam Ó Briain uair 'of Larkin it is incontestable that he revived an almost extinct flame of nationalism in thousands of Dublin workmen.' Bhí an bharúil céanna ag an bPiarsach nuair a dúirt sé sa bhliain 1913 go raibh níos mó déanta ag an Lorcánach chun Caisleán Bhaile Átha Cliath a leagadh agus réim iasachta a scrios taobh istigh de sé míosa ná éinne eile le leath-chéád blian. Ach caithfear admháil freisin go raibh dhá Lorcánach ann .i. an laoch agus an buachaill báire. Bhí nós meidhreach aige-sin i gcónaí fabhailscéal a mheascadh ina chuid cainte agus go minic mheasc sé an fhírinne fós leis an bhfabhailscéal.

Mar a dúirt R.M. Fox: 'He was a great romanticist and a great romancer. This always put his more mundane critics and enemies in a rage. But Larkin could not help seeing himself as the centre of a thrilling saga. Usually he did hold this position so there was a fundamental truth about his attitude, however uncertain the details might be'. Agus go cinnte b'íontach na 'details' úd!

Ach ar an dtaobh eile den scéal, do bhí an *saga féin* níos iontaí arís. I mBéal Feirste sa bhliain 1907 rinne se míorúilt nach ndearna éinne roimhe sin ná ó shin. Mharbhaigh sé fearmad creidimh sa chathair sin maol marbh agus shiúil Caitiliceach agus Protastúnach, Finíní agus Fir Oráiste guala ar ghualainn fana gcuid bratacha féin agus iad go léir aontaithe i gcúis an Lucht Oibre.

Innesofar mar chuimhne ar an Lorcánach go deo an gníomh do rinne sé nuair a labhair sé o chéimeanna Theach an Chustaim i mBéal Feirste ar an 12 lá de mhí Iúil 1907 leis na sluaite comhaontaithe sin. 'Ní raibh a leithéid ann riamh ná ó shin', arsa Alice Milligan uair, 'ní raibh an fearmad chomh marbh céanna ariamh, ní raibh lucht oibre chomh cáirdiúil le chéile, ní raibh an spiorad náisiúnta ariamh chomh láidir is do bhí 'sna laethe sin'.

Ag seo giota de óráid do thug Ó Lorcáin uaidh ós comhair na cúirte a dhaor é mar 'criminal anarchist' agus é ina dheoraí ins an Oileán Úr:

And so at an early age I took my mind to this question of the ages – why are the many poor? It was true to me, but it came to me in a flash. The thing was wrong because the basis of society was wrong ... How did I get the love of comrades, only by reading Whitman? How did I get this love of humanity except by understanding men like Thoreau and Emerson and the greatest men I have lived with, the real Americans. It is not the Americans of the mart and the exchange, the men who would sell their souls for money and sell their country, too, if need came.

Ach ní raibh Ó Lorcáin ró-sholúnta ar feadh na trialach féin. Léadh cúpla abairt dhó ó fhorfógra Left Wing éigin agus cuireadh ceist air an é a bhí ciontach leis.

'Ní mise do scríobh na focla sin in aonchor. Is maith is eol dom an duine do scríobh iad, agus tig libh é chur san bpríosún más féidir libh. Karl Marx is ainm do, ach faraor fuair sé bás fadó!'

Comhar (Baile Átha Cliath), Deire Fomhair 1957

Sliochtanna eile as an óraid úd ó Séamus Ó Lorcáin san chúirt:

I went to school for three and a quarter years altogether, and a great deal of that time I was welcome as a part-timer. It was an English Catholic School. It was a poverty-stricken school, and I was taught the truth of eternal justice, and I was taught the brotherhood of man was a true and living thing. And then I had occasion to go out in the world and found out that there was no fatherhood of God, and there was no brotherhood of man, but every man in society was compelled to be like a wolf or a hyena, trying to tear down the other man's sufferings, or by the other man's sorrow, or, which was more important, the sorrow of his wife, the sorrow of his children.

Deasún Ó Riain, see Desmond Ryan (page 288)

Sir William Orpen

I used to go down to the dirt and filth of Liberty Hall and sit in Jim Larkin's office in the afternoons just for the interest of watching the man. He was always sincere, always modest, always thinking of others, during those terrible strike times when he was out against 'graft', drink and starvation in the city. The poverty in Dublin during that time of riots and strikes was terrible, and the basements of Liberty Hall were used as soup kitchens.

I remember a few things that may show some reason for my admiration for this man. On a certain Saturday afternoon I was with him. A letter had come in saying that the Roman Catholic Archbishop was going to speak against him from the pulpit on Sunday morning. After 4.30, up came a man and said a priest from some village near Dundalk insisted on seeing him. 'Show him up,' said Jim. In came a very excited priest. 'Well,' said Jim, 'what is it all about?' 'About!' he shouted. 'I hear they are going to speak against you from the pulpit tomorrow, and that your people are going to have a procession through the city. I want you to let me lead them. You are the Saviour of Dublin.' Jim rang his bell. A man came in. He muttered something to him and the man departed. Jim lit a cigar slowly and said, 'I thank you from my heart for your goodwill, and what you wish to do for me, but I cannot allow you to do it. Now, will you really trust me and do what I tell you?' 'Surely,' said the priest. 'Then,' said Jim, 'you are to go back to your village at once and carry on your duties there, and forget that you ever came to Liberty Hall.' Then turning to one of the clerks he said, 'Show His Reverence downstairs. There is a cab waiting at the door. Take him to Amiens Street Station and see him off in the train to Dundalk.' Then turning to the priest he said, 'Goodbye, Father. This is the best thing you can do for me and for yourself. Pray for me.' And out went the poor priest in tears, with his head bowed.

One of the next visitors that afternoon was a high prelate of the Church. He thundered at Jim. Did he not realise that on the morrow he was going to be spoken against from the pulpit; that 'the Church' had ordered him not to hold his meeting on that Sunday afternoon in the Phoenix Park; that if he did he was defying the Church? So he railed on at him for a long time, his arms flying about, and occasionally thrusting his forefinger close to Jim's face. All this time Larkin was sitting back in his chair puffing his cigar, with his clear eyes fixed on the prelate. Not a move did he make. When the prelate's outburst ceased from want of breath, Jim got slowly out of his chair and said very gently, 'Pray God, Holy Father, that when you rise tomorrow morning you will be able to say your prayers to your God with the same peace of mind that I will say mine.' And turning to one of his men he said, 'Show the Holy Father the way out'. And he departed amid great silence. And Jim continued his work and his cigar.

Stories of Old Ireland and Myself *(London, 1924)*

William Orpen (1878-1931) was born in Stillorgan, Co. Dublin. He was knighted in 1918 as one of the official war artists. In a letter to Sir William Rothenstein, the painter and principal of the Royal College of Art in London, Orpen wrote 'Larkin is the greatest man I ever met'.

Pádraig Pearse

I calculate that one-third of the people of Dublin are underfed; that half the children attending Irish primary schools are ill-nourished. I suppose there are twenty thousand families in Dublin in whose domestic economy milk and butter are all but unknown: black tea and dry bread are their staple articles of diet. There are many thousand fireless hearth-places in Dublin in the bitterest days of winter.

Twenty thousand families live in one-room tenements. It is common to find two or three families occupying the same room; and sometimes one of the families will have a lodger! There are tenement rooms in which over a dozen persons live, eat and sleep.

High rents are paid for these rooms, rents which in cities like Birmingham would command neat four-roomed cottages. The tenement houses are so rotten that they periodically collapse upon their inhabitants and if the inhabitants collect in the street to discuss matters police baton them to death.

These are the grievances against which men in Dublin are beginning to protest. Can you wonder that the protest is crude and bloody? I do not know whether the methods of Mr James Larkin are wise methods or unwise methods (unwise, I think in some respects), but this I know, that there is a most hideous wrong to be righted and the man who attempts honestly to right it is a good man and a brave man.

Irish Freedom *(Dublin), October 1913*

James Plunkett

James Joyce spoke of Dublin as the centre of paralysis. It was a total paralysis, blinding conscience and soul. It remained to Jim Larkin to see the slum dweller as a human being – degraded, yet capable of nobility; perceptive, capable of living with dignity, capable even, of music and literature. That was the message he began to address to the city at large – a message of love, delivered, one must concede, by a man swinging wildly about him with a sword.

In the course of forty years of social agitation Jim Larkin earned a reputation that was universal. Yet he was no doctrinaire revolutionary in the Continental sense and he was not a great theorist. Perhaps the employers of Dublin found the best name for his movement when they labelled it Larkinism. His lifelong concern was not with theory, but with the immediate needs of the underprivileged, the sweated men, the struggling mothers, the little children born to a life of drudgery in a sunless world. In his efforts to help them he was sometimes arrogant, sometimes unfair to colleagues and often rash beyond the justification of his most indulgent admirers.

Leaders and Workers *(Cork, 1986)*

James Plunkett (1920 –). Novelist and short story writer. His novels include Strumpet City *(1969), set in Dublin in 1913,* Farewell Companions *(1977), and* The Circus Animals *(1990). He is the author of the radio play,* Big Jim, *and the play,* The Risen People.

James Plunkett was an official of the Workers' Union of Ireland from 1946 to 1955 and during that period worked with both Jim Larkin and James Larkin Junior. He contributed 'Sean O'Casey and the Trade Unions' to the Thomas Davis Lectures in 1980, The O'Casey Enigma, *edited by Micheal Ó hAodha (Cork, 1980), and to the Thomas Davis Lecture series,* Trade Union Century *(1994).*

Desmond Ryan

Larkin had fanned up the smouldering discontent of the masses and breathed a new spirit into Irish trade unionism and labour political bodies in general. Jim Larkin had much kindliness of heart, and Elizabethan directness of diction, a love for the poetry of Walt Whitman and Francis Thompson, an immense power of gripping popular audiences. He aroused the vague, incoherent and almost helpless masses and wielded them into harmonious union, articulate, organised and militant.

Jim Larkin, not unjustly struck the popular eye as the inspiration, and indeed, as the fomenter of the revolt. From an open window in Liberty Hall the well-known figure of the strike leader dominated the scene – a strong, sturdy, fighting frame, a face of rare determination and purpose, with fierce blue eyes that drop before no man's, a voice that seemed as the long silent voice of the underpeople, ringing out with a rude, eloquent beauty upon a hitherto listless, now startled world.

Night after night, this husky scaring giant of labour thunders out the strangest talks that have ever stirred a multitude: no balanced periods, no favourite whimsicalities, no cleverly prepared surprises. Nay, none of these, nor the recondite philosophy of a Karl Marx, the subtle triflings of a George Bernard Shaw, the sentimental trenchant appeals of a Keir Hardie; but rather facts known to the audience, the virtues of temperance, bowelless employers, white-livered curs, adjectived scabs, and other obnoxious individuals. Above all, what was to be done that night, tomorrow, next week. Dublin workers tightened their belts to an enthusiastic murmur: 'Good luck to you Jim Larkin! We will fight on!'

James Connolly: His Life, Work and Writings (*Dublin and London, 1924*)

Desmond Ryan (1893-1964). Author of The Man Called Pearse *(1919),* James Connolly *(1924),* Remembering Sion *(1934),* Unique Dictator [Eamon de Valera] *(1936),* The Phoenix Flame *(1937), and* The Rising *(1949). He edited three volumes of the writings of James Connolly (Dublin) 1948-51.*

Desmond Ryan was the son of W. P. Ryan.

W.P. Ryan

Jim Larkin is the greatest figure in Irish Labour mythology. I well remember the swift, strange growth of the marvel, the dire magic of the sinister, tremendous 'Larkin' of the legend, several months before I met the human 'Jim' in the actual world.

By the hostile he was deemed rude, domineering, turbulent, prone to passion and exaggeration; to the detached he seemed vigorous, reckless, racy; to the sympathetic he was often somewhat distressing, and by no means definite and conclusive in his social and industrial philosophy. What were his ideals, and where lay his goal? His harangues and exhortations suggested different conclusions. He advised, exhorted, struggled, and struck from instinct, from an intense pity for the slave class amongst which he had grown; yet from a feeling of pride in its manhood, depressed and distorted though it might be; and from a stern determination to secure fair play. He did not come with any shapely social scheme, he had not learning or leisure in the way of Utopias; but he had a burning desire to right the immediate wrong, and to go on battling against the next.

He called ugly things by their names, his more than childlike simplicity in this regard being mistaken for calculated daring and the desire to give offence. He said rude blunt things when he and his were cheated and hurt; the life circumstances did not tend to bring a naturally strong and earnest character, the doubtful graces of finesse and circumlocution. Through all this two of his most decided characteristics were liable to be obscured: his genuine kindliness of heart and – although he was not always easy to work with – his faculty of conciliation.

Larkin went straight to the men in the workshops and the unions – though he also talked to them in ringing tones abroad – and dwelt far more on what was pressing and painful at the moment than on what might be permanently true or ideally right. He told them home-truths on the subject of their own faults and weaknesses; he spared them no more than the masters. He did not suggest the student or the thinker, though he had studied and thought to some purpose, loving poetry at least as much as economics. His experiences in the terrible human (or inhuman) school through which he had passed gave him a unique mould and driving force. Below and beyond all there was a magnetic power not easily described. But the undermen felt it from the first, and that made all the difference.

Jim Larkin, moving amongst despised dockers, carters and land-slaves, lit fires that at one and the same time were beacons, bewildering portents and irritants. It took a long time for even idealists to see that the flame he brought was but part of the Gleam and the Ideal that had never died in his race. The Kingdom of Heaven is within us, we know from the Gospel; but who had sought for it hitherto amongst the slums and unskilled slaves of Dublin?

The Irish Labour Movement from the 1820s to our Own Day
(Dublin and London, 1968)

William P. Ryan [Liam P. Ó Riain] (1867-1942). Author of The Irish Literary Revival *(1894),* The Pope's Green Island *(1912),* The Irish Labour Movement *(1919). He wrote novels, plays and poetry in Irish and English. After a time spent in London, he returned to Ireland at the end of 1906, editing, successively, the* Irish Peasant, The Peasant *and the* Irish Nation. *He returned to London in 1911 becoming assistant editor of the* Daily Herald *with which he remained up to his death in 1942.*

Sir James Sexton

Jim Larkin, crashed upon the British public with the devastating force and roar of a volcano exploding without even a preliminary wisp of smoke. He swept down upon us, indeed, with the startling suddenness of the eruption of Mount Pelée, and, proportionally, his activities were hardly less serious in their results.

I have myself been called an 'agitator' and of being a mob orator who could use only the wildest language. Believe me, however, in my earliest and hottest days of agitating, I was more frigid than a frozen mill pond in comparison with Larkin, whilst in the matter of language I was feeble, tongue-tied, almost dumb.

In Belfast he actually succeeded in calling out the members of the Royal Irish Constabulary and holding a strike meeting in the yard of their own barracks. I happened to be present at that meeting – surely unparalleled in all the history of Labour effort – and I still marvel at the power Larkin then revealed, however brief its duration may have been.

Agitator: The Life of the Dockers MP. An Autobiography (London, 1936)

Sir James Sexton was the general secretary of the Liverpool-based National Union of Dock Labourers when Jim Larkin was appointed organiser in 1905. It was Sexton who sent Larkin to Belfast in 1907 to organise the dockers there.

Francis Sheehy Skeffington

Almost every one of the Labour leaders involved has in some way or other helped the Suffrage cause, or shown his adhesion to it. Mr Larkin was the initiator of the vigorous resolution passed by the Irish Trades Union Congress, last Whitsuntide, in condemnation of the Government's attack upon freedom of speech and freedom of the press.

He has also assisted to carry suffragist resolutions at the Dublin Trades Council and his paper, the *Irish Worker*, has repeatedly attacked the Government for its coercive policy towards the suffragists. The men of Mr Larkin's union also frequently interfered, at the rowdy meetings in Dublin last year, to protect Suffragettes from the hooligans of the AOH – the body that is now organising strike-breakers.

Irish Citizen *(Dublin), 6 September 1913*

Francis Sheehy Skeffington (1878-1916). Author of the Life of Michael Davitt *(1908). Editor of the* Irish Citizen *(Dublin), a feminist weekly journal. He was the Irish correspondent of the socialist papers, the* Daily Herald *(London) and* Humanité *(Paris).*

Both Francis and his wife Hanna, were actively involved with the workers in the Dublin lock-out in 1913. Francis was shot by a British army officer during the Easter Rising in 1916. The officer was subsequently found to have been insane. On hearing of his death, the poet, James Cousins (1873-1956), who had been editor of the Irish Citizen, *wrote from India:*

> *You whom no power or pride e're awed;*
> *Whose hand would heal where sharp it fell*
> *Smite error on the throne of God*
> *And smile on Truth though found in Hell.*

W. P. Ryan described Sheehy Skeffington as the 'champion of so many good causes who was heart and soul with Labour in its ideals, its activities, and its crises, above all in 1913'.

Owen Sheehy Skeffington

I think of a magnificent Jim Larkin speech at a meeting of the TCD Historical Society in 1931 which made us all feel that if he had asked us there and then to storm the Dáil we would at once have done so.

Owen Sheehy Skeffington (1909-70), the son of Francis and Hanna Sheehy Skeffington, was Lecturer and Reader in French in Trinity College Dublin, from 1935. The extract is from an article, 'Hist Memories', in The Irish Times, 5 March 1970.

R. M. Smyllie

My journalistic career has brought me into contact with many great orators. I think that during the last thirty years I have heard most of the world's most famous public speakers, from President Woodrow Wilson to Mr Winston Churchill. I have listened to them all. But I never heard anybody who moved me quite so much as Jim Larkin.

Of course I was very young at the time. It was in 1912. Naturally I was impressionable. I had just come to Dublin from the country as a student. But I fell for Larkin's spell-binding oratory. And I was not altogether in bad company. He was a wonderful speaker. I happened to be in Sackville Street – now O'Connell Street – when he made his famous appearance on the balcony of the old Imperial Hotel. I also heard him speaking outside Liberty Hall, outside the Ballast Office and in various other places: and I came to the youthful conclusion that Jim Larkin was one of the greatest men in the world.

Doubtless, that was youthful enthusiasm. But ever since I have had a hankering respect for a man who seemed to me at the time to be a single-minded idealist. I may be wrong; but, somehow, I do not think so even now. Larkin was a queer, wayward creature, who never sought popularity, although he achieved it in abundant measure.

He had a terrific personality. His detractors say that he was merely a mob orator, which he probably was; but there was more to him than that. He believed in what he was doing, and had the knack of making other people believe in it as well.

Nichevo, An Irishman's Diary, The Irish Times, *1 February 1947*

'Nichevo' was Robert Maire Smyllie (1894-1954), editor of The Irish Times *from 1934 to 1954.*

James Stephens

By bettering your own conditions you are going to better the condition of everyone. Every great human movement, every crusade that had an idea or an ideal for its banner was inaugurated and carried to victory by your class in the teeth of precisely the same opposition as is arrayed against you today.

Be very proud of what you are doing. The whole weary earth is hanging on your fortitude. You are as truly the liberators of the world today as were those twelve other working men who long ago threw up their jobs to follow the penniless Son of the Carpenter and your battle will not be a bit easier than theirs was. Your leader was in jail through as contemptible a piece of political and social treachery as can be imagined. Every lie that malignity could invent has been used against him for the past seven years. Are you going to desert him? He did not desert you. Was it any fun for Larkin to be rusting in Mountjoy Jail? If he could have been bought his price would have been paid ages ago; but thank heaven, there are still poor men who are not for sale. Can you be bought away from him? If so, there is money and soft soap for the traitor; but one can live to the height of one's intellect and soul and be a proud man even if one is a hungry man.

Irish Worker, *13 December 1913*

James Stephens (1882-1950) was Register of the National Gallery of Ireland, 1915-1925. Author of many books, most notably, The Crock of Gold, *published in 1913. The article from which the above extracts have been taken was sent to the* Irish Worker *from Paris.*

John Swift

Then came Larkin and his co-workers. Soon thousands of the despised rabble became ennobled with the dignity of trade union organisation. Larkin taught them the duty of struggle, the imperative of rebelliousness. He breathed fire into the dead eyes and the cringing breasts of slaves. They heard him, and their supplications to their masters became defiance, their despair became a challenge. He taught them self-reliance. They followed Larkin because he had convinced them in his person and in his teaching that there was no more noble duty or destiny for men and women than that of raising themselves from bondage.

Some of us are old enough to remember how Dublin throbbed to Larkin's fiery slogans. A Titan of a man, he needed no banners on which to scroll his burning poetry. He made banners of the air: his voice wrought magic patterns compelling attention and exultation. In the city's gutter, in the fetid slum, in the stinking holds of ships, on the quayside, where men fawned and flunkeyed for wretched bread, in the poorhouse, even, and the prison, there was exultation when Larkin spoke. Men and women, made dumb and abject by injustice and destitution, listened. What new hurricane from the heavens was this that said: 'The great appear great because we are on our knees. Let us rise.' Or:

> Who is it speaks of defeat?
> I tell you a cause like ours
> Is greater than defeat can know
> It is the power of powers!

This man of power was loved by little children and was himself throughout his life, in many ways a child. He was a great artist, working towards the ideal that consumed him. His music was livid thunder, hurtled at injustice and hypocrisy. At times his harmonies were strange, as of forces eruptive and elemental. But who could doubt the main chords of the symphony he sought to fashion, with its tones and overtones that told of chains breaking and dungeons tottering, and the wild elation of serfs made free! Let us stand to honour Larkin – Larkin who taught the despised rabble to stand erect, unafraid and hopeful.

Extract from John Swift's Presidential Address to the fifty-third annual meeting of the Irish Trade Union Congress, Olympic Ballroom, Waterford, 29 July 1947.

John Swift (1896-1990). *General Secretary of the Irish Bakers', Confectioners' and Allied Workers' Amalgamated Union, was a member of the National Executive of Congress from 1944 to 1958 and Treasurer from 1950 to 1958.*

He was the author of History of the Dublin Bakers and Others *(Dublin, 1948). His biography, by John P. Swift,* John Swift: an Irish Dissident, *was published in 1991. There is an obituary essay by Francis Devine in* Saothar, 15, 1990, *the journal of the Irish Labour History Society. John Swift was a prime mover in the formation of the Society in 1973 and was Honorary President from 1977 till his death in 1990.*

Bertram D. Wolfe

Big Jim Larkin appeared in our midst surrounded by legend. The year was 1917. He was a big-boned, large-framed man, broad shoulders held not too high nor too proudly, giving him an air of stooping over ordinary men when he was speaking to them. Bright blue eyes flashed from dark heavy brows; a long flashy nose, hollowed-out cheeks, prominent cheek bones, a long thick neck, the cords of which stood out when he was angry, a powerful stubborn chin, a head longer and a forehead higher than in most men, suggesting plenty of room for the brain pan. Big Jim was well over six feet tall. Long arms and legs, great hands like shovels, big rounded shoes shaped in front like the rear of a canal boat, completed the picture.

When Larkin spoke, his blue eyes flashed and sparkled. He roared and thundered, sputtered and – unless a stage separated him from the public – sprayed his audience with spittle. Sometimes an unruly forelock came down on his forehead as he moved his head in vigorous emphasis. Impulsive, fiery, passionate, swift at repartee, highly personal, provocative, and hot-tempered in attack, strong and picturesque of speech, Larkin's language was rich in the terms of Irish poetic imagery sprinkled with neologisms of his own devising. Particularly in front of an Irish or an Irish-American audience, or an audience of bewildered foreign-born socialists unprepared for poetry and religion in Marxist oratory, he was the most powerful speaker in the left-wing socialist movement. An Irish nationalist to the core of his being, he was at the same time a revolutionary socialist and internationalist. Combative by nature, he was reflective, too, and a romantic who always saw himself as the spokesman and leader of some gallant fight. No one ever heard foul language from his lips. He could be as hot-tempered as any man, indeed hotter, but the temper expressed itself in withering repartee, angry condemnation, and scorn, sputtering, unforgettable epithets, never in obscenity.

He had no taste for theory at all, but made up for that by a strong sense of justice, and a belief in his personal mission to lead men in combat, in all manner of struggles for a better life, a little more dignity, a little more freedom. He made no appeal to reason, advanced no theories, only recited wrongs and outrages in angry tones, labour's wrongs and Ireland's together.

He never seemed to prepare a speech, being always ready with invective and his ad libs. Acoustics, whether of hall or roaring streets, were of no moment. His voice was strong and strident, and at climatic points turned to withering scorn or exultant roar.

Strange Communists I have Known *(London, 1966)*

Bertram Wolfe was one of the founders of the American Communist Party.

The Lion Will Roar no More

Sean O'Casey

It is hard to believe that this 'lion' of the Irish Labour movement will roar no more. When it seemed that every man's hand was against him the time he led the workers through the tremendous days of 1913 he wrested tribute of Ireland's greatest and most prominent men. Yeats, George Russell, Orpen and George Bernard Shaw proclaimed him to be the greatest Irishman since Parnell. And so he was; for all thoughts and all activities surged in the soul of this Labour leader. He was far and away above the orthodox Labour leader, for he combined within himself the imagination of the artist, with the fire and determination of a leader of a down-trodden class.

He was the first man in Ireland – and, perhaps, in England, too – who brought poetry into the workers' fight for a better life. Lectures and concerts, and other activities, he brought into Liberty Hall, and the social centre he organised in Croydon Park coloured the life of the Dublin workers, and was a joyous experience they had never known before, and won for Jim the admiration of many who had but scanty interest in the labour movement.

Before all others, Jim Larkin brought into the Dublin labour strife an interest in the hearts of humanity never associated before with the life of those who had to work hard and long for a living; and today this interest has grown to tremendous proportions, and the workers are swarming to enjoy and to understand the finer things of life.

So Jim Larkin, as well as being a great leader of men and an imaginative artist himself, was a foreseer of things to come. He was the man who first introduced to me the great name of Eugene O'Neill just after that playwright had had his *Hairy Ape* produced in New York. He fought for the loaf of bread as no man before him had ever fought; but, with the loaf of bread, he also brought the flask of wine and the book of verse.

He had the eloquence of an Elizabethan, fascinating to all who heard him, and irresistible to the workers. He was familiar with the poetry of Shakespeare, Whitman, Shelley and Omar Khayyam, and often quoted them in his speeches. In all his imaginative speeches there ran the fiery thread of devastating criticism not only of the employers, but of the workers themselves.

Jim Larkin never hesitated to expose and condemn the faults of his followers. No man ever did more since the days of Father Matthew to persuade the workers to live a more sober and sensible life than this Jim.

Many were jealous of his great fight and of his influence on the working class, and many still are, but the life of this man, so great, so unselfish, so apostolic, will live for ever in the hearts and minds of those who knew him and in the minds of those who will hear of the mission to men, and of all he did to bring security and decency and honour to a class that never knew of these things until Jim Larkin came.

There was a man sent from God whose name was Jim, and that man was Larkin. Jim Larkin is not dead, but is with us, and will be with us always.

The Irish Times, *31 January 1947*.

Feartlaoi

Micheál Ó Maoláin

A Shéamuis shiubhlas le t'ais ar shráideanna Loch Garmain i 1911 nuair a tháinig oibridhthe an bhaile sin amach le fáilte a chur rómhat fhéin agus roimh Pádraig Ó Dálaigh a chaith ráithe i bpríosún ar a son; bhí mé do chuideachtain go Sligeach i 1912 nuair a bhunuigheamar beirt Chraobh de'n Transport Union ar a mbaile sin; chaitheas téarma i bpriosún i Mountjoy comh maith leat féin i 1913 agus b'iomdha cruinniughadh eile dár fhreastal sinn beirt chomh maith. B'iomdha seanchas agus b'iomdha sáruidheacht a bhíodh againn le chéile faoi neithibh a bhain le lucht oibre agus le Éirinn.

Labhair mé leat san osbidéal cúpla lá sul dar d'éag thú a Shéamuis. Tá tú imighthe uainn anois agus is uaigneach an chathair i Bláth Cliath id'éagmais. Tá roinnt mhór dar sheas leat sa ngluiseacht fadó imighthe freisin ach feiceamuíd a chéile arís agus déanfamuíd seanchas 'sa' machaire glórmhor ar an taoibh thall de na Réalta. Go dtí sin a Shéamais 'mo ghuidhe-sa féin

298

agus guidhe Mhic Mhuire leat' agus go mba soillseach t'ionad i measc na naingeal agus na naomh. Leagaim an fhleaschuimhne seo ar t'uaigh.

Ar Aghaidh, *Márta 1947*

Translation

Jim, I walked with you through the streets of Wexford in 1911 when the workers of the town came out to welcome you and Patrick Daly who had been in prison on their behalf; I was with you in Sligo in 1912 when we set up a branch of the Transport Union in the town; I was with you in prison in Mountjoy in 1913, and many other meetings too we had together. Many were the yarns we had, and many the arguments about matters affecting the working class and Ireland.

I spoke with you in the hospital a few days before you died, Jim. You have left us and lonely is Dublin city now that you have gone. A great many of those who stood with you in the movement long ago have now departed but we'll see one another again and we'll talk together in that bright glade beyond the stars. Till then, Jim, 'My prayer and the prayer of Mary's Son be with you'; and may your place be radiant among the angels and the saints. I lay this garland of memories on your grave.

***

Micheál Ó Maoláin who was born in the Aran Islands in 1881, was a colleague of Larkin from 1911 and a regular contributor to the *Irish Worker*. In 1913 he was appointed North County Dublin organiser of the ITGWU and was involved in the agitation there among farm workers which culminated in a strike at harvest time. In August, the Farmers' Association agreed to increase wages from 14s to 17s for a 66-hour week. (A ballad by G.K. Chesterton about an incident on the Swords Road during the strike is on page 323). Ó Maoláin was later transferred to the insurance section of the Union where he worked with P. T. Daly.

After Larkin's arrest in America in 1921 on a charge of 'criminal anarchy', Ó Maoláin, with Delia Larkin and P. T. Daly, organised the Release Jim Larkin Committee, with Sean O'Casey as secretary. In a letter from the Banba Hall, Parnell Square in November 1921, appealing for Christmas greetings to be sent to Jim Larkin in Sing Sing in Ossining in New York, O'Casey wrote:

> There can hardly be any necessity to appeal to you to assist us in this effort to show Jim we have not forgotten one who did so much for Liberty and Truth. His present condition testifies to his unbreakable fealty to the Cause of the People. His is a prison cell, the convict garb, and the felon's cap. He never sold the workers for a handful of silver, nor even left them for a riband to stick in his coat.

At the time, O'Casey shared a room at 35 Mountjoy Square in Dublin with Ó Maoláin whom he made the model for Seamus Shields in his play, *The Shadow of a Gunman* (1923). Later, in a letter to Jack Carney (18 April 1942) O'Casey was to refer to Ó Maoláin as 'The Aran man who gave me a shake-down in his room'. He was the founder of Coiste na bPáistí scheme in the 'thirties which raised funds, mainly from trade unions, to send poor children for summer holidays in Irish-speaking areas in Connemara (the Connacht Gaeltacht).

Ó Maoláin contributed to various labour and nationalist papers over almost half a century including an article in *Feasta*, about a year before his death, in which he gave his version of what happened on the night of the Black and Tan raid in 1920, the incident O'Casey used in his play. He was also a regular broadcaster on Radio Éireann. Ó Maoláin was still living in the same 'return room' in Mountjoy Square when he died in 1956. (A picture of Ó Maoláin in the room appeared in the American magazine, *Life*, 26 July 1954).

The 1911 census of population return for the Larkin household living at 27 Auburn Street, Dublin now in the National Archives, was filled in in Irish in Gaelic script. It is likely that the census return was completed by Micheál Ó Maoláin.

Big Jim Crosses the City

Liam MacGabhann

There were crowds at Jim Larkin's funeral – just as there were crowds in Jim Larkin's life. A half century of history marched through Dublin yesterday morning. The years were crowded between Haddington Road and Glasnevin.

You couldn't think of Larkin being in that flower-covered coffin with its Starry Plough flag, just dead.

They all came out, men in dungarees with overcoats buttoned up to the throats, marching erectly as he told them to march. It could have been a Citizen-Army-cum-Irish-Volunteer parade, only for the slowness. The very air of the city seemed to be muffled. You had the feeling that the people were magnetised into the funeral 'as by common instinct'.

And the men in the dungarees and the women grown old who have borne children since they struck instinctively at the 400 bosses at Larkin's will, seemed to be there because they just had to be there.

Just because Big Jim was crossing the city.

Then you wanted to see a big black slouch hat on the coffin and a big black pipe beside it, because all the time you visualised Larkin swinging his huge shoulders, going to a meeting in the North City.

That flag on the Ballast Office symbolised death yet did not stress it.

What does it bring back? Words tramp through the slush of the streets, undertone the music of the dead: –

And Connolly watches ships go out through flags at Kingstown
    pier;
A starving Dublin sends its toll of guard and fusilier;
The Citizen Army is out to-day and if you wonder why,
Go, ask the lords of the finance boards why the men go out to die.

The south-easterly gale blows up the turbulent river, crashing on the O'Connell Bridge arches like Larkin's fist at the council table.

Boots, heavy and grimy and dirty; boots polished and shiny, tramp, tramp, tramp, joining the long, long crowd, step and slither through the snowy slush.

As the procession passes, blinds come down over the windows, people come out of the shops, swell the funeral.

Groups that line the sidewalks, waiting, saying nothing, move out, walk after the old grey men of the Citizen Army, after the tired women of the hopeful eyes of the Citizen Army.

Children gather around the huge lorry of flowers, red and yellow and blue and lily white.

At Beresford Place the bands cry back through the years. Up from the docks small, stocky men walk. They stand beside the coffin as it halts near Liberty Hall.

The deep-sea men seem grimly proud to stand as guard-of-honour.

301

(Larkin ... tied to a ship's stanchion ... planning revolution ... that's what you're thinking.)

The parade moves on, by the Workers' Union old headquarters. Women on tenement steps – (there are brand new bricks on the buildings now) – hold up children to see the parade.

Moladh go deó le Dia! A Kerry policeman is straightening out the crowd and that's not rain on his cheeks. Praise be! At Larkin's funeral I have seen a policeman on duty ... crying!

Corporation men were cleaning slush an hour ago. There are men in the funeral with shovels – and they handle them like military weapons. That band rings through the high houses and the words plod by the horses' feet –

The Citizen Army is out to-day and if you wonder why,
Go ask the lords of the finance boards if the cash returns are high;
It isn't the bosses that bear the brunt and 'tisn't you or I,
'Tis the women and kids whose tears are hid as the Army marches by.

But that is old ... out by O'Connell Street you can't help thinking of Bloody Sunday. Crowds waiting, a D.M.P. man to every two workers and somewhere, silent and disguised, there is hope – *Big Jim is crossing the City!*

So fifty years of history have marched on and so have the D.M.P.

Gardaí in blue are lining the way for Jim Larkin's funeral.

There are wreaths on the coffin from people in Britain too, people who wear dungarees – and frock-coats – girls in offices, men in mines.

The principal men of the State he helped to build, when the foundation stones were being laid, are behind the great coffin that still looks small because one thinks of the fierce statuary of Big Jim.

The Last Post sounds and rifles crash a volley. The people tramp back through the slush and snow, a bit dazed.

They seem dimly aware that above the muffled throbbing of the drums, above the lament of the bugle, and the dull thudding of the marching thousands it was really a voice that called them. Larkin's voice shouting to the people about the history of things they had lost and gained.

Like a thousand times before when the battles were won, he had shouted with a proud command in his words: 'Go back to the job'. Back to the job ... Big Jim has crossed the city.

The Irish Press, *5 February 1947*

302

Liam MacGabhann, one of the Kerry poets of the 1930s, was among the out-standing journalists of his time. His best-known poems are: Connolly – The man was all shot through that came today/Into the barrack square. *(In the poem, it is a young Welsh 'Tommy', one of the firing-squad, who is speaking);* and, The Poor of the World:

> *I have seen rich men go feasting and making din,*
> *I have seen the rich men's homes and the wealth therein,*
> *And I would that their wealth and wares to the winds were hurled*
> *For the poor o' the world, O Christ, the poor o' the world.*

Inscriptions on a Monument

The great appear great because we are on our knees. Let us rise.

Ní uasal aon uasal ach sinne bheith íseal: éirimís!

Les grands ne sont grands que parce que nous sommes à genoux: Levons-nous!

These inscriptions, in English, Irish and French, are inscribed on the front of the base of the Jim Larkin Monument in O'Connell Street, Dublin.

The motto, 'The great appear great to us, only because we are on our knees. Let us Rise', appeared on the masthead of the the *Workers' Republic*, the organ of the Irish Socialist Republican Party, which was published in Dublin between 1896 and 1903. The ISRP was founded by James Connolly when he came to Ireland in 1896 at the age of twenty-eight years. An Irish trans-lation of the motto used on the masthead was: 'Is dóigh linn gur mór iad na daoine móra mar atámaoid féin ar ár nglúnaibh. Eirghmís'.

The slogan is usually attributed to Camille Desmoulins (1760-1794), the French revolutionary and one-time friend of Robes-pierre, who was executed on 2 April 1794. The slogan was used by *Le Journal des Révolutions de Paris* which was published from 1789 and which was edited by Louis Marie Prudhomme. While Desmoulins was associated with *Le Journal* and it ceased publica-tion after his death, the slogan has been attributed to the editor, Prudhomme (*Dictionary of Quotations, French and Italian*, by P.B. Harbottle, London, 1901). The text given by Harbottle is 'Les grands ne paraissent grands que parce que nous sommes à genoux. Levons-nous'.

In *Les Citations françaises: Receuil de passages* célèbres, *phrases familières, mots historiques* by Othon Guerlac (Paris: A. Colin, 1953), the slogan is given as a motto which appeared at the head of Prudhomme's newspaper, *Les Révolutions de Paris*. Guerlac states that some attribute the slogan to Vergniaud, others to Loustalot, the chief editor of Prudhomme's paper, and that it seems to have been inspired by a similar phrase used in 1652 by Dubosc-Montandré, in his pamphlet, *Le point de l'ovale*.

The text given in Guerlac is that inscribed on the Larkin Monument.

The Irish text used on the Larkin Monument is by Seán MacRéamoinn.

On the west side of the base of the Larkin Monument there is a quotation from a poem by Patrick Kavanagh (1905-1965):

And Tyranny trampled them in Dublin's gutter
Until Jim Larkin came along and cried
The call of Freedom and the call of Pride
And Slavery crept to its hands and knees
And Nineteen Thirteen cheered from out the utter
Degradation of their miseries.

Kavanagh's poem, 'Jim Larkin', was first published in *The Bell* (editor, Peadar O'Donnell), March 1947.

On the east side of the Larkin Monument there is a quotation from Sean O'Casey (1880-1964):

... he talked to the workers, spoke as only Jim Larkin could speak, not for an assignation with peace, dark obedience, or placid resignation; but trumpet-tongued of resistance to wrong, discontent with leering poverty, and defiance of any power strutting out to stand in the way of their march onward.

The quotation is from *Drums under the Window* (London, 1945).

The figure of Jim Larkin that stands on the base of the Monument is by Oisín Kelly (1915-1981). The Monument was unveiled by the President of Ireland, Dr Patrick J. Hillery, on 15 June 1979.

A Literary Footnote

Has any other Irish figure this century inspired so much literary and artistic work as Jim Larkin? A subject for street ballads and verse from the time he came to Belfast in 1907, Larkin had created his own place in the hearts of Irish workers and in the minds of writers, poets and artists.

The American writer, James T. Farrell, visited Larkin in Dublin in 1938 and has described the ageing leader kneeling on the floor of the flat where he lived, searching for a book he wanted to give to his guest:

> His books were in dusty cabinets along the floor. Nothing was in order. He flung out piles of books. One's throat became dry and one almost choked because of the dust in the room. And Jim kept looking ... This seemed to go on endlessly. Finally, he grunted with pleasure.

Larkin had found the book he was searching for. It was a play by Daniel Corkery, *The Labour Leader.* Jim was the model for the hero of the play.

In the first act of the play, Tim Murphy, the representative of the coal porters on the Strike Committee, mocking the suggestion that the strike leader, Davna, be given a secretary, asks:

> And if ye give him a secretary his job will be to cut Davna off when he's giving us the history of Ireland in the tenth century, or giving us Shelley: 'Rise like lions after slumber'; 'Shake your manes like thunder'; 'Ye are many, they are few': He was a great lad, that Shelley, and he only a poor sheep of an Englishman and all. And what would we know about him only for Davna? Or about the Red Flag? Or about anything at all.

Corkery's play was produced by Lennox Robinson at the Abbey Theatre on 30 September 1919 and published the following year.

Daniel Corkery (1878-1964) was the author of several plays, short stories and a novel, *The Threshold of Quiet* (1917). He is best known as the author of *The Hidden Ireland* (1925).

Larkin was also to be the inspiration for characters in two of Sean O'Casey's later plays. Already the real-life Larkin had been much written about by O'Casey, notably in the third volume of his autobiography, *Drums Under the Windows* (1945):

Through the streets he strode, shouting into every dark and evil-smelling hallway. The great day of change has come; Circe's swine had a better time than you have; come from your vomit; out into the sun. Larkin is calling you all!

O'Casey dedicated *The Star Turns Red* (1940) to 'the men and women who fought through the great Dublin lock-out in nineteen hundred and thirteen'. The second act of the play takes place in the headquarters of the General Workers' Union where a streamer proclaims 'An Injury to One is the Concern of All!' (This motto appeared at the top of the editorial in the *Irish Worker*) . In response to the Brown Priest's question as to why he should stay with the workers in revolt, Red Jim answers, 'To be with us when the star turns red; to help us carry the fiery cross. Join with us. March with us in the midst of the holy fire.'

In the final act of the play, Red Jim declares:

We fight on; we suffer; we die; but we fight on.
Till brave-breasted women and men, terrac'd with strength,
Shall live and die together, co-equal in all things;
And romping, living children anointed with joy, shall be banners
    and bannerols of this moving world!
In all that great minds give, we share;
And unto man be all might, majesty, dominion, and power!

In *Red Roses for Me* (1942), which is autobiographical, Sean O'Casey again evokes the spirit of Larkin and 1913, when the young strike leader, Ayamonn Breydon, asserts: 'Let us bring freedom here, not with sounding brass an' tinkling cymbal, but with silver trumpets blowing, with a song all men can sing, with a palm branch in our hand, rather than with a whip at our belt, and a headsman's axe on our shoulders', and later, in the third act, when he speaks to the women on the darkened bridge:

Friend, we would that you should live a greater life; we will that all of us shall live a greater life. Our strike is yours. A step ahead for us today; another one for you tomorrow. We who have known, and know, the emptiness of life shall know its fullness. All men and women quick with life are fain to venture forward. (To Eeada) The apple grows for you to eat. (To Dympna) The violet grows for you to wear. (To Finnoola) Young maiden, another world is in your womb.

At the end of the third act, as the scene darkens and nothing is heard but the sound of tramping feet, through this threatening sound comes the sound of voices singing quietly:

We swear to release thee from hunger and hardship,
From things that are ugly and common and mean;

306

Thy people together shall build a great city,
The finest and fairest that ever was seen.

When, towards the end of the fourth act of the play, Inspector Finglas of the Mounted Police responds to a remark that Ayamonn's end was 'a noble an' a mighty death', with the dismissive 'It wasn't a very noble thing to die for a single shilling', Ayamonn's lover, Sheila, replies, 'Maybe he saw the shilling in th' shape of a new world'.

Earlier in the play, Ayamon had referred to the shilling:

A shilling's little to me, and less to many; to us it is our schechinals, showing us God's light is near; showing us the way in which our feet must go; a sun ray on our face; the first step taken in the march of a thousand miles.

A.E. (George Russell), whose searing indictment of the Dublin employers in his famous letter written in 1913 is among the classics of literary protests, based the character Culain, the socialist, in *The Interpreters* (1922) on Larkin. Culain is 'a mystic motivated by an absolutely Christian compassion for the slum dwellers of the city', to quote the American critic, William Irwin Thompson, who adds: 'A.E. knew Larkin well and his portrait of Larkin's religious nature is true to life'.

In *The Interpreters*, A. E. describes Culain as he enters the prison to join the other prisoners:

The figure which emerged from the shadowy into the red air was massive, noble and simple. It might have stood for an adept of labour or avatar of the Earth spirit incarnated in some grand labourer to inspire the workers by a new imagination of society. To the workers this Culainn appeared an almost superhuman type of themselves, a clear utterer of what in them was inarticulate. That deep, slow, thrilling voice myriads had listened to as the voice of their own souls.

A.E.'s fellow-poet and colleague on the *Irish Homestead* journal which he edited, Susan Mitchell, published her poem, 'To the "Villas of Genteel Dastards"', in the *Irish Worker* in November 1913.

No prouder sight has Ireland seen since banded peasants stood
Upon her fields for freedom than this famished brotherhood,
Who in their leader's message have caught a distant gleam
Of that far off Holy City, our glory and our dream.

Almost a decade later in New York, a Dublin-born American poet, Lola Ridge, the theme of whose poetry was the martyrdom of the downtrodden, wrote her poem, 'To Larkin', then in Sing Sing gaol:

> One hundred million men and women go inevitably about their
>   affairs
> In the somnolent way
> Of men before a great drunkenness ...
> They do not see you go by their windows, Jim Larkin,
> With your eyes bloody as the sunset
> And your shadow gaunt against the sky ...
> You, and the like of you, that life
> Is crushing for their frantic wines.

Frank O'Connor's poem, 'Homage to Jim Larkin' was first published in *The Irish Times* towards the end of 1944, just two years before Larkin's death:

> Roll away the stone, Lord, roll away the stone
> As you did when last I died in the attic room;
> Then there was no fire as well, and I died of cold
> While Jim Larkin walked the streets before he grew old.

A month after Larkin's death, Patrick Kavanagh's poem, 'Jim Larkin', was published in *The Bell*:

> And Tyranny trampled them in Dublin's gutter
> Until Jim Larkin came along and cried
> The call of Freedom and the call of Pride
> And Slavery crept to its hands and knees
> And Nineteen Thirteen cheered from out the utter
> Degradation of their miseries.

The same month, Breandán Ó Beacháin (Brendan Behan) published his poetic tribute in *Comhar*:

> Ag leanúint a chónra tré chlab na cathrath aréir
> An sinne a bhí sa chónra?
> Níorbh eadh; bhíomar sa tsráid ag máirseáil,
> Beó-bhuidheach do'n mharbh.

> (Following the coffin through the city's open mouth last night/Was it we ourselves who were in the coffin?/No; we were on the streets marching/The living grateful to the dead.)

Austin Clarke's 'Inscription for a Headstone', in his *Collected Poems* (1974), opens with the line 'What Larkin bawled to hungry crowds', and concludes:

> His name endures on our holiest page,
> Scrawled in a rage by Dublin's poor.

Many ballads have been written by anonymous scribes of the people about Larkin, and Dublin's women and men who scrawled the heroic tale that was 1913. Two of the many are reproduced in this Miscellany:

We rose in sad and weary days
To fight the workers' cause
We found in Jim, a heart ablaze,
To break down unjust laws.
But 'tis a sin to follow him
Says Murphy and his crew,
Though true men, like you men,
Will stick to him like glue.

The Dublin lock-out of 1913 and the towering figure of Larkin provide the background to James Plunkett's powerful novel, *Strumpet City* (1969) on which was based a notable RTE television series. Plunkett also wrote the radio play, *Big Jim*, broadcast by Radio Éireann in 1954. His stage play about 1913, *The Risen People*, was produced by the Abbey Theatre in 1958.

Two other stage productions have commemorated 1913 and Larkin. A masque, *Let Freedom Ring*, by Donagh McDonagh (1912-68) was produced at the Gate Theatre, Dublin in 1963 to commemorate the fiftieth anniversary of the 1913 lock-out and in 1974, the fiftieth anniversary of the founding of the Workers' Union of Ireland was celebrated by a production in the Gaiety Theatre, Dublin of *The Ballad of Jim Larkin*, by Eoghan Harris.

Larkin figures in Part Five (The Great Lock-out) of *The Non-Stop Connolly Show*, by Margaretta D'Arcy and John Arden. The six plays which comprise the Show were published in five volumes in 1977 and in a one-volume edition in 1986. The six plays were first given in a twenty-four hour performance in Liberty Hall, Dublin in 1975.

Jim Larkin is publicly commemorated in his adopted city by the life-size bronze statue by Oisin Kelly (1915-1981) that stands on a granite base, the Larkin Monument, in O'Connell Street, Dublin, between the GPO on one side of the street and on the other side, a department store which in 1913 was the Imperial Hotel, owned by Larkin's great antagonist, William Martin Murphy, at the window of which a disguised Larkin addressed the proclaimed meeting which was to lead to the police baton charges on what came to be known as Bloody Sunday, 31 August 1913.

In the Lane Municipal Gallery of Modern Art in Parnell Square, Dublin there is a head of Larkin by the American sculptor Mina Carney (died 1974). She was married to Jack Carney, the close friend and comrade of Larkin over three decades in Ireland and in America. Both had been involved together in some of the great working-class struggles of the time and had endured prison spells for their activities.

A frequent visitor to Liberty Hall in 1913 was the artist, William Orpen, RA, who made drawings of the food kitchen there and of Larkin. One drawing of Larkin at work in Liberty Hall was reproduced in Orpen's book of reminiscences, *Stories of Old Ireland and Myself*, published in 1924. Another drawing of Larkin by Orpen done around the same time was reproduced in the catalogue for the William Orpen Centenary Exhibition in the National Gallery of Ireland in Dublin in 1978. On the drawing, Orpen had written: 'I can't draw him – He's more like your El Greco man and 6 ft 4" high.'

A cartoon drawing of Larkin by the artist Grace Gifford was published in *Irish Opinion*, 12 December 1913. Grace Gifford married Joseph Mary Plunkett on the eve of his execution in Kilmainham Jail on 4 May 1916.

There are other drawings of Larkin including one by Sean O'Sullivan, RHA (1906-1964) which was done in 1942 when Larkin was sixty-eight and which is in the National Gallery of Ireland, and a pastel drawing by Sean Keating (1889-1977) done in 1946, the year before Larkin's death, which is now in Liberty Hall. Stamps (7p and 11p) designed by Peter Wildbur and incorporating the portrait of Larkin by Sean O'Sullivan were issued by the Post Office on 21 January 1974.

There are numerous representations of Larkin on posters and banners, notably the huge banner of the Workers' Union of Ireland done by Peter Broughal in 1949. The maroon border is inscribed in gold, above the name of the union and below 'An Injury to One is the Concern of All'.

There was a wall painting by Nano Reid (1905-1981), 'Larkin speaking in College Green, Dublin', in the Four Provinces House, Harcourt Street, Dublin, the head office of the Irish Bakers', Confectioners' and Allied Workers' Amalgamated Union, now demolished. A colour slide of the mural is in the Irish Labour History Museum, Dublin.

The March of the Workers

What is this, the sound and rumour? What is this that all
    men hear,
Like the wind in hollow valleys when the storm is drawing
    near,
Like the rolling on of ocean in the eventide of fear?
                         'Tis the people marching on.

Whither go they, and whence come they? What are these of
    whom ye tell?
In what country are they dwelling 'twixt the gates of heaven
    and hell?
Are they mine or thine for money? Will they serve a master
    well?
                        Still the rumour's marching on.

    Hark the rolling of the thunder!
    Lo the sun! and lo thereunder
    Riseth wrath, and hope, and wonder,
    And the host comes marching on.

Forth they come from grief and torment; on they wend
    toward health and mirth,
All the wide world is their dwelling, every corner of the
    earth
Buy them, sell them for thy service! Try the bargain what 'tis
    worth,
                      For the days are marching on.

These are they who build thy houses, weave thy raiment,
    win thy wheat,
Smooth the rugged, fill the barren, turn the bitter into sweet,
All for thee this day – and ever. What reward for them is
    meet
                    Till the host comes marching on?

    Hark the rolling of the thunder!
    Lo the sun! and lo thereunder
    Riseth wrath, and hope, and wonder,
    And the host comes marching on.

311

Many a hundred years passed over have they laboured deaf
and blind;
Never tidings reached their sorrow, never hope their toil
might find.
Now at last they've heard and hear it, and the cry comes
down the wind,
And their feet are marching on.

O ye rich men hear and tremble! for with words the sound is
rife:
'Once for you and earth we laboured; changed henceforward
is the strife.
We are men, and we shall battle for the world of men and
life;
And our host is marching on.'

Hark the rolling of the thunder
Lo the sun! and lo thereunder
Riseth wrath, and hope, and wonder,
And the host comes marching on.

'Is it war, then? Will ye perish as the dry wood in the fire?
Is it peace? Then be ye of us, let your hope be our desire.
Come and live! for life awaketh, and the world shall never
tire;
And hope is marching on.'

'On we march then, we the workers, and the rumour that ye
hear
Is the blended sound of battle and deliv'rance drawing near;
For the hope of every creature is the banner that we bear,
And the world is marching on.'

Hark the rolling of the thunder!
Lo the sun! and lo thereunder
Riseth wrath, and hope, and wonder,
And the host comes marching on.

William Morris (1834-1896)

*These verses were quoted by Labour speakers at meetings and demonstrations.
Jim Larkin frequently quoted from the poem in speeches and in the* Irish
Worker.

312

The Red Flag

The people's flag is deepest red,
It shrouded oft our martyr'd dead,
And ere their limbs grew stiff and cold,
Their heart's blood dyed its every fold.

Then raise the scarlet standard high –
Within its shade we'll live and die!
Though cowards flinch and traitors sneer,
We'll keep the Red Flag flying here!

Look round! – the Frenchman loves its blaze,
The sturdy German chants its praise;
In Moscow's vaults its hymns were sung,
Chicago swells the surging song.

It waved above our infant might
When all ahead seemed dark as night;
It witnessed many a deed and vow –
We must not change its colour now!

It well recalls the triumphs past,
It gives the hope of peace at last;
The banner bright – the symbol plain
Of human right and human gain.

It suits today the weak and base,
Whose minds are fixed on pelf and place,
To cringe before the rich man's frown
And haul the sacred emblem down.

With head uncovered swear we all
To bear it onward till we fall;
Come dungeon dark or gallows grim,
This song shall be our parting hymn:

Jim Connell (1852-1929)

Jim Connell was born in Killskyre, County Meath. The Red Flag was first published in the Christmas 1889 edition of Justice, the organ of the Social Democratic Federation in Britain. Connell told Tom Mann that in writing it he had been 'inspired by the Paris Commune, the heroism of the Russian Nihilists, the firmness of the Irish Land League, the devotion to death of the Chicago anarchists'. *The immediate occasion for Connell writing the verses was the great London dock strike of 1889 for the 'dockers' tanner'.*

The Red Flag was sung at the end of Congress annual meetings in the late 1920s.

Be Moderate

'Be Moderate', the timorous cry,
    Who dreads the tyrant's thunder,
    'You ask too much, and people fly
From you aghast in wonder'.
    'Tis passing strange, and I declare
Such statements cause me mirth,
For our demands most moderate are,
We only want *the earth*.

Our masters all – a godly crew
    Whose hearts throb for the poor –
    Their sympathies assure us, too,
If our demands were fewer.
Most generous souls, but please observe,
What they enjoy from birth,
Is all we ever had the nerve
To ask, that is, *the earth*.

The Labour Fakir, full of guile,
    Such doctrine ever preaches,
And, whilst he bleeds the rank and file,
Tame moderation teaches.
Yet, in his despite, we'll see the day
When, with sword in its girth,
Labour shall march in war array,
To seize its own, *the earth*.

For Labour long with groans and tears
    To its oppressors knelt,
    But, never yet to aught save fears
Did hear of tyrant melt.
We need not kneel; our cause is high,
Of true men there's no dearth,

314

And our victorious rallying cry
Shall be, *we want the earth.*

James Connolly (1868 -1916)

'Be Moderate' was included in James Connolly's Songs of Freedom *published in New York in 1907.*

James Connolly wrote: 'No revolutionary movement is complete without its poetical expression. If such a movement has caught hold of the imagination of the masses, they will seek a vent in song for the aspirations, the fears and hopes, the loves and hatreds engendered by the struggle. Until the movement is marked by the joyous, defiant, singing of revolutionary songs, it lacks one of the distinctive marks of a popular revolutionary movement; it is a dogma of a few, and not the faith of the multitude'.

Bread and Roses

As we come marching, marching,
In the beauty of the day,
A million darkened kitchens,
A thousand mill lifts gray,
Are touched with all the radiance
That a sudden sun discloses,
For the people hear us singing,
'Bread and roses, Bread and roses.'

As we come marching, marching,
We battle too for men,
For they are women's children,
And we mother them again.
Our lives shall not be sweated
From birth until life closes,
Hearts starve as well as bodies,
Give us bread, but give us roses.

As we come marching, marching,
Unnumbered women dead
Go crying through our singing
Their ancient cry for bread.
Small art and love and beauty
Their drudging spirits knew.
Yes, it is bread we fight for –
But we fight for roses, too!

As we come marching, marching,
We bring the greater days.
The rising of the women means
The rising of the race.
No more the drudge and idler –
Ten that toil where one reposes,
But a sharing of life's glories:
Bread and roses! Bread and roses!

James Oppenheim

Delegates to the ICTU Women's Conference sing this song at the conclusion of the conference.

The song came out of a famous strike in the United States in 1912. On their marches the strikers carried banners with the slogan 'We want bread and roses too,' and it was this that inspired the song. The music was composed by Caroline Kohlsaat.

'It was the first strike I ever saw which sang,' a journalist wrote, 'I shall not soon forget the curious lift, the strange sudden fire of the mingled nationalities at the strike meetings when they broke into the universal language of song. And not only at the meetings did they sing, but in the soup houses and in the streets. I saw one group of women workers who were peeling potatoes at a relief station suddenly break into the swing of the 'Internationale'''.

'The strikers were always marching and singing', wrote another journalist, 'The tired, gray crowds ebbing and flowing perpetually into the mills had waked and opened their mouths to sing'. Carrying their picket signs with the slogan 'We Want Bread and Roses Too', they sang, as they marched, Jim Connell's The Red Flag, the Marseillaise, Hold the Fort, Joe Hill's Casey Jones, and On the Good Old Picket Line.

On one occasion when the IWW leader, Bill Haywood (who, a year later, was to address mass meetings in Britain with Jim Larkin in support of the locked-out Dublin workers) spoke to a crowd of 25,000 on Lawrence Common, the strikers sang the 'Internationale' in each of their many languages in turn.

The strike at the Lawrence mills of the American Woolen Company involved 23,000 workers of at least 25 different nationalities and languages. Teen-age girls made up half the strikers from the four mills. A young woman, Anna LoPezzi, was killed by police fire as they tried to break up a picket line.

The cause of the strike was the decision of the employers to cut weekly wages by two hours' pay when a new state law reduced weekly hours from 56 to 54 for women and children under 18. 'Better to starve fighting than to starve working', was their battle cry. The workers won a great victory after nearly three months. The employers agreed to increase wages by at least 5% (15% for the lower-paid), to pay time-and-a-quarter for overtime and to rehire strikers without discrimination.

Elizabeth Gurley Flynn – her mother, Annie Gurley, was born in Loughrea, Co. Galway and her paternal grandfather was also Irish-born – then 22 years old, was a leader of the strike. She held special meetings for the women and spoke in the eastern cities in support of the workers. She was 'The Rebel Girl' for whom Joe Hill wrote his famous song. She met him for the first time in his cell in May 1915. It was to her that he wrote his last letter at 10 p.m, 18 November 1915, a few hours before he was executed in Utah State Prison in Salt Lake City. 'You have been more to me than a Fellow Worker', he wrote, 'You have been an inspiration and when I composed The Rebel Girl you were right there and helped me all the time. As you furnished the idea I will, now that I am gone give you all the credit for that song'. As she left the jail, Hill said to her: 'I'm not afraid of death, but I'd like to be in the fight a little longer.'

Jim Larkin was the main speaker at Joe Hill's funeral in Chicago (in accordance with his wish 'not to be found dead in the state of Utah'. the IWW had brought his body there for cremation). The Rebel Girl was not there: she was awaiting trial in Patterson, New Jersey, on charges arising from a strike of silk workers in 1913.

At his last interview, Joe Hill was asked by a reporter about his will. He scribbled on a piece of paper:

My will is easy to decide,
For there is nothing to divide.
My kin don't need to fuss and moan -
'Moss does not cling to a rolling stone'.

My body? – Oh! – if I could choose,
I would to ashes it reduce,
And let the merry breezes blow
My dust to where some flowers grow.

Perhaps some fading flower then
Would come to life and bloom again.
This is my last and final will.
Good luck to all of you.

Joe Hill was executed on 19 November 1915 by firing squad at the Utah state prison. More than 30,000 people marched in the funeral procession. His wish that the breezes blow his dust to 'where some flowers grow' was honoured by his comrades. His ashes were scattered in various parts of America. One container, however, was held by a postmaster who would not deliver 'subversive' mail. Somehow the container ended up in the National Archives in Washington. On 19 November 1988, exactly seventy-three years after Joe Hill's execution, the National Archives forwarded the ashes to the office of the IWW in Chicago.

In 1979, the AFL-CIO made an appeal to the Governor of Utah seeking a pardon for Joe Hill that would 'remove the stain of injustice that surrounds the memory of Joe Hill'. (In 1977, fifty years after their execution, Sacco and Vanzetti were vindicated by a proclamation from the Governor of Massachusetts, Michael Dukakis). The Governor of Utah did not respond to the AFL-CIO appeal.

Still, as the song by Alfred Hayes and Earl Robinson goes:

Joe Hill ain't dead, he says to me, Joe Hill ain't never died.
Where working men are out on strike, Joe Hill is at their side.
From San Diego up to Maine, in every mine and mill
Where workers strike and organise, says he, you'll find Joe Hill.

The Watchword of Labour

Oh, hear ye, the Watchword of Labour,
The slogan of they who'd be free
That no more to any enslaver
Must labour bend suppliant knee.
That we, on whose shoulders is borne,
The pomp and the pride of the great,
Whose toil they repay with their scorn,
Must challenge and master our fate.

Then send it aloft on the breeze boys
The slogan the grandest we've known
That Labour must rise from its knees boys,
And claim the broad earth as its own.

Oh, we who've oft won by our valour
Empires for our rulers and lords
Yet kneel in abasement and squalor
To the thing that we've made by our swords
Now valour with worth will be blending
When answering labour's command
We arise from our knees and ascending
To manhood, for freedom take stand.

Then out from the fields and the factories,
From workshop, from mill and from mine,
Despising their wrath and their pity
We workers are moving in line
To answer the Watchword and token
That Labour gives forth as its own
Nor pause till our fetters we've broken
And conquered the spoiler and drone.

James Connolly (1868-1916)

This verse appeared in the Irish Worker, *December, 1913 as 'Watchword, A
Rallying Song for Labour', with music by Frank Doyle. This was a pseudonym
for J.J. Hughes (Seamus Hughes). Hughes became an official of the ITGWU in
1917 and was assistant secretary when he resigned in 1921. He later became
the first general secretary of the Cumann na nGael party. In 1924 he was
appointed the first announcer in the new radio station, Dublin 2RN, later
becoming assistant director of Radio Eireann. He died in 1942.
'The Watchword of Labour' was sometimes sung at the conclusion of
Congress meetings.*

September 1913

What need you, being come to sense,
    But fumble in a greasy till
And add the half pence to the pence
    And prayer to shivering prayer, until
You have dried the marrow from the bone;
    For men were born to pray and save:
Romantic Ireland's dead and gone,
    It's with O'Leary in the grave.

Yet they were of a different kind,
  The names that stilled your childish play,
They have gone about the world like wind,
  But little time had they to pray
For whom the hangman's rope was spun,
  And what, God help us, could they save?
Romantic Ireland's dead and gone,
  It's with O'Leary in the grave.

Was it for this the wild geese spread
  Their grey wing upon every tide;
For this that all that blood was shed,
  For this Edward Fitzgerald died,
And Robert Emmet and Wolfe Tone,
  All that delirium of the brave:
Romantic Ireland's dead and gone,
  It's with O'Leary in the grave.

Yet could we turn the years again,
  And call those exiles as they were,
In all their loneliness and pain,
  You'd cry 'Some woman's yellow hair
Has maddened every mother's son':
  They weighed so lightly what they gave,
But let them be, they're dead and gone,
  They're with O'Leary in the grave.

W. B. Yeats (1865-1939)

To the 'Villas of Genteel Dastards'

*'[A city of bellowing slaves! Villas of genteel dastards!' –
John Mitchel in* Jail Journal.]

It was a glorious civic boast – *civis Romanus sum!*
But we – we want no citizens, we have no Orange drum;
We have the Ancient Order and ratepayers of renown,
And publicans and peelers all over Dublin town.

Oh mean and crafty Dublin, the sons you've flung away!
The tale of your iniquity you're filling up today;

You cringe and slink before the lash, I know you for a cur
Who turned on a Lord Edward, who fawned upon a Sirr.

You stood aside while Emmet died, you let John Mitchel go
Across the seas of exile, nor struck one manly blow
To save the ardent hearts who would have set you up on
     high:
You found the paid informer, you cheered the pensioned
     spy.

You sit within your villas, genteely, as of yore,
Unheeding the fierce life that throbs a stone's throw from
     your door:
Have you no blood to nerve your arm to do the selfless
     deed?
The portents that surround you have you no eyes to read?

I see a band of shabby men, down in a shabby street,
I see the light in eyes upturned a leader's eyes to meet:
I know that spark of holy fire and bend a reverent knee
Before the light unquenchable of man's divinity.

No prouder sight has Ireland seen since banded peasants
     stood
Upon her fields for freedom than this famished brotherhood,
Who in their leader's message have caught a distant gleam
Of that far off Holy City, our glory and our dream.

These are the sons whom Dublin should gather to her breast,
Those – these her citizens to spread her glory East and West,
Ye cannot quench the spirit, but oh, consider well,
Lest ye should turn the torch of God to light the fires of hell.

                              Susan Mitchell (1866-1926)

Susan Mitchell worked as sub-editor on the Irish Homestead *edited by A.E.,
and subsequently the* Irish Statesman. *Her books of poems include* The Living
Chalice (1908).

Who Fears to Wear the Blood Red Badge?

Who fears to wear the blood red badge
Upon his manly breast?
What scab obeys the vile command
Of Murphy and the rest,
He's all a knave, and half a slave
Who slights his Union thus
But true men, like you men,
Will show the badge with us.

They dared to fling a manly brick
They wrecked a blackleg tram,
They dared give Harvey Duff a kick,
They didn't care a damn.
They lie in gaol, they can't get bail,
Who fought their corner thus,
But you men, with sticks men,
Must make the Peelers 'cuss'.

We rose in sad and weary days
To fight the workers' cause,
We found in Jim, a heart ablaze,
To break down unjust laws.
But 'tis a sin to follow him
Says Murphy and his crew,
Though true men, like you men,
Will stick to him like glue.

Good luck be with him, he is here
To win for us the fight;
To suffer for us without fear,
To champion the right.
So stick to Jim, let nothing dim
Our ardour in the fray,
And true Jim, our own Jim,
Will win our fight today.

This ballad by 'Maca', was published in the Irish Worker, *11 October 1913.
The ITGWU badge in 1913 was the Red Hand of Ulster.*

A Song of Swords

'A drove of cattle came into a village called Swords and was stopped by the rioters'. (Daily Paper)

In a place called Swords on the Irish road
It is told for a new renown
How we held the horns of the cattle, and how
We will hold the horns of the devil now
Ere the lord of hell, with the horn on his brow,
    Is crowned in Dublin town.

Light in the East and light in the West,
And light on the cruel lords,
On the souls that suddenly all men knew,
And the green flag flew and the red flag flew,
And many a wheel of the world stopped, too,
    When the cattle were stopped at Swords.

Be they sinners or less than saints
That smite in the street for rage,
We know where the shame shines bright: we know
You that they smite at, you their foe,
Lords of the lawless wage and low,
    This is your lawful wage.

You pinched a child to a torture price
That you dared not name in words;
So black a jest was the silver bit
That your own speech shook for the shame of it.
And the coward was plain as a cow they hit
    When the cattle have strayed at Swords.

The wheel of the torment of wives went round
To break men's brotherhood,
You gave the good Irish blood to grease
The clubs of your country's enemies,
You saw the brave man beat to the knees:
    And you saw that it was good.

The rope of the rich is long and long –
The longest of hangmen's cords;

But the kings and crowds are holding their breath,
In a giant shadow o'er all beneath
Where God stands holding the scales of Death,
    Between the cattle and Swords.

Haply the lords that hire and lend,
The lowest of all men's lords,
Who sell their kind like kine at a fair,
Will find no head of their cattle there;
But faces of men where cattle were;
    Faces of men – and Swords.

And the name shining and terrible,
The sternest of all man's words,
Still mark that place to seek or shun,
In the streets where the struggling cattle run –
Grass and a silence of judgement done
    In the place that is called Swords.

                G.K. Chesterton (1874-1936)

This ballad refers to an incident during a strike of farm workers in North County Dublin in 1913 which was led by Jim Larkin. The ballad was first published in the Daily Herald (London), 11 October, 1913.
    The Daily Herald in 1913 was edited by George Lansbury, the assistant editor was W. P. Ryan (see page 289) and the Dublin correspondent was Francis Sheehy Skeffington (see page 291).

Solidarity Forever

When the union's inspiration through the workers' blood
    shall run,
There can be no power greater anywhere beneath the sun.
Yet what force on earth is weaker than the feeble strength of
    one?
But the union makes us strong.

    Solidarity forever!
    Solidarity forever!
    Solidarity forever!
    For the union makes us strong.

All the world's that's owned by idle drones is ours and ours
alone.
We have laid the wide foundations; built it skyward stone by
stone.
It is ours not to slave in, but to master and to own,
While the union makes us strong.

They have taken untold millions that they never toiled to
earn.
But without our brains and muscle not a single wheel can
turn.
We can break their haughty power; gain our freedom when
we learn
That the union makes us strong.

In our hands is placed a power greater than their hoarded
gold;
Greater than the might of armies, magnified a thousand-fold.
We can bring to birth a new world from the ashes of the old.
For the union makes us strong.

Ralph Chaplin (1887-1961)

*Ralph Chaplin wrote this famous labour song in 1915 to the tune of 'Battle
Hymn of the Republic' and it soon became the anthem of the IWW – Industrial
Workers of the World – known throughout the world as the Wobblies. In the
1930s it became the organising song of the CIO. Next to Joe Hill, Chaplin was
the IWW's foremost poet and songwriter. (He was the author of the verses with
which Cathal O'Shannon ended his Presidential address to the Irish Labour
Party and Trades Union Congress in 1922 – see page 191).*

*Big Bill Haywood, one of the founders of the IWW in 1905 and in 1914 its
general secretary, spoke with Jim Larkin on his Fiery Cross campaign in
Britain in 1913. (See page 268.) Two years later Larkin and Haywood were the
main speakers at the funeral of Joe Hill in Chicago in November 1915. It was
Larkin who spoke the last words: 'Let his blood cement the many divided
sections of our movement and our slogan for the future be: Joe Hill's body lies
mouldering in the grave, but the cause goes marching on.' It was Larkin who
first quoted Joe Hill's last words, 'Don't mourn for me: organise!'*

*James Connolly was a member of the IWW in 1905 and one of its New
York organisers in 1907. He met Ralph Chaplin in Chicago. Connolly had just
completed his pamphlet,* Socialism Made Easy, *and Chaplin was drawing the
cover design for the publishers, the Kerr Company. 'Any suggestions?',
Chaplin asked him. 'None at all boy, just so it's plenty Irish', Connolly replied.
The cover was full of runic decorations, shamrocks and an Irish harp. Connolly
was so delighted that he asked Chaplin to chair one of his open-air propaganda
meetings. So it was that at Sixty-third and Halsted streets in Chicago, Chaplin
delivered his first soapbox oration.*

To Larkin

Is it you I see go by the window, Jim Larkin – you not look-
    ing at me or anyone,
And your shadow swaying from East to West?
Strange that you should be walking free – you shut down
    without light,
And your legs tied up with a knot of iron.

One hundred million men and women go inevitably about
    their affairs,
In the somnolent way
Of men before a great drunkenness ...
They do not see you go by their windows, Jim Larkin,
With your eyes bloody as the sunset
And your shadow gaunt upon the sky ...
You, and the like of you, that life
Is crushing for their frantic wines.

Lola Ridge (1871-1941)

*Lola Ridge was born in Dublin and went to America in 1907. Her first volume
of poems,* The Ghetto and Other Poems, *was published in 1918. This was
followed by* Sun-Up *(1920);* Red Flag *(1927);* Firehead *(1929), which was
inspired by the execution of Sacco and Vanzetti; and* Dance of Fire *(1933).
The consistent theme of her poetry was the martyrdom of the downtrodden.*
    Lines from Lola Ridge's poem were quoted in an editorial in The Nation
*(New York), 2 May 1923 following 'Big Jim's' deportation from the United
States as an 'undesirable' a few months after Governor Smith's pardon. The
editorial stated:*

> *Deportation is always a petty process; it somehow seems doubly petty in
> the case of such an epic figure as gaunt, gray-haired, long-limbed James
> Larkin ... We seldom agree with Larkin. But there is a genuine bigness of
> soul behind his bigness of body. He is one of those rare things – a born
> leader of men, with a sense of the pain of life. Lola Ridge understood the
> man ...*

Song of the Workless

Opening of the Dáil Session, October, 1932

In the heart of the city,
Not craving for pity
Nor for charity, as cold as icy blast,
Children of the land
In serried ranks we stand
Asking - aye demanding, how long is this to last?

    Rally, Rally! Mate and brother,
    Our banner and no other
    Floats out upon the wind this bitter day.

Do they dare to sneer - 'work shy',
We throw them back their lie!
Gladly will we take any work that comes our way.
Let but this hunger cease,
This ache of care decrease,
And there'll open out before us the dawn of a new day.

Barely, barely can we live
On the meagre dole they give
In kind, they kindly say, lest we drink it all away.
Shelter, light and fire,
'Twere futile to desire;
To live in decent comfort one must pay, pay, pay.

At last in desperation, to those who rule the nation
We sent out our demand and awaited their reply;
At length the answer came;
'We are not', they say, 'to blame;
Have patience! We have much to do: we'll right you bye-
    and-bye'.

Tomorrow and tomorrow
Today, dull pain and sorrow;
Must this go on for ever? Sternly, we answer 'NO!'
Brave Belfast, valiant Birkenhead.

In their passion fight for bread
Have shown to us, the workless, along what path to go.

    Chorus
    Rally, Rally! Mate and brother,'
    Our banner and no other
    Floats upon the wind this bitter day.

Charlotte Despard (1844-1939)

These verses were written by Charlotte Despard in her eighty-eighth year. Mrs Despard was one of the remarkable band of Labour pioneers who in the early years of the century blazed a trail of agitation in Britain and Ireland. Born in 1844, she played many roles, agitating in the slums of Battersea in London's East End in the 'nineties; a leading figure in the women's suffrage movement; a pacifist in the First World War. Active in support of the independence movement in Ireland (her brother was Lord French, Viceroy of Ireland 1918-1921) and in campaigns with Maud Gonne McBride for the release of prisoners during the Civil War, she worked with the Labour movement in Dublin in the 'twenties and in Belfast in the 'thirties. She died in Belfast in 1939 and was buried in Dublin.

She spoke at the Albert Hall Rally for Dublin in 1913 and in her diary noted how Larkin 'who was simply splendid' had quietened the students who tried to create a disturbance. In Dublin in the late 1920s, she lamented that 'In the Labour world it is all hideous chaos – splits, suspicions, mutual recriminations everywhere.' In Belfast she worked with the unemployed movement and against sectarianism.

For more about Charlotte Despard, see An Unhusbanded Life, Charlotte Despard, *by Andro Linklater (1980) and* Charlotte Despard, *by Margaret Mulvihill (1989).*

To Belfast: In Memory of 11 October 1932

The streets are grimed with dirt, O dismal town,
The belching smoke adulterates the air,
Foul Poverty stalks along with gloomy frown,
Leaving on many a man his mark of care.
Poor little capital of a puppet state,
Police-controlled and politician-ridden,
And all revolt diverted by the great –
The flag of freedom is no longer hidden.
Some men have lost all fear of hell damnation,
And strive to make this isle a worker's home.
Where social justice is the inspiration,

328

And not the creeds of Luther or of Rome.
O men of Belfast, will you lead the free
To found the workers' state of liberty!

Patrick Rowe

This poem was written in memory of workers killed and injured in disturbances in Belfast during the Outdoor Relief campaign in Belfast in 1932. In July, an Outdoor Relief Workers Committee had been set up to seek better pay and conditions, the abolition of payment in kind, and outdoor relief for single people. On 3 October, 2,000 men on relief work went on strike. That evening an estimated 20,000 people marched through the city in support of the strikers. There were serious disturbances on 11 October when the police tried to prevent a banned march. The police met the demonstrators with gunfire, killing two men and wounding fifteen.

For more about the Outdoor Relief campaign in Belfast in 1932 see Paddy Devlin's Yes We Have No Bananas *(Belfast, 1981). One of the leaders of the campaign was Betty Sinclair.*

6 p.m. Belfast

The Albert strikes, the sirens scream,
    The hammer and the pen are downed,
And out there pours a living stream
    Of toilers, homeward bound.

From every art and part they come,
    From leafy lane and squalid street,
Or from suburban villadom
    The poor and the elite.

And yet it matters not if they
    Be coated o'er with silk or grime,
They are but fellows who obey
    The call of supper-time.

Yes, fellow toilers, every one,
    Amid the city's din and strife,
Co-workers, yet who fight alone
    For daily bread and life.

Ruddick Millar

The two poems of the Belfast poets, Patrick Rowe and Ruddick Millar, were published in Good-Bye, Twilight. Songs of the Struggle in Ireland, *edited by Leslie H. Daiken (London, 1936).*

The book was dedicated to 'Tom Mooney, still prsioner 31921 San Quentin Prison, San Francisco, USA'. (See page 249.)

Leslie Daiken (1912-64). Poet, playwright, broadcaster, was an authority on children's games and toys. Author of Children's Games Throughout the Ages *(1953),* The Lullaby Book *(1959) and a collection of Dublin street rhymes,* Out Goes She *(1963).*

Homage to Jim Larkin

Roll away the stone, Lord, roll away the stone
As you did when last I died in the attic room;
Then there was no fire as well, and I died of cold
While Jim Larkin walked the streets before he grew old.

Larkin was a young man then, all skin and bone;
Larkin had a madman's eyes, I saw them through the stone;
Larkin had a madman's voice, I don't know what he said,
I just heard screeches ringing in my head.

Something screeched within my head as in an empty room;
I felt the lightning of the pain run through every bone;
I couldn't even scream, Lord, I just sobbed with pain;
I didn't want to live, Lord, and turned to sleep again.

But with the screeches in my head I couldn't settle right,
At last I scrambled to my knees and turned to the light;
Then I heard the words he spoke, and down crashed the
    stone
There was I with blind man's eyes, gaping at the sun.

Things are much the same again, damn the thing to eat;
Not a bloody fag since noon and such a price for meat;
Not a bit of fire at home all the livelong day –
Roll the stone away, Lord, roll the stone away!

Frank O'Connor (1903-1966)

This poem was first published in The Irish Times, *9 December, 1944. It was recited by Harry Craig, assistant editor of* The Bell, *at the first Jim Larkin Memorial Meeting and Concert which was held in the Olympia Theatre, Dublin on 1 February 1948.*

Jim Larkin, RIP

Come listen a while you Irish men, and hear my mournful
    news,
Although it is quite sorrowful, I'll know you'll me excuse,
Come join my lamentation for one who was our friend,
He led the tortured workers and made the bosses bend.

A great man like Jim Larkin, we never can replace,
He fought our fight in dark '13 when the Peelers he did face,
We lost our fight, but still we won, for Jim was not outdone,
And as the troubled years rolled on, his fight and ours he
    won.

When Ireland honours heroes bold, who fought to make her
    free,
The name of brave Jim Larkin will be there for all to see,
He fought to save the working man from bondage and from
    woe,
And his name will long be honoured no matter where you
    go.

He was treated to the batons by the Forces of the Crown;
But bullies' guns or batons they could never keep him down,
The worker is a free man now by his persevering fight,
And his prospects for the future have never been so bright.

So, God rest your soul, Jim Larkin, may Heaven be your
    home,
May St Patrick take you to the Land from where you'll never
    roam,
And when a day in Ireland dawns that North and South are
    free,
We will think of one great fighting man and just say: R.I.P.

This Dublin street ballad was included by Colm Ó Lochlainn in More Irish
Street Ballads *(1965). Ó Lochlainn states that it was sold in the streets of
Dublin on the day of Larkin's funeral.*

Jim Larkin

Ba mise é – ba gach mac máthar againn é,
Sinn féin – láidir mar dob áil linn bheith,
Mara b'eól dúinn bheith,
Sé ag bagairt troda 's ag bronnadh fuasgailt,
Ag leanúint a chónra trí chlab na cathrach bhéil,
I mbéice móra feirge.

Ag leanúint a chónra tré chlab na cathrach aréir
An sinne a bhí sa chónra?
Niorbh eadh; bhíomar sa tsráid ag máirseáil,
Beó-buidheach do'n mharbh.

Breandán Ó Beacháin (1923-1964)

This poem by Brendan Behan was first published in Comhar *(Dublin), March 1947.*
      Brendan Behan was the author of Borstal Boy *(1958),* Brendan Behan's Island *(1962),* Hold Your Own and Have Another *(1963),* Brendan Behan's New York *(1964) as well as a number of plays notably, in Irish,* An Giall *(1958), and in English,* The Quare Fellow *(1954) and* The Hostage *(1958).*

English version by Manus O'Riordan (1949 –)

He was us! He was me!
Each and every mother's son!
We ourselves. Self-reliant. Strong.
As we would wish ourselves to be
Knowing such strength could make us free.

Himself fist-clenched confronting oppression
To release from servitude's knee-bending servility
Ourselves to mourn in his funeral procession
Those great angry roars through this open mouth city.

Last night as we followed his coffin
Through Dublin's garrulous din
Were we ourselves in that same coffin?
Not so: on the streets were now marching our ranks
Alive Alive Oh! To the Dead we give thanks.

Jim Larkin

Not with public words now can his greatness
Be told to the children, for he was more
Than a labour-agitating orator –
The flashing flaming sword merely bore witness
To the coming of the dawn: 'Awake and look!
The flowers are growing for you, and wonderful trees
And beyond are not the serf's grey Docks, but seas –
Excitement out of the Creator's poetry book.
When the Full Moon's in the River and the ghost of bread
Must not haunt all your weary wanderings home,
The ships that were dark galleys can become
Pine forests under winter's starry plough
And the brown gantries will be the lifted head
Of man the dreamer whom the gods endow.'

And thus I heard Jim Larkin above
The crowd who wanted to turn aside
From Reality coming to free them. Terrified
They hid in the clouds of dope and would not move.
They eat the opium of the murderer's story
In the Sunday newspapers; they stood to stare
Not at the blackbird but at a millionaire
Whose horses ran for Serfdom's greater glory.
And Tyranny trampled them in Dublin's gutter
Until Jim Larkin came along and cried
The call of Freedom and the call of Pride
And Slavery crept to its hands and knees
And Nineteen Thirteen cheered from out the utter
Degradation of their miseries.

Patrick Kavanagh (1905-1967)

This poem was first published in The Bell, *March 1947.*

Inscription for a Headstone

What Larkin bawled to hungry crowds,
Is murmured now in dining-hall
And study. Faith bestirs itself,
Lest infidels in their impatience
Leave it behind. Who could have guessed
Batons were blessings in disguise,
When every ambulance was filled
With half-killed men and Sunday trampled
Upon arrest? Such fear can harden
Or soften heart, knowing too clearly
His name endures on our holiest page,
Scrawled in a rage by Dublin's poor.

Austin Clarke (1896-1974)

This poem was first published in Collected Poems *(Dolmen Press, Dublin 1974).*

Congress: An Outline History

From its foundation in 1894 until 1914, the name of the organisation was the Irish Trades Union Congress (sometimes it was described as the Irish Trades Congress). Following the decision at the 1912 Annual Meeting to include amongst the objects of Congress, 'the independent representation of Labour upon all public boards', a motion was passed at the 1913 Annual Meeting instructing the Parliamentary Committee 'to draft a constitution and such alterations in the Standing Orders' as the change rendered necessary. In accordance with this decision the 1914 Annual Meeting adopted a constitution which included the title 'Irish Trades Union Congress and Labour Party'.

A new constitution adopted at a Special Conference in Dublin on 1 November 1918 changed the title to 'Irish Labour Party and Trade Union Congress'. With the decision in 1929 to dissolve the conjoint organisation, a new constitution which included the title 'Irish Trade Union Congress' was adopted and came into operation on 1 March 1930.

In 1945 a number of unions disaffiliated from the Irish TUC and formed the Congress of Irish Unions. After fourteen years, the two Congresses were reunited in 1959 under the title 'Irish Congress of Trade Unions'.

Objects

For many years the Congress operated on the basis of Standing Orders for the Annual Meeting and there was no formal constitution. The first constitution was adopted in 1914. The objects of the Congress were stated to be:

> To organise and unite the workers of Ireland in order to improve their status and conditions generally, and to take such action in the Industrial and Political fields, with that end in view as may be decided upon at its Annual Meetings.
>
> In addition, it shall be the duty of the National Executive to assist in adjusting all differences, on the request of the trade affected, between employers and employees and to aid affiliated bodies in their efforts to improve the conditions of employment.

The objects set out in the constitution adopted at the Special Conference held in the Mansion House, Dublin on 1-2 November 1918 were as follows:

(a) To recover for the Nation complete possession of all the natural physical sources of wealth of this country.

(b) To win for the workers of Ireland, collectively, the ownership and control of the whole produce of their labour.

(c) To secure the democratic management and control of all industries and services by the whole body of workers, manual and mental, engaged therein, in the interest of the Nation and subject to the supreme authority of the National Government.

(d) To obtain for all adults who give allegiance and service to the Commonwealth, irrespective of sex, race or religious belief, equality of political and social rights and opportunities.

(e) To abolish all rights and privileges, social and political, of institutions or persons, based upon property or ancestry, or not granted or confirmed by the freely-expressed will of the Irish people; and to insist that in the making and administering of the laws, in the pursuit of industry and commerce, and in the education of the young, property must always be subordinate to humanity, and private gain must ever give place to the welfare of the people.

(f) With the foregoing objects in view, to promote the organisation of the working class industrially, socially and politically e.g. in Trade Unions, in Co-operative Societies (both of producers and consumers), and in a Political Labour Party.

(g) To secure labour representation on all national and local legislative bodies.

(h) To co-ordinate the work of the several sections of the working class movement.

(i) To promote fraternal relations between the workers of Ireland and of other countries through affiliation with the international Labour movement.

(j) To co-operate with that movement in promoting the establishment of democratic machinery for the settlement of disputes between Nations; and in raising the standard of social legislation in all countries to the level of the highest;

(k) Generally to assist the efforts of the working class of all Nations in their struggle for emancipation.

In 1926, the Constitution was revised and the following changes were made in the Objects as set out above:

(1) In (e), 'powers' was substituted for 'rights' on the first line.
(2) In (f), the words 'e.g. in Trade Unions, in Co-operative Societies (both of producers and consumers), and in a Political Labour Party' were deleted.
(3) In (g), the words 'and administrative' were inserted before 'bodies' on the second line.
(4) In (i), the words 'through affiliation with the international Labour movement' were deleted.
(5) The following was substituted for (j): 'to promote international co-operation, the establishment of machinery for the settlement of disputes between nations, and the raising of the standard of social legislation in all countries.

The objects as set out in the constitution of the Irish TUC adopted at the Special Congress on 28 February and 1 March 1930 were as follows:

(a) To secure the reconstruction of the social and economic system of Ireland so as to further the interests of the community as a whole and to secure for all workers, subject to the general interest, adequate control of the industries or services in which they are engaged.
(b) To safeguard and improve the standards of wages, hours and other conditions of workers.
(c) To assist the organisation of workers in Trade Unions and the co-operation of Trade Unions one with another.
(d) To promote fraternal relations between the workers of Ireland and of other countries, and to co-operate with similar organisations in other countries for the purpose of raising the standard of social legislation and social conditions in all countries.
(e) To secure the realisation of such measures in furtherance of these Objects as the Congress may from time to time approve.
(f) To co-operate with the Irish Labour Party in matters of common concern.

The objects of the Irish Congress of Trade Unions as set out in the Constitution adopted by the CIU and the Irish TUC in 1959, as amended in 1973, were as follows (Clause (b) below, was inserted in 1973):

(a) To uphold the democratic character and structure of the Trade Union Movement, to maintain the right of freedom of association and the right of workers to organise and negotiate and all such rights as are necessary to the performance of trade union functions and in particular, the right to strike.
(b) To ensure full equality in all aspects of employment and to oppose discrimination on any such grounds as colour, ethnic or national origins, politics, race, religion or sex.
(c) To support the democratic system of government and promote the social and economic policies and programme of the workers of Ireland as expressed from time to time by the Irish Trade Union Movement.
(d) To encourage and assist the application of the principle of co-operation in the economic activities of the nation.
(e) To seek the full utilisation of the resources of Ireland for the benefit of the people of Ireland and to work for such fundamental changes in the social and economic system as will secure for the workers of Ireland adequate and effective participation in the control of the industries and services in which they are employed.
(f) To promote fraternal and co-operative relations with trade unions and trade union federations and congresses in other countries for the purpose of furthering the common interests of workers in all countries; and further to co-operate with other types of democratic organisations in supporting progressive endeavours intended to safeguard and strengthen justice, peace and freedom throughout the world.

Annual Conferences

Annual Meetings of Congress, sometimes referred to as Annual Conferences or Annual Congresses, were held from 1894 to 1991 with the exception of the year 1915 when no conference was held. The Irish Congress of Trade Unions held its first biennial conference in 1993.

The annual conferences of Congress have been held in twenty centres throughout Ireland. In the case of the Irish TUC

(1894-1959), its sixty-five annual meetings were held in the following cities and towns: Cork and Dublin (ten each), Galway and Waterford (five each) Belfast, Derry, Killarney, Limerick and Sligo (four each), Drogheda (three), Dundalk and Newry (two each), Athlone, Bangor, Bundoran, Clonmel, Kilkenny, Portrush, Tralee and Wexford (one each).

In the case of the ICTU (1959-1991), its thirty-four annual conferences were held in the following cities and towns: Cork and Galway (six each), Belfast and Killarney (five each), Bundoran and Dublin (three each), Limerick (two), Portrush, Tralee and Waterford (one each). The first biennial conference of the ICTU was held in Galway.

The numbers of delegates to the annual meetings accredited from trade unions, Trades Councils and other labour organisations totalled 119 in 1894 and 121 in 1895. Over the following twenty-one meetings the numbers of delegates ranged from a low of sixty-two in 1899 to a high of 111 in 1917, averaging eighty-one over the period.

The numbers of delegates accredited increased greatly in the years after 1917. Over the six years 1918 to 1923, the numbers varied between 220 in 1919 and 250 in 1921. There was a decline to 201 in 1924 and 160 in 1925. Between 1926 and 1935 the number of delegates averaged 132. It rose to 191 in 1936 and averaged 208 over the period 1937 to 1944, the year before the split in Congress.

Over the six years following the setting up of the CIU, the number of delegates to the annual conferences of the Irish TUC averaged 178 (1945-1950). Thereafter the numbers increased significantly, ranging from 188 in 1950 to a high of 233 in 1958. Over the nine years 1951 to 1959, the number of delegates averaged 217.

In the case of ICTU annual conferences, the number of delegates accredited at its first conference was 321. The number increased each year rising to 436 in 1969 and 608 in 1979. The number rose further to 658 in 1982 when a decision was made to adjust the basis of representation at annual conferences. As a result of the change, the number of delegates accredited to the 1983 conference was reduced to 460. The number remained at around this figure in the following five years, averaging 449 over this period. The number increased again, however, in the following years totalling 553 in 1991 and 554 in 1993.

Executive Council

A Parliamentary Committee was elected by the delegates attending the Annual Meetings of Congress. The duties of the Committee, as set out in the Standing Orders, were to endeavour to give practical effect to the resolutions of Congress; to watch all legislative measures directly affecting the question of Labour in Ireland; and to initiate such legislative and other action as Congress might direct. Up to 1914 the Committee also had the duty 'generally to support the Parliamentary Committee of the United Trades Congress upon all questions affecting the workers of the United Kingdom'.

The Parliamentary Committee originally consisted of nine members including the Secretary. The number was increased to twelve in 1913 including the Secretary and the Treasurer. Not more than one member of the same trade or occupation was entitled to sit on the Committee which submitted a report to the Annual Meeting.

In the constitution adopted in 1914 the name of the Parliamentary Committee was changed to National Executive and its duties set out as follows: to endeavour to give effect to the decisions of the annual meetings; to watch all legislative measures affecting Labour in Ireland; to initiate such legislative and other action as might be necessary and as the Annual Meeting might direct; to endeavour to secure the independent representation of Irish Labour in Parliament and upon all Public Boards; and generally to co-operate with the organised workers in other countries towards the common advancement of Labour. It was also stated to be the duty of the National Executive to assist in adjusting all differences, on the request of the trade affected, between employers and employees, and to aid affiliated bodies in their efforts to improve the conditions of employment.

The constitution of the Irish Labour Party and Trade Union Congress adopted in 1918 increased the members of the National Executive to fourteen consisting of a Chairman, Vice-Chairman, Treasurer and Secretary and ten other members elected at the Annual Meeting.

The National Executive was to be the administrative authority of the organisation and responsible for the conduct of its general work. Specifically it was to give effect to the decisions of the National Congress, watch all legislative measures affecting labour in Ireland, initiate such legislative and other action as was deemed necessary, and generally promote the objects of the organisation in the most effective manner within its power. It was also to ensure that Labour was represented by a 'properly constituted organisation in each constituency in which this is found practicable'.

The 1930 constitution of the Irish TUC provided for the election by the Annual Congress of a National Executive consisting of a President, Vice-President, Treasurer and twelve other members. Subject to the control and directions of the Congress, the National Executive was to be the administrative authority responsible for the general work of the organisation and for giving effect to the decisions of the Congress. It was to assist and advise in the work of affiliated trade unions and Trades Councils, and promote co-operation and close contact between them. It was to watch all legislative and administrative action affecting Labour and promote such legislation as it might deem necessary.

The constitution of the Irish Congress of Trade Unions, adopted in 1959, provided that the executive authority of the Congress was the Executive Council which was responsible for the implementation of all decisions of Annual and Special Delegate Conferences and for the conduct of the general business of Congress. In particular it was to assist and advise trade unions and local councils and promote co-operation between them; watch all legislative and administrative action affecting workers and promote such legislation as it might deem necessary.

The Executive Council was to consist of a President, Vice-President, Treasurer and sixteen other members elected at the Annual Delegate Conference. Not more than one member of an affiliated trade union could be elected to the Executive Council otherwise than as officers. However a trade union having more than 50,000 members could have not more than two members elected. A person nominated for election had to be a delegate to the conference. (Under the Standing Orders of Congress a nomination could only be made by a trade union, not by a Trades Council).

A number of amendments to the section of the Constitution dealing with the Executive Council have been made since its adoption in 1959. In 1970 the limit on ordinary membership was raised from sixteen to twenty and the restriction on the number of members that could be elected from one trade union removed. In 1971 a limit of two was imposed on the number of members from a trade union that could be elected other than as officers. In

1983 the number of ordinary members to be elected to the Executive Council was increased to twenty-four, with two of the seats reserved for women members to be elected by separate ballot. The size of the Executive Council was again increased in 1991, the number of ordinary members being increased to twenty-six with four of the seats being reserved for women members.

Executive Council Members

The names of all the members of the Executive Council of Congress since 1894 are given in alphabetical order from page 442. Over the one hundred years there have been 321 members, including elected officers. Of these, twenty-three were women including nine elected to reserved seats which were introduced in 1983.

Sixty-one members were Belfast residents when first elected to the Executive Council of Congress.

The twenty members with the longest service on the Executive Council of Congress (including the Central Council of the CIU) were: William McMullen (28 years), W. J. Fitzpatrick (27), James Larkin Junior (25), William O'Brien (25), Sam Kyle (24), J Harold Binks (23), Michael Drumgoole (23) Fintan Kennedy (23) Norman Kennedy (23), Denis Cullen (22), Andrew Barr (21), John Conroy (21), Dan Murphy (20) John Carroll (19), Robert Smith (19), Seán P. Campbell (18), John Cassidy (18), Gerard Doyle (18), Dominick F. Murphy (18) and Jack Macgougan (17).

Of the twenty, only one, Dan Murphy, was an Executive Council member in the Congress centenary year: he was elected at the 1993 biennial conference.

The woman member with the longest service on the Executive Council was Louie Bennett with thirteen years' service.

Secretariat

The Congress organisation had no full-time staff up to 1921. A Secretary was elected at each annual meeting. (The honorarium was fixed at £5 in 1901 and was £20 in 1917). The first Secretary was John Simmons of the Associated Society of Carpenters and Joiners who held the position up to 1899. (Simmons was secretary of the Dublin Trades Council for thirty years from its inception in 1886 to 1916).

Simmons was succeeded by Hugh McManus, Belfast (Irish organiser of the Typographical Association from 1894 to 1910) as Secretary in 1900. Another printer, E.L. Richardson (Dublin Typographical Provident Society) was Secretary from 1901 to 1910 when he retired on his appointment as the first manager of the Board of Trade Labour Exchange in Dublin. He had been twice President of the Dublin Trades Council, in 1895 and 1903.

Richardson was succeeded by another member of the DTPS, P.T. Daly, a delegate to the Congress from the Dublin Paviours. He was re-elected unopposed as Secretary each year until 1918 when (he was then a delegate from the Dublin Fire Brigade Men's Union) he was defeated by William O'Brien, a delegate from the Dublin Trades Council, by the slim margin of 114 votes to 109. (Daly was Secretary of the Dublin Trades Council from 1919 till his death in 1943 and President of Congress in 1939).[1]

William O'Brien was Secretary of Congress in 1919 and 1920. He had first attended the Congress in 1909 as a delegate from the Amalgamated Society of Tailors and in subsequent years was a delegate from the Dublin Trades Council. He was a member of the Parliamentary Committee/National Executive from 1911 to 1929. He was again a member of the National Executive from 1939 to 1945. O'Brien was President of Congress four times, in 1913, 1918, 1925 and 1941.[2]

In 1918 it was decided that the position of Secretary should be full-time. Thomas Johnson, a delegate from the National Amalgamated Union of Shop Assistants and Clerks in Belfast was elected Secretary in 1921 and was re-elected annually until his resignation at the end of 1928. Johnson had been President of Congress in 1916. (He again acted as Secretary of the Irish TUC for some months in 1945 following the resignation of the then Secretary).[3]

Following the dissolution of the conjoint organisation in 1930, the constitution of the Irish TUC provided for the Secretary of the organisation to be appointed by the National Executive.

---

1. See: 'The Remarkable P.T. Daly', by Seamus Cody, *Obair*, January 1985.
2. See: *Forth the Banners Go: the Reminiscences of William O'Brien as told to Edward MacLysaght* (1969); 'William O'Brien 1881-1968 and the Irish Labour Movement', by Arthur Mitchell, *Studies*, 20, 1971; 'The Rake's Progress of a Syndicalist: the Political Career of William O'Brien', by D. R. O'Connor Lysaght, *Saothar*, 9 , 1983.
3. See: *Thomas Johnson 1872-1963: First Leader of the Labour Party in Dáil Éireann*, by J. Anthony Gaughan (1980).

The first appointed Secretary was Eamonn Lynch who had been an organiser for the ITGWU in Cork from the early 1920s. He took up duties in September 1930 and was Secretary until he resigned in 1940.

Lynch was succeeded by Cathal O'Shannon, also a long-time official of the ITGWU, who was Secretary until 1945 when he resigned to become the first Secretary of the Congress of Irish Unions. He had been President of the Irish TUC in 1922. (In 1946 Cathal O'Shannon and Thomas Johnson were appointed the first Workers' Members of the Labour Court set up under the Industrial Relations Act 1946).

Ruaidhri Roberts was appointed Secretary of the Irish TUC from October 1945 and remained in that office until his appointment, with Leo Crawford, the Secretary of the CIU, as Joint Secretaries of the ICTU in 1959. Following the retirement of Crawford in 1966, Roberts was appointed General Secretary. He retired at the end of 1981 and was succeeded by Donal Nevin who had been appointed research officer of the Irish TUC early in 1949. On Nevin's retirement in 1989, Peter Cassells, who had been on the staff of Congress from 1975, was appointed General Secretary.

Staff

From the setting up of a secretariat in 1921 up to the dissolution of the Irish TUC and the CIU in 1959, the staff of the Congress was tiny. In the 1920s – when the Congress was a conjoint organisation covering both the political and the industrial sides of the Labour Movement – it employed, apart from the Secretary, an Assistant Secretary and one/two clerical staff. The Assistant Secretary from 1922 to 1930 was R. J. P. Mortished. He resigned in 1930 to take up a position with the International Labour Office in Geneva. (Mortished was to be the first Chairman of the Labour Court in 1946. He died in 1957).

During the 1930s and 1940s apart from the Secretary, there was only one other staff member employed by Congress. At the beginning of 1949 the staff consisted of the Secretary, Ruaidhri Roberts, and Colette Tierney. That year they were joined by Donal Nevin as Research Officer and in 1950 by Shirley Lowe. In the case of the CIU, the staff throughout the 1950s consisted of the Secretary, Leo Crawford, and Marie Flavin.

On the establishment of the ICTU in 1959, the total staff at the head office in Dublin consisted of the Joint Secretaries and four other staff members.

At the beginning of 1994, there was a total of twenty-seven full-time employees on the staff of the ICTU in Dublin and eight in Belfast.

Up to 1911, the Congress address was the home address of the Secretary. In 1911 it was the Trades Hall in Capel Street, Dublin and in 1912-13, Liberty Hall in Beresford Place. It was again the Trades Hall from 1914 to 1918.

From 1920 the Congress occupied offices at 32 Lower Abbey Street. It moved to 32 Nassau Street (corner of Dawson Street) in October 1933 and remained there until 1956 when it transferred to Merrion Building, Lower Merrion Street, together with the CIU which transferred from 85 Grafton Street where it had had its office since 1945. The offices at Lower Merrion Street were also the office of the Provisional United Trade Union Organisation from 1956 to 1959, and of the ICTU from 1959.

In 1964, the ICTU acquired premises at 19 Raglan Road, Ballsbridge, Dublin.

Northern Ireland

A special committee of the National Executive of the Irish TUC was set up in 1943, consisting of Robert Getgood, M.J. Keyes T.D., Senator Sean Campbell, Senator Sam Kyle, William McMullen, William O'Brien and the Secretary of Congress, Cathal O'Shannon, to examine the position of affiliated trade unions operating in Northern Ireland and their relation to Congress.

The special committee's recommendations, which were adopted by the National Executive, included 'the setting up as a tentative measure of a Committee on Congress membership in Northern Ireland'. The functions of the Committee were to include (a) considering resolutions and decisions of Congress and of the National Executive affecting members in Northern Ireland, (b) watching industrial legislation and administration in Northern Ireland, (c) assisting as a co-ordinating body for trade unions in Northern Ireland, and (d) acting as an advisory and consultative body under the authority of the National Executive.

In adopting the special committee's recommendations, the National Executive agreed that 'normally the advice of the Northern Ireland Committee would be acted upon'. It decided, as a 'temporary and experimental procedure', that the Northern Ireland Committee should consist of the President of Congress, two members of the National Executive, and four members of trade unions resident in Northern Ireland, with the Secretary of Congress acting as secretary of the Committee.

The members of the Northern Ireland Committee originally nominated by the National Executive in 1944 were: the President of Congress, Robert Getgood (ATGWU); members of the National Executive: Senator Sam Kyle (ATGWU) and William McMullen (ITGWU); members resident in Northern Ireland: George Porter (National Society of Painters), David Madden (Amalgamated Engineering Union), Robert Morrow (Plumbers', Glaziers' and Domestic Engineers' Union) and Herbert Trotter (Amalgamated Engineering Union). Later, Herbert Trotter found himself unable to act and William Boyd (National Union of Vehicle Builders) was nominated in his place. Subsequently, Robert Morrow was elected to the National Executive at the 1944 Congress, and the resulting vacancy on the Northern Ireland Committee was filled by the appointment of Armand Wallace (Amalgamated Society of Woodworkers).

The members of the Northern Ireland Committee for 1944-45, as given in the Fiftieth Annual Report of Congress, were: Senator Thomas Kennedy (President of Congress), Senator Sam Kyle, William McMullen, William Boyd, David Madden, George Porter, Armand Wallace and Cathal O'Shannon (Secretary). The Committee does not seem to have met before the secession from Congress of a number of affiliated unions in 1945 and the resignation from the National Executive of Senator Thomas Kennedy, William McMullen and of the Secretary, Cathal O'Shannon.

A conference of affiliated organisations having members in Northern Ireland held in Belfast on 3 November 1945 was attended by forty-one delegates representing nineteen trade unions, as well as the Belfast Trades Union Council. This Conference recommended the setting up of a Northern Ireland Committee which would be a sub-committee of the National Executive and which would be empowered to act on its behalf in matters peculiar to Northern Ireland.

The names of the ten delegates forwarded to the National Executive for ratification as members of the Northern Ireland Committee were: Jack Beattie M.P. (Irish National Teachers' Organisation), J. Harold Binks (Clerical and Administrative Workers' Union), William Boyd (National Union of Vehicle

Builders), James Brown (Irish Bakers' Union), Robert Getgood M.P. (ATGWU), David Madden (Amalgamated Engineering Union), Jack Macgougan (National Union of Tailors and Garment Workers), George Porter (Amalgamated Society of Painters), J. Scott (Plumbers', Glaziers' and Domestic Engineers' Union) and Armand Wallace (Amalgamated Society of Woodworkers).

The Conference decided that the Northern Ireland Committee should consist of these ten members, together with the President, Vice-President and Secretary of Congress. These decisions of the Conference were ratified by the National Executive and the first meeting of this Northern Ireland Committee was held on 30 November, 1945.

John McAteer, an official of the National Union of Printing, Bookbinding and Paper Workers, and Secretary of the Belfast Trades Council, was appointed Secretary of the Northern Ireland Committee in November 1945 and served on a voluntary basis until 1953. John McAteer was elected President of Congress that year and was succeeded in 1954 as Secretary of the Northern Ireland Committee by John Kerr (ATGWU) who served, also on a voluntary basis, until 1956.

In 1956, the National Executive of Congress decided to appoint a full-time Northern Ireland Officer. William J. Leeburn (ATGWU) was appointed to the position in June 1956 and served until 1959. Following his resignation he was succeeded as acting NIO for a year by J.E. Sloan (ATGWU).

William J. Blease (created Lord Blease of Cromac in 1978) was appointed Northern Ireland Officer from August 1960. He retired in July 1975 and was succeeded by Terry Carlin.

The first offices of the Northern Ireland Committee were at 138 North Street, Belfast. In 1962, Congress moved to 9 Donegall Square South and in 1969 to 236 Antrim Road. Due to repeated attacks on this building, the staff moved in 1981 to temporary accommodation in Transport House, High Street and after a year there, to 1/9 Castle Arcade in April 1982. In 1988 the Congress offices moved to 3 Wellington Park.

The annual Northern Ireland Conferences have been held most frequently in Belfast but also in Bangor, Ballymena, Coleraine, Craigavon, Derry, Downpatrick, Enniskillen, Newry, Portadown, Portrush and Whiteabbey.

The Constitution of Congress now provides for a Northern Ireland Committee consisting of fifteen members of affiliated trade unions with members in Northern Ireland to be elected every two years at a specially-convened Northern Ireland Conference. The President and General Secretary of Congress are *ex officio* members of the Northern Ireland Committee. Two seats on the Committee are reserved for women members elected from the delegates to the Northern Ireland Conference by separate ballot.

There have been twenty-eight chairpersons of the Northern Ireland Committee since it was set up in 1944. The first chairperson was William Boyd of the National Union of Vehicle Builders who held office for four years. He was followed by J. Harold Binks of the Clerical and Administrative Workers' Union and he was chairperson for fourteen years from 1949-50 to 1963-64. (He was again chairperson in 1975-76 and 1976-77). Since 1990, chairpersons of the Northern Ireland Committee have been elected for a two-year term of office.

There has been only one woman chairperson of the Northern Ireland Committee, Inez McCormack, National Union of Public Employees, who was elected in 1984. (In 1980 she was the first woman from Northern Ireland to be elected to the Executive Council of Congress.)

There have been reserved seats for women on the Northern Ireland Committee since 1988. Up to 1992 there was one reserved seat. Monica McWilliams (ATGWU) was elected in 1988 and 1989 and Avila Kilmurray (ATGWU) in 1990 and 1991. Since 1992 there have been two reserved seats. Carol O'Malley (Northern Ireland Public Service Alliance) and Betty Dickey (GMB) were elected in 1992 for a two-year term, and Avila Kilmurray (ATGWU) and Rosaleen Davidson (UNISON) in 1994.

A list of the chairpersons of the Northern Ireland Committee is given on page 446.

Congress Presidents

There have been eighty-five Presidents of the Irish TUC and the Irish Congress of Trade Unions over the 100 years of the Congress' existence. In the early years from 1894 to 1902 (except in 1901), the President of the local Trades Council of the city in which the annual meeting of Congress was held, was elected President. In 1903 and in subsequent years, the chairperson of the Parliamentary Committee, selected by its members, was elected President, holding office for one year and presiding at the next annual meeting.

A list of the Presidents of Congress over the last 100 years is given on pages 437 to 440. The year shown is that in which the person presided at the annual Congress, with four exceptions. The President elected in 1936, Helena Molony, was ill and unable to preside at the Congress the following year. The Presidents elected in 1944 and 1976, Thomas Kennedy and Brendan Harkin respectively, resigned before the next Congress was held while the President elected in 1971, Jim Cox, died in office.

There have been eleven Presidents of the Irish TUC/ICTU who were elected twice or more, viz. Louie Bennett (1932, 1948), Denis Cullen (1926, 1931), John Conroy (1959, 1968), Luke J. Duffy (1923, 1924, 1939), Sam Kyle (1940, 1950), Norman Kennedy (1957, 1961), James Larkin, Junior (1949, 1952, 1960)), James McCarron (1899, 1907, 1910), Jack Macgougan (1959, 1963), Thomas MacPartlin (1917, 1921) and William O'Brien (1913, 1918, 1925, 1941).

Thus William O'Brien was President four times and Luke Duffy, James McCarron and James Larkin, Junior, three times.

Three women have been Presidents of Congress: Louie Bennett in 1932 and 1948, Helena Molony in 1937 and Helen Chenevix in 1951. All were officials of the Irish Women Workers' Union. It may be noted also that they were all Presidents of the Irish TUC. There has never been a woman President of the Irish Congress of Trade Unions: this can be largely explained by the fact that every President of the ICTU has been a full-time trade union official, usually the chief official of the union in Ireland.

Since 1899 delegates from Trades Councils have been elected President of Congress on eight occasions: Belfast (1904, 1908), Cork (1902, 1909, 1953), and Dublin (1913, 1918, 1939).

In the first nine years of the Congress' existence, the Presidents were members of craft unions; by trade carpenter, printer (two), pork butcher, tailor (two), plasterer, flax dresser, and bootmaker. The first non-craft union member to be elected was Walter Hudson, an official of the Amalgamated Society of Railway Servants, who was President in 1903. He was followed by seven Presidents from craft unions whose trades were: carpenter, saddler, baker, tailor, printer and coachmaker. In 1911, David Campbell was the first President from a non-manual union, the National Union of Assurance Agents. He was followed in 1912 by M.J. O'Lehane from the Irish Drapers' Assistants' Association.

The President in 1913, William O'Brien, was then a member of the Amalgamated Society of Tailors.

The first President from a general union was James Larkin, general secretary of the Irish Transport and General Workers' Union, in 1914.

Over the twenty-five years from 1894 to 1919, all but four of the Presidents were members of craft unions, the exceptions being Campbell, O'Lehane, Larkin, referred to above, and Thomas Johnson, a member of the National Amalgamated Union of Shop Assistants, Warehousemen and Clerks, who was President in 1916.

In the seventy-five years since 1919 all but four of the Presidents of Congress have been full-time trade union officials. The exceptions were Jeremiah Hurley T.D. (1938), Michael J. Keyes T.D. (1943), Con Connolly (1953) and Walter Carpenter (1959).

There have been thirty-four Presidents of the Irish Congress of Trade Unions. Only one has been President on two occasions, John Conroy. Thirteen of the Presidents of the ICTU have been from Belfast.

All of the thirty-four men who have been President of the ICTU have been full-time officials of their unions: fifteen of them in general unions, ten in white-collar unions, six in craft unions and four in industrial unions. Nine of the Presidents have been from public service unions.

Of the ninety-six persons who have been Presidents of Congress (Irish TUC, CIU and ICTU) over the last hundred years, thirty-one of them were at one time or other, a member of the House of Commons at Westminster in London, the Stormont Parliament in Belfast, or one of the Houses of the Oireachtas in Dublin. One of them, William McMullen, had been an MP at Stormont and later a member of Seanad Éireann, while another, Thomas Johnson, had been a TD and later a Senator.

The President who was a Westminster MP was Walter Hudson who was President of the Irish TUC in 1903. Of the three Stormont MPs, Robert Getgood was President of the Irish TUC in its golden jubilee year 1944 and Sam Kyle in 1940 and 1950 while William McMullen was President of the CIU in 1953. Norman Kennedy, a Stormont Senator, was President of the Irish TUC in 1957 and President of the ICTU in 1961.

Eleven Congress Presidents were TDs: Denis Cullen (1926 and 1931), Thomas Johnson (1916), Michael Keyes (1943), Jeremiah Hurley (1938), Denis Larkin (1974), James Larkin (1914),

James Larkin, Junior (1949, 1952 and 1960), Gilbert Lynch (1946), William O'Brien (1913, 1918 and 1941), T. J. O'Connell (1930) and Cathal O'Shannon (1922).

The fifteen Congress Presidents who were members of Seanad Éireann were – Seán P. Campbell (1933), Michael Colgan (1950), Luke Duffy (1923-24), Michael Duffy (1934), James Dunne (1969), Thomas Farren (1920), Thomas Foran (1921), Thomas Johnson (1916), Fintan Kennedy (1966), Thomas Kennedy (1947) Chris Kirwan (1991), William McMullen (1953), Thomas MacPartlin (1917), Dominick F. Murphy (1965) and J. T. O'Farrell (1927).

One family's record of service on the Congress executive over three generations might be noted. James Larkin was first elected to the Parliamentary Committee of the Irish TUC in 1908 and was also a member from 1911 to 1914. His eldest son, James Larkin Junior, was on the National Executive of the Irish TUC and the Executive Council of the ICTU from 1945 to 1969 while his second son Denis, was on the National Executive of the Irish TUC from 1956 to 1959 and on the ICTU Executive Council from 1969 to 1976. Young Jim Larkin's daughter, Hilda Breslin, was elected to the Executive Council of the ICTU in 1990 and in 1991.

Another family record that might be mentioned is that of Thomas Kennedy who was on the National Executive of the Irish TUC for fourteen years and on the Central Council of the CIU for two years while his son, Fintan Kennedy, was on the Executive Council of the ICTU, either as an officer or an ordinary memeber, for thirteen years.

Congress Treasurers

There have been twenty-two Treasurers of the Irish TUC, CIU and ICTU over the last one hundred years. The longest-serving were Walter Beirne who was Treasurer of the CIU 1947-59 and the ICTU in 1959; Fintan Kennedy who was Treasurer of the ICTU 1968-81 and Seán P. Campbell who was Treasurer of the Irish TUC 1934-44 and the CIU 1945-46.

The names and unions of the Congress Treasurers are on page 441.

Congress Membership

The affiliated membership of trade unions affiliated to the Irish TUC from 1894 to 1959 and the ICTU from 1960 to 1994 are given on pages 433 to 436. Attention is drawn to the notes to the tables.

Finance

In the early years of Congress its income was derived from contributions from the Trades Councils and from the larger trade unions. The financial requirements of Congress were limited given that the only expenditure was in respect of the annual meeting and the expenses of the Parliamentary Committee which usually met quarterly. It was not until 1905 that a scale of payment was provided for in Standing Orders. The affiliation fee was then fixed at one penny per member per annum for small unions with 250 members or less; £1 8s 4d for unions with between 250 and 500 members; and £1 10s for unions with 500 to 1,000 members with an additional £1 for each 1,000 members after the first 1,000.

This affiliation fee remained unchanged until 1919 when it was fixed at two pence per member per annum. In 1924 the fee was increased to three pence and it remained at this level until 1948 when it was raised to four pence. Successive increases brought the fee to 16d (old pence) in 1969 or less than seven new pence. The high inflation in the 1970s had pushed the fee up to 63p (new pence) by 1982. It was held at this level until 1988 when it was raised to 70p. From January 1994 the fee has been 96p, to increase to £1 in 1995, or less than 2p per week per member.

In 1901 the total income of Congress was £177 which would be equivalent to about £12,000 in terms of 1993 prices. By 1922-23, Congress income had increased to £2,317 (£76,000 in 1993 prices) but in 1939-40, Congress income at £1,970 was less than it was seventeen years earlier. In 1948-49, three years after the setting up of the Congress of Irish Unions, the income of the Irish TUC was £3,608 (£69,000 in 1993 prices). Ten years later in its final year, 1958-59, the Irish TUC's income had about doubled to £6,966 (£91,000 in 1993 prices).

The income of the Irish Congress of Trade Unions in its first full year, 1960-61, totalled £14,652 (£190,000 in 1993 prices). Ten years later, in 1970-71, total income was £56,761 (£454,000 in 1993 prices). However in that year, for the first time, income other than from affiliation fees represented a significant proportion (28%) of total income: grants amounting to £15,621 were paid to Congress by the Irish National Productivity Committee, later the Irish Productivity Centre.

The proportion of Congress income represented by grants reached a peak in 1981 when it amounted to £555,000 out of total Congress income of £1,162,000. These grants, made by the Department of Labour in the Republic and the Department of Economic Development in Northern Ireland, were in respect of the provision by Congress of education and training courses and advisory services for affiliated unions.

In 1982, affiliation fees (£366,000) represented about one-fourth (26%) of the total income of Congress which amounted to £1,419,000. Ten years later in 1992, affiliation fee income at £594,000 represented 27% of total income of £2,224,000.

In 1993 the total income of Congress amounted to £2,344,000 made up of affiliation fees (£612,000), grants from the Department of Labour (£700,000), grants from the Northern Ireland Department of Economic Development (£143,000) and other income, mainly payment by unions for education and training courses (£776,000).

From an income in 1901 equivalent to £12,000 in 1993 prices and an income of £190,000 (at 1993 prices) in 1960-61, the first full financial year of the ICTU, the income of Congress in 1993 was £2,344,000.

Over the period 1960 to 1993, the income of Congress rose from under £15,000 to £2.3 million. This dramatic increase over thirty-three years is, of course, a reflection of the low income of Congress a third of a century ago and the fact that Congress now provides a wide range of services to its affiliated unions to an extent that could not have been even contemplated in the past. From a staff of two in 1944 and a staff of nine in 1960, the staff of Congress in its centenary year was thirty-five.

Trades Councils

Unlike the British Trades Union Congress which ended Trades Council representation at its annual conferences in 1895, the Irish

TUC always provided for trade union delegates to attend and vote at its annual meetings.

Trades Councils provided the first five Presidents of the Congress: Dublin in 1894, Cork in 1895, Limerick in 1896, Waterford in 1897 and Belfast in 1898. Thereafter Trades Council delegates were Presidents at the Congresses held in 1904 and 1908 (Belfast), 1902, 1909 and 1953 (Cork) and 1913, 1918 and 1939 (Dublin).

In the first decade of the century, Belfast, Cork, Dublin, Kilkenny and Limerick Trades Councils were represented at virtually all the annual meetings. Other councils that were occasionally represented in those years were Athlone, Derry, Newry and Sligo.

Many of the Trades Councils enjoyed varying fortunes over the century and the number of councils affiliated to Congress fluctuated greatly. In 1917 there were only four councils affiliated to Congress but in the following year the number rose to fifteen.

In 1939 sixteen Trades Councils were affiliated to the Irish TUC but the number had fallen to eleven by 1944. In the last year of the Congress in 1959 there were sixteen councils affiliated including nine in Northern Ireland.

There were only seven Trades Councils affiliated to the ICTU in 1963 but there were seventeen councils registered: these were not eligible to appoint delegates to the annual Congress. By 1973 there were still only seven councils affiliated but the number registered had risen to twenty-four.

By 1983, however, there were forty-six Trades Councils affiliated, seventeen of them in Northern Ireland, and there were four registered councils.

In 1993 there were thirty-seven Trades Councils affiliated to the Irish Congress of Trade Unions, twenty-eight in the Republic and nine in Northern Ireland as follows:

Republic: Athlone, Ballina, Bray, Carlow, Castlebar, Clare, Clonmel, Cork, Drogheda, Dublin, Dundalk, Dungarvan, Galway, Kildare, Kilkenny, Killarney, Letterkenny, Limerick, Longford, Meath, Monaghan, Mullingar, Sligo, Tralee, Tullamore, Waterford, Wexford, Wicklow.

Northern Ireland: Antrim, Belfast, Coleraine, Craigavon, Derry, North Down and Ards, Dungannon, Fermanagh, Newry.

Under the constitution of Congress, Trades Councils may appoint delegates, who must be members of affiliated trade unions, to biennial conferences, one delegate where the council has up to 6,500 members and two delegates where it has over 6,500 members. Trades Councils may not nominate persons for election as officers or members of the Executive Council.

At the first biennial conference of the ICTU held in 1993, there were twenty-six delegates from nineteen Trades Councils out of a total 554 delegates attending.

International Affiliation

Up to 1945, the Irish TUC had not affiliated to any of the international trade union organisations. In that year it affiliated to the World Federation of Trade Unions which was set up in London that year and to which the AFL-CIO, the British Trades Union Congress and the central organisation of the trade unions of the USSR were also affiliated. When the WFTU split in 1949 and the International Confederation of Free Trade Unions was established, the Irish TUC withdrew from the WFTU. In subsequent years Congress maintained friendly relations with the three international trade union organisations, ICFTU, WFTU and the World Confederation of Labour, with representatives of these three organisations attending the annual conferences of Congress.

Following the accession of Ireland to the European Community from 1 January 1973, the ICTU affiliated to the European Trade Union Confederation. Denis Larkin was the Congress representative on the executive committee of the ETUC from 1974 to 1979, Ruaidhri Roberts in 1980 and 1981, Donal Nevin from 1982 to 1988 and Peter Cassells from 1989.

The biennial conference of the ICTU held in 1993 decided that Congress should affiliate to the International Confederation of Free Trade Unions (ICFTU). It affiliated in 1994.

Irish TUC Publications

Apart from the reports of the National Executive of the Irish TUC and reports of the proceedings of the annual congresses, which were published annually from 1895 to 1959, there were few other publications on trade union matters issued by the Congress over its sixty-five years.

355

The main publications of the Irish TUC were:

1919: Ireland at Berne. Reports and memoranda presented to the International Labour and Socialist Conference held at Berne. February 1919. (52pp)
1924: Unemployment 1922-24. The record of the Government's failure. (16pp)
1930: Report of the Special Committee on Re-organisation and the proceedings of the Special Congress held on 28 February and 1 March 1930. (42pp)
1939: Irish Trade Union Congress and Unemployment. Reply to Mr Lemass. (24pp)
1939: Report of the Trade Union Conference 1939 with memoranda of the Commission of Enquiry set up by the National Executive in 1936. (52pp)
1952: Unemployment. A constructive approach to the problem of unemployment in Northern Ireland. (16pp)
1955: Repeal the Trades Disputes Act (Trade Disputes and Trade Union Act (Northern Ireland) 1927). With decorations by Rowel Friers. (16pp)

In 1954, a Joint Committee of the Irish TUC and the CIU issued a Joint Memorandum on Trade Union Unity (32 pp) and in 1956 the Provisional United Trade Union Organisation, representing the Irish TUC and the CIU, published a thirty-two page booklet, *Planning Full Employment. A Trade Union Approach.*

The Irish Labour Party and Trade Union Congress, as the Congress was then called, published a weekly paper, *The Irishman* from 14 May 1927 to 25 October 1930. It was edited by R. J. P. Mortished who was the Assistant Secretary of the Congress, up to March 1930. He was succeeded as editor on a part-time basis by Cathal O'Shannon on secondment from the ITGWU.

The paper's name was changed to *The Watchword* from 1 November 1930. It ceased publication on 24 December 1932.

The first issue of the Irish TUC journal, *Trade Union Information* was published in May 1949. As an Irish TUC publication it ran to ninety-two issues over the following ten years. A new series was issued by the ICTU in April 1960 which ran to 172 issues. The last issue was Winter 1980-81.

The Irish TUC and the ICTU series of *Trade Union Information* ran to 264 issues over thirty-one years. The editor of the journal throughout was Donal Nevin.

Women and the Trade Union Movement

Four women, two from Belfast and two from Dublin, have a special place in the history of trade unionism in Ireland. They were delegates to the first meeting of the Irish Trades Union Congress held in the Trades Hall, Capel Street, Dublin in April 1894. Two of them were among the six delegates from the Belfast Trades Council, Miss Morris and Miss McCrory. The two delegates from Dublin represented the bookfolder members of the Irish National Labour Union, Miss Valentine and Miss Stanley. (The list of delegates does not give the first names of the women delegates).

Thus four of the 119 delegates at that first Congress meeting were women.

Miss Morris it was who moved the historic motion from the Belfast Trades Council that noted with pleasure the attempts then being made in Belfast and elsewhere, to form unions of women workers engaged in the textile and other industries. The motion, recognising the necessity for organisation, called on all Irish trade unionists to support those engaged in the prosecution of this work. The motion was seconded by Miss McCrory. These two delegates were the first women to address an Irish Congress.

There was no woman delegate at the next three Congresses but in 1898 the efforts at organising women workers in Belfast referred to in the motion adopted four years earlier, had begun to bear fruit. The newly-affiliated Textile Operatives Society of Ireland in Belfast sent two women delegates to the Congress, Lizzie Bruce and Mary Galway.

Together with William Walker, later to be President of Congress, Mary Galway organised the Textile Operatives Society in Belfast in 1893 and three years later led 8,000 women and girls in a strike against the Truck Acts which was successful in achieving changes in the regulations on fines in the textile mills.

Mary Galway was to become the most prominent woman trade unionist in Ireland over the next two decades. At the 1898 Congress she called for the appointment of women factory inspectors, a call she was to make almost annually over the next decade. Though there were 70,000 women working in industry in the North, she reminded the delegates, and 40,000 in Belfast alone, there was not one woman factory inspector.

The Textile Operatives seem not to have been represented at the next two Congresses but in the 1901 report we find Mary Galway denouncing the disgraceful conditions of the houses of the working classes as well as again calling for women factory inspectors to be appointed. Her fellow delegate from the Society that year was Miss McKenna, and in 1902, Julia Lee.

At the Congresses in 1903 and 1905 to 1913, the second delegate from the Textile Operatives was Elizabeth McCaughey; in 1908, for the first and only time, there was a third delegate, Sarah Ogle.

In 1905, Mary Galway called for the abolition of overtime for women and in 1907 supported a motion moved by James Larkin on the Belfast dock lock-out. She condemned the system of instant dismissal in the drapery trade, spoke on the ventilation and sanitary inspection of factories and on amending the Truck Acts, referring to a girl in a textile factory, who, out of a wage of 11s 7d, had to pay 6s 4d in fines even though it had been proved that the loom was at fault.

Mary Galway was a frequent contributor to Congress debates. In 1908, she spoke on the depression in the linen trade, fines under the Truck Acts and the sweated industries. At this Congress she urged that women should have the same political rights as men and that they should be admitted to Parliament. In 1909, she again called for the extension of the franchise to all adults, men and women, and spoke also on the recently introduced Trade Boards Bill. At the Congresses in 1910 to 1913, she again raised the questions of the Truck Acts, the Factories Acts, sweated industries and adult suffrage – issues of concern to all workers, men and women, at the time.

Mary Galway was the occasion for the Chief Secretary, Augustine Birrell, expressing his opinion on the position of women in Ireland. When she was a member of a deputation to the Chief Secretary from the Parliamentary Committee of Congress in Dublin Castle on 9 November, 1907, she was introduced by the Secretary of Congress, E.L. Richardson, who boasted that the Irish Congress had been ahead of the English Congress in having elected a 'lady member', to which Birrell replied that he thought 'ladies had not yet been given the place to which they are entitled in this country'.

In 1907, Mary Galway was elected to the Parliamentary Committee in third place, a remarkable achievement in the circumstances. She was re-elected in 1908 (again in third place), 1909 (in second place), 1910 (in third place), 1911 (in first place) and in 1912 (in seventh place). At the last Congress that she was to attend, in 1913, she was defeated in the election for ten members of the Parliamentary Committee.

Mary Galway was selected as Vice-Chairperson by her colleagues on the nine-member Parliamentary Committee in 1909 and 1910. According to William O'Brien, a member of the Committee at the time (letter to *The Irish Times*, 2 February 1955) she refused the Presidency when it was offered to her.[1]

The Textile Operatives Society was the only trade union to appoint women delegates to Congress between 1894 and 1910 (there was also a woman delegate from the Lurgan Hemmers and Veiners, in 1911, Minnie Rodgers). In 1912, Delia Larkin, sister of James Larkin, was a delegate from the Irish Women Workers' Union, which appointed two delegates the following year, 1913, Delia Larkin and Ellen Gordon from Belfast (later to be an organiser for the Irish Textile Workers' Union). That year saw the biggest number of women delegates to date at a Congress – four! – a figure to be exceeded in 1918 when there were nine women delegates though out of a total of 240 delegates as against only ninety-nine delegates in 1913.

Helena Molony was first present at an Annual Meeting of Congress in 1914 when she led a deputation from the Citizens Housing League. Three years later she was a delegate from the IWWU together with Louie Bennett, Ellen Cross and Madeleine Ffrench Mullen. Helen Molony spoke on juvenile offenders, called for the ending of the system of half-timers and the extension of the Trade Boards to women workers in the printing and allied trades. She spoke scathingly about the conditions in laundries in Dublin being a real scandal with 'girls having to work in some places in which other people would not place their animals'.

Interestingly, Helena Molony also moved a motion in almost identical terms to that which had been passed by the first Congress in 1894 calling on all unions to take steps to organise

---

1. For further information about Mary Galway, see article on her by Peter Collins in *Labour History News* (Irish Labour History Society), September 1991; and 'Early slaves of the linen trade', by Francis Devine, in *Liberty* (ITGWU), February 1976.

women employed in their respective trades, either into their own unions or into the IWWU.[2]

At the Congress in 1918 there were, as has already been noted, nine women delegates from three unions: four from the IWWU, three from the newly-affiliated Irish National Teachers' Organisation and two from the Amalgamated Union of Tailors and Tailoresses. Significantly, a woman delegate from the INTO, Rose Timmon, was elected to the National Executive, heading the poll in the election with 164 votes: there were 240 delegates at the Congress.

At the 1918 Congress, which was dominated by political discussion, the women delegates spoke on the urgent need for educational reform, demanding that 'Labour men and women be appointed on all educational committees'; on the need for additional women factory inspectors, housing, a State system of pensions for mothers, a 48-hour working week and at least one week's annual holiday with full pay. Louie Bennett seconded a motion calling on the workers of all countries to make a determined effort to bring about peace and proclaiming the adherence of Congress to 'the Russian formula of a peoples' democratic peace'.

In 1919 there were no delegates at the Congress from the IWWU. Notwithstanding this, there were five women delegates, three of the them new delegates: Cissy Cahalan (Irish Drapers' Assistants' Association) who spoke on trade union organisation, Mary Clinton (International Tailors, Machinists and Pressers' Union) and Mrs Mortished from the Irish Nurses Union, then associated with the IWWU, who spoke on education and on the employment conditions of nurses. An INTO delegate, Miss Tierney, moved a motion demanding full civil rights for civil servants. Rose Timmon was re-elected to the National Executive.

A record sixteen women delegates attended the 1920 Congress from seven unions and a Trades Council: IDAA, Irish Union of Tailors and Tailoresses (two), Amalgamated Society of Tailors and Tailoresses (five), IWWU (three), INU, and ITGWU (two). Women delegates spoke on a variety of subjects: closer union between unions, income tax, land policy, a 48-hour week for trained nurses (who then worked 76-84 hours a week); a working week of 24 hours for boys and girls under seventeen;

---

2. For further information about the IWWU delegates to Congress see *These Obstreperous Lassies: a History of the Irish Women Workers Union*, by Mary Jones (1988).

housing utility organisations; co-ops. One of the ITGWU delegates, Nora Connolly, was elected a teller at the 1920 Congress.

Between 1901 and 1920, the average number of women delegates was three. The number peaked in 1920 when there were sixteen women delegates. During the 1920s, the number declined considerably, averaging only seven between 1921 and 1930, the delegates coming mainly from the IWWU which usually sent five delegates. Unions that occasionally sent one or two women delegates during the 1920s were the INTO, Amalgamated Transport and General Workers' Union, Irish Nurses Union and Irish Union of Distributive Workers and Clerks. Over this period, the biggest union in Congress, ITGWU, did not include any woman in its delegation after 1922.

The position in relation to women delegates improved somewhat during the 1930s when the average number rose to ten. The IWWU accounted for about half this average. The unions that fairly regularly appointed one or two women as delegates during this period were INU, INTO and the National Union of Tailors and Garment Workers. Throughout these ten years the ITGWU only once appointed a woman on its large delegation and that was in 1935: Miss McDonald, was one of thirty-three delegates from that union. Interestingly, the Textile Operatives Society of Ireland which re-affiliated to Congress in 1938 appointed two women delegates each year up to 1942.

During the six years 1939 to 1945, the situation as regards women delegates attending Congress was scarcely any better than in the 1930s. Over the five years prior to the split the average number of women delegates was twelve. At the last Congress before the split in 1944, of the two biggest unions – both with a sizeable women's membership – the ATGWU included one woman and the ITGWU, none. Apart from the delegates from the IWWU, notable women delegates to Congress during the 1940s were Saidie Patterson (ATGWU), Belfast, and Betty Sinclair from the Belfast Trades Council who was first a delegate to Congress in 1942.[3]

At the first annual conference of the Irish Congress of Trade Unions in 1959 there were seventeen women delegates out of a total of 316 delegates, or 5% of the total. Eight of the women delegates were from the Irish Women Workers' Union, three

---

3. For more about these two women see: *Saidie Patterson: Irish Peacemaker*, by David Bleakley (Belfast, 1980); and 'Betty Sinclair: a Woman's Fight for Socialism', by Hazel Morrissey (Belfast, 1983).

from the ITGWU and one each from ATGWU, Civil Service Clerical Association, Irish Shoe and Leather Workers' Union, National Union of Tailors and Garment Workers, and Workers' Union of Ireland.

The number of women delegates rose slightly in the early 1960s but then declined. At the 1969 conference there were twenty-one women delegates, less than 5% of the total. The unions that accredited women delegates were: IWWU (8), NUTGW (3), ITGWU (2), Northern Ireland Civil Service Alliance, Civil Service Executive and Higher Officers' Association, EETU-PTU, Irish Local Government Officials' Union, Post Office Workers' Union, ASTI and INTO (one each).

By 1980, there were fifty-seven women delegates, or 9% of the total of 653 delegates. The women were from twenty-one trade unions and four Trades Councils, including NICSA (seven), IWWU (six), NUPE (five), ASTMS and ITGWU (four each), IUDWC, LGPSU and ASTI (three each).

In 1983, a survey of delegates to the annual conference was made by Michael Barry and Kevin Quinn S.J. of the then College of Industrial Relations, Dublin. Over two-fifths of the 457 delegates replied to the questionnaire. The survey indicated that about one in six of the delegates (17%) were women. Amongst Northern Ireland delegates, 18% were women while 16% of the delegates from the Republic were women.

At the first annual conference of the ICTU, six women delegates spoke. They were: Kay Fallon (WUI), Betty Sinclair (Belfast Trades Council), Sara Cunningham (National Union of Tailors and Garment Workers) and Kay McDowell, Elizabeth Caffrey and Maura Breslin (IWWU).

Ten years later in 1969, eight women delegates spoke: Betty Sinclair and Kay McDowell; Evelyn Owens and Joan Fortune (Irish Local Government Officials' Union), Betty Irwin (Northern Ireland Civil Service Alliance), Frances Maguire (National Union of Tailors and Garment Workers), Mrs Byrne (IWWU) and Carmel Dunlea (Civil Service Executive and Higher Officers' Association).

In 1979, twenty years after the setting-up of the ICTU, there were still only ten women speakers at its twenty-first annual conference: Francis Maguire (NUTGW), Patricia Redlich (ASTMS), Helen Corcoran and Mary McCarthy (ASTI), Inez McCormack (NUPE), Patricia McKeown (Northern Ireland Musicians' Association), Betty Dillon (Local Government and Public

Services Union), Mary Byrne (TASS) and Maura Breslin and Mai Clifford (IWWU).

Over the 1980s however there was a big increase in the number of women speakers at the annual conferences. In 1989 there were twenty-eight women speakers who between them made forty-four speeches: they came from twelve trade unions and three Trades Councils.

A constitutional change made in 1990 obliged unions with from 500 to 1,000 women members and appointing two or more delegates, to appoint at least one woman delegate. Unions with between 1,000 and 5,000 women members had to appoint at least two women delegates; between 5,000 and 10,000 at least three; between 10,000 and 15,000 at least four; between 15,000 and 20,000 at least five. At least one woman delegate was to be appointed for each 5,000 women members above 20,000

As a result of this change there was a substantial increase in the number of women delegates. Of the 545 delegates at the 1991 conference, 137, or 25%, were women. The number of women speakers at the conference increased considerably as compared with previous years. The total number of speakers (other than Congress officers and staff) was 155 of whom 110 were men and forty-five were women. Thus women speakers constituted three in ten of the speakers at the conference. More importantly, they came from as many as nineteen trade unions out of the seventy-one unions that accredited delegates to the conference.

There were 145 women delegates from thirty-four unions at the second biennial conference of Congress held in 1993. This represented just over a quarter (26%) of the total delegates, numbering 554 from seventy unions.

The eleven unions accrediting more than five women delegates were SIPTU (fifteen), INO (twelve), NIPSA (eleven), IDATU (ten), GMB (nine), NUPE (nine), COHSE (seven), MSF (seven), ATGWU (six), INTO (six) and IBOA (six).

Since the first annual conference of the ICTU in 1959, the proportion of women delegates has increased five-fold. In 1959 women represented 5% of the delegates. The figure ten years later in 1969 remained 5%. By 1980 the proportion had almost doubled to 9% and by 1983 had virtually doubled again to 17%. Ten years later, in 1993, the proportion of women delegates was 26%. One hundred years ago there were four women delegates out of 119 or under 4%.

So, while for almost three-quarters of a century, the proportion of women delegates to Congress annual conferences remained at about one in twenty, over the last quarter of a century the proportion has increased to one in four, a five-fold increase.

At the ICTU Northern Ireland Conference held in the Guildhall, Derry in April 1994, exactly one-third of the delegates were women (sixty-five out of 196).

Women on Congress Executive

Only eight women were elected to the National Executive of the Irish TUC over the period 1894 to 1959. Mary Galway of the Textile Operatives Society, Belfast was the first woman to be elected to the Parliamentary Committee of the Congress, as the executive of the organisation was called up to 1914. She was a member from 1907 to 1912. Other women elected subsequently to the National Executive were (the years shown are the years they were elected):

Rose Timmon, INTO, 1918 to 1921
Helena Molony, IWWU, 1921, 1933 to 1937
Cissy Cahalane, IUDWC, 1922, 1923
Elisabeth O'Connor, IWWU, 1924, 1925
Louie Bennett, IWWU, 1927 to 1932, 1945 to 1950
Lily Lennon, IWWU, 1935
Helen Chenevix, IWWU, 1950 to 1952, 1955 to 1957

Five of the eight women elected to the National Executive of the Irish TUC over the sixty-five years were members of the IWWU. The three women Presidents, Louie Bennett, Helena Molony and Helen Chenevix were also members of that Union.

Helena Molony was an actress at the Abbey Theatre, a friend of the Countess Markievicz and Maud Gonne MacBride, and a helper at Liberty Hall during the lock-out. In 1915 she was Secretary of the Irish Women Workers' Union with which she was to be associated for more than forty years.

As a member of the Irish Citizen Army, she took part in the attack on Dublin Castle on Easter Monday 1916 when her close friend, Captain Sean Connolly, an Abbey Theatre actor, was killed.

She was a delegate to the annual meetings of Congress either from the IWWU or from the Dublin Trades Council for many years and was elected to the National Executive in 1921 and 1933 to 1936. She was elected President of Congress in 1936 but did not preside at the annual meeting in 1937 because of illness. Helena Molony died in 1967 at the age of eighty-three.

Louie Bennett (1869-1956) a pacifist and feminist from an early age, first became associated with the Irish Women Workers' Union in 1916. The daughter of a prosperous professional family, with Helen Chenevix, she founded the Irish Women's Suffrage Federation in 1911 and later the Irish Women's Reform League. At the end of 1916, following the imprisonment of Helena Molony, who was the Secretary of the Union, which had been founded by Jim Larkin and his sister, Delia Larkin, in 1911, Louie Bennett became one of the union's Vice-Presidents. When the union was first registered as a trade union in March 1918, Louie Bennett and Helen Chenevix were honorary secretaries. The following year, Louie Bennett was made General Secretary of the union. She retired in 1955 at the age of eighty-six and died the following year.

Louie Bennett was a member of the National Executive of the Congress in 1927-32 and 1944-50 and was President in 1932 and 1948. She was the first woman to be elected President of Congress and one of only eleven Presidents in a hundred years to be elected more than once.

Helen Chenevix, the daughter of a Church of Ireland bishop and a graduate of Trinity College Dublin, was associated with the Irish Women Workers' Union as an official from 1917 and was appointed General Secretary in 1955. She retired in 1957 and died in 1963.

She was a member of the National Executive of the Irish TUC from 1949 to 1956 and was President in 1951.

For more about the trade union activities of the only three women Presidents of Congress – all officials of the IWWU – see the history of the Irish Women Workers' Union, *These Obstreperous Lassies* (1988) by Mary Jones.

Other material on Louie Bennett is in R. M. Fox's *Louie Bennett, Her Life and Times* (1958) and in the essay on Louie Bennett by Medb Ruane in *Ten Dublin Women* (1991). There is an article by Ellen Hazelkorn, 'The Social and Political views of Louie Bennett', in *Saothar* 13, 1989.

There is information about the activities of Louie Bennett and Helen Chenevix in the suffrage movement in Rosemary

Cullen Owens' *Smashing Times. A History of the Irish Women's Suffrage Movement 1889-1922* (1984).

Over the thirty-four years 1959 to 1993, there were only five women elected as ordinary members of the Executive Council of the ICTU. The first was Kay McDowell (IWWU), who was elected in 1959. The others were Margaret Skinnider, INTO (1962-63), Maura Breslin, IWWU (1971-72 to 1973-74), Inez McCormack, NUPE (1980-81, 1981-82, 1987-88 to 1993-95) and Patricia McKeown, NUPE (1984-85, 1985-86).

In 1983, a motion to amend the Constitution of Congress to provide that two seats on the Executive Council should be reserved for women to be elected by direct ballot, was before the annual conference.

The question of positive discrimination in favour of women had been a matter of controversy at previous conferences. In 1980 and again in 1982, motions calling for reserved seats for women were lost. In the course of the debate on the motion from the Irish Women Workers' Union in 1982, it was pointed out on behalf of the Executive Council that in its consideration of the recommendations received from the Sub-Committee on Equality, the Council had considered the matter and had decided to reject a proposal that there should be reserved seats for women.

At the 1983 annual conference, the motion on reserved seats for women on the Executive Council was moved by Inez McCormack of the National Union of Public Employees and seconded by Padraigín Ní Mhurchú of the Irish Women Workers' Union. In a controversial debate, described by the President, Paddy Cardiff, as 'very rational and unemotional', ten trade unions spoke on the motion proposed by NUPE. Seven were in favour of the motion and three against. In the event the motion was passed by 195 votes to 186.

The Congress constitution was again amended in 1992 to provide for four reserved seats for women. The Executive Council now consists of a President, Vice-President, Treasurer and twenty-six other members. Thus four out of twenty-nine places, or 14% are reserved for women.

The women elected to reserved seats on the Executive Council of Congress were (years are those of election to the Council):

Hilda Breslin, SIPTU 1990 and 1991
Claire Bulman, FWUI 1988

Mary Burke, SIPTU 1989
Eileen Fitzsimmons UNISON 1993
Mairin Ganly TUI 1984-89
Noirin Greene ITGWU 1984-87; SIPTU 1993
Avila Kilmurray, ATGWU 1991 and 1993
Ann McGonagle, NUPE 1991
Lenore Mrkwicka, Irish Nurses' Organisation 1991 and 1993
Alice Prendergast TUI 1990

Women's Committee

At the first annual conference of the ICTU in 1959, Kay Fallon moved, on behalf of the Workers' Union of Ireland, a motion directing the Executive Council to appoint a Women's Advisory Committee for the purpose of furthering trade union organisation among women workers generally and acting as an advisory committee on economic, industrial and social matters of special concern to women workers.

In her speech, Kay Fallon pointed out that very little support was given to women to help them overcome their problems. Women were playing a more important role in industrial and community life than in the past and this had created problems not only for women but for their families, the community and for society. It was necessary that the trade union movement work out a co-ordinated policy to deal with the situation, in particular, the lack of progress in organising women.

Betty Sinclair of the Belfast Trades Council seconded the motion, stating that the movement's job was to bring women into everything to do with the movement and drew attention to the absence of women from the conference (only seventeen of the 316 delegates were women).

The motion, the first taken at the first annual conference of the ICTU, was passed without dissent. Before the end of the year it had been implemented by the Executive Council. Nine women were appointed to the Women's Advisory Committee: Elizabeth Caffrey (IWWU), J. Califf (Irish Shoe and Leather Workers' Union), May Finane (NUTGW), Sheila French (ATGWU), Frances Lambert (ITGWU), Hilda Larkin (WUI), M.E. Maguire (CSCA), Margaret Skinnider (INTO) and Ella Stokes (IUDWC).

The first meeting of the Women's Advisory Committee was held on 8 April 1960 when Margaret Skinnider was elected Chairperson and Frances Lambert, Secretary. The first chairperson of the Northern Ireland Women's Advisory Committee was M. R. C. Shanks (INTO).

Other chairpersons in the early years of the WAC included Eileen Liston (INTO), Evelyn Owens[4] (Irish Local Government Officials' Union), Sylvia Meehan[5] (ASTI) and Brid Horan (ASTMS). Francis Maguire (National Union of Tailors and Garment Workers) was for many years chairperson of the Northern Ireland Women's Advisory Committee. Apart from Francis Lambert who was secretary of the WAC for many years, others who acted as secretary to the committee included Carmel Dunlea (Civil Service Executive Union), Carmel Colclough (Institute of Professional Civil Servants), Mai O'Brien (ITGWU), and Janet Hughes (FWUI).

Equality

In 1980 the annual conference of Congress adopted a motion expressing concern at the continuing discrimination against women in employment and declaring that this must be resolved through trade union action. It called on trade unions, *inter alia*, to examine ways and means of increasing participation at an active level by women members and to take positive steps to assist this. The following year, the annual conference called on the Executive Council to consider specific proposals for the elimination of discrimination against women. A sub-committee on equality was set up to prepare a report for the 1982 conference. The members of the sub-committee were drawn from the Executive Council and the Women's Advisory Committees (Carmel Colclough, Janet Hughes, Lily Kerr and Patricia McKeown) with Peter Cassells and Donal Nevin.

The report of the sub-committee, which was accepted by the Executive Council, was in two parts, one part dealing with issues to be pursued by Congress at national level with government and employers, and the second part dealing with a programme of positive action to be pursued by trade unions and by Congress.

A number of recommendations were made for action by Congress in promoting the greater involvement of women in the trade union movement. The recommendations included the changing of the name of the WAC to Women's Committee and

---

4. Appointed first woman Chairperson of the Labour Court in 1994.
5. First Chief Executive of the Employment Equality Agency.

368

that an annual Women's Conference be held comprised of delegates from all affiliated organisations. Unions were to be actively encouraged to increase the number of women among their delegation to annual conference and a section of the agenda of the conference was to be devoted to women's affairs.

The first annual Women's Conference was held in February 1983. It was attended by 155 delegates from forty-two trade unions and ten Trades Councils. The agenda included forty motions submitted by eighteen trade unions and four Trades Councils.

A survey by Congress of the breakdown of affiliated membership between men and women, revealed that the number of women members in affiliated unions in the Republic and in Northern Ireland at the end of 1982 was 216,000, or 34% of total membership of 642,000. Of the eighty-nine affiliated unions, seventeen of them accounted for 88% of the total women membership. The unions with the biggest membership among women were ITGWU (47,300), ATGWU (17,700), Confederation of Health Service Employees (16,600), FWUI (16,500), INTO (16,500), IUDWC (10,500) and NUPE (10,000). Four of these unions had a majority of women in their total membership, viz. NUPE (84%), COHSE (83%), INTO (73%) and IUDWC (53%).

A Congress survey of trade union officials in 1983 showed that the fifty affiliated unions with one or more full-time officials had a total of 328 officials engaged in negotiating with employers but only nineteen of these were women, a mere 6% of the total. (A similar survey in 1979 showed that only 4% of trade union officials were women).

The Equality Report which had been adopted by the annual conference in 1982 was monitored in the following years and a review of the overall positive action programme was undertaken in 1987 when an Equality Review Group was set up by the Executive Council consisting of members of the Council with the officers of the Women's Committees and Peter Cassells and Patricia O'Donovan. The Group's recommendations relating to the role of Congress included one that the annual Women's Conference be extended to two days. The report, noting that women represented only 12% of delegates to the Congress annual conference, recommended that over the following five years this should be increased to about one-third. It also recommended that steps be taken to ensure the proportionate representation of women on the Executive Council over the next five years, if necessary by extending the existing provision for reserved seats to provide for proportionate representation of women (two reserved seats for women were introduced in 1983). The Review Group's report was accepted by the 1987 annual delegate conference.

In February 1988, a further programme of positive action on equality was issued by Congress covering a six-year period, *A Programme for Progress*, and in 1993, a third Equality Programme, *Mainstreaming Equality*, was submitted to the annual conference. It set out the priorities in relation to equality for Congress and for trade unions over the period 1993-1998.

Trade Union Organisation

At the founding meeting of the Irish Trades Union Congress held in 1894, there were fifty-two trade unions or trade societies represented. Their membership as returned to the organising committee was 20,600. There were thirty-seven trades represented by separate unions, from bakers, basket makers, blacksmiths, boiler-makers, bookbinders, book-folders, bootmakers, brush-makers and butchers to whitesmiths and wiremakers.

Other trades represented by separate unions were cabinet-makers, carpenters, confectioners, coopers, cork-cutters, coach-makers, flax dressers, glass bottle-makers, litho printers, mill sawyers, newspaper machinists, organ builders, printers, plasterers, plumbers, painters, paper cutters, poulterers, rope makers, slaters, shirt cutters, saddlers, silk weavers, smiths, stereotypers, tailors.

Other unions represented brewery labourers, coal labourers, dockers, general labourers, railway staff, tramway men, assurance agents, purveyors' assistants, press dispatch assistants, and hotel and club assistants.

The fifty-two trade unions represented (in most cases they were local unions) had a membership of some 20,600. Contrary to the widely-held belief, only 9,700 of these were in craft unions: there were 10,900 in non-craft unions, mainly unions of labourers and other manual workers though there were also what would now be referred to as white-collar unions, represented. However, while there were sixty-three craft union delegates at the first Congress, there were only twenty-nine delegates from other unions.

Also represented at this 1894 Congress were five Trades Councils: Belfast, Cork, Drogheda, Dublin and Limerick. There were eight delegates from the Dublin council and six from the Belfast council including two women.

Other labour bodies represented were the Knights of the Plough, the Irish National Labour League, the Irish National Labour Association and the Irish Democratic Labour Federation.

As might be expected, since the meeting was held in Dublin, a large majority of the delegates were from that city, eighty out of a total of 119 delegates. There were fifteen delegates from Belfast, seven from Cork and four from Limerick.

Six of the unions represented had over 1,000 members: the Amalgamated Society of Railway Servants (4,000), Amalgamated Union of Labour, Belfast (2,300), United Labourers of Ireland, Dublin (1,500), Flax-dressers, Belfast (1,250), Typographical Society (1,200) and the Amalgamated Carpenters and Joiners (1,200).

The membership of affiliated unions was not given in the annual reports of Congress until 1919. However ten years after the founding of Congress, the largest unions based on delegate fees paid, in 1904 were: Amalgamated Society of Railway Servants, Typographical Society, Amalgamated Society of Tailors, United Kingdom Association of Coachmakers and the Dublin Typographical Provident Society – all but the first-mentioned, were craft unions.

In 1914, twelve unions paid affiliation fees of more than £2 suggesting that they had a membership of over 2,000. These were: ITGWU, NUR, Irish Drapers' Assistants, Typographical Society, Amalgamated Union of Tailors and Tailoresses, Postmen's Federation, DTPS, Irish Women Workers' Union, Amalgamated Society of Painters and Decorators, Railway Clerks' Association, Belfast and Dublin Locomotive Drivers and Mechanics and the United Kingdom Society of Coachmakers. Only five of these twelve unions were craft unions.

The biggest delegations in 1914 were from the ITGWU – its General Secretary, James Larkin, was President of Congress that year (sixteen delegates); Amalgamated Society of Tailors and Tailoresses (five), NUR (four), Typographical Society (four) and IWWU (three).

The 1919 Congress report was the first to give the membership of each affiliated union. There were twelve unions affiliated for 2,000 members or over (membership figures are here rounded to the nearest one hundred): ITGWU (66,000), NUR (17,800), INTO (10,500), Flax Roughers and Yarn Spinners, Belfast (9,600), Amalgamated Society of Carpenters and Joiners (8,000), Irish Clerical Workers' Union (6,000), Irish Drapers' Assistants' Association (4,000), Postmen's Federation (3,000), Amalgamated Society of Operative House and Ship Painters (2,200), Irish National Agricultural and General Workers' Union (2,000), (Irish) National Amalgamated Union of Bakers (2,000). Only one of these twelve unions, the INTO, was still in existence in 1994. Of the twelve largest unions in 1919, only four were craft unions.

In the twenty years between the wars, 1919 to 1939, affiliated membership reached a peak in 1920 when it totalled 229,000. However, half of the increase over the previous year was accounted for by the increase of 34,000 in ITGWU membership to 100,000. Thus this union represented well over two-fifths (44%) of Congress total membership.

By 1930, when the conjoint organisation, the Irish Labour Party and Trade Union Congress was dissolved and the Irish TUC came into existence, the membership of the ITGWU had plummeted to 20,000, or just one-fifth of the total membership of Congress which by now had declined to 102,000.

In 1930, the ten biggest unions affiliated to the Irish TUC were: ITGWU (20,000), ATGWU (15,000), NUR (10,200), INTO (9,700), ASW (7,200), IUDWC (6,100), POWU (4,000), RCA (2,600), IWWU (2,500) and ASPD (2,200). Only two of these unions were craft unions while three were white-collar unions. It might be noted that the Workers' Union of Ireland which was not affiliated to Congress, had about 14,000 members at this time making it the third biggest union in the country. Only two of these unions, ATGWU and INTO, were still in existence in 1994.

In 1944, the year before the withdrawal of a number of unions from Congress, the membership of the Irish TUC was 162,000, a strong recovery from the lowest figure of 98,000 recorded in 1929. In 1944, the ten biggest unions affiliated were: ITGWU (36,000), ATGWU (35,000), IUDWC (9,900), ASW (9,400) INTO (9,000), NUR (8,000), IWWU (6,000), National Union of Tailors and Garment Workers (4,100) and Irish Seamen's and Port Workers' Union (4,000). There was only one craft union among these ten unions. Again only two of these unions, ATGWU and INTO, were in existence in 1994.

The Congress of Irish Unions which was set up in 1945 did not include the membership of affiliated trade unions in its annual reports. However the Joint Memorandum on Trade Union Unity prepared by a Joint Committee of the Irish TUC and the CIU, for Trade Union Conferences held by the two Congresses in April 1954 gave the membership of unions affiliated to the CIU. There were five unions in the CIU with 3,000 or more members. These were: ITGWU (148,400), IUDWC (14,700), National Union of Vintners', Grocers' and Allied Trades' Assistants (3,800), Irish Engineering and Foundry Union (3,000) and Irish Seamen's and Port Workers' Union (3,000). None of these unions were still in existence in 1994. The remaining seventeen unions in the CIU had less than 3,000 members.

In the Joint Memorandum, the total membership of the CIU is given as 189,000 and the membership of the Irish TUC as 211,000.

The membership of trade unions affiliated to the Irish TUC over the period 1894 to 1959 is given on page 433. In 1959, the Congress of Irish Unions and the Irish TUC united in the Irish Congress of Trade Unions. The membership of the ICTU for each year 1960 to 1994 is given on page 435.

In its first year, the membership of the Irish Congress of Trade Unions totalled 432,000. Ten years later, in 1970 it had increased by 18% to 510,000 and by 1980 by a further 30% to 661,000. There were small downward changes in some years of the 1960s, 1970s and 1980s but membership increased in most years and by 1990 had reached 679,000, the highest figure reached up to that year, and 3% higher than ten years previously. The peak of Congress membership was reached in 1991 when membership was 682,000. By 1994 it had fallen back fractionally to 681,000.

A breakdown of the affiliated membership of Congress between the Republic and Northern Ireland is available since 1984. The figures for certain years are shown in the table on page 375. Membership in the Republic has risen from 423,000 in 1980 to 467,000 in 1994, or by 8%, and in Northern Ireland has declined from 238,000 to 214,000, or by 10%.

The ten largest unions in Congress in 1994 were as follows: SIPTU (198,500), ATGWU (60,200), NIPSA (36,000), UNISON (31,500), MSF (31,000), IMPACT (27,000), GMB (26,300), MANDATE (26,100), AEEU (24,400) and INTO (24,100).

The five largest unions in the Republic were: SIPTU (190,500), IMPACT (27,000), MANDATE (26,100), MSF (21,000), and INTO (19,800). The eight unions with more than 15,000 members in the Republic constituted three-quarters (74%) of the total while the twenty-three smallest unions with fewer than 5,000 members accounted for 8% of the total.

In Northern Ireland, the five largest unions in 1994 were: ATGWU (42,100), NIPSA (36,000), UNISON (31,500), GMB (26,300) and AEEU (19,200). The six unions with over 10,000 members represented over three-quarters (77%) of the total while the twenty-three smaller unions with under 5,000 members accounted for 12%.

SIPTU constituted two-fifths of the membership of Congress in the Republic in 1994 and the sixteen public sector unions for over a quarter (127,600). The five largest unions accounted for three-fifths (61%) of the total.

In Northern Ireland there were thirty-three trade unions affiliated to Congress in 1994. The two main general unions (ATGWU and GMB) accounted for 67,600 members, or about one-third (32%) of the total and the eleven public service unions with 80,300 members for almost two-fifths (38%).

In 1994, women members totalled 173,700 in the Republic, 37% of the total membership, and 90,400 or 42% of the total in Northern Ireland. The women membership in Ireland was 264,100, or two-fifths of the total membership in Congress.

ICTU Membership in Republic and Northern Ireland
1980-1994

	Republic	Northern Ireland
1980	423,000	238,000
1985	436,000	217,000
1990	456,000	223,000
1991	459,000	224,000
1992	455,000	218,000
1993	464,000	215,000
1994	467,000	214,000

Profiles

William O'Brien

Daniel Corkery wrote many years ago in *The Leader* that the tragedy of Jim Larkin's life was the failure of a leader of the democracy to find lieutenants. This was indeed a prophetic flash of insight into the weakness of the Labour movement in Ireland: it concentrates on the bread and forgets the circus, leans to the prosaic and safe, and dislikes the intellectual and the poet as much as it fears the independent mind and the definite act.

Corkery, indeed like A. E., saw with his poet's eye the demoniac force in Larkin, but there was something else he did not stress, even if, in his play *The Labour Leader*, he dropped a hint: there is a suggestion in the conflict of the hero in that play of a clash between mediocrity and genius, but in Larkin there was also the charlatan and the egoist as much as the genius and the leader. If men make movements it is their fate sometimes to unmake them, as the chronicle of our own Civil War may remind us. There are cynics who would amend Corkery's version of the Larkin tragedy to read that Larkin's real tragedy was that he tolerated only lieutenants who were automatons and like Pope's Turk, would never tolerate a rival near the throne.

When Jim Larkin, in the autumn of 1914, left Ireland for a nine-years' exile in the United States amid the shadows of European War, the threat of coming Irish revolution, and the wreckage of the bitter industrial dispute of 1913, which had broken his great union's power, membership and resources, he left at least two able lieutenants and rivals behind him, James Connolly and William O'Brien. Today, only one of the uneasy triumvirate survives, the subject of this profile, William O'Brien, beyond doubt one of the keenest minds and most efficient organisers any movement has produced in the country in the last forty years.

On a first meeting with this reserved, witty, astute, methodical and most subtle man, the question irresistibly rises to the mind of the thoughtful observer as to what the devil ever brought him into the revolutionary and Labour galley, although such is his force and social philosophy that the thoughtful observer understands very well why he eventually played so effectively the Cat among the Quiet Mice. He is a businessman to his fingertips and whatever he has talked, it has never been non-sense. Facts, documents, neatness, punctuality and efficiency to the point of pedantry characterise him, and this excess of virtues too rare amongst us explains the heat, conflict and unpopularity he has provoked in his critics and his enemies and his followers for many years.

There is a parallel between himself and Michael Collins in this stickling for order and system, and the same impatience with good intentions and sayers of words who are slack in performance, even if O'Brien prefers the expressive look and the terse epigram rather than the flourished fist and full blooded oath as the fit vehicle for communication. And if he lacks Mr de Valera's infinite patience with bores and long-winded nitwits, he lacks, too, mastery of the Taoiseach's capacity of rising after long sessions of such gentry's most painful exhibitions, and talking them all to a submissive standstill with the charm of a seraph – albeit a seraph with an iron fist in reserve.

William O'Brien prefers a straight yea and nay, yet his chairmanship of the most cliché-ridden, passionate and stormy Labour congress is masterly and never more so than when he himself has been the target of the most envenomed and unruly onslaughts. After the uproar during a Congress at the time of the Trade Union Bill controversy (1941), when the massed invective and insult of the Left Wing had played on his personality and record, O'Brien sarcastically quoted from a novel of Walter Scott's 'hold me over Hell's mouth, give me a good shaking, but don't drop me in', then smiled and said he had one wish: to attend his own funeral, and discover what they really thought of him.

His critics have been very definite as to what they will say both before and after his funeral, of which there are certainly no very imminent signs (O'Brien died fifteen years after the profile was written) since William O'Brien retired some years ago from his post as General Secretary of the Irish Transport and General Workers' Union to such placid sidelines as a Directorship of the Central Bank and editorship of the Devoy papers and visits abroad to social conferences.

It is to be hoped that the rumour is true that he is writing his memoirs, although it may be that he has contented himself with the reflection that time, after all, tells best and that the encomiums of the mourners at his funeral, attended or unattended by his shade, will chime in vindication to the verdict of posterity.

His memoirs would certainly be a contribution to much inner and significant political and social history in the last half century, and, above all, a valuable gloss on the varying fortunes of the Labour and Trade Union movements in Ireland.

O'Brien was one of the earliest colleagues of James Connolly and a member of the Irish Socialist Republican Party in the 1890s. It is mainly due to O'Brien's care and industry that Connolly's writings have been preserved, published in book and pamphlet, and kept in circulation. Moreover, in a very practical manner, Connolly's syndicalist or industrial unionist theorising has been translated by O'Brien into the sea change of that certainly very big and efficient machine, the ITGWU.

And the success of that most formidable organisation owes much to O'Brien's iron insistence on system, concentration, good staff work, rules, regulations, sound finance, strict auditing of accounts which has certainly spared the Transport Union from those ugly peculations which every now and then disturb the trade union world elsewhere. To be sure, the very success of the organisation, and the menace of its strength to weaker bodies, has created envy, distrust and the once popular slogan of One Big Union sounds like a knell of doom in many proletarian ears. Yet, whatever the merits of this controversy, it must be conceded that O'Brien's industry and foresight forged a very formidable weapon.

More controversial and problematical, to be sure, is the famous split in the Labour and Trade Union movements in which William O'Brien and the ITGWU, cheered on by a most diverse collection of gallant allies, but relying in the first instance on their own strength, struck in full confidence of victory, with our pathetic little local collection of Communists as the ostensible *casus belli*. There has been stalemate, not victory – or perhaps both sides won. Certainly both sides, with their volubility and self-righteousness, have bored the general public into indifference or, perhaps, into the feeling that family quarrels are not for outsiders even if such a potentially valuable political force as the Labour Party is neutralised, and the perpetual inter-union wrangles threaten to blunt, if not break, the weapon which, in a memorable phrase of Connolly himself, found the Irish workers on their knees and raised them to their feet.

Certainly, Mr William O'Brien is not so much at fault in all this, except that, when he was in the fray, he was a very bonnie fighter; and if he had one fault, it was to go on fighting beyond the finish. It is very arguable that, in his dispute with Larkin when that great man returned in 1923 – and lost a fight with the odds heavily in his favour – O'Brien was nearly a hundred per cent right, and that, when you fight a force of nature, you had better fight with the buttons off the foils. And above all, the future biographer of Larkin or the historian of the Labour movement here must note with particular care the amazing rise of the ITGWU in 1917-18 from ten branches and a membership of 5,000 to 100,000 and 210 branches, with a proportionate increase in its prestige and financial resources, with room in its ranks for nearly every category of workers, gains consolidated and maintained with the exception of agricultural workers for a season wooed, won and then lost by mutual consent after a sensational flash in the pan.

Mr O'Brien was the main agent who worked on the favourable post-Rising circumstances, aided by such helpers as Foran and O'Shannon, an ability to recruit an army of hardworking and able trade union officials, and the shrewd political leadership of Thomas Johnson. O'Brien was an active and ubiquitous co-ordinator in those years, and could blend the Red Flag with the Papal Encyclicals, a speech at a political meeting with the launching of yet another branch of his union, Wormwood Scrubbs and the Mansion House Anti-Conscription conference. Then came – after the virtual Labour-Republican alliance in the War of Independence, where O'Brien is well known to have been the vital link – the Free State, Civil War, the return of Larkin to Ireland and its sequel.

William O'Brien's selection as Labour representative on the Central Bank in recent years was a wise and inevitable choice. It is known that his colleagues, even those most conservative in outlook, have grown to respect his keen mind, organising grasp, quickness of decision and economy of words. He is the perfect committee man, always five minutes early for a meeting, ready to rap out a date, a figure, the apt statistics for the asking. He invariably answers a letter by return, and his memory and capacity for documents relevant and awkward have long seemed disconcerting to his enemies. Jim Larkin once paid him the compliment of saying that William O'Brien was the only colleague of his who ever really worked; and even if Larkin with a rare discretion, paid that particular compliment privately, it was praise indeed.

379

Slightly abridged version of an unsigned Profile of William O'Brien published in The Leader *(Dublin), 31 January 1953. The writer of the Profile was Professor T. Desmond Williams, Professor of Modern Irish History, University College Dublin, 1949-83.*

James Larkin T.D.

James Larkin's unusual abilities soon marked him as the most intelligent member of his party. But how did he compare with members of other parties? In the select company of, perhaps, the two ablest members of the Dáil, he seemed less shrewd but scarcely less persuasive than Mr Lemass, and Mr McGilligan, whose own luminous intellect is quick to perceive another trained mind (even if trained in a different school) was soon keeping his eye on the new TD.[1]

Larkin's speeches were devoid of rhetoric, well-structured, authoritative in factual content and original in conception. Sometimes his delivery seemed forced and mechanical as if he was trying to inject a synthetic substitute for the emotional element that was so conspicuously missing. His appeal was to reason and he has always disdained the oratorical devices which some TDs use in attempts to embellish their words or conceal their lack of thought.

But Larkin's speeches are in no sense mere impersonal cascades of economic facts and figures. One remembers him addressing the Trinity College Fabian Society over ten years ago and sounding more academic and intellectual than any of the members. But one remembers, too, his diffident kindliness, on that occasion, towards the percipient but innocent enquiries of a young woman, whose attractions were not exclusively intellectual. The careful observer in the Dáil gets telling glimpses of the man in occasional mannerisms. When an argument is failing to carry conviction he adopts a more personal tone suggestive of greater frankness; it is often accompanied by a thin, slow, shy smile that seems to reflect a private appreciation of the ironies of life rather than high spirits or good humour to be shared with others. He rarely repeats himself and always commands an attentive audience. He has never made a bad speech in the Dáil. His reputation was quickly recognised outside the House, but as

1. Seán Lemass was Minister for Industry and Commerce from 1932 to 1948, except for a period during the war years when he was Minister for Supplies. Patrick McGilligan was Minister for Finance from 1948 to 1951.

a public speaker on the platform he disappointed some who said: 'If only he had his father's personality and if only "Big Jim" had had "Young Jim's brains".'

Like McGilligan in Fine Gael, he is a contributor to policy and in no sense a leader of a Parliamentary Party. It is not suggested, of course, that he aspires to leadership, or has the capacity for it. It is hard to define his position in his party as it was to define that of his late father, in the labour movement. His ultimate interests may not be in politics at all but in trade union activity in which, as General Secretary of the Workers' Union of Ireland, his efforts compel the admiration of members and earn the respect of those employers who 'know where they stand with Jim Larkin'.

Mr Larkin is certain to hold his seat in the Dáil for as long as he wants it but it would cause little surprise if, secretly, he were to attribute his success more to his own personal merits, reputation and achievements than to the present banner of the Party he serves with such loyalty and distinction.

Mr Larkin's views were well set out in his Presidential address to the fifthy-fifth annual meeting of the Irish Trade Union Congress in Belfast in 1949. 'Not so many years ago,' he said, 'not only was it permissible to criticise the capitalist system, but it was regarded as a perfectly intelligent and normal course.' 'Today,' he continued, 'criticism is constrained and limited, because criticism, valid though it might be, of an economic system which has exposed its own defects a thousand times over, is denounced as criticism – political and ideological criticism – of the international plans and organisations offered to us as the salvation of all our post-war problems.' He went on to say that capitalism, as an economic system, no longer served the requirements of society and that changes would have to be made to cover its defects. He pointed to the need for organising collective effort, and remarked that even the Marshall Plan as a form of collective effort was 'completely contrary to the very basis of capitalism'.

When the first Inter-Party budget was introduced in May 1948, Mr Lemass taunted the Labour Party on its new-found allies. In a defence of his position, Mr Larkin began by saying: 'In a short and somewhat uneventful life, I have often had occasion to be thankful that I had some small sense of humour.' 'Fianna Fáil', he said, 'was no longer the Government because it had not been able to adjust itself to a new situation. The Labour Party

381

may have had to choose between alternatives it did not like, but after sixteen years of Fianna Fáil it preferred the Inter-Party position.' 'We may change our minds some day,' he said, 'and in due course we will notify the Fianna Fail party of the change and they can then take advantage, but at the moment it looks as if there will not be a change for quite a long time.'

To a large section of the public Mr Larkin is more than a deputy who makes able speeches in the Dail, who contributes ideas, if not a policy, to his party and who is a principal officer of a trade union. To many he is primarily his father's son. What must it be like, one wonders, to be the favourite son and political heir of such a famous father? 'Big Jim's' standards were high and a man of such great gifts must inevitably have imposed almost insuperable tests of adequacy on others – particularly on members of his family. He must have instilled in his son a severe degree of self-criticism. He also sent him to Patrick Pearse's school, Saint Enda's, and gave him other advantages for educational and intellectual development of which he had been deprived himself. No doubt, young Jim was grateful; he has always been proud of his father and deeply loyal to him. But outstripping him in intellectual attainments and having been groomed to follow in his public footsteps did not make it any easier for a middle-aged man to take his place in the Dublin labour movement where he was destined to be known as 'Young Jim' even if he lived to be the age his father was.

The public had its impression of the father: the gifted and successful Labour leader with a wonderful physical presence, vitality even in old age, and all the public virtues of political anger, kindliness, encouragement for the young and enthusiastic and the kind of humour that suits a crowd. His instinct for communicating his fiery and turbulent personality to an audience is remembered by those who cannot recall a word of what he said. But the special gifts that made him larger than life in public were not necessarily assets in family relationships. To love such a parent, to be proud of him may well make it all the more difficult to fit oneself for his shoes.

From the grave 'Big Jim' has good reason to be well satisfied with his son. 'Young Jim' has shown himself to be a man of integrity, sincerity and, when the occasion arises, courage. If he is sometimes shy and aloof, perhaps it is because he is always mindful of being measured, no matter what he does. Will he retain his ideals through expedient methods? It is too soon to answer all these questions, but, unlike other people who embraced similar ideals in their youth, Mr Larkin will not be permitted by his friends, or his enemies, to forget about his. He has obviously always felt the weight of other people's expectations, and in circumstances that might have defeated his father's resourcefulness, he has tried hard to do what seemed best to him. Once, at least, he fulfilled an historic role: when he published his letter appealing for Labour unity after his father's death.[2] One may doubt whether 'Big Jim' would have tolerated such rivalry from his chosen son during his own life. But 'Big Jim' lived until his son had already passed the adaptable stage of early youth; in fact, he was no longer young when the torch was passed to his hand.

Extracts from an unsigned Profile in The Leader *(Dublin), 27 March 1954. The writer of the Profile was Professor T. Desmond Williams, Professor of Modern Irish History, University College Dublin, 1949-83.*

James Larkin was born in Liverpool in 1904, the son of Elizabeth Brown and James Larkin. He went to school at Scoil Eanna in Rathfarnham, Dublin, a school run by Padraig Pearse and his brother, Willie. He studied in Moscow 1928-30. On his return to Dublin he was elected to the Dublin City Council of which he was a member until June 1933.

During the 1930s and up to his father's death in 1947, he was in effect assistant general secretary of the Workers' Union of Ireland. In 1947 he was elected General Secretary, a position he held until his death in 1969.

James Larkin was first elected to Dáil Éireann in 1943 for the Dublin South Central Constituency and was re-elected at the 1944, 1948, 1951 and 1954 general elections. He was for a time chairperson of the Parliamentary Labour Party. He did not contest the 1957 election.

He was a member of the National Executive of the Irish TUC 1945-1959 and the Executive Council of the ICTU from 1959 until his death. He was President of Congress in 1948-49, 1951-52 and 1959-60.

James Larkin was the Secretary of the Provisional Committee of the ICTU in 1959.

Ruaidhri Roberts

Ruaidhri Roberts was the fourth full-time secretary of the Irish Trade Union Congress when he was appointed from October 1945, his predecessors being Thomas Johnson (1921-28), Eamonn Lynch (1930-40) and Cathal O'Shannon (1940-45). Following the dissolution of the Irish TUC and the Congress of Irish Unions in 1959, he and Leo Crawford, the secretary of the CIU, were

2. *The text of James Larkin's letter to* The Irish Times *is on pages 405-7.*

appointed Joint Secretaries of the new Irish Congress of Trade Unions. On the retirement of Leo Crawford in 1966, Ruaidhri Roberts was appointed the first General Secretary of the Congress, a position he held until his retirement at the end of 1981, becoming the longest-serving chief official of a national trade union centre in the world.

At the thirty-five annual conferences that he attended between 1946 and 1981, as well as the many special conferences held over this period, it was Roberts who normally presented the executive council's position on major policy matters and who highlighted the main developments affecting trade unions. Over this period he would have made over one hundred major contributions to the discussions at annual conferences on important issues. These contributions ranged over wide areas of trade union, industrial, economic and social policy issues. For example, his first speech to an annual meeting in 1947 dealt with an administrative matter, co-ordination between Congress and the Lower Prices Council set up by the Dublin Trades Council. His last speech to an annual conference in 1981 dealt with the National Understandings.

In 1959 there were three Congress conferences. In February, at the Irish TUC Special Congress, Ruaidhri Roberts gave a detailed explanation of the main provisions in the draft constitution of the ICTU. At the last annual meeting of the Irish TUC in July, his speeches covered several topics including firstly, apprenticeship legislation; secondly, a dispute with the then Minister for Health, Mr Sean MacEntee, arising from the insistence of Congress that it had the right to nominate a trade union representative to the National Health Council rather than, as the Minister wanted, submit a panel of names from which the Minister would select; and thirdly, the need for an economic planning body.

In the same year 1959, the first annual conference of the ICTU was held in September at which Ruaidhri Roberts presented a major report on economic development and the general approach of the trade union movement to economic problems as outlined in *Planning Full Employment* that had been prepared by the Provisional United Organisation of the Irish Trade Union Movement. At that conference he also spoke about the need to develop and expand trade union education and training services, something that he was to pursue vigorously over the following years as he had in his years as Secretary of the Irish TUC, having been the founder of the People's College in 1946.

For over twenty years, Ruaidhri Roberts was the Irish Workers' Delegate to the annual International Labour Conference held in Geneva.

Ruaidhri Roberts was a member of many Government Commissions and other bodies, including the Commission on Emigration and Other Population Problems 1948-54; Commission on Workmen's Compensation; Capital Investment Advisory Committee; National Industrial Economic Council and the National Economic and Social Council. He was closely associated with the setting up of the Irish National Productivity Committee (later the Irish Productivity Centre) and was its chairperson for many years.

Ruaidhri Roberts' last substantive speech to the annual conference in 1981 was on economic policy from which the following are extracts:

> The deep involvement of the Irish trade union movement in the business of government in all the areas in which Congress has an interest has been a result of developments under the two National Understandings on Social and Economic Development.
>
> These have brought about a dramatic change in the position of the trade union movement vis-a-vis Government and the developments which have taken place in recent years represent an unprecedented breakthrough in establishing the position of the movement in the planning of changes in our economic and social affairs. Employment, investment, taxation, training, social insurance, health, problems of the handicapped, pensions, child care, education, housing, have all been included in the Government-Congress discussions and programmes.
>
> Employment is at the core of the National Understanding. But we are also concerned with the shape of future negotiations on pay. What is now contained in the new Government's Programme 1981-86, gives us considerable cause for concern. We propose to seek discussions with the Taoiseach so that we can determine whether the National Understanding will be properly honoured by the Government and secondly, to determine whether the Government is prepared to continue with the collaborative approach and involve the trade union movement in real consultation and a part in the planning by consent of our economic and social development.
>
> If we obtain satisfaction on these questions we will report to affiliated unions. If we cannot obtain this satisfaction, and if future economic and social policy is to be determined by a flock of economists, then the future is dismal indeed.

Thus in his last speech to conference, Ruaidhri Roberts was prophetic indeed.

At this 1981 conference, Roberts' last as General Secretary, the President, Dan Murphy paid this tribute to him:

His contribution to the Irish Trade Union movement has been an outstanding one. His greatest achievement was undoubtedly the prominent role he played in the discussions in the years 1956 to 1959 leading to the re-establishment of trade union unity. His contribution to the successful negotiations on the various National Pay Agreements and National Understandings over the last decade also was enormous. He has always fought with courage and tenacity, particularly in the interests of the weakest sections of our movement. The whole Irish Trade Union movement owes Ruaidhri Roberts a great debt of gratitude.

Trade Unions and Social Policy

This seminar prompts the question as to how effective has been the role of the trade union movement in the formation of social policy in Ireland. There is a social aspect to much of what trade unions seek to achieve through their normal activities. Obviously too, there is a beneficial social fallout from trade union action. Above all, however, trade unions have influenced the climate of thinking about social policy. Then, in more practical terms, there have been the many submissions on social policy made by Congress to Governments, particularly in the context of the annual Budget, and from time to time considerable pressure is exercised on individual Ministers for the implementation of particular aspects of social policy.

It should also be pointed out that in the triad of policy objectives that the trade union movement has consistently put forward over recent years – namely, full employment, the improvement of social services, the raising of the living standards of our members – that the development and expansion of the social services has been the second priority, after full employment, and before that which is the main direct purpose of trade unions which is to look after the interests of their members in respect to their employment.

The second point I would make concerns the National Economic and Social Council. Congress played a significant role in the setting up of the NESC and has been a major influence on the evolution of the thinking of the Council, especially the development of social policy initiatives. Congress has also had a major input into the identification of the social issues that the Council has examined and researched.

Many reports of the NESC have contained radical ideas and proposals that represent a rich vein for us to exploit, a resource to utilise. They provide the basis for pressure by the movement for the implementation of progressive social policies. It goes without saying that the recommendations made by the Council are concerned with economic structures as they are and as they are likely to continue for some time, and with society as it is. To that extent they are limited in their espousal of revolutionary changes in society. And they may not be the worse for that.

My third point relates to the implementation of social policy through the means open to the trade union movement. Here I refer specifically to the National Understanding for Social and Economic Development. (Note that 'social' came first). I doubt if there is as yet a full realisation among our members of the major change in trade union policy that is implied in the acceptance of the principle of the National Understanding. It would seem to me that in accepting overwhelmingly, the National Understanding, trade unions have consciously, and in a major way, added an important string to the traditional collective bargaining bow.

In a sense the National Understanding has institutionalised a new dimension to our trade union activity. It was not merely a pay agreement. It was a pay agreement made in the context of negotiations with the Government on diverse economic and social matters including employment, taxation and social services. Here one should note that the trade union commitment to full employment as its first priority, has an important social dimension because unemployment is a major source of poverty and inequality in our society. In other areas covered by the National Understanding such as social welfare, health eligibility, education, the progress made may have been limited but what seems to me to be of extreme importance is the fact that these elements were there, that Congress negotiated with the Government changes in the social services – these being changes that would not have been brought about if Congress had not been involved in the discussions on the National Understanding.

It is up to the trade union movement to consider how this significant departure in trade union policy can be extended and developed and, if there is to be another such National Understanding, what specific elements of social policy ought to be included in any new draft proposals.

My fourth point relates to the difficulties that arise for the trade union movement through its involvement in the development of social policy. There is no use pretending that problems do not arise for us, problems that can at times be embarrassing, awkward, disturbing. For example, we all can accept that redistribution from the rich is all right. But when you go beyond the rich and seek some form of redistribution from those who are not so rich, that seems to be another matter.

It is clear that redistribution, whether through the taxation system alone or in combination with social security, can be a painful process for some and we do experience in our trade union work resistance to that form of redistribution. Then again the awkward question arises at to who should pay the cost of economic difficulties that can assail us from time to time. I have the suspicion that those who will bear the cost will be those who lose their jobs. To what extent will the rest of us be prepared to share the cost?

Then there are the problems that arise in social policy through upsetting the status quo, or as it has been referred to, the divine right of differentials – I refer not to differentials between craft workers, say, and other workers but am using the term to cover differences in income between different categories of employees.

On the question of the social wage, John Blackwell has pointed out at this seminar that, on an admittedly crude calculation, the social wage per person at work in 1979 was about £1,700. That represents almost one-third of the gross earnings of a male industrial worker and half the average earnings of all industrial workers, men and women. One might ask what recognition do we give in practice to this factor of the social wage when seeking adjustments in general pay rounds, and, more importantly perhaps, what is our attitude to the social wage when we come to consider matters relating to taxation.

We have been told here that our standard of living has broadly doubled in the last twenty years. Should we ask ourselves whether we have made the best use of the opportunity provided by the doubling of our living standards, to remedy some of the ills that have plagued our society? Have we effectively opted for more consumer spending rather than smaller school classes, or whatever other social priority you may have in mind?

On the question of discrimination against groups, which clearly emerges as a significant feature of society in relation to women workers, can we say that trade unions have been as aggressive in pursuing pay equalisation as between men and women as we might have been?

Finally, some uncomfortable ideas have emerged from this seminar – for example, that the causes of poverty or inequality have to do with the distribution of power in society and that the characteristic of the poor that emerges again and again is their powerlessness. So it is that a transfer of power to the poor might not be without complications for other sections of society. We are not now dealing with a 'Strumpet City' society, though features

389

of it still persist, but the reality is that there are more than the Bradshaws among the 'haves' in our present-day society.[1] If, as in 1913, the trade union movement is not committed to the fight against poverty, inequality and injustice, what then can it be seen to be committed to?

I would like to conclude with the words of the great Italian socialist, Antonio Gramsci, who said:

'The poor have no power, they only have their friends'.

I would suggest that we, the trade union movement, must be those friends. No doubt our collective trade union heart is in the right place. It is up to us to see that the actions we pursue are in tune with that and that we avoid advocating simplistic approaches that flow from the heart and which tend to be concerned with vague abstract concepts that might or might not develop in some revolutionary future. Options is what it is all about, and grasping nettles, and, unfortunately, the selection of particular options necessarily involves the rejection of others and in grasping nettles, we run the risk of being stung.

Extracts from summing-up remarks of Donal Nevin, Assistant General Secretary, Irish Congress of Trade Unions, at final session of seminar on Trade Union Priorities in Social Policy, organised by the Federated Workers' Union of Ireland, 19-20 April 1980.

---

1 The Bradshaws were the wealthy family in the novel about 1913 by James Plunkett, *Strumpet City*.

Trade Union Membership

For the first time, a comprehensive survey of trade union membership in the Republic was undertaken by the Central Statistics Office as part of the Labour Force Survey in 1992. The questionnaire which was completed by 46,500 households comprising 153,900 persons (4.4% of the total population) included a question about membership of trade unions or staff associations.

The survey indicated that in April/May 1992, the number of persons who were members of trade unions or staff associations totalled 479,400. Of these, 301,700 (63%) were men and 177,700 (37%) were women.

Of the total, 42,600 were either unemployed or retired. Accordingly, the estimated number of persons at work who were trade union members was 436,800, including 267,000 men (61%) and 169,800 women (39%). There were 18,500 part-time workers who were members of trade unions, or 4% of the total: 80% of these part-time workers in trade unions were women.

The breakdown of the 436,800 trade union members working in the main economic sectors was as follows: manufacturing, etc (125,100), professional services [includes the health and education sectors] (104,600), commerce, insurance, finance and business services (60,700), public administration and defence (51,000), transport, communication and storage (71,000), building and construction (25,900) and other sectors [mainly personal services, catering, hotels, agriculture, forestry] (28,300).

Exactly half of all employees at work in 1992 were members of trade unions or staff organisations. Trade union density, that is the proportion of a particular group who were members of trade unions, in the main sectors was: public administration and defence (73%), transport, etc. (71%), professional services (60%), manufacturing, etc. (55%), building and construction (49%), commerce [mainly distribution], insurance, finance and business services (34%) and personal services, etc. (26%).

By main occupations, the Labour Force Survey indicated that trade union density was highest among professional and technical workers, such as teachers and health service staff, with 61% of such employees organised, and transport and communication workers, also with 61% organised. These two groups were closely followed by producers, makers and repairers with 60% of such employees organised.

Less than half of the employees in the other main occupational groups were in trade unions: clerical workers (49%), service workers (42%) and commerce, insurance and finance workers (29%). In the remaining occupational groups [agricultural workers, labourers and 'others'] trade union density was 38%.

According to the LFS survey, women trade unionists were concentrated mainly in the following sectors: professional services (69,700), manufacturing (36,100), commerce, insurance, finance and business services (26,500) and public administration (16,200). The remaining sectors accounted for 21,300 women trade unionists.

By occupational group, women trade unionists were concentrated mainly in professional and technical occupations (58,500), clerical workers (47,400), producers and makers (25,000) and commerce, insurance and finance workers (19,000). Three in five women trade unionists were in non-production occupations.

The proportion of employees at work who were in trade unions in 1992 was 52% for men and 47% for women. Trade union density among men was highest in the transport and communication sector and in public administration, 72% in both these sectors. Next highest were professional services (63%), manufacturing (56%) and building and construction (51%). By contrast, the proportion of men organised in the commerce, insurance, finance and business services area was only 35%.

In the case of women, trade union density was highest in public administration (76%), professional services (59%) and manufacturing (52%). The proportion of women organised in the commerce, insurance, finance and business services sector was 32% and in the remaining sectors, 30%.

Trade union density, by occupational groups was highest among clerical workers (65%), transport and communication workers (61%), producers (60%), professional and technical workers (56%) and service workers (55%). It was lowest among commerce, insurance and finance workers (32%).

In the case of women, trade union density was highest among professional and technical workers (65%) and producers (62%). Trade union density among women clerical workers was 44% and among service workers, 33%. It was lowest among women workers in commerce, insurance and finance (27%).

The distribution of trade union membership among the planning regions in 1992 was as follows: Dublin, 175,100; rest of East

Region (Kildare, Meath, Wicklow), 39,900; South-West Region (Cork, Kerry), 68,600; South-East Region (Carlow, Kilkenny, Tipperary South, Waterford, Wexford), 47,800; North-East Region (Cavan, Louth, Monaghan), 24,700; Mid-West Region (Clare, Limerick, Tipperary North), 38,100; Midlands Region (Laois, Longford, Offaly, Roscommon, Westmeath), 30,500; West Region (Galway, Mayo), 32,200 and North-West Region (Donegal, Leitrim, Sligo), (22,500).

Almost half (45%) of trade union members in 1992 were in the East Region (Dublin and the three adjoining counties Kildare, Meath and Wicklow) while a further 14% were in the South-West Region and 10% in the South-East Region: almost 70% of trade union members were therefore in these three regions (eleven counties) with the remaining 30% in the other sixteen counties.

ICTU Surveys

Seven surveys of trade union membership were undertaken by the ICTU in the 1960s and 1970s and published in various issues of *Trade Union Information*.[1] These estimates of trade union membership in the Republic for certain years were: 359,400 in 1966, 386,800 in 1970, 441,000 in 1974 and 498,900 in 1979.

Estimates for total trade union membership in the Republic have also been made by W.K. Roche and Joe Larragy of University College Dublin.[2] For the seven years for which Congress estimates are available, the variation between the two sets of figures averages 0.1%. The Roche and Larragy estimates for certain other years were: 1930 (99,500), 1940 (151,600), 1950 (290,600), 1960 (312,600), 1970 (408,600) and 1980 (527,200).

Northern Ireland

The United Kingdom Labour Force Survey has also included a question on trade union membership. Figures for Northern Ireland are available from this survey.[3]

1. The ICTU estimates of trade union membership in the Republic were given in the following issues of *Trade Union Information*: August 1967 (1966), December 1968 (1968), June 1971 (1970), November-December 1975 (1974), Spring 1978 (1976), Summer 1980 (1979).
2. The data collected by Roche and Larragy was part of a study of the Development of Trade Unions in European Societies (DUES) undertaken by the University of Mannheim.
3. *Employment Gazette* (HMSO, London), January 1993.

The LFS indicated that trade union membership in Northern Ireland in 1991 (Spring) for all employees was 233,000. Of these, 131,000 (56%) were men and 102,000 (44%) were women. There were 210,000 trade union members in full-time employment and 23,000 (10%) in part-time employment.

Trade union density in Northern Ireland among all employees in 1991 was 47%. It was 50% for men and 44% for women. Among non-manual workers, trade union density was 49% and among manual workers, 46%. In the manufacturing sector it was 52% compared with 46% in the other sectors.

Among full-time workers, trade union density was 52% and among part-time workers, 24%. In establishments employing six to twenty-four workers, trade union density was 24% but in enterprises employing over twenty-four workers it was 58%.

International Comparisons

A survey by the Organisation for Economic Co-operation and Development in *Employment Outlook*, July 1994, indicates that trade union density (the per cent of wage and salary earners in trade unions) in Ireland was the sixth highest of the eighteen OECD countries for which comparable statistics were available.

Trade union density in Ireland in 1990 was 50 per cent, a figure exceeded only by the four Scandinavian countries Sweden (83%), Finland (72%), Denmark (71%) and Norway (56%), and marginally, by Belgium (51%). The figure for Ireland was substantially higher than in Japan (25%) and the United States (16%) and in EC countries such as France (10%), Spain (11%), Netherlands (26%) and Germany (33%) and higher too than in Britain and Italy (39%).

Industrial Disputes 1922-1993

In fourteen of the seventy-two years 1922 to 1993, over half a million days were lost through industrial disputes, strikes and lock-outs, in the Republic. Three of these years were in the pre-war period (1922, 1923 and 1937), two were in the 1950s (1951 and 1952) four were in the 1960s (1964 to 1966, 1969) and five in the 1970s (1970, 1974, 1976, 1978, 1979).

The following are the fourteen years in which over 500,000 days were lost through industrial disputes and the main disputes occurring in those years:

1922 – 705,000 days. Postal dispute, whole State; railway workers, Dublin; building workers, Dublin; creamery workers, Tipperary, Waterford; drapery shop assistants, Dublin; dockers, Dublin; coal mines, Arigna.

1923 – 1,209,000 days. Dockers, main ports; bacon factories, Limerick, Waterford; flour mills (national dispute); general workers, Cork; shipyard workers, Dublin; bottlemakers, Dublin; fertiliser industry, Dublin, Cork.

1937 –1,755,000 days lost including 1,437,000 in building trade dispute, Dublin and Cork, which lasted from April to October; clothing workers, Dublin (138,000).

1951 – 545,000 days. Banks (144,000); transport (110,000).

1952 – 529,000 days. Printing, Dublin (240,000); hotels and restaurants, Dublin.

1964 – 545,000 days. Building industry (421,000).

1965 – 556,000 days. Printing industry (316,000).

1966 – 784,000 days. Banks (327,000); paper mills (154,000).

1969 – 936,000 days. Maintenance craftsmen dispute (629,000), secondary teachers (115,000).

1970 – 1,008,000 days. Banks (791,000).

1974 – 552,000 days. CIE Buses (247,000).

1976 – 777,000 days. Banks (482,000).

1978 – 613,000 days. Transport (174,000); food industry (143,000).

1979 – 1,465,000 days. CIE Buses (1,206,000).

The table on page 396 gives for each of the fourteen five-year periods between 1922 and 1993, the average annual numbers of industrial disputes, days lost and workers involved in disputes and, in the final column, the average number of days lost per worker.

The period with the greatest frequency of disputes was 1972-76 with an average of 163 disputes per year, followed by 1947-51 with 157 and 1977-81 with 143. The periods with the lowest frequency were 1987-91 with fifty-seven disputes and 1927-31 and 1957-61, both with sixty disputes.

The highest average annual number of days lost was in the period 1977-81 (673,000) and this was followed by the 1967-71 period (561,000).

The highest number of workers ever involved in industrial disputes in any year was in 1985 when 168,700 workers were involved: this, however, was because of a one-day strike in the public services when virtually all public servants stopped work in protest at the government's threat to the public service arbitration schemes. Apart from this exceptional year, the highest numbers of workers involved in disputes were in the years 1969 (61,800), 1966 (52,200), 1986 (50,200) and 1979 (49,600) while the lowest numbers were in the years 1928 (2,200), 1927 (2,300), 1930 (3,400), 1926 (3,500) and 1989 (3,700).

Industrial disputes in Republic 1922-1993
(annual averages)

	No.	Days lost	Workers involved	Days lost per worker
1922-26	94	519,000	15,826	33
1927-31	60	121,000	3,575	34
1932-36	93	179,000	8,305	22
1937-41	108	460,000	13,949	33
1942-46	85	122,000	7,024	17
1947-51	157	348,000	18,399	19
1952-56	80	192,000	9,310	21
1957-61	60	160,000	11,742	14
1962-66	84	445,000	28,498	16
1967-71	121	561,000	38,820	14
1972-76	163	408,000	33,780	12
1977-81	143	673,000	35,764	19
1982-86	139	373,000	82,067	5
1987-91	57	153,000	13,683	11
1992	38	191,000	13,107	15
1993	47	61,000	12,764	5

Source Irish Trade Journal (1926-37), Irish Trade Journal and Statistical Bulletin (1938-63), Irish Statistical Bulletin (1964-94). The statistics on industrial disputes are compiled by the Central Statistics Office.

Leaving aside the exceptional five-year period 1982-86, the highest average number of workers involved in the other five-year periods were 1967-71 (38,800), 1977-81 (35,800), 1977-81 (35,800) and 1962-66 (28,500). By contrast, the highest annual average number of workers involved prior to the 1960s was 18,400 in the 1947-51 period followed by the 1922-26 period with 15,800. The lowest incidence of workers involved in disputes was in the periods 1927-31 (3,600), 1942-46 (7,000) and 1932-36 (8,300).

Throughout the period the main causes of industrial disputes related to wages and the dismissal of workers. A table in the Report of the Commission on Industrial Relations (1981) showed that over the years 1923 to 1979, 43% of disputes related to wages while 27% arose out of the dismissal of workers. A further 24% of disputes related to other matters concerning conditions of employment.

The average annual number of days lost in industrial disputes over the fourteen five-year periods 1922-26 to 1987-91 and in the years 1992 and 1993 are shown in the accompanying diagram.

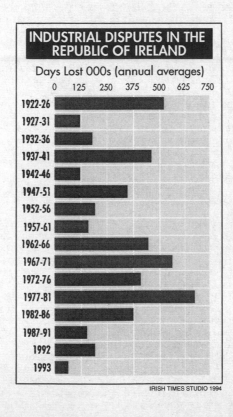

IRISH TIMES STUDIO 1994

The Testimony of Josephine Soap

In 1945, women workers in the public laundries in Dublin, members of the Irish Women Workers' Union, voted for strike action to secure a fortnight's holiday. Their weekly wages were 38s 6d. On 21 July, the 1,500 workers withdrew their labour. The strike lasted fourteen weeks.

On 13 September 1945, *The Irish Times* diarist, Quidnunc, included the following in 'An Irishman's Diary':

I, Miss Soap, Testify –

My name is Josephine Soap, laundress. There are a number of different tasks that I can perform in my laundry: but none of them enables me to get sufficiently far away from your shirt.

If you reach a point with your shirt whereat you can no longer bear the fried egg on the collar, how do you think that I feel about it, who had nothing to do with throwing the egg around? Why, in fact do you think that I press your handkerchief – the one used for cleaning bicycles – to my breast, whispering, 'Parfum d'amour'?

The plain truth of the matter is that I love your dirty linen far less than you do. The other plain truth of the matter is that large heaps of dirty linen provide the most depressing sight in Europe.

It would, perhaps not be so bad if it were new dirty linen. I might feel pleasure in restoring it to its true beauty. But when it's a pink (faded) shirt, with small, green stars, patched on the shoulder with a piece from the seat of a pair of khaki cycling shorts, I feel I do myself an injustice if I do not throw it out of the window. If I do throw it out of the window, the owner of the shirt writes to the management in terms suggesting that the Crown Jewels have been broken up, and buried.

That I Can Sort –

If I wish, in my laundry, I can sort. The ghastly parcels walk in and we corner them and tear off their wrappings, and then beat them into different piles of sheets and shirts, socks, jumpers, jerseys, and the rest of the litter, and send the whole lot along to the washing department. Some of the customers suck the laundry mark off their handerchiefs, and we have to mark them over again.

Contemplate with what pleasure you burrow in search of his laundry, into the boot locker of your husband's wardrobe on a Monday morning, as if into a nest of ferrets. And then think how I feel about sorting *his* laundry, and your man's laundry, and the brother's laundry, and here's your sal volatile.

If I wish, I can work in the washing department. Here I bung bundle after bundle of old clothes into long steaming cylinders, shut the hatch to stop them jumping out, turn the switch that causes the cylinders to revolve, and then sit down to contemplate the absolute horror of what is going on inside. It might be tolerable,

398

with morphia, if there were but one cylinder; but I have many to empty and refill. For this diverting pastime I wear rubber boots and overalls, and look like a lady out of a slaughterhouse.

Or Dry –

If I wish, in my laundry, I can work in the drying department. Here I pack the sodden relics from the washing cylinders into perforated bins. I touch a switch, and the bins revolve at high speed casting the water out of the garments by centrifugal force. I sit, quietly crying, watching the water running out of the channels at the base of the bin. After a time I dry my eyes, shut off the power, and dig the laundry out of the dryer. It's been packed like concrete by the whirling motion. I think it might be nice to put old men who drop port on their jerseys into the dryer, just for a time, to see what would happen.

Or, perhaps, it might be my laughing pleasure to attend the eight-roller ironing machine. Here hour after hour, with mounting excitement I feed sheets and blankets, pillowslips and bedspreads onto an endless belt. The belt draws these delightful items beneath the rollers, the whole thing is superheated with steam and the sheets and so on come out the other end all fresh and lovely. I remain where I am and I suppose it is amusing in a way, that my hair keeps falling over my face. I consider the cause of that to be the steam and I hope you did not burn your leg too severely on the pipe.

Or Iron –

Or, perhaps if I were very, very good, I might be allowed into the ironing department. Come follow, follow, follow, while I give this shirt what's coming to it.

See this polished metal arm. This is for drying shirt sleeves. I draw the sleeve over the arm, pulling it down till the sleeve is tight, possibly burning my hand. Oh no, *you* burn *your* hand! Well, somebody was bound to. That's how it goes.

This thing here is for drying and pressing collars and cuffs. I clamp the left cuff in here, the collar in the middle, and the right cuff here, so that the shirt seems to be held in the stocks. Would it not be agreeable if the owner of the shirt were in it too? But the owner of the shirt has his spare one on, and at this moment has his head back, pouring sevenpence worth of stout over the front of it.

With these hand irons I can attempt to flatten the belts of dresses, used last week for strangling husbands; and the hard collars that the husbands use for strangling themselves.

Finally, in the packing department I can blind myself deciphering laundry marks, and send everybody back their own oddments; although I cannot tell why anybody would wish to see this stuff again.

And Don't Like It

I, Josephine Soap, laundress, have spoken, but I haven't nearly finished. I am waxy. I am waxy about having to stand around knee-deep all day in old clothes – no rose garden, believe me, Claud. But specially best I'm waxy about this – that as soon as I've washed the

399

clothes the customers go out and get 'em dirty all over again. I, Josephine Soap, feel that I am probably digging a hole and filling it up and digging a hole and filling it up and digging a hole and filling it up and that all this is leaving me very little time, in my span upon earth, for contemplation of the Exhibition of Living Art, Clark Gable, and Merrion Strand with the tide out.

I, Josephine Soap, respectfully present my compliments to the Federated Union of Employers – (linen not quite so spotless as usual, eh, boys?) – and suggest that they release me from my treadmill for a period of fourteen days in the year.

I close now, with best thanks to you dear –

***

Marches by the women strikers, intense lobbying by the Union, support from other unions and by the public, sustained morale over the slowly-passing months and compensated in part for the depleted coffers of the IWWU and the modest strike pay. On the picket lines and on the marches through the centre city, the strikers proclaimed their determination in song to the tune of 'Lilli Marlene':

> Then they gave us one week,
> But we wanted two,
> And we well deserved it
> For the work we had to do.
> There for a long nine hours a day
> In heat and steam we have to stay
> And then they gave us one week out of fifty-two.

The strike was won. On 30 October, an agreement between the IWWU and the Federated Union of Employers conceded two weeks' holidays with pay. It was a victory not just for the laundry workers but for all trade unionists who soon followed the women workers' example and secured two weeks' holidays.

The Union subsequently wrote to Quidnunc of *The Irish Times*, thanking him for his support in their struggle. He replied: 'I am keeping your letter as evidence of the fact that I once served some slightly useful purpose. It was easy to write about people with such immense spirit.'

The diarist, Quidnunc, was Patrick Campbell (1913-80), later Lord Glenavy, the author of many books and a noted broadcaster.

Congress Manifestoes and Documents

1919 To the Employers of Labour and Property Owners of Ireland

We desire to address you in the names of the organised working class in Ireland. We wish to state clearly what is the cause of the so-called unrest amongst the workers, why we are dissatisfied with the conditions of employment, rates of wages, hours of labour, and to explain where lies the responsibility for the deplorable conditions in which the great majority of the workers of Ireland live and labour.

For several years before the outbreak of war there had been an upward movement in prices; the cost of living had been steadily rising, until in July 1914, the workers had to pay 23s for the same amount of food that they were able to buy in 1904 for 20s. The prices of clothing, boots, and sundry household requisites had risen even higher.

[The Manifesto cited a study of poverty in Cork by Father McSweeney, of 1,010 working-class families (5,058 persons). Of these families, 495 (2,524 persons) were in receipt of a total income averaging below 21s per week; 354 families (1,832 persons) were in receipt of an average income, per family, of only 13s 9d per week!

The Manifesto also quoted from a memorandum by Smith-Gordon and Cruise O'Brien in *Food, Famine and the Workers*, published in May 1917, that in Dublin the average pre-war wage of organised unskilled workers was 22s 6d per week, and of unorganised casual workers, 20s per week when employed. It pointed out that in estimating annual income, allowance must be made for periods of unemployment owing to temporary slackness.

The Manifesto also quoted a report by the Department of Agriculture in 1916 that the average wages paid in Ireland for different grades of agricultural workers, i.e. general labourers, cattlemen, ploughmen, ranged from 12s to 16s 6d per week 'for men who do not live in free cottages or receive allowances of any kind'].

Such was the position at the outbreak of war. Do you consider it was satisfactory? Was the agricultural labourer to remain content with his 12s to 16s per week, or the town labourer with 13s 9d to 21s? Bear in mind this, that the food requirements alone to keep an average family in health, according to the conservative estimate of the most competent authority (Mr Seebohm Rowntree) could not at that time be bought for less than 15s per week.

After the outbreak of war, prices rose daily. Farmers prospered; merchants, shopkeepers, manufacturers, all found their bank balances growing rapidly. Wealth came to you unconsciously, as the dew from heaven.

Did you voluntarily share your new-found wealth with your workers? No. You waited until compulsion was applied by the power of their trade unions, the threat to strike, and the regulations of the State. And, after all the advances in rates of wages which have thus far been forced from your hands, what is the position of the workers today? This: (1) that as compared with July 1914, the cost of living for the working-class family has increased 115 per cent.: 20s in 1914 would purchase as much food, clothing and household requisites as 43s will purchase today; (2) that, with the exception of a few industries closely connected with providing munitions of war, rates of wages have not kept pace with the advance in the cost of living.

We find, therefore, that the workers today are actually in a worse financial position than they were in the days before the war, a position which was even then intolerable.

The present claim which we make on behalf of the workers is for a higher standard of life than that which they suffered in 1914.

We insist that in cases where men were employed in 1914 at starvation rates, i.e. below 20s per week, that these rates must be deemed to have been raised to the minimum level of 20s per week and that we now require an advance over and above the real-wage standard represented by that 1914 minimum.

In these and in all other cases we claim that money wages must be raised to a point that will more than equal the increase in the cost of living.

Ireland and all its natural resources belong by inalienable right to the whole people of Ireland. You, the present generation of employers and property-owners have usurped authority over the material resources of this country. You have sought your own profit at all times without regard to the people's welfare.

402

You care nothing for the condition of the workers. You think of them as men and women whose destiny is to work for your profit, and when you do not see the prospect of a profit to be got out of their labours, you cease to employ them. Their future is no concern of yours; their children are allowed to go hungry, unclothed, and uneducated.

The present methods of industry and trade are doomed; the existing economic relations between men cannot long continue. It is not our duty to propound a remedy. Any remedy we could suggest must inevitably involve a complete alteration in the basis of your system, must end in giving control of the processes of wealth production and distribution to the people engaged in those processes in the interests of the community, not by virtue of ownership, but of service. We would eliminate the motive of profit-making from industry, and direct our energies to organising the production of goods for the use and service of the people. Such a course would solve at the same time both the political and economic problem. The present political system could not long survive a revolution in the economic system.

For the moment you, the legal proprietors and employers, are the people whose duty it is to lift the country out of the economic and social bog into which you have driven it. And you fail at your peril!

Extracts from a Manifesto issued by the National Executive of the Irish Labour Party and Trade Union Congress, 1 May 1919.

1934 Manifesto to the Workers of Ireland

The Irish Trade Union Congress and the Irish Labour Party take a serious view of the growth of Fascism in this country; and the pronouncements of Fascist advocates regarding the Trade Union and Labour Movement. These pronouncements representing the opinions of prominent men in the political life of the country, cannot be ignored. They constitute a grave danger to the free existence of trade unions as well as pointing to the overthrow of democratic government.

The present world economic situation is considered by the Fascists in this country to have created a suitable setting and environment to push forward the violent principles of Fascist reaction. Through the exploitation of economic distress the disappointed remnants of the Cumann na nGaedheal Party, by coalescing with other reactionary political elements, adopting new theories and party cries, and promoting a semi-military political organisation, hope to disguise their past, and rehabilitate themselves once more as a Government.

In this aim and objective these disappointed politicians have the support of every reactionary element which sees in the national and social advance of the people the loss of a privileged class position that has been enjoyed since the conquest. These anti-national elements are centring their hostility to the people under the banner of Fascism. In this attack on the principles of democracy and trade unionism the forces of landlordism and reaction, linked with disappointed party politicians avaricious for power, are massing themselves under Fascist leadership. These Fascist preparations portend the gravest menace the workers of Ireland have ever been called on to face. On the issue of this struggle will depend whether the people of Ireland, and the workers in particular, will maintain the political and social advancement secured through centuries of sacrifice.

The Fascist movement is developing in this country on lines similar to those followed in Continental countries – inflammatory oratory, spectacular parades, the glamour of uniforms, appeals to youthful enthusiasm, political gasconading, promises of material reward – and behind it all the backing of a private political army. The advocates of Fascism by such means emulate their confreres on the Continent and hope thereby to secure power and control in the State.

Once seated in the saddle of Government the mask will be thrown aside, and by the suppression of democratic organisations and democratic rights, Fascism will reveal itself as elsewhere – the oppressor of liberty and the effective instrument of heartless capitalism.

Largely because the mass of the people failed to appreciate the significance of its aims, Fascism in Continental countries succeeded in gaining control of the State by means of specious promises, the savage suppression of opposition and, to an extent, the apathy of public opinion. Today in the Fascist countries the trade unions and other popular organisations are destroyed, their buildings stolen, their funds confiscated, and their leaders in gaol or in their graves. Such are the methods by which Fascism alone can succeed. These are its approved methods in all countries where it has obtained control of the State machine.

Anyone who has studied the growth of the Fascist Movement elsewhere will recognise the same methods, phrases, and party slogans; the salutes, uniforms and badges of its counterpart in the Blueshirt Movement here. That Movement, like Fascism in other European countries, adopts an 'Economic' code, and sets out to advocate the so-called 'Corporate State' in furtherance of which trade unionism must be destroyed. To replace the Trade Unions, puppet organisations will be established with constitutions and rules drafted by the government, who will appoint the officers and control their policy. Here is the graveyard of civil liberty.

Fascism has nothing to recommend it to the people. Its trail across the face of civilised Europe has been one of violent upheaval, bloodshed and terrorism.

Cognisant of the dangers which confront the workers of Ireland, we urge the masses of the people to distinguish between spurious promises and the realities of Fascism as expressed in the Blueshirt Movement. The issue is one of life and death for democracy and trade unionism.

To crystallise the hostility of the Trade Union and Labour Movement to the realities of Fascism, public meetings are to be organised throughout the country, commencing on the 6th May 1934. Trades Councils and Labour Party branches are, therefore called upon to make the requisite arrangements for holding demonstrations in their areas.

This call is addressed not alone to the working class, but to every hater of arrogance and lover of liberty.

Shortened version of the Manifesto to the Workers of Ireland on the Fascist Danger, issued by the Irish TUC and the Irish Labour Party in May 1934.

1947 Labour Unity

To the Editor of *The Irish Times*

Sir,
It is necessary for me to seek the courtesy of your columns because, in the first place, this letter is not and cannot, by its very purpose, be addressed directly to any person or organisation,

and in the second place, it is of concern to so many who can only become aware of it through the medium of the Press.

This day a man was laid to rest with the great dead of our race. Of his claim to that resting-place many tongues have spoken during these past few days, and a deep and wide-flung emotional wave has swept over great numbers of people. That common emotion, that appreciation of loss, has been keenest among working men and women and the organisations, political and industrial, in which they associate. Whatever be the measure of his claim to their thoughts and feelings, Jim Larkin has been mourned and his passing deeply regretted by persons and organisations in every section and division of the Irish Labour movement. Stirred by a common emotion, these diverse groups and persons have found that they hold in common certain simple, yet great, beliefs, which have been brought sharply to the surface by the death of this man. They have found that they possessed a common bond, because being of the Labour movement, they found their common heritage added to by the unique service of the dead man, and the essential unity of Labour has been indicated by the value placed by them on his lifework in the broad stream of Irish Labour.

If it be true that Irish workers have suffered a great loss, and if in that loss something common to all in the working-class movement has been manifest, surely now at this moment that which is most essential to Irish Labour can be given to Irish working men and women – a Labour movement, united in purpose, in struggle, and in its objectives. Unity is not such a great benefit that it may be purchased at any price, but today unity of Labour, industrial and political, is so urgently required that the price, even it be costly, can, and should, be paid by those who are in a position to make sacrifices.

The great mass of working men and women who constitute the Irish Labour movement most ardently desire that their strength and purpose should be added to a thousandfold by all that flows from unity, and those in whose hands lies the giving or the withholding of that unity should not deny the living vibrant mass of Labour, made up of the bodies, minds and spirits of living men, that which they need so urgently.

Irish people are emotional, and, perhaps, our common emotion this day may give us that unity we need, where reason and argument has failed in the past.

I have no doubt of the truth of my statement when I declare that unity is the single quality sought for by the working men and women who constitute, and who are, the Irish Labour movement. Why, therefore, when so little stands between them and the unity they desire, should they be denied it.

With this great man's death, the last of the great figures of Irish Labour has passed, and we who remain are little people. If among those of us who occupy leading positions in the Labour movement there be individuals who, for one reason or another, represent obstacles or barriers to unity, let us grow in stature by stepping aside so that unity may be realised; if there are difficulties of policy standing in the way, let us, as we did this day, find the simplest common denominator in policy, and agree upon that as an immediate objective; if there are difficulties of organisation to be overcome, let us overcome them in the understanding that our organisations were built to serve Labour, not to shackle it.

Who shall make the first step? Naturally, those whose devotion to Labour is greatest. If the greater measure of devotion is not expressed by those of us who by chance are playing leading roles, then let the real and living body of Labour – the rank and file– show us and compel us to do our duty; but let it be quick and decisive, whoever takes the first step.

I have, as I stated above, written this letter because I feel it should be written now on this day of mourning and deep and common emotion. I have consulted no person. I speak for no organisation, neither the union of which I am a member nor the political party I support. Neither do I write it because of the name I bear, which is mine by accident of birth, but, being the only possession this dead man had to leave me, an obligation devolves on me of putting in words that which tens of thousands of working men and women felt this day – their common emotion spreading from their common needs and striving in this life and united in that which is known as 'Irish Labour.' – Yours, etc.

James Larkin

Thomas Ashe Hall,
5a College Street, Dublin,
Monday, February 3rd, 1947

1959 To All Trade Unionists

The Irish Congress of Trade Unions now formally inaugurated, greets the workers of Ireland on the occasion of the restoration of unity in the trade union movement.

The division which had persisted for over fourteen years weakened all unions and retarded the full development of the movement. That division is ended and our movement can now take its proper place in the nation's life, speaking with one voice and concentrating its undivided endeavours towards the achievement of working-class ideals and aspirations.

Recognising the traditional sense of loyalty of Irish workers to the principles of trade unionism and their unyielding militancy in defence of trade union interests, we confidently appeal for the support of workers in all unions throughout Ireland, north and south, in the tasks that lie before the united Congress.

Unity is not an end in itself but a means towards a stronger and more effective trade union movement. Our movement, here as in all the countries of the world, has over the years won tremendous advances for workers. Apart from material standards of real wages, hours and conditions, trade unionism has been the most potent instrument for winning dignity, self-respect and freedom for the workers. Nevertheless a long road stretches out before our ultimate goal is reached.

Towards the achievement of that goal of freedom and security for all our people in a peaceful and prosperous Ireland, the work of the Irish Congress of Trade Unions is dedicated.

The Congress is pledged to uphold democracy in the trade union movement, to maintain the right of freedom of association and the right of workers to organise and negotiate, and, in particular, the right to strike. It will support the democratic system of government and endeavour by all means open to it to promote such social and economic policies as are in the interests of Irish workers and which may from time to time be formulated by the trade union movement.

We will seek the full utilisation of the resources of Ireland for the benefit of the people of Ireland and will work for such fundamental changes in the social and economic system as may be necessary for the attainment of our objectives. In particular, Congress policy will be directed towards the solution of the problems of unemployment and emigration, north and south.

The primary purpose of trade unions is to protect the interests of members. The Irish Congress of Trade Unions will support unions in this purpose and will seek to ensure that workers' living standards, particularly their real wages, employment standards and working conditions, are maintained and improved. The Congress will also seek to promote the interests of the weaker sections of the community, the aged, the unemployed, the sick, and will strive to secure adequate social services that will ensure at least modest comfort for them. Radical improvements in educational facilities and opportunities, and in the health services will also be sought.

In the international sphere, the aim of the Irish Congress of Trade Unions is to promote fraternal and co-operative relations with the trade union movement in other countries for the purpose of furthering the common interest of all workers. It will co-operate with other democratic organisations in supporting progressive endeavours to safeguard and strengthen justice, peace and freedom in the world.

Unity in the trade union movement will mean an incalculable accession of strength to all unions in Ireland. The ninety unions affiliated to the CIU and the Irish TUC have been invited to apply for affiliation to the united Congress. We extend the hand of welcome to them.

Text of statement issued following the first meeting of the Provisional Committee of the ICTU, 12 February 1959.

1969 Programme for Peace and Progress in Northern Ireland

The Northern Ireland Committee of the Irish Congress of Trade Unions represents 215,000 trade union members in Northern Ireland and is the most representative body covering all sections of religious and political opinions.

The primary functions of the Committee are to protect and improve the wages and working conditions of trade unionists and to promote economic and social progress through full employment, equality of opportunity and rising standards of living.

The Committee has consistently sought to influence the government and the community to pursue progressive policies in the interests of all the people in Northern Ireland; in particular we have sought the acceptance of full democratic and civil rights for all citizens.

Northern Ireland is constituted as an integral part of the United Kingdom, and this position cannot be changed except by the democratic decision of the majority of the people of Northern Ireland. This is the constitutional position and all citizens, whatever their political view, should reject the use of physical force as a means of achieving political objectives. All citizens should be free to advocate change by democratic means. People should be assured that there are effective means of protecting the State and its people against the use of force from any quarter.

In normal circumstances, all police forces should be unarmed and be seen to be in an impartial civilian force for the protection of order and the safeguarding of the liberties and rights of all citizens.

Legislation should guarantee all citizens the basic human rights contained in the United Nations Declaration of Human Rights and provide machinery to make a reality of this guarantee.

An impartial Community Relations Board should be constituted so as to ensure its acceptability by all sections of the community in Northern Ireland. The Board should endeavour to eliminate the causes of discrimination by means of conciliation, but should have power to take legal action where this may be necessary to secure redress. Appointments in the public service should be made in such a way as would assure all citizens that appointments are made on the basis of merit and suitability.

The basis of allocation of public housing accommodation should be on a points system. It is urgently necessary that a crash programme of new housing be undertaken without delay. Positive steps should be taken to avoid segregation in new housing projects: this is of paramount importance.

The provision of jobs is a primary need if one of the basic causes of community tensions and unrest is to be removed. The programme for the attraction and establishment of new industries must be pressed forward with urgency. The Northern Ireland Committee will continue to extend its full support to the manpower and industrial training programmes. All means of providing work for the unemployed whether by public or private enterprise should be fully explored.

The extension of the local government franchise to all adult citizens must be implemented and the reorganisation of local government areas carried through without delay. The criteria for local government reorganisation should be service to the people and efficient administration. The new local government authorities must be determined to serve all the people in their areas.

Representatives of civil authorities, Churches and educational bodies should jointly examine ways and means of achieving greater co-operation and co-ordination between all schools with a view to achieving ultimately an integrated and comprehensive educational system which would provide full protection for all religious and cultural interests and in which the educational interests of the children would be paramount.

We recognise that a democratic state requires powers to protect its security and the liberty of its citizens. Legislation appropriate to this purpose, which protects the principle of innocence until guilt is proven, should take the place of the Civil Authorities (Special Powers) Act (Northern Ireland) 1922.

The Northern Ireland Committee acknowledges the strenuous efforts of trade union officials, shop stewards and members during the recent difficult period to maintain calm, order and solidarity.

Conscious of the influence which can be exerted by the trade union movement on community affairs by reason of the magnitude of its membership and the widespread nature of its organisation, the Northern Ireland Committee calls on all trade unionists to accept the responsibility of using their influence to the full in support of the Programme for Peace and Progress in Northern Ireland.

In present circumstances the trade union movement has a very special opportunity of making an immense contribution to an improvement in community relations. The opportunity should be taken.

The Programme for Peace and Progress in Northern Ireland, from which the above extracts have been taken, was issued by the Northern Ireland Committee of the ICTU in August 1969.

411

1971 Peace, Employment, Reconstruction

The Northern Ireland Committee of the ICTU has repeatedly advocated that all citizens, whatever their political views, should reject the use of force as a means of achieving political objectives, but should be free, without intimidation of any form to advocate change by democratic means.

Because of the situation and the demand by trade unionists in Northern Ireland for equality of citizenship, the Northern Ireland Committee made representations to the Northern Ireland Government in September 1966 about a number of basic reforms, including electoral reform and boundary revision in Stormont and local government elections; representation of minority groups on government-appointed public bodies; measures to diminish discrimination on religious or political grounds in employment and on religious grounds in the allocation of houses; and the appointment of an Ombudsman.

At that time the Northern Ireland Government refused to concede these reforms which would have helped substantially towards modernisation and democratisation in Northern Ireland. The Northern Ireland Committee continued to press the Government for the acceptance of their views. Unfortunately, the intransigence of the Government led to the subsequent breakdown in community relations with the tragic events of August 1969.

All people should be assured that there are effective means within the State for the protection of all its citizens against the use of force and all forms of violence from whatever quarter this may originate. The Northern Ireland Committee also condemns all forms of sectarianism and intimidation, and the persons who perpetrate such vile practices.

There is a need to establish, as more than a paper concept, the security of the rights of all citizens. We call for the introduction of a Bill of Human Rights, incorporating the machinery necessary for its full implementation. Such a Bill of Human Rights should be based on the Universal Declaration of Human Rights adopted in 1948 by the United Nations, and the European Convention of Human Rights 1950.

[The Programme went on to set out proposals to ease the unemployment situation and create new jobs; economic reconstruction; public enterprise; housing].

The trade union movement, by reason of its membership, can and must exert a constructive influence on the community. It is the working people who suffer most through civil unrest. In the end, it is the working people who will have to resolve the differences, and find solutions to our common problems.

The Northern Ireland Committee acknowledges with pride, the strenuous efforts made by many trade union officials, shop stewards and members, to maintain the high standard of human dignity and respect of others on which the unity of the trade union movement is based.

We commend these efforts to keep the civil strife out of industry and to spread peace in the streets and to the community at large.

Extracts from the Programme for Peace, Employment, Reconstruction issued by the Northern Ireland Committee of the ICTU in 1971.

1976 A Better Life for All

We the people of Northern Ireland support the trade union campaign for 'A Better Life for All' and pledge our efforts in our homes, work-places and in our community, to seek the achievement of the following rights:

- the right to live free from violence, sectarianism, intimidation and discrimination;
- the right to security of employment and well-paid work;
- the right to associate freely and to advocate political change by peaceful means;
- the right to good housing accommodation;
- the right to equality of educational opportunity;
- the right to adequate social services to protect the well-being and living standards of the aged, the young, the sick, the unemployed and the socially deprived.

We, therefore, call on all individuals and organisations engaged in violence in any form, whether by word or deed, to cease all violence immediately, and avoid further misery for the people of Northern Ireland.

We pledge ourselves individually to work for the aims of this Campaign, to enable the community to devote all its energy and resources towards the betterment of society.

***

At a Mass Peace Rally organised by the Trade Union 'Better Life For All' Campaign, held in Belfast on 20 November 1976, the following resolution was passed:

This rally reiterates its commitment to work for the implementation of a peaceful society in Northern Ireland.

Such a society must ensure equality and adequate provision for the social and economic needs of all its citizens.

We reject totally the gunman, the bomber, the assassin and the intimidator.

We extend our sympathies to the families and friends of all those who have suffered and died at their hands.

We recognise that peace is not just the absence of violence but the establishment of a society in which all can play their full part, free from the scourges of unemployment, sectarianism, inadequate housing and inequality whether in freedom of speech, educational or employment opportunities, social services or other aspects of community life.

We pledge our efforts to work for the aims of the 'Better Life For All' campaign to enable the community to devote all its energy and resources towards the betterment of our society.

1985 Youth Charter

The ICTU recognises and affirms the right of Youth to participate fully in the social, economic, political and cultural life of the community in conditions of peace, prosperity, freedom and dignity, regardless of sex, race, creed or political opinion.

Congress identifies the right to work as the most pressing social need of our time, so that young persons can have a basis for financial independence, social status and participation in society.

Congress affirms the urgent need for special measure to alleviate the particular difficulties faced by young women, young travellers, the homeless young, disabled youth, and disadvantaged youth.

Employment

The right to work which can only be achieved by Government implementing the trade union policies for radical changes in the economy and in society.

A national statutory minimum wage to protect young persons from exploitation.

Reorganisation and reduction in working hours, thereby improving employment opportunities for young persons.

Equality of access to a comprehensive, publicly-funded and accountable, democratically-controlled education system at all levels. In particular finance must be provided and measures taken to increase the participation of working-class youth in third-level education.

A scheme of educational allowances to enable working-class youth to remain on at second-level education.

Reform of education curricula, so as to eliminate sexism, promote an understanding of social, economic and political issues including trade unionism, encourage the development of a critical and evaluative mind, and lay the foundation for education as a life-long process.

Action to ensure that the education system does not reinforce existing class structures.

The reduction in pupil/teacher ratios through the employment of unemployed teachers.

Youth Schemes

A single agency should have responsibility for the co-ordination and supervision of Youth Schemes.

The introduction of a single framework Youth Scheme incorporating integrated modules for training, work experience and relevant education related to the target group, with guaranteed places for *all* unemployed youth.

Special provision should be made for second-chance education for early school-leavers and disadvantaged youth.

Adequate allowances must be provided for trainees who should have the right to join trade unions.

Training

Expansion of quality training programmes for youth which should include training in new technology and provide for the acquisition of transferable skills and an end to sex stereotyping.

Extension of the designated apprenticeship system to additional skill areas.

Guarantee for all apprentices and trainees of the opportunity to complete their training.

Youth and Law

Removal of the status of illegitimacy.

Freedom from discrimination arising from sexual orientation.

An end to the constitutional ban on divorce and the introduction of divorce legislation.

Provision of special treatment centres for drug abusers in custody.

Increased emphasis on non-custodial sanctions and community rehabilitation for young offenders.

The age of criminal consent to be raised to fifteen years of age.

Health and Social Welfare

Young persons to be eligible for the full range of welfare and health benefits.

Provision of a comprehensive programme of sex education and family planning services.

A programme of health education for young persons with particular emphasis on prevention of substance abuse (e.g. alcohol, drugs, etc.).

Extracts from Youth Charter drawn up by the ICTU Youth Committee, which was adopted by the ICTU in 1985.

1986 Divorce is a Trade Union Issue

Four years ago, at its Annual Conference in July 1982, the ICTU adopted a motion recognising that because the irretrievable breakdown of marriage does occur, divorce should be recognised as a civil right. The Conference of 650 delegates from the Republic and Northern Ireland, representing eighty-eight trade unions and thirty-six Trades Councils, called on the Congress to campaign for the removal of the Constitutional ban on divorce.

Why Trade Unionists should vote YES

The constitution of the ICTU pledges support for democracy and opposition to all forms of discrimination and sectarianism.

The ban on divorce and remarriage is:

– undemocratic, in that it denies what is a basic human and civil right to that minority of citizens whose marriages have failed.
– it discriminates against those who in conscience accept divorce.
– it is tainted with sectarianism in that it is in conflict with the religious views of sections of our people.

The removal of the Constitutional ban on divorce will extend the liberty of citizens and rescue scores of thousands from the shadow of the irretrievable breakdown of their marriage.

Why Divorce is necessary

The ban on divorce has not prevented marital breakdown, nor does it solve any of the problems created by such breakdown. A significant number of our fellow-citizens – particularly younger people – are caught in this constitutional trap. Their freedom to act in accordance with their conscience on the matter of divorce depends on this Amendment to the Constitution being carried.

The conditions for divorce proposed in the Amendment must be considered extremely conservative and in no way provide for easy or quick divorce. The rights of spouses and children are fully protected.

For all these reasons the Irish Congress of Trade Unions is calling on all trade unionists to VOTE YES in the Referendum and to uphold the civil rights of citizens and eliminate this discrimination and sectarianism.

Statement issued by the Executive Council of the ICTU on the Constitutional Referendum on Divorce in 1986.

1986 Stand Together for Peace, Work and Progress

Within the Trade Union Movement, workers pledge a special loyalty not just to themselves and their own interests but also to the interests of others. Whilst the primary objectives of the Trade Union Movement are industrial and economic, we also campaign on many issues which are of interest to the wider community.

By definition, the word 'community' implies the same concept of loyalty to one's neighbour and fellow-citizens. When people attack their fellow-citizens, they not only attack the individual victim – they attack the whole concept of living together in a community.

As trade unionists therefore we must speak out clearly and unanimously against violence directed at anyone in our community. We must not support any group which seeks to promote violence, intimidation or sectarianism – in any form.

If we in the Trade Union Movement stand back and tolerate or condone threats to our colleagues, we undermine the whole concept of 'community'. More directly we cheapen and sully the name of trade unionism. Given the purpose of trade unionism, our members should have a special understanding that the first loyalty of anyone must be the loyalty to one's fellow human beings.

It is that loyalty which gave birth to our Movement. Without it we are an empty shell. We must protect it and protect any fellow worker who is under threat. No trade unionist should ever be guilty of offending or threatening fellow-workers because of their religion, because of whom they serve, or because their jobs take them into certain areas or locations, such as police stations.

It is, of course, perfectly legitimate for trade unionists to have other loyalties as well and to seek to promote them by participating in, for example, voluntary organisations, campaigning groups and political parties. There is a limit however to the methods which are legitimate in pursuit of these objectives. We must withdraw support from all those who advocate violence against others in pursuit of their objectives. That includes disowning those who do not appear to advocate violence but, by their statements, implicitly support or excuse its use, those who promote hostile living and working environments, and sectarian divisions among workers.

There are no 'justifications' – no 'legitimate targets' – no 'acceptable levels of violence'. These are false excuses and do not serve the interests of working people, whether Catholic, Protestant, or Dissenter.

Workers who in any way assist, promote, or contribute financially to those who threaten these rights are not threatening anonymous, faceless groups of people. In reality they are threatening their fellow-workers, their trade union colleagues and their livelihoods.

The current political unrest is undoubtedly causing great tension in the community and the workplace, and there are elements, both sinister and mischievous, who are seeking to exploit that situation for their own ends. Amongst the tactics currently being employed in many areas of the Province is that of intimidation of workers, either in collective groups or of one religion or other, or named individuals.

Some of our members are now threatened with a sentence of death from the paramilitaries for doing nothing more than, for example – emptying dustbins, driving buses, fixing telephone exchanges, serving in canteens, delivering meals-on-wheels, belonging to one religious background or the other, building houses or administering housing programmes, delivering public services.

We re-assert the demands of the 'Better Life for All' campaign of the 1970s and in particular the right of everyone to security of employment and well-paid work, and the right to live free from violence, intimidation, sectarianism and discrimination – no matter what their forms or from where they come.

The Trade Union Movement recognises that it cannot achieve these objectives by itself and we urge and encourage every constructive element in our society to seek to influence

419

their members to subscribe to and support the principles outlined in this statement.

For example, we would hope that the churches would continue their efforts to bring home to their members the inhumanity involved in all kinds of sectarianism and intimidation as well as in more overt acts of violence.

Equally we hope that employers and their organisations will do all they can to promote a positive response to their places of work. In particular, we would expect that they would take the necessary steps to ensure the elimination of intimidation, sectarianism and discrimination at work, and to promote their places of work as areas where workers from different backgrounds do not feel under threat as they carry out their tasks.

We would also urge the political parties to rid themselves of any vestige of support for violence and to spare no effort to devise political arrangements which meet the needs and aspirations of the working people of Northern Ireland and which ensure the effective and impartial protection of the personal security of the people of Northern Ireland, the elimination of poverty, of poor housing conditions and of deprivation of all kinds.

The Northern Ireland Committee ICTU believes that Government has a duty not just to seek to eradicate social and economic deprivation. They also have a duty to promote the positive protection of the rights of citizens who subscribe to the principles outlined above. For that reason we have long supported and confirm that support, for a Bill of Rights for the people of Northern Ireland. We believe that a positive commitment by Government to the Bill of Rights would assist those who seek to promote constructive progress in various ways in the community.

In conclusion, we wish therefore to reassert to all our members in Northern Ireland that if, as a Trade Union Movement, we are to have any hope of achieving our primary social and economic objectives of full employment and improved living and social standards for all, it is imperative that:

WE STAND TOGETHER FOR PEACE, WORK AND PROGRESS
AND
WE STAND TOGETHER AGAINST VIOLENCE AND INTIMIDATION

A Statement of Principles issued by the Northern Ireland Committee ICTU, October 1986.

1988 Women's Charter

The Irish Congress of Trade Unions recognises and demands the right of everyone, irrespective of race, ethnic origin, creed, political opinion, age, sex, marital status or sexual orientation to have the means to pursue their economic independence and to full participation in the social, cultural and political life of the community in conditions of freedom, dignity and equal opportunity. Congress further recognises that the elimination of past and present sex discrimination requires positive action and therefore resolves to pursue a programme of positive action to achieve full equality for women in society.

The ICTU will therefore campaign for the following Charter of Rights for Women and calls on all trade unionists to do their utmost to further the principles set out in this Charter:

The *right of women to work* regardless of marital status, including the right to return to work after a period of absence.

Equal pay for work of equal value and the introduction of *a national statutory minimum wage* to alleviate the real problem of low pay.

Equality in conditions of employment and the elimination of all forms of direct and indirect discrimination with regard to *sick pay* and *pension schemes.*

Equal access to job opportunities, promotion and work experience.

Full statutory protection and pro-rata pay and benefits for part-time workers.

Elimination of *discriminatory age-limits* in the public and private sectors.

Equal access to all levels of education, the elimination of all forms of sexism and a positive programme aimed at promoting equality and ensuring equal opportunities for both sexes.

Special training programmes to encourage more women into higher skilled jobs and non-traditional occupations.

The working environment to be adapted to ensure the health, safety and welfare of women workers.

The *re-organisation of working time* through the introduction of more flexible working arrangements and an overall reduction in working hours.

421

Twenty-six weeks maternity leave on full pay, the latter 12 weeks to be taken by either parent. A minimum period of 15-20 days *leave for family reasons*.

Eradication of *sexual harassment* in all its forms.

Protection of women's health by dealing with the major issues affecting it, including stress, domestic violence, pre-menstrual tension and menopause. The provision of a comprehensive service for women's health to be made available on a local basis, this service to incorporate contraception, antenatal and post-natal care, comprehensive screening facilities for cancer and other diseases and a health education service.

Recognition of *divorce* as a basic civil right. An end to the constitutional ban on divorce and the introduction of divorce legislation.

An end to the *portrayal of women by the media* in a sexist and stereotyped manner.

The provision of *comprehensive childcare* facilities to be provided free and controlled by the State including after-school and holiday care facilities and school meals.

The elimination of all forms of direct and indirect discrimination against women in the *social welfare code*. A fundamental review of the concept of dependency which would recognise the independent status of each individual.

Provision of *comprehensive contraception* freely available and accessible to all. All necessary measures should be adopted to ensure women have access to the necessary information and means to exercise their basic right to control their fertility.

That all appropriate measures should be taken to ensure that *civil and criminal law* protects and supports the rights of women.

1994 Community Situation in Northern Ireland

The Northern Ireland Committee ICTU at its meeting today reaffirmed its policies of working towards a unifying peace in our community in line with the principles of the Congress' 'Peace Work and Progress Campaign'.

Any reduction in violence is a step towards our objective of healing the wounds in our divided society and creating an atmosphere in which the grave social and economic problems which beset our community, can be tackled.

Today's announcement would appear to be in line with our repeated demands for a cessation of all terrorist violence.

The Northern Ireland Committee ICTU reaffirms that no cause can justify the taking of human life or the destruction of places of employment or recreation and calls on all paramilitaries to end their campaigns of murder and destruction.

Statement issued by the Northern Ireland Committee ICTU on 31 August 1994.

Towards a New Century

Peter Cassells
General Secretary, Irish Congress of Trade Unions

When I look out my office window here at Raglan Road, I see a row of restored 'mews' residences on Raglan Lane. It isn't difficult to imagine what was happening on this lane one hundred years ago when Congress was founded and these houses were homes for horses and the people who worked with them. Some stable staff may well have been feeding, cleaning and harnessing some of the horses that took the conference delegates on their carriage drive to Lucan through the Phoenix Park on Saturday, 28 April 1894.

I look around the office and think that if this was 1894 there would be no phone on my desk, no fax, no word processor, no stack of video tapes or file of computer discs, not even a biro or an electric bulb or switch. One of the few experiences shared by the people who resided in this elegant building and those who lived with the horses was that both were oblivious of the vast array of changes the next century would bring for all classes.

Change, Change and More Change

Looking forward to the new century is not as easy as looking out the window for a glimpse of the past. I will start with the only predication that I can be certain about which is that the new century will be a time of 'change, change and more change'.

Change is not new but the speed at which change is happening is faster than at any time in the history of human kind. These fundamental changes affect not only the content of the trade union agenda but also the methods we use for pursuing that agenda. Our mission in the radically different circumstances of 1994 has to be different than it was in 1894.

Today we are in the midst of a technological revolution where the microchip is transforming work on a scale similar to the impact of the steam engine during the industrial revolution. Globalisation of economic activity is rapidly producing a commercial global village where the video in my living-room may be the result of the accumulated labour of workers in five continents and my toughest competitor may be operating at the far side of the world.

Innovation is now a key element in gaining competitive advantage and opportunities for innovative activity exist at all levels within the workforce. Today's educated workforce are not prepared to leave their brains behind them when they go to work and they also know that for a company or organisation to compete successfully every member of the team must be given the opportunity to play their part.

Labour market changes are also producing a 'new' and growing workforce of part-time, temporary, casual, contract and home workers. Many of these workers are badly-paid with poor conditions who need the most basic service and representation that unions offer their members. Most of the workers in this 'new' category are women who are contributing to the feminisation of the workforce and of trade unions. The changing composition of the workforce is changing the content of the trade union agenda which in turn is changing how we process that agenda.

Linking Workers with Jobs and Those with None

One of the other challenges that unions have had to respond to because of the dramatic changes in the labour market is the totally unacceptable levels of unemployment. Our response to this crisis will continue to be based on a two pronged approach – firstly, pursuing policies for job creation at national and local level and secondly, working to ensure that those who are without jobs have a decent standard of living and a good quality of life.

The development by Congress since 1986 of thirty unemployed centres around the country has helped to build links between workers with jobs and those with none. Congress unemployed centres have also helped to change the perception and the reality of what kind of services unemployed people expect and need. While people who are long-term unemployed will continue to take precedence, changing patterns of employment has meant that more people are spending periods between jobs when they can derive great benefit from the range of services provided by the unemployed centres in the Congress Network.

Lobbying for adequate State provision for unemployed people and their families is one of several areas of social policy and social welfare reform that Congress pursues with governments and other decision makers. This agenda for social reform and progressive change will continue to be pursued in a variety of ways, including national negotiations, pre-budget submissions and public campaigns. The philosophy behind Congress' commitment to social reform has not changed significantly from that outlined by my predecessor, Donal Nevin, elsewhere in this book. This commitment is central to trade union values and there is no evidence that the need to be concerned with social policy will be any less necessary in the new century.

Beyond Pay and Conditions

Unions today recognise the importance of the social wage and the need to extend the scope of service and representation beyond pay and conditions. Issues such as taxation, pensions, PRSI, public services like health and education, training, health and safety, job sharing, gender equality, career development, job satisfaction, flexible working time, worker participation, company restructuring and retirement planning are all part of what workers today are concerned about and which they expect their unions to take on board.

Management too are changing their approach from the old Taylorist model to managing human resources with a variety of new forms of work organisation and techniques from quality circles to team working with the main focus on the worker as an individual. While management's motives for HRM may vary from company to company, the new emphasis on the worker as a human resource provides us with the opportunity of advancing the long-held union objective of securing dignity for the worker as an individual in her or his own right.

Individual – Not a Cog in Machine

Unions have always rejected the notion of the worker as a cog in the company machine and sought recognition for the unique value of each worker's contribution. The need for unions to negotiate collective agreements which apply to large categories of workers in order to improve wages and living standards should not obscure our primary concern with the individual worker. From time to time it may be necessary to remind ourselves that while the principle of collective organisation is sacrosanct the main purpose of our collective action is to enhance the lives of the individual women and men who give us our collective strength. Our willingness and ability to meet that challenge will be a major determinant of our relevance to the needs of working people in the twenty-first century.

In the past, the emphasis was mainly on the liberation of individual workers through the liberation of their class. The future will see a bigger emphasis on worker solidarity as an instrument for the enrichment of the quality of life for individual workers.

New Agenda for a New Century

Part of the trade union agenda for the new century will be to relate the aspirations of working people to the new ways in which goods and services are produced.

Speaking in London this year at the launch of the British TUC publication *The Future of Trade Unions*, Jacques Delors said that unions 'often confused the legitimate defence of rights won by the workers with a determination to preserve old habits and ways of thinking and that now after a period of critical self-analysis it is time to explore new avenues'.

Congress began to explore new avenues with the publication of *Trade Unions and Change* (1989); *Ireland 1990-2000 – A Decade of Development, Reform and Growth* (1990); *Irish Political Economy – The Case For Consensus* (1992); *New Forms of Work Organisation* (1993); *Developing Our Human Resources – A Partnership for Work* (1993) and *The Intelligent Island* (1994). The new century will see this exploration given concrete expression through changes in the form and content of trade union activity. We will neither change for the sake of change nor cling to the past for the sake of the past. Our criteria for change will be relevance and effectiveness.

The need for unions is not in doubt. As the General Secretary of the British TUC said recently: 'Workers today need the support of trade unions as much as at any time in the past one hundred years'. Our experience shows that workers in Ireland also need union support and the current growth in union membership in the Republic shows that they are willing to seek that support. It is up to this generation of union leaders to ensure that workers see the support unions have to offer as relevant to their modern needs and effective in its delivery of concrete results.

Telling the Truth

Our first duty in maintaining our relevance is to tell the truth. It may be easier to get up on a canteen table and condemn Human Resource Management as the latest tool of capitalist manipulation than to quietly discuss the complex issues involved in developing a strategy for using the opportunities provided by HRM to enhance the job satisfaction of individual workers without undermining their collective strength. Workers know that yesterday's slogans do not put bread on today's table. They also need to know that competitiveness is part of commercial reality and not a piece of capitalist fantasy.

Unions should acknowledge and appreciate the vital role of genuinely entrepreneurial capitalists whose enterprise and initiative helps to generate real wealth and create worthwhile jobs. The people that unions have to confront are those who single-mindedly set out to exploit the labour of others to satisfy their own greed. But to equate genuine enterprise and risk-taking with greed and meanness is wrong and unfair. Similarly for employers to equate unions with confrontation and obstruction is unfair. All the successful countries in the world and the vast majority of successful companies in this country respect the rights of workers to join unions and recognise the right of those unions to represent these workers.

Innovation

As we approach the new century, Irish business and Irish society in general faces important choices about the way we go about our business in this country. The choices we make will have far ranging effects not only on our industrial relations but also on our ability to compete and therefore on the standard of living of all our citizens. Put very simply, the choice is to play as a team or go on a solo run. In this instance the metaphor is very close to the reality.

Innovation which is the key to growth and survival in the new century is no longer about one big idea thought up by one entrepreneur and implemented by thousands of workers on an assembly line. Ideas are no longer conceived and produced like a baby Ford. For innovation to be effective it will have to transform ideas into the development of new and better products

428

quickly and efficiently. This development follows an evolutionary path. For example, vacuum-tube radios evolved into transistors which were followed by pocket stereos, compact discs and optical discs. So instead of one big idea which comes in a complete package and stands alone we are now dealing with a continuum of ideas providing incremental changes which continually improve products and processes and result from the collective inputs of several different workers with a variety of skills and insights which may take place simultaneously.

As the dividing line between those who 'come up with ideas' and those who 'produce the goods' becomes less clear so also will the distinction between those who manage and those who are managed. In the workplace of the future we will have to acknowledge that entrepreneurship is not confined to individuals but that it also embraces the notion of collective entrepreneurship. 'Collective Entrepreneurship' is defined by Robert B. Reich as 'endeavours in which the whole of the effort is greater than the sum of individual contributions' and he urges Americans to honour their teams more and their aggressive leaders and maverick geniuses less.

Highways or Byways

In dealing with the challenge of global competition, the consequences of the technological revolution and our approach to entrepreunership we are faced with two broad options – we can take the highway or the byway.

Byway: This approach is based on cutting costs especially labour costs by reducing both the numbers of workers employed and their wages. Automation is seen primarily as a means of reducing the size of the workforce to get costs down. Innovation, to the extent that it exists at all, is driven by the need to reduce costs rather than improve quality or develop the product or service. Tenders for materials or services will be judged mainly or exclusively on costs alone. Diversification, if it takes place, will very often take the form of takeovers of other companies that are going cheap because of their low performance and may be involved in totally different businesses.

The management approach to industrial relations on the byway is to threaten to close down or, if it's an international company, to move to a cheaper location. Since workers are seen exclusively as a cost factor to be minimised rather than a resource to be developed, management will use HRM techniques as a tool for manipulation rather than an instrument for development.

Workers on the byways will feel that their jobs are 'permanently' insecure, their contribution constantly under-valued, their wages and conditions under threat, their ideas neither wanted nor respected and their interests very low on management's list of priorities.

In these circumstances the workers and their unions will be reluctant to co-operate with change, will be deeply sceptical of management's warnings, will see new technology as a threat to their livelihoods and new work practices as another attempt by management to get more for less.

Survival on the byway may be possible in the short term but in the long term it leads to nowhere.

It has to be acknowledged that in a small number of cases some union people may be content to operate in this adversarial system and rely on muscle rather than reason to match management's heavy-handed approach. It is certainly not the preferred option of the vast majority of union activists or the people they represent.

The Highway: The highway presents very different challenges and opportunities for both unions and management. It may not always be an easy way to reach but it will take us safely into the new century. The highway is based on high standards of work, high levels of co-operation and high levels of trust between management and unions. A relevant analogy for this new approach is the Irish Football team in recent years. The Irish team works well because Jack Charlton trusts the players, the players trust Jack and they trust each other. His style of management is firm but it is fair and is seen to be fair. The contribution of each player is valued and everything possible is done to develop their individual skills and talents. Their ideas and opinions are sought and respected.

The workers on Jack Charlton's team as individuals have set *themselves* high standards and neither their management nor their supporters begrudge them their high wages and top-class conditions of employment. Jack's approach may well be influenced by his involvement with the Amalgamated Transport and General Workers' Union campaign in Britain against low wages. His common sense approach to management tells him that if you pay low wages and provide low quality conditions you cannot expect to get high standards and high quality performance.

Back in the world of Irish industrial relations the highway or Irish team approach means increasing the value of our workers' input rather than lowering their rewards. This involves constantly retraining the workforce to update their skills to enable them to add more value to the tasks they perform and to perform more complex tasks. It also means using new technology to reduce rather than increase the amount of routine tasks. This will free up time to develop the creative potential of all workers and their capacity to contribute to the advancement of their company as well as to their personal development. This approach has already been adopted by some of the most successful companies in Ireland and abroad.

Management on the Highway

On the highway management accepts that responsibility for innovation and initiative does not rest with a few individuals at the top but is dispersed throughout the organisation. Management also recognises that workers must benefit from increased productivity especially through profit-sharing schemes. Job retention must replace job-shedding as one of management's top priorities with a jobs audit forming part of company reports. Management structures must reflect the right of workers to participate in decisions about the future of the company and to have their interests represented alongside shareholders' interests.

Unions on the Highway

On the highway workers will still need the protection, support and representation that union organisation provides. But the content and form of this representation will be different from that required by workers trapped on the byway with their backs to the wall.

In the highway organisation whether it be involved in manufacturing or services, unions will be required to co-operate with positive flexibility. By 'positive' I mean flexible workers that will boost productivity and improve job satisfaction. Rigid job demarcation will have no place on the highway to the new century where new, and often more demanding work practices will be required.

In return for increased involvement, recognition and rewards unions will encourage workers to take more responsibility for its welfare. I do not underestimate the enormity of this change or the difficulties it will involve for some of our own people.

If we are demanding radical changes in management's approach we will have to be willing to change ourselves, and change is never easy. It takes courage and confidence to leave the past behind us and start out on a new journey. Courage has never been lacking in our movement and after one hundred years our roots are deep enough to give us confidence in ourselves to face the challenges of the new century.

When the next centenary will be celebrated, I have no doubt that that generation will be able to look back with the same pride on the new departures of 1994 as we do on the foresight and courage of the 113 men and women who assembled in Capel Street at the end of April 1894. Let us ensure that we put our stamp on the new century with the same courage and commitment that they did on this one.

Congress Membership 1894 – 1994

Irish Trade Union Congress 1894 – 1959

1894	21,000	1920	229,000	1940	163,000
1901	67,000	1921	196,000	1941	173,000
1902	n.a.	1922	189,000	1942	164,000
1903	71,000	1923	183,000	1943	183,000
1904	72,000	1924	175,000	1944	187,000
1905	73,000	1925	149,000	1945 *	146,000
1906	68,000	1926	123,000	1946	147,000
1907	75,000	1927	113,000	1947	151,000
1908	70,000	1928	103,000	1948	181,000
1909	89,000	1929	92,000	1949	196,000
1910	n.a.	1930	102,000	1950	197,000
1911	50,000	1931	102,000	1951	210,000
1912	70,000	1932	95,000	1952	214,000
1913	100,000	1933	95,000	1953	209,000
1914	110,000	1934	115,000	1954	211,000
1915	n.a.	1935	125,000	1955	218,000
1916	120,000	1936	134,000	1956	221,000
1917	150,000	1937	146,000	1957	222,000
1918	250,000	1938	161,000	1958	226,000
1919	270,000	1939	162,000	1959	224,000
1919	159,000				

Year CIU broke from Irish TUC.

Note 1

1894: The membership of the trade unions that accredited delegates to the first Congress as given in a pre-Congress publication issued by the Dublin United Trades Council and Labour League which had organised and convened the Congress. In addition to trade unions and trade societies, other labour organisations including Trades Councils were represented at this first meeting.

1901-1910: These are the figures of the total membership of affiliated organisations as reported by the Standing Orders Committee to the Annual Meetings. They include the membership of affiliated Trades Councils and therefore involve a degree of double counting.

1911-1918: These figures have been taken from *Ireland at Berne: Being the Reports and Memoranda presented to the International Labour and Socialist Conference held at Berne, February 1919*, which was issued by the National Executive of the Irish Labour Party and Trade Union Congress, and which states that they are 'the official figures' of the affiliated membership of the organisation at each annual Congress. The figures include therefore the membership of affiliated Trades Councils and involve double counting of trade union membership.

1919: The first figure shown is the total membership of affiliated organisations including Trades Councils and other labour organisations. It corresponds with the figures given for previous years. The second figure shown for 1919 is the total membership of affiliated trade unions. Separate figures for each affiliated trade union were given for the first time in the Congress report for 1919.

1920-1959: The total of the individual trade union membership figures as given in the Congress annual reports. For most years the total membership figures were reported by the Standing Orders Committee to the annual meeting specifically as the membership of affiliated trade unions. This has been confirmed by reference to the figures given for each trade union.

Note 2

The total membership figures are very much influenced by the membership of the large general unions as returned to Congress as the basis for the calculation of the affiliation fees.

The membership of the ITGWU as returned was 66,000 in 1919; 100,000 in the years 1920 to 1923; 89,000 in 1924; 61,000 in 1925; 40,000 in 1926; 30,000 in 1928; 20,000 in the years 1929 to 1933; 25,000 in 1934; 30,000 in 1935 and 1936; 32,000 in 1937 and 36,000 in the years 1938 to 1944; the Union withdrew from Congress in 1945.

The membership returns of the ITGWU to the Registrar of Friendly Societies for certain years, as at the beginning of the year, were as follows (figures shown to nearest hundred): 1930 (33,400), 1935 (30,000), 1940 (36,000), 1945 (53,200), 1950 (116,300), 1953 (119,400).

The first year that the financial membership of the ITGWU was given in its annual report was in 1937 when the figure was 33,100. The figures for certain other years (rounded to nearest hundred) were as follows: 1939 (33,600), 1942 (30,600), 1944 (38,000), 1946 (46,500), 1951 (87,000) and 1956 (84,300).

The membership of the ATGWU (mainly in Northern Ireland) was 8,000 in 1922 (its first year of affiliation); 5,000 in 1923; 6,000 in 1924; 8,000 in the years 1925 to 1927, [membership was not given in 1928 or 1929]; 15,000 in 1930 to 1933; 25,000 in 1934 to 1936; 35,000 in 1938 to 1940; 33,000 in 1941 and 1942 and 35,000 in 1943 and 1944.

From 1945 the two main general unions affiliated to Congress were the ATGWU and the Workers' Union of Ireland. The membership of the ATGWU as returned was 35,000 in the years 1945 to 1947 and 40,000 in 1948 to 1959.

The affiliated membership of the WUI as returned to Congress was 8,000 in the years 1945 to 1947; 15,000 in 1948 to 1950 and 25,000 in 1951 to 1959.

The membership returns of the WUI to the registrar of Friendly Societies for certain years, as at the beginning of the year, were as follows (figures shown to nearest hundred): 1925 (15,800), 1930 (16,200), 1947 (13,200), 1952 (28,000), 1957 (28,700).

Irish Congress of Trade Unions, 1960 – 1994

1960	432,000	1972	539,000	1984	643,000*
1961	439,000	1973	547,000	1985	652,000
1962	440,000	1974	570,000	1986	666,000
1963	441,000	1975	576,000	1987	670,000
1964	453,000	1976	550,000	1988	670,000**
1965	465,000	1977	564,000	1989	663,000**
1966	472,000	1978	604,000	1990	679,000
1967	483,000	1979	621,000	1991	682,000
1968	491,000	1980	661,000	1992	679,000
1969	499,000	1981	663,000	1993	679,000
1970	510,000	1982	641,000	1994	681,000
1971	523,000	1983	640,000*		

* Excluding CPSSU suspended from Congress.
** Excluding IDATU suspended from Congress.

Membership figures have been rounded to the nearest thousand.

Note

The membership of the three main general unions affiliated to the ICTU in respect of which afiliation fees were paid to Congress was as follows:

ATGWU: 50,000 in the years 1960 to 1972, 60,000 in 1973 to 1981, 50,000 in 1982, 55,000 in 1983 to 1985, 70,000 in 1986 to 1991, 60,000 in 1992 to 1994.

ITGWU: 150,000 in the years 1960 to 1989. The financial membership of the ITGWU for certian years as given in the Union's annual reports, was as follows (figures to nearest hundred): 1961 (91,300), 1966 (100,800), 1971 (117,000), 1976 (141,100), 1981 (169,800), 1986 (136,400), 1989 (126,300).

WUI/FWUI: 30,000 in the years 1960 to 1973, 35,000 in 1974 to 1979, 50,000 in 1980 to 1984, 51,000 in 1985 to 1987, 54,000 in 1988 and 55,000 in 1989.

SIPTU: 205,000 in 1990, 206,000 in 1991, 198,000 in 1992, 197,500 in 1993 and 198,000 in 1994. (The ITGWU and the FWUI merged in 1990 to become the Services Industrial Professional Technical Union).

Congress Presidents 1894 – 1994

The name of the trade union or Trades Council represented by the President at the Congress is shown in brackets. The President's place of residence is also given: Dublin unless otherwise stated. The year shown is the year that the President presided at the annual meeting except for 1937 when the President, Helena Molony, was absent due to illness.

Irish Trade Union Congress 1894 – 1959

1894: Thomas O'Connell (Dublin Trades Council)
1895: J. H. Jolley (Cork Trades Council), Cork
1896: James D'Alton (Limerick Trades Council), Limerick
1897: P. J. Leo (Waterford Trades Council), Waterford
1898: Richard Wortley (Belfast Trades Council), Belfast
1899: James McCarron (Amalgamated Society of Tailors), Derry (d 1918)
1900: George Leahy (Dublin Operative Plasterers' Society)
1901: Alexander Bowman TC (Belfast Municipal Employees' Society), Belfast
1902: Alderman William Cave (Cork Trades Council), Cork
1903: Walter Hudson MP (Amalgamated Society of Railway Servants)
1904: William Walker (Belfast Trades Council), Belfast (d. 1918)
1905: James Chambers (Dublin Saddlers' Society)
1906: Stephen Dineen (Irish Bakers' Amalgamated Union), Limerick (d. 1939)
1907: James McCarron (Amalgamated Society of Tailors), Derry (d. 1918)
1908: John Murphy (Belfast Trades Council), Belfast
1909: M. J. Egan (Cork Trades Council), Cork
1910: James McCarron (Amalgamated Society of Tailors), Derry (d. 1918)
1911: David R. Campbell (National Union of Assurance Agents), Belfast
1912: Michael J. O'Lehane (Irish Drapers Assistants' Association) (d. 1920)
1913: William O'Brien (Dublin Trades Council) (d. 1968)
1914: James Larkin (Irish Transport and General Workers' Union) (d. 1947)
1915: No Congress held
1916: Thomas Johnson (National Amalgamated Union of Shop Assistants, Warehousemen and Clerks), Belfast (d. 1963)
1917: Thomas MacPartlin (Amalgamated Society of Carpenters) (d. 1923)
1918: William O'Brien (Dublin Trades Council) (d. 1968)
1919: Thomas Cassidy (Typographical Society), Derry
1920: Thomas Farren (ITGWU)
1921: Thomas Foran (ITGWU) (d. 1951)
1922: Cathal O'Shannon T.D. (ITGWU) (d. 1969)
1923/24: Luke J. Duffy (Irish Union of Distributive Workers and Clerks)
1925: Alderman William O'Brien (ITGWU) (d. 1968)
1926: Denis Cullen (Irish Bakers' Amalgamated Union) (d. 1971)
1927: Senator J. T. O'Farrell (Railway Clerks' Association) (d. 1971)

1928: William McMullen M.P (ITGWU), Belfast (d. 1982)
1929: Luke J. Duffy (Irish Union of Distributive Workers and Clerks)
1930: Thomas J. O'Connell (Irish National Teachers' Organisation) (d. 1969)
1931: Denis Cullen (Irish Bakers' Amalgamated Union) (d. 1971)
1932: Louie Bennett (Irish Women Workers' Union) (d. 1956)
1933: Seán P. Campbell (Dublin Typographical Provident Society) (d. 1950)
1934: Senator Michael Duffy (ITGWU)
1935: P.J. Cairns (Post Office Workers' Union)
1936: Michael Drumgoole (Irish Union of Distributive Workers and Clerks) (d. 1960)
1937: Helena Molony (Irish Women Workers' Union) (d. 1967)
1938: Jeremiah Hurley T.D. (Irish National Teachers' Organisation), Cork (d. 1943)
1939: P.T. Daly (Dublin Trades Union Council) (d. 1943)
1940: Sam Kyle (Amalgamated Transport and General Workers' Union) (d. 1962)
1941: William O'Brien (ITGWU) (d. 1968)
1942: Michael Colgan (Irish Bookbinders and Allied Trades Union) (d. 1953)
1943: Michael J. Keyes TD (National Union of Railwaymen), Limerick (d. 1959)
1944: Robert Getgood (Amalgamated Transport and General Workers' Union), Belfast (d. 1964)
1945/1946: Gilbert Lynch (Amalgamated Transport and General Workers' Union) (d. 1969)
1947: John Swift (Irish Bakers', Confectioners' and Allied Workers' Union) (d. 1990)
1948: Louie Bennett (Irish Women Workers' Union) (d. 1956)
1949: James Larkin TD (Workers' Union of Ireland) (d. 1969)
1950: Sam Kyle (Amalgamated Transport and General Workers' Union) (d. 1962)
1951: Helen Chenevix (Irish Women Workers' Union) (d. 1963)
1952: James Larkin TD, (Workers' Union of Ireland) (d. 1969)
1953: Con Connolly (Cork Trades Council), Cork (d. 1981)
1954: John McAteer (National Union of Printing, Bookbinding and Paper Workers), Belfast
1955: Robert Smith (Plumbing Trades Union) (d. 1961)
1956: J. Harold Binks (Clerical and Administrative Workers' Union), Belfast (d. 1986)
1957: Norman Kennedy (Amalgamated Transport and General Workers' Union) (d. 1983)
1958: Jack Macgougan (National Union of Tailors and Garment Workers), Belfast
1959: Walter Carpenter (Amalgamated Society of Woodworkers) (d. 1970)

Congress of Irish Unions 1945 – 1959

1945/1946: Gerard Owens (Electrical Trades Union (Ireland)
1947: Senator Thomas Kennedy (Irish Transport and General Workers' Union) (d. 1947)

1948: William J. Whelan (Dublin Typographical Provident Society) (d. 1960)
1949: Owen Hynes (Building Workers' Trade Union) (d. 1970)
1950: Senator Michael Colgan (Irish Bookbinders' and Allied Trade Union) (d. 1953)
1951: John Conroy (ITGWU) (d. 1969)
1952: Walter H. Beirne (Irish National Union of Vintners', Grocers' and Allied Trades Assistants) (d. 1959)
1953: Senator William McMullen (ITGWU) (d. 1982)
1954: Gerald Doyle (Operative Plasterers' Trade Society) (d. 1979)
1955: John O'Brien (Irish Engineering, Industrial and Electrical Trade Union) (d. 1967)
1956: Michael Mervyn (Electrical Trade Union Ireland) (d. 1960)
1957: Laurence Hudson (United House and Ship Painters' and Decorators' Trade Union of Ireland)
1958/1959: Terence Farrell (Irish Bookbinders' and Allied Trade Union) (d. 1961)

Irish Congress of Trade Unions 1959 – 1994

1959: John Conroy (Irish Transport and General Workers' Union) (d. 1969)
1960: James Larkin (Workers' Union of Ireland) (d. 1969)
1961: Norman Kennedy (Amalgamated Transport and General Workers' Union) (d. 1983)
1962: William J. Fitzpatrick (Irish Union of Distributive Workers and Clerks) (d. 1990)
1963: Jack Macgougan (National Union of Tailors and Garment Workers), Belfast
1964: Charles McCarthy (Vocational Teachers' Association) (d. 1986)
1965: Dominick F. Murphy (Transport Salaried Staffs' Association)
1966: Fintan Kennedy (ITGWU) (d. 1984)
1967: Robert Thompson (General and Municipal Workers' Union), Belfast (d. 1968)
1968: John Conroy (ITGWU) (d. 1969)
1969: James Dunne (Marine, Port and General Workers' Union), (d. 1986)
1970: James Morrow (Amalgamated Union of Engineering and Foundry Workers), Belfast (d. 1986)
1971: Maurice Cosgrave (Post Office Workers' Union)
1972: Jim Cox (Amalgamated Society of Woodworkers) Elected President in 1971. Died April 1972
Stephen McGonigle (ITGWU), Derry
1973: Stephen McGonigle (ITGWU), Derry
1974: Denis Larkin (Workers' Union of Ireland) (d. 1987)
1975: Andy Barr (National Union of Sheet Metal Workers, Coppersmiths, Heating and Domestic Engineers), Belfast
1976: Matt Griffin (Irish National Teachers' Organisation) (d. 1978)
1977: Brendan Harkin (Northern Ireland Civil Service Association), Belfast. Elected President in 1976. Resigned October 1976
John Mulhall (Irish National Painters' and Decorators' Trade Union) (d. 1981)

1978: John Mulhall (Irish National Painters' and Decorators' Trade
        Union) (d. 1981)
1979: Harold O'Sullivan (Local Government and Public Services Union)
1980: Jack Curlis (General and Municipal Workers' Union), Belfast (d.
        1988)
1981: Dan Murphy (Civil Service Executive Union)
1982: David Wylie (Union of Shop, Distributive and Allied Workers),
        Belfast
1983: Patrick Cardiff (Federated Workers' Union of Ireland)
1984: James Graham (Amalgamated Union of Engineering Workers –
        Engineering Section), Belfast (d. 1985)
1985: Matt Merrigan (Amalgamated Transport and General Workers'
        Union)
1986: Jim McCusker (Northern Ireland Public Service Alliance), Belfast
1987: John F. Carroll (ITGWU)
1988: Billy Wallace (National Union of Tailors and Garment Workers),
        Belfast
1989: Gerry Quigley (Irish National Teachers' Organisation)
1990: Jimmy Blair (Amalgamated Engineering Union), Belfast
1991: Chris Kirwan (Services Industrial Professional Technical Union)
1992: No Congress held
1993: (First Biennial Conference) Tom Douglas (General Municipal
        Boilermakers and Allied Trade Union), Belfast
1995: Philip Flynn (Irish Municipal Public and Civil Trade Union,
        Dublin (Elected in 1993 for two-year term).

1996

1997

1998

1999

Congress Treasurers 1894 – 1994

Irish Trade Union Congress

1894: Patrick Dowd (Dublin Trades Council)
1895-97: J. H. Jolly (Typographical Association)
1898-9: P. J. Tevenan (Amalgamated Society of Railway Servants)
1900-01: Alex Taylor (Irish Linenlappers' Trade Union)
1902-04: George Leahy (Operative Plasterers)
1905-09: E. W. Stewart (Shop Assistants)
1910-12: M. J. O'Lehane (Drapers Assistants)
1913-18: David R. Campbell (Assurance Agents)
1919-20: Thomas Johnson (Amalgamated Shop Assistants)
1921-24: William O'Brien (ITGWU)
1925: Archie Heron (ITGWU)
1926-29: William O'Brien (ITGWU)
1930: Denis Cullen (Irish Bakers' Amalgamated Union)
1931-33: Luke J. Duffy (Irish Union of Distributive Workers and Clerks)
1934-44: Seán P. Campbell (Dublin Typographical Provident Society)
1945-49: J. T. O'Farrell (Railway Clerks' Association)
1950-58: John Swift (Irish Bakers' and Confectioners' Amalgamated
          Union)
1959: D. F. Murphy (Trasnport Salaried Staffs' Association)

Congress of Irish Unions

1945-46: Seán P. Campbell (Dublin Typographical Provident Society)
1947-59: Walter H. Beirne (Irish National Union of Vintners', Grocers'
          and Allied Trades' Assistants)

Irish Congress of Trade Unions

1959: Walter H. Beirne (Irish National Union of Vintners, Grocers' and
          Allied Trades' Assistants)
1960-67: John Conroy (ITGWU)
1968-81: Fintan Kennedy (ITGWU)
1982-84: Patrick Clancy (ITGWU)
1985-89: Chris Kirwan (ITGWU)
1990-94: Edmond Browne (ITGWU/SIPTU)

Congress Executive Council Members 1894 – 1993

Paul Alexander 1960-62, 1969-71
Bob Allen* 1972-77
Brian Anderson 1982-83, 1985-91, 1993
Richard S. Anthony 1924
W. A. Attley 1984-91, 1993

Andrew Barr* 1956-63, 1965-66, 1968-78
James Barry 1940-42, 1944-50
Dave Begg 1987-91, 1993
Walter Beirne [1945-58, 1959]
William Bell 1959-65
J. H. Bennett 1917
Louie Bennett 1927-32, 1944-50
J. Harold Binks* 1950-66, 1968-69, 1971, 1974-76
James Blair* 1984-89
Nicholas Boran [1953-58]
Alexander Bowman* 1899-1901
William Boyd* 1930
Desmond Branigan [1955-56]
Peter P. Brennan [1952-53]
Hilda Breslin 1990-91
Maura Breslin 1971-73
Edward D. Browne 1985-91, 1993
Nicholas S. Broughall 1988-91
Claire Bulman 1988
Mary Burke 1989

Jack Cagney 1986
Cissy Cahalane 1922-23
P. J. Cairns 1930-49
David R. Campbell* 1909-14, 1916-18
John Campbell* 1932
Seán P. Campbell 1930-44, [1945, 1947-48]
J. P. Candon 1962
Patrick Cardiff 1972-73, 1977-83
Walter Carpenter 1949-60
James Carr 1921, 1931-32
John F. Carroll 1971-1989
John Carter 1894
Des Casey 1978-79
James M. Casey 1934-39, 1945-46
Seán Casey 1955-58
John Cassidy [1948-51], 1959-67, 1970-74
Patrick Cassidy 1900

Thomas Cassidy 1914, 1916-18, 1924-34, 1936
William Cave 1902
James Chambers 1900-06
Helen Chenevix 1949-56
Patrick J. Clancy 1977-84
Joseph Clarke 1910-11
Paul Clarke 1993
Michael Cleary 1964-66, 1968-69, 1971-72, 1974-75, 1977
George Coates 1904
Michael Colgan 1938-43, [1945-52]
James Collins 1927
Con Connolly 1951-53
James Connolly* 1914
John Conroy [1947-58], 1959-68
Jimmy Cosby* 1977-82
Maurice Cosgrave 1966-72
Patrick Costello [1953]
M. Courtney* 1928-29
Jim Cox 1965-71
Leo Crawford 1943, [1945-46]
Patrick Crowley 1958, 1964
Denis Cullen 1920-1938, 1940-42
John Cullen 1968-70
William Cummins 1920
Hugh J. Curlis* 1972-80
Owen Curran 1978-79, 1981
Bertie Curtain [1949]

James D'Alton 1896
P. T. Daly 1905, 1910-18, 1935-39
T. C. Daly 1918-20
Murray Davis* 1895-1899
Richard Deasy 1951-52, 1954
Séamus De Paor 1977-79, 1982-86
Christopher Devine 1977-81
Eamonn Devoy 1993
Edward Dignam [1956-58]
Stephen Dineen 1903-08
William Donohue 1957
Con Donovan 1970-71
Dermot Doolan 1968-69
James Doolan [1949-51]
Jim Dorney 1991, 1993
Tom Douglas* 1981-91
Patrick Dowd 1894
Gerard Doyle [1947-58], 1959-60, 1963-65, 1967

Patrick Doyle 1953-55
Michael Drumgoole 1931-44,
 [1945-53]
Kevin Duffy 1981-87
Luke J. Duffy 1920-33
Michael Duffy 1926-27, 1932-36
Patrick Duffy 1977
Martin Dummigan* 1989-91
James Dunne 1960, 1962-64, 1966-
 71
Seán Dunne 1948-49

Michael Egan 1906-10, 1913-14,
 1916-18
Jim Eadie 1982-84, 1993
Robert Emmet 1953

Terence Farrell [1954-58]
Thomas Farren 1918-26
Andrew Faulkner 1954-59
Andrew Fenlon 1950
E. Fitzgerald 1927-28
John Fitzpatrick 1896-98
William J. Fitzpatrick [1954-58],
 1959-64, 1966-78, 1980-82
Eileen Fitzsimmons* 1993
Gerard Fleming 1988-91
Philip Flynn 1984-91, 1993
Frank Foley 1944-47
Thomas Foran 1916-17, 1920-24
J. P. Forrestal 1943-48, 1953-54
John Freeman* 1974-76, 1986-91,
 1993

Mary Galway* 1907-12
Mairin Ganly 1984-89
Tom Garry 1991
T. Gavin 1895
Robert Getgood* 1940-46
John Gibbons 1901
George F. Gillespie 1930
Patrick Golden 1896
Dawson Gordon* 1910, 1916,
 1919, 1926-29, 1931
Jimmy Graham* 1978-83
Malachy Gray* 1947-49
Noirin Greene 1984-87, 1993
William P. Greene 1935, 1938-39
George Greig* 1906-08, 1911
Matt Griffin 1965-77

John Hall 1979-86
Brendan Harkin* 1970-76
Tadgh Harrington 1985-86
Noel Harris 1972-77
E. P. Hart 1939-45

Michael Hartney 1937
Matthew Harvey 1909
Edward Healy [1945-51]
Tom Heery 1973, 1975-76, 1978,
 1980-81, 1983
James Hennessy 1894
Archie Heron 1924-26, 1928-29
Michael Hill 1923
W. E. Hill 1913-14
Maurice Holly 1974
Patrick Holohan 1933-34
Laurence Hudson [1948-49, 1953-
 58]
Walter Hudson 1901-06
Charles D. Hull* 1973-74
Jeremiah Hurley 1930-39, 1941-42
Owen Hynes 1924-25 [1946-55]

Thomas Irwin 1924, 1926
William A. Irwin* 1959

J. H. Jolley 1894-97
Thomas Johnson* 1913-14, 1916-
 28

Michael J. Keating 1978
Alf Keery* 1990-91
Fintan Kennedy 1959-81
Norman Kennedy 1951-73
Thomas Kennedy 1923-24, 1930-
 33, 1936-40, 1942-44, [1945-
 46]
Laurence Keegan 1924
Michael J. Keyes 1937-48
Avila Kilmurray* 1991, 1993
James Kirkwood* 1993
Chris Kirwan 1983-90
Sam Kyle 1932-55

George Lamon 1979-80
Denis Larkin 1956-59, 1969-76
James Larkin 1908, 1911-13
James Larkin, Junior, 1945-68
Luke J. Larkin 1919-23, 1927-28
George Leahy 1900-05, 1907
William J. Leahy 1900-02
William J. Leeburn* 1953-55
Charles Lennon 1991, 1993
Lily Lennon 1935
P. J. Leo 1896-98
Brian Leonard 1968
William Liddell* 1901
William Lindsay* 1976-77
Michael P. Linehan 1930
Colin C. Lowry* 1983-91
Eamonn Lynch 1926

Gilbert Lynch 1941-56
Patrick Lynch 1917
W. A. Lynch 1972-81, 1985-87

Dan MacAllister* 1960-63
John McAteer* 1946-58
Ernie McBride* 1983-84, 1993
James McCarron 1895-09
Pat McCartan* 1983-84
Charles McCarthy 1960-63, 1965-70
T. McConnell* 1910, 1912-13
Aidan McCormack 1989-90
Inez McCormack* 1980-81, 1987-91, 1993
Jim McCusker* 1978-91, 1993
Kay McDowell 1959
Stephen McGonagle 1964-72
Nicholas McGrath 1961-62, 1967
Jack Macgougan* 1951-52, 1954-68
M. J. McGowan 1924-25
Patricia McKeown* 1984-85
C. J. McLean [1950-52]
Hugh McManus* 1894, 1900-04
William McMullen* 1925-44, [1945-52]
R. S. McNamara 1903
William J McNulty 1917
Thomas MacPartlin 1912-14, 1916-20
Thomas McPartlin [1949]
James McQuane 1929
James J. MacSweeney [1954]
Michael Mackin [1948-49]
Patrick Malone 1964
Joe Matthews 1975
Greg Maxwell 1985-90
Kevin Meehan 1973
Matt Merrigan 1977-79, 1982-86
Michael Mervyn [1949-58], 1959
Hugh Miskelly* 1988-90
John Mitchell 1982-86
Joseph Mitchell 1918
Joseph Mitchell [1948]
Helena Molony 1921, 1933-37
Robert F. Morgan 1947-50
Dermot A. Morrissey 1951-52
James Morrow* 1963-69
Robert Morrow* 1933-41, 1944
Michael Moynihan [1952]
Lenore Mrkwicka 1991, 1993
John Mulhall [1948], 1971-77
Michael Mullen 1973-76, 1982
Kieran Mulvey 1982-90

Dan Murphy 1972-75, 1977-85, 1987-91, 1993
Dominick F. Murphy 1949-55, 1957-59, 1961-68
John Murphy* 1906-08
Patrick Murphy 1965, 1971-73, 1975, 1977, 1979, 1981-85, 1987
Rory Murphy 1986
Seán Murphy [1950-57]
Tom Murphy 1990-91
William Murphy 1910

George Nason 1920-22
William Norton 1926-29
Owen Nulty 1993

John O'Brien (1945-49, 1952-56)
Joseph O'Brien 1897-99
William O'Brien 1911-14, 1916-29, 1939-44, [1945]
Richard O'Carroll 1911-14
Thomas O'Connell 1894-95
Thomas J. O'Connell 1922-29
Elizabeth O'Connor 1924-25
Frank O'Connor [1956-58], 1960-61, 1969-71
James C. O'Connor 1919
Richard P. O'Connor 1894, 1897-1900
Seamus O'Donnell 1991
John O'Dowd 1988-91, 1993
J. F. O'Farrell 1919
J. J. O'Farrell 1920
J. T. O'Farrell 1918-19, 1921-29, 1944-48
Patrick O'Farrell 1978
John O'Flynn [1956]
Thomas O'Gorman [1949, 1953-55]
James O'Keeffe 1944-45
Michael J O'Lehane 1909-14, 1918-19
Edward O'Mahony 1919
Seán O'Moore [1945-52]
Seán Ó Murchu [1950-51, 1958]
Matt O'Neill 1962-64
Noel O'Neill 1989-91, 1993
Frank O'Reilly 1987-91, 1993
James O'Reilly* 1991
Cathal O'Shannon 1918-20, 1922, 1928
Patrick O'Shaughnessy 1990, 1994
J. O'Shea [1949]
Harold O'Sullivan 1967-72, 1974-75, 1977-83
John O'Sullivan 1913

Martin O'Sullivan 1930-33
Joe O'Toole 1991, 1993
Gerard Owens (1945, 1947-48)
Hugh M. Pollock 1990
Alice Prendergast 1990
Frank Purcell [1953-58]

E. G. Quigley 1978-90
Terry Quinlan 1973-74, 1977-84

Edward Reid [1956-58]
Robert P. Rice 1979-80, 1982,
    1984-88
Nathan Rimmer 1916
E. L. Richardson 1994, 1901-1909
Henry Rochford 1909, 1917
Bernard Rorke 1986-87
A. J. Ryan* 1934
Ciaran Ryan 1993
T. Ryan 1925

W. A. Scott 1936-38
Patrick Shanley 1988
J. A. Sheehy 1975
Richard Sheldon* 1894-95
John Simmons 1894-99
Margaret Skinnider 1961-62
James E. Sloan* 1957-58, 1960
Robert Smith 1940-58

Jimmy Somers 1993
Alexander Stewart* 1922-23
E. Q. Stewart 1904-09
Michael Somerville 1922-23, 1925-
    26, 1930-31, 1934, 1939
John Swift 1944-57

Alexander Taylor* 1896-1901
Patrick J. Tevenan 1895-99
Bob Thompson* 1961, 1963-6
John Tierney 1987-88, 1993
Rose Timmon 1918-21
William R Trulock 1975
Edward J. Tucker 1947
Anthony P. Tuke (1958)
James Tully 1955-58, 1960-61,
    1963
Robert Tynan 1929

M. Walker 1946
William Walker* 1902-1904
William Wallace* 1980-87
Seán Walsh 1972, 1974
Seán F. Walshe 1943
Cecil D. Watters 1926-31
William J. Whelan [1945-58]
Richard Worley* 1898
David Wylie* 1967-68, 1970-71,
    1977, 1979-81

*Belfast resident when first elected

The years shown are those in which the members were elected, or, in a few cases, co-opted, either as President, Vice-President, Treasurer, Secretary or member of the Executive Council of Congress (in the case of the Irish TUC, the Parliamentary Committee from 1894 to 1913 and the National Executive from 1914 to 1959).

The years in square brackets refer to membership of the Central Council of the Congress of Irish Unions (1945-58).

No Congress was held in 1915 or in 1992. Conferences were held annually from 1894 to 1991. The first biennial conference was held in 1993.

Northern Ireland Committee Chairpersons 1945 – 1994

1945-46 to 1948-49: William Boyd (National Union of Vehicle Builders)

1949-50 to 1963-64: J. Harold Binks (Clerical and Administrative Workers Union)

1964-65: David Wylie (Union of Shop, Distributive and Allied Workers)

1965-66: James Sloan (ATGWU)

1966-67: Andrew Barr (National Union of Sheet Metal Workers and Coppersmiths)

1967-68: James Morrow (Amalgamted Engineering Union)

1968-69: Stephen McGonagle (ITGWU)

1969-70: Bob Allen (Amalgamated Society of Woodworkers)

1970-71: Cecil Vance (ATGWU)

1971-72: Brendan Harkin (Northern Ireland Civil Service Association)

1972-73: Senator Norman Kennedy (ATGWU)

1973-74: Charles Hull (Amalgamated Union of Engineering and Foundry Workers)

1974-75: Jack Curlis (General and Municipal Workers' Union)

1975-76, 1976-77: J. Harold Binks (Association of Professional, Executive, Clerical and Computer Staff)

1977-78: William Lindsay (NUTGW)

1978-79: John Freeman (ATGWU)

1979-80: James Cosby (Union of Construction, Allied Trades and Technicians)

1980-81: Jim McCusker (NICSA)

1981-82: James Graham (Amalgamated Union of Engineering Workers (Engineering Section)

1982-83: William Wallace (NUTGW))

1983-84: W. F. Jackson (COHSE)

1984-85: Inez McCormack (National Union of Public Employees)

1985-86: Roger Jeary (Association of Scientific Technical and Managerial Staff)

1986-87: Al Mackle (Irish National Teachers' Organisation)

1987-88: Tom Douglas (General Municipal Boilermakers and Allied Trades Union)

1988-89: Joe Bowers (AUEW-TASS)

1889-90: Pat McCartan (APEX)

1990-91: Hugh Miskelly (COHSE)

1992-94: Jack Nash (SIPTU)

1994-96: Bobby Gourley (Union of Shop, Distributive and Allied Workers)

Trade Union Banners

Trade Union Banners carried at Labour Day Demonstration held in Dublin on 6 May 1894 to mark the first meeting of the Irish Trades Union Congress:

Amalgamated Ironfounders: Fane, enclosing three illustrations of iron-founder's work, supporting allegorical figure mining ore; figures of Justice and Hope on either side; scroll with name of trade.

Amalgamated Painters: Poplin, with name of trade. Reverse, Irish wolf dog and round tower.

Amalgamated Society of Railway Servants: Engine in front. Four corners illustrated with representations of the several grades of railway work. Motto: 'All grades united to support; not combined to injure.' Reverse, emblems of unity – the fagot, encircled with wreath of shamrocks, roses, and thistles. Motto: 'All grades, all creeds, and no distinctions'.

Bookbinders: Arms of the trade. Beneath an arch, supported by pillars, is a shield on which is emblazoned a book containing date 1782, being the year in which several members of the craft were prosecuted in London for illegal combination, and sentenced to long terms of imprisonment. A shield, supported by two journeymen, with hands clasped. Above hovers a dove bearing in its bill an olive branch. Mottoes: 'Bind right with might'; 'United to support, but not combined to injure'. Arms of the four Provinces in corners. Reverse, a large oval, representing a monk seated in his cell engaged in illuminating manuscript. Among the centre-piece are oval portraits of Swift, Moore, Davis, Burke, Griffin and Goldsmith.

Bottlemakers: Representation of men working at bottlemaking, with various implements of the trade. Reverse, figure of Erin.

Brassfounders: Descriptive design in brass, with emblems of trade. King Solomon receiving Cherubs from King Hiram on completion of Temple of Jerusalem.

Brush Makers: Triumphal arch, surrounded by the arms of the trade, supported by the wild boar and hunter. Through arch is seen the Custom House and Quays of Dublin. Reverse, scene in Killarney, with Erin and wolf dog.

Cabinet Makers: Arms of the trade, supported by figures of Justice and Truth. Reverse, emblems of the Union, supported by Science and Art.

Coach Builders: Arms of trade, with painting of a coach.

Coal Labourers: Life-size figure of Daniel O'Connell.

Confectioners: Silk poplin, with name of trade in gold letters.

Corkcutters: Arms of the trade: to the left the figure of Justice; to the right a figure leaning on shield, and holding a spear in right hand. Cork tree in centre. Underneath, hands joined, with the motto 'United to support; not combined to injure'. Reverse, figure of Erin, with sentiment 'Ireland for the Irish'.

Dockers' Union: Life-size figure of St Laurence O'Toole; heading representing sunburst in carved wood.

Dublin and District Tramway Men's Union: Miniature tramcar and horses. Reverse, painting of Glendalough. Motto: 'Union is strength.'

Farriers: Emblematic representation and arms of trade, surrounded with various devices.

Fishermen: Representation of the Miraculous Draught of Fishes.

Hairdressers' Trade Union: Arms of the trade, with inscription 'De Praeseientia Dei'. Motto: 'United to protect; not combined to injure.' Reverse, figure of Brian Boroimhe.

Letterpress Printers: Printing press enclosed in a fane of Ionic order, with a superscription, 'Associated to protect our rights, not to infringe on those of others.' In the centre of fane is a shield supported by winged figures, on which is inscribed the motto of the trade – 'The Light of the World.' Medallions of Caxton and

Schoffer above. On the reverse, a figure of Erin, with the legend, 'Behold we bring the Second Ark.'

Lithographic Printers: Silk, with portrait of Lenefelder (inventor of lithography) in centre. Right and left top corners representations of litho presses. Two shields bearing lithographic instruments supported by the figure of a youth (representing the comparative youth of the art), and the motto, 'Saxa loquitur' (the stone speaks). Figures to represent body and soul in bottom corners.

Operative Bakers: Arms of the trade, supported by two figures representing plenty, surmounted by the American and Irish arms combined; also the arms of the city. Reverse, figures of Erin, Irish Cross, and Wolf Dog in background; the arms of the four Provinces. Motto: 'May liberty for ever shine.'

Operative Butchers: Rich cardinal and green watered tabinet, raised letters 'Operative Butchers Trade Union, 1890.' Reverse, 'Guild of Blessed Virgin Mary'; Lamb of God bearing cross resting on book, with seven seals, surrounded by cherubins. Brass wands and battle-axes.

Operative Plasterers: Shields, supported by two griffins. Motto: 'United we stand, divided we fall'. Reverse, figure, patron of Guild of St Bartholomew.

Operative Slaters: Arms of the trade, representing two slaters in ancient costume, supporting a shield emblazoned with drawings of the tools of the craft; underneath is a second shield and panel, with the clasped hands and heart, and a ribbon bearing the motto, 'By love and harmony we support'. Reverse, a large oval medallion, with the figure of Erin weeping over the harp, with the wolf dog at her feet; in the background, round tower and church.

Operative Smiths: Arms of trade surmounted by figure of Vulcan seated on anvil, supported by representations of Justice and Hope. Mottoes; 'Union is strength' – 'By hammer in hand all arts do stand'.

449

Plumbers: Green ground, with gold letters, crossed plumbing irons in centre, and clasped hands underneath; brass standards and cross rail.

Pork Butchers: Arms and name of Society; emblems of trade.

Poulterers: Arms of trade, surmounted by harp. Reverse, Erin, harp, and wolf dog. Mottoes: 'Peace, plenty, and unity'. 'All hail with joy the golden days of Erin'.

Regular Glass Cutters, Glaziers and Lead Sash Makers: Green poplin, with yellow fringe, and the name of the trade in gold.

Saddlers: Shield, supported by rampant horses (1791). Mottoes: 'Our trust is in God'; 'We unite for home trade'.

Sailors' and Firemen's Union: Union flag, with ships in centre, and the emblems of the United Kingdom, with motto 'Pull together'.

Silkweavers: Arms of trade: shield, Fleur-de-lis and leopards' heads, with shuttle in mouth, and supported by two griffins; top, St Patrick, French crown and Irish harp. Motto: 'Nihil sine Labore'.

Stationary Engine Drivers: Arch, supported by Herculean figures enclosing a stationary engine, and figure of Erin, surrounded by winged-angels holding scroll, with name of trade union. Reverse, representation of large beam engine, with medallions of Watt and Stephenson.

Stone Cutters' Union of Ireland: Representation of the Temple of Jerusalem, with life-size figure of Hiram, the Architect, bearing a scroll inscribed with the plan of the temple. Opposite Hiram is a modern stonecutter, holding in his hands the implements of the trade. Reverse, full-size figure of Brian Boru clad in armour, leading his soldiers to victory, surmounted by the legend, 'Remember the glories of Brian the Brave'. Beneath is inscribed, 'Sons of Hiram, proceed and prosper'.

Tailors: Arms of trade, on shield, supported by two camels (spotted), surmounted by clasped hands. Motto: 'Nundus et operuistis me'.

United Labourers of Ireland: Large figure of Erin; rural landscape and Celtic Cross, surrounded by figures working at different branches of unskilled labour. Reverse, Coat of Arms of the four Provinces, surrounded by figure same as front.

Upholsterers: Painting of St Paul on green poplin. Motto: 'Uphold the truth'. Reverse, the arms of the trade.

Source: Publication issued by the Dublin United Trades Council and Labour League in connection with the holding of the first Irish Trades Union Congress in Dublin, 27 and 28 April 1894, and the Labour Day Demonstration, 6 May 1894.

Bibliography of Trade Unions and Trade Unionism in Ireland

The main sources for the Bibliography of books, articles and pamphlets on trade unions in Ireland were:

(a) the invaluable bibliographies on Irish labour history, 1973-1993, compiled by Deirdre O'Connell, Humanities/Social Sciences Librarian, University College Dublin and published annually in *Saothar*, the journal of the Irish Labour History Society, 5 (1979) to 19 (1994)

(b) the ten-year retrospective bibliography, 1963-1972, compiled by Mary E. Flynn, Librarian at University College Dublin and published in *Saothar*, 14 (1989) and a retrospective bibliography, 1960-72 in *Saothar* 16 (1991).

(c) bibliographies published in various issues of *Trade Union Information* (ICTU), particularly the Spring 1978 issue.

Generally, the Bibliography does not cover writings on the political Labour Movement in Ireland nor on industrial relations. However a few books dealing with industrial relations as well as reports by the National Industrial Economic Council and the National Economic and Social Council which had important implications for trade union policies have been included.

The main areas covered by the Bibliography are: trade union history, trade union organisation, trade union law and biographies of trade union leaders.

Publications by the Irish TUC and the ICTU are given separately. (See pages 355 and 470 respectively).

Books

Asmal, Kader, *Sources of labour law in Ireland*, Brussels: European Commission, 1973.
Asmal, Kader, *The Law on Collective Agreements in Ireland*, Brussels: European Commission, 1977.
Asmal, Kader, 'The Constitution, the law and industrial relations', in Donal Nevin (editor), *Trade Unions and Change in Irish Society*, Dublin: Mercier Press/RTE, 1980.

Bew, Paul, 'Politics and the rise of the skilled working man', in J. C. Beckett *et al*, *Belfast: the Making of the City, 1800-1914*. Belfast: Appletree Press, 1983.

Boyd, Andrew, *The Rise of the Irish Trade Unions 1729-1970*. Tralee: Anvil Books, 1972. [Second edition 1985]

Boyle, John W., *The Irish Labour Movement in the Nineteenth Century*, Washington DC: Catholic University of America Press, 1988.

Bradley, Daniel G., *Farm Labourers' Irish struggle, 1900-1976*. Belfast: Athol Books, 1988.

Breen, Richard; Hannan, Damien; Rottman, David B. and Whelan, Christopher T., 'Understanding Contemporary Ireland: State, Class and Development in the Republic of Ireland', Chapter 8, *Industrial Relations and the State*, Dublin: Gill and Macmillan, 1990.

Brennan, A. and Nolan, W., 'Nixie Boran and the colliery community of North Kilkenny', in W. Nolan and K. Whelan, *Kilkenny: History and Society*. Dublin: Geography Publications, 1990.

Cahill, Liam, *Forgotten Revolution: Limerick Soviet 1919*, Dublin: O'Brien Press, 1990.

Campbell, John, *A Loosely Shackled Fellowship: a History of Comhaltas Cána (Association of Higher Officers of Customs and Excise)*, Dublin: Public Service Executive Union, 1989.

Carr, A., *The Early Belfast Labour Movement. Part 1: 1885-93*. Belfast: Athol Books, 1974.

Cassells, Peter, 'The organisation of trade unions in Ireland', in *Industrial Relations in Ireland: Contemporary Issues and Developments*, Dublin: Department of Industrial Relations, University College Dublin, 1989.

Chubb, Basil (editor), *Federation of Irish Employers 1942-1992*, Dublin: Gill and Macmillan, 1992.

Clancy, Paul and MacKeogh, Kay, 'Gender and Trade Union Participation', in Chris Curtin, Pauline Jackson and Barbara O'Connor (editors) *Gender in Irish Society*, Galway: Galway University Press, 1987.

Clarkson, J. Dunsmore, *Labour and Nationalism in Ireland*, New York: Columbia University, 1925.

Cody, Seamus; O'Dowd, John and Rigney, Peter, *The Parliament of Labour: One Hundred Years of the Dublin Council of Trade Unions*, Dublin: Dublin Council of Trade Unions, 1986.

Commission of Inquiry on Industrial Relations (Chairman: Seamus Ó Conaill) *Report*. Dublin: Stationery Office, 1981.

Connolly, James, *Labour in Ireland: Labour in Irish history (1910): The re-conquest of Ieland* (1915); Dublin: At the Sign of the Three Candles, 1950. (A previous edition of the two books in one volume was dated 'October 1916,' and this was reissued in 1922).

Coolohan, John, *The ASTI and Post-primary Education in Ireland, 1909-1984*, Dublin: Association of Secondary Teachers Ireland, 1984.

Cradden, Terry, *Trade Unionism, Socialism and Partition: the Labour Movement in Northern Ireland 1939-1953*, Belfast: December Publications, 1993.

Curriculum Development Unit, Dublin. *Divided City: Portrait of Dublin 1913*. Dublin: O'Brien Educational, 1978. [New edition Dublin 1913: A Divided City (1982)]

D'Arcy, Fergus and Hannigan, Ken, *Workers in Union: Documents and Commentaries on the History of Irish Labour*, Dublin: National Archives, 1988.

Daly, George F., *Industrial Relations: Comparative Aspects with Particular*

Reference to Ireland, Cork: Mercier Press, 1968.

Daly, Mary E., 'Women, work and trade unionism', in Margaret MacCurtain and Donncha Ó Corráin (editors), *Women in Irish Society: the Historical Dimension*, Dublin: Arlen House, 1978.

Deasy, Joseph, *The Fiery Cross: the Story of Jim Larkin*, Dublin, 1963.

Enright, Michael, *Men of Iron: Wexford Foundry Disputes 1890 and 1911*, Wexford: Wexford Council of Trade Unions, 1987.

Fox, Robert M., *Louie Bennett: her Life and Times*, Dublin: Talbot Press, 1958.

Fox, Robert M., *Jim Larkin; the Rise of the Underman*, London: Lawrence and Wishart, 1957

Gaughan, J. Anthony, *Thomas Johnson, 1872-1963: First Leader of the Labour Party in Dáil Éireann*, Dublin: Kingdom Books, 1980.

Graham, Brian, *The History of TASS in Ireland: Chronicle of a Union in Action*, Dublin: MSF, 1991.

Gray, John, *City in Revolt: James Larkin and the Belfast Dock strike of 1907*, Belfast: Blackstaff Press, 1985.

Greaves, C. Desmond, *The Life and Times of James Connolly*, London: Lawrence and Wishart, 1961.

Greaves, C. Desmond, *The Irish Transport and General Workers Union: the Formative Years 1909-1923*, Dublin: Gill and Macmillan, 1982.

Hardiman, Niamh, *Pay, Politics, and Economic Performance in Ireland, 1970-1987*, Oxford: Clarendon Press, 1988.

Hardiman, Niamh, 'The State and Economic Interests: Ireland in Comparative Perspective', in John H. Goldthorpe and Christopher Whelan, *The Development of Industrial Society in Ireland*, Oxford: Oxford University Press for the British Academy, 1992.

Hillery, Brian; Kelly, Aidan and Marsh, Arthur, *Trade Union Organisation in Ireland*, Dublin: Irish Productivity Centre, 1975.

Hillery, Brian, 'The Irish Congress of Trade Unions', in *Industrial Relations in Ireland: Contemporary Issues and Developments*, Dublin: Department of Industrial Relations, University College Dublin, 1989.

Holton, B., 'British Syndicalism, 1900-14: Myths and reality', Chapter 14, *Syndicalism and Larkinism*, London: Pluto Press, 1976.

Irish Transport and General Workers' Union, *The Attempt to Smash the Irish Transport and General Workers' Union*, Dublin: ITGWU, 1924.

Jones, Mary, *These Obstreperous Lassies: a History of the Irish Women Workers' Union*, Dublin: Gill and Macmillan, 1988.

Keogh, Dermot, *The Rise of the Irish Working Class: the Dublin Trade Union Movement and Labour Leadership, 1890-1914*. Belfast: Appletree Press, 1982.

Kelly, Aidan, 'White-collar trade unionism', in Donal Nevin (editor), *Trade Unions and Change in Irish Society*, Dublin: Mercier Press/RTE, 1980.

Kelly, Aidan and Brannick, Teresa, 'Strikes in Ireland: measurement, incidence and trends', in *Industrial Relations in Ireland: Contemporary Issues and Developments*, Dublin: Department of Industrial Relations, University College Dublin, 1989.

Kerr, Tony and Whyte, Gerry, *Irish Trade Union Law*. Abingdon: Professional Books, 1985.

Kerr, Tony, 'Trade unions and the law', in *Industrial Relations in Ireland: Contemporary Issues and Trends*, Dublin: Department of Industrial Relations, University College Dublin, 1989.

Larkin, Emmet, *James Larkin 1876-1947: Irish Labour Leader*. London: Routledge Kegan Paul, 1965. [Also London: Pluto Press, 1990]

Lee, J. J., 'Worker and society in modern Ireland', in Donal Nevin (editor), *Trade Unions and Change in Irish Society*, Dublin: Mercier Press/RTE, 1980.

Levenson, Samuel, *James Connolly: a Biography*, London: Martin Brian and O'Keefe, 1973.

Loftus, Belinda (compiler), Marching Workers: an Exhibition of Irish Trade Banners and Regalia, Belfast and Dublin: Arts Councils of Ireland, 1978.

Lynch, Patrick, 'The social revolution that never was', in T. Desmond Williams (editor), *The Irish Struggle 1916-1926*. London, 1966.

Lynch, Patrick and Hillery, Brian, *Ireland in the International Labour Organisation*, Dublin: Stationery Office, 1969.

Mapstone, R., *The Ulster Teachers' Union: an Historical Perspective*, Coleraine: University of Ulster Academic Publications Committee, 1986.

McCartney, J.B., 'Strike Law and the Constitution in Eire,' in Otto Kahn-Freund (editor), *Labour Relations and the Law: a Comparative Study*, London: Stevens, 1965.

McCarthy, Charles, *Trade Unions in Ireland, 1984-1960*, Dublin: Institute of Public Administration, 1977.

McCarthy, Charles, 'The development of Irish trade unions', in Donal Nevin (editor), *Trade Unions and Change in Irish Society*, Dublin: Mercier Press/RTE, 1980.

McCarthy, Charles, 'James Larkin as the embodiment of the working classes 1907-1913', in *Discussion Papers in Industrial Relations*, Vol. 2, Dublin: School of Business and Administrative Studies, Trinity College Dublin, 1984.

McCarthy, W. E. J.; O'Brien, J. F. and Dowd, V. G., *Wage Inflation and Wage Leadership: a Study of the Role of Key Wage Bargains in the Irish System of Collective Bargaining*, Dublin: Economic and Social Research Institute, 1975.

McGovern, Patrick G., 'Union recognition and union avoidance in the 1980s', in *Industrial Relations in Ireland: Contemporary Issues and Developments*, Dublin: Department of Industrial Relations, University College Dublin, 1989.

McNamara, Gerry; Williams, Kevin and West, Des., *Understanding Trade Unions, Yesterday and Today*, Dublin: ICTU/O'Brien Educational, 1988.

Merrigan, Matt, *Eagle or Cuckoo? The Story of the Amalgamated Transport and General Workers' Union in Ireland*, Dublin: Matmer Publications, 1989.

Mitchell, Arthur, *Labour in Irish Politics, 1890-1930: the Irish Labour Movement in an Age of Revolution*, Dublin: Irish University Press, 1974.

Morgan, Austen, *Labour and Partition: the Belfast Working Class 1905-1923*, London: 1991.

Morrissey, T.J., *A Man Called Hughes: the Life and Times of Seamus Hughes 1881-1943*, Dublin: Veritas, 1991.

Mulvey, Charles, Report of Inquiry into Strikes in Bord na Mona. Dublin: Stationery Office, 1969.

Murphy, Con, Report on Dispute between FUE and Maintenance Craft Unions. Dublin: Stationery Office, 1969.

Murphy, Patrick, The Federation of Rural Workers 1946-1979. Dublin: Federated Workers' Union of Ireland, 1988.

Murphy, Tom, 'The union committee at the workplace', in *Industrial Relations in Ireland: Contemporary Issues and Developments*, Dublin:

Department of Industrial Relations, University College Dublin, 1989.

National Industrial and Economic Council, Report on Economic Planning. Dublin: Stationery Office, 1965.

National Industrial and Economic Council, Report on Full Employment. Dublin: Stationery Office, 1967.

National Industrial and Economic Council, Report on Incomes and Prices Policy. Dublin: Stationery Office, 1970.

National Economic and Social Council, A Strategy for Development, 1986-1990. Dublin: Stationery Office, 1986.

Nevin, Donal (editor), 1913: Jim Larkin and the Dublin Lock-out. Dublin: Workers' Union of Ireland, 1964.

Nevin, Donal, 'Labour and the political revolution' in Francis MacManus (editor), The Years of the Great Test 1926-39,. Dublin: Mercier Press/RTE, 1967.

Nevin, Donal, 'Industry and labour', in Kevin B. Nolan and T. Desmond Williams (editors), Ireland in the War Years and After 1939-51, Dublin: Gill and Macmillan, 1969.

Nevin, Donal (editor), Trade Unions and Change in Irish Society, Dublin: Mercier Press/RTE, 1980

Nevin, Donal, 'Trade unions and social policy', in Donal Nevin (editor), Trade Union Priorities in Social Policy, Dublin: Federated Workers' Union of Ireland, 1981.

Nevin, Edward, Wages in Ireland 1946-1962, Dublin: Economic Research Institute, 1963.

Northern Ireland Department of Manpower Services, Industrial Relations in Northern Ireland: Report of the Review Body, 1971-74. (Chairman: Dr. W.G.H. Quigley). Belfast: HMSO, 1974.

Organisation for Economic Co-operation and Development, Wage Policies and Collective Bargaining Developments in Finland, Ireland and Norway. Paris: OECD, 1979.

O'Brien, James F., A Study of National Wage Agreements in Ireland, Dublin: Economic and Social Research Institute, 1981.

O'Brien, William, Forth the Banners Go. Reminiscences of William O'Brien as told to Edward MacLysaght, Dublin: The Three Candles Press, 1969.

O'Connell, Thomas J., One Hundred Years of Progress: the History of the Irish National Teachers' Organisation 1868-1968, Dublin: INTO, 1968.

O'Connor, Emmet, Syndicalism in Ireland: 1917-1923, Cork: Cork University Press, 1988.

O'Connor, Emmet, A Labour History of Waterford. Waterford: Waterford Council of Trade Unions, 1989.

O'Connor, Emmet, A Labour History of Ireland 1824-1960. Dublin: Gill and Macmillan, 1992.

O'Higgins, Paul, Irish Labour Law: Sword or Shield? Dublin: Irish Association for Industrial Relations, 1979.

O'Mahony, David, Industrial Relations in Ireland: the Background, Dublin: Economic Research Institute, 1964.

O'Neill, T.P., 'Irish trade banners', in Caoimhín Ó Danachair (editor), Folk and Farm, Dublin: 1976

O'Reilly, James, and Redmond, Mary, 'Cases and Materials on the Irish Constitution', Chapter 17 Freedom of Association. Dublin: Incorporated Law Society of Ireland, 1980.

O'Shannon, Cathal, Fifty Years of Liberty Hall: the Golden Jubilee of the ITGWU 1909-1959, Dublin: The Three Candles Press, 1959.

Owens, Rosemary Cullen, Smashing Times: a History of the Irish Women's

Suffrage Movement 1889-1922 (Labour links, pp. 74-94). Dublin: Attic Press, 1984.

Patterson, Henry, *Class Conflict and Sectarianism: the Protestant Working Class and the Belfast Labour Movement 1868-1920*. Belfast: Blackstaff Press, 1980.

Patterson, Henry, 'Industrial labour and the labour movement', 1820-1914 in Liam Kennedy and Philip Ollerenshaw (editors), *An Economic History of Ulster, 1820-1939*. Manchester: Manchester University Press, 1985.

Pimley, Adrian, 'The working-class movement and the Irish revolution 1896-1923', in D.G. Boyce *The Revolution in Ireland*, London, 1988.

Plunkett, James, 'Jim Larkin', in John W. Boyle (editor), *Leaders and Workers*, Cork: Mercier Press, 1966.

Plunkett, James, 'Sean O'Casey and the trade unions', in Micheál Ó hAodha, *The O'Casey Enigma*. Cork: Mercier Press, 1980.

Pratschke, John L., 'Business and labour in Irish society 1945-70', in J.J. Lee, *Ireland 1945-70*, Dublin: Gill and Macmillan, 1979.

Redmond, Mary, 'The law and workers' rights', in Donal Nevin (editor), *Trade Unions and Change in Irish Society*, Dublin: Mercier Press/RTE, 1980.

Redmond, Mary, 'The law and workers' right', in *Industrial Relations in Ireland: Contemporary Issues and Developments*, Dublin: Department of Industrial Relations, University College Dublin, 1989.

Redmond, Mary, *Redmond's Guide to Irish Labour Law: Labour Law and Industrial Relations in Ireland*, Dublin: Bridgefoot Press, 1984.

Redmond, Sean, *The Irish Municipal Employees Trade Union 1883-1983*, Dublin: IMETU, 1983.

Roberts, Ruaidhri, *The Story of the People's College*, Edited and additional material incorporated by R. Dardis Clarke. Dublin: O'Brien Press/People's College, 1986.

Roche, William K. and Quinn, F., *Trends in Irish Industrial Relations*, Dublin: College of Industrial Relations, 1981.

Roche, William K. and Larragy, J., 'The trend of unionisation in the Republic of Ireland' in *Industrial Relations in Ireland: Contemporary Issues and Developments*, Dublin: Department of Industrial Relations, University College Dublin, 1989.

Roche, William K., 'The liberal theory of industrialism and the development of industrial relations in Ireland', in John H. Goldthorpe and Christopher T. Whelan *The Development of Industrial Society in Ireland*, Oxford: Oxford University Press for the British Academy, 1992.

Ruane, Medb, Louis Bennett in *Ten Dublin Women*, Dublin: Women's Commemoration and Celebration Committee, 1991.

Rumpf, E. and Hepburn, A.C., *Nationalism and Socialism in Twentieth Century Ireland*, Liverpool: Liverpool University Press, 1977.

Ryan, Desmond, *James Connolly: his Life, Work and Writings*, Dublin: Talbot Press, 1924.

Ryan, Desmond (editor), *The Workers' Republic: a Selection from the Writings of James Connolly*. Introduction by William McMullen, Dublin: At the Sign of the Three Candles, 1951.

Ryan, Desmond (editor), *Socialism and Nationalism: a Selection from the Writings of James Connolly*. Introduction by editor. Dublin: At the Sign of the Three Candles, 1948.

Ryan, W.P., *The Irish Labour Movement from the Twenties to Our Own Day*, Dublin: Talbot Press, 1919.

Schregle, Johannes, *Restructuring the Irish Trade Union Movement*,

Geneva: International Labour Office, 1975.

Sexton, Sir James, *Sir James Sexton Agitator. The Life of the Dockers' MP. An Autobiography*. London: Faber and Faber, 1936. [Chapter XXIX. James Larkin and his Work].

Shillman, Bernard, *Trade Unionism and Trade Disputes in Ireland*, Dublin: Dublin Press, 1960.

Steele, Richard, 'Labour law in action', in Hugh M. Pollock (editor), *Reform of Industrial Relations*, Dublin: O'Brien Press, 1982.

Strauss, E., *Irish Nationalism and British Democracy*, London: Metheun, 1951.

Sweeney, Gary, *In Public Service: a History of the Public Service Executive Union 1890-1990*, Dublin: PSEU/IPA, 1990.

Swift, John, *History of the Dublin Bakers and Others*, Dublin: Irish Bakers', Confectioners' and Allied Workers Union, 1948.

Swift, John P., *John Swift: an Irish Dissident*, Dublin: Gill and Macmillan, 1991.

Thomason, George F., *The Individual, the Trade Union and the State – Some Contemporary Issues*, Dublin: Irish Association for Industrial Relations, 1978.

Thomson, Lucinda, 'Strikes in Galway', in David Fitzpatrick (editor), *Revolution? Ireland 1917-1923*, Dublin: Trinity History Workshop, 1990.

Von Prondzynski, Ferdinand, and McCarthy, Charles, 'Employment Law', Chapter 1: *Irish Labour Law and Industrial Relations*, London: Sweet and Maxwell, 1984.

Von Prondzynski, Ferdinand, 'Collective Labour Law in *Industrial Relations in Ireland: Contemporary Issues and Developments*, Dublin: Department of Industrial Relations, University College Dublin, 1989.

Wallace, Joseph and O'Shea, F., *A Study of Unofficial Strikes in Ireland*, Dublin: Stationery Office, 1987.

Wayne, Naomi, *Labour Law in Ireland*, Dublin: Irish Transport and General Workers' Union, 1980.

Wright, Arnold, *Disturbed Dublin: the Story of the Great Strike*. London: Longmans Green, 1914.

Histories of Trade Unions

There are references to trade union branches in Ireland in the following trade union histories:

They also Serve. The Story of the Shop Worker, P. C. Hoffman. London: Porcupine Press, 1941.

The Typographical Association. Origins and History up to 1949, A. E. Musson. Oxford: Oxford University Press, 1954.

The Woodworkers 1860-1960, T. J. Connelly. London, 1960

A History of the Association of Engineering and Shipbuilding Draughtsmen, J. E. Mortimer. London: AESD, 1960.

The Railwaymen. Vol. 1, P.S. Bagwell. London: Allen and Unwin, 1963.

The Needle is Threaded 'The History of an Industry', Margaret Stewart and

Leslie Hunter. (History of National Union of Tailors and Garment Workers). London: Heinemann, 1964.
A History of the Transport and General Workers' Union. Vol. 1 The Making of the TGWU: The Emergence of the Labour Movement 1870-1922. *Part 1 1870-1911 From Forerunners to Federation. Part II. 1912-1922 From Federation to Amalgamation.* Ken Coates and Tony Topham. London: Basil Blackwell, 1991.

Journals

Administration (Institute of Public Administration, Dublin)
McCarthy, Charles, A review of the objectives of National Pay Agreements in 1970-1977, Spring 1977.
Whitaker, T. K. Industrial relations – is there a better way?, Vol. 27, No.. 3, 1979.
Von Prondzynski, Ferdinand, Unofficial strikes: myth and reality, Vol 29, No. 4, 1982.

British Journal of Industrial Relations (London)
Sams, K. I. Government and trade unions – the situation in Northern Ireland, July 1964.
Brown, M. H., Labour and incomes policy in the Republic of Ireland, March 1965.
Sama, K. I., The Appeals Board of the ICTU, July 1968.

Bulletin of the Society for the Study of Labour History (Sheffield) [now *Labour History Review*]
Moran, B., The Dublin lock-out 1913, Autumn 1973.
Patterson, Henry, The new unionism and Belfast, Autumn 1977.
Boyle, John W., The Irish TUC: A review essay of Charles McCarthy, 'Trade unions in Ireland 1894-1960', Autumn 1980.

Capuchin Annual (Dublin)
Keogh, Dermot, The 'new unionism' and Ireland: the Dublin coal porters' strike 1890, 1975.
Keogh, Dermot, Michael J. Lehane organises the drapers' assistants, 1976.
Keogh, Dermot, William Martin Murphy and the origins of the 1913 lock-out, 1977.

Civil Service Review (Public Service Executive Union, Dublin)
Sweeney, Gary, When the Dublin carters struck [1905], May-June 1974.
Sweeney, Gary, The rise and fall of Larkinism, July-August, September-December 1976.
Sweeney, Gary, Belfast and its workers, July-August, November-December, 1981.

Economic and Social Review (Dublin)

McCarthy, Charles, From division to dissension: Irish trade unions in the 1930s, 5 (3) and 5 (4), 1974.

Hillery, Brian, Trade union finance in the Republic, April, 1974.

Barlow, A. C., Trade union organisation in Ireland: a review of recent publications, October 1975.

Robertson, N. and Sams, K., The role of the full-time trade union officer in Northern Ireland, October 1976.

Brannick, Teresa and Kelly, Aidan, The reliability and validity of Irish strike data and statistics, Vol. 14, No. 4, 1983.

Callan, Tim and Reilly, Barry, Unions and the wage distribution in Ireland, July 1993.

European History Quarterly (London)

Newsinger, John, 'A lamp to guide your feet': Jim Larkin, *The Irish Worker* and the Dublin working class, January 1990.

Historical Journal (London)

O'Higgins, Rachel, Irish trade unions and politics, 1830-1850, IV, 2, 1961

IBAR – Journal of Irish Business and Administrative Research (Dublin)

Kelly Aidan, Unionism of white-collar employees, October 1980.

Murphy, Tom, The trade union committee at the workplace: a case analysis of its role, activities and influence in union decision making, October 1981.

Hardiman, Niamh, Trade union density in the Republic of Ireland 1960-1979, October 1983.

Kelly, Aidan and Brannick, Teresa, The pattern of strike activity in Ireland 1960-1979, April 1983.

Kelly, Aidan and Brannick, Teresa, Voluntarism in trade unions: union officials' attitude to unofficial strike action, April 1984.

Kelly, Aidan and Brannick, Teresa, The changing contours of Irish strike patterns 1960-1984, Vol. 8, Part 1, 1986.

Kelly, Aidan and Brannick, Teresa, Strike trends in the Irish private sector, Vol. 9, 1988.

Black, Boyd, Trade union density in Northern Ireland, Vol. 13, 1992.

Cradden, Terry, Trade unions and HRM (human resource management): the incompatibilities, Vol. 13, 1992.

Roche, William K., Modelling trade union growth and decline in the Republic of Ireland, Vol. 13, 1992.

Tipping, Brian, Patterns of union membership and collective bargaining: the Northern Ireland experience, Vol. 13, 1992.

Industrial Law Journal (Oxford)

Black, Boyd, Trade union democracy and Northern Ireland, December 1984.

Industrial and Labour Relations Review (Cornell, New York)

Cradden, Terry, Trade unionism, social justice and religious discrimination in Northern Ireland, Vol. 46, No. 3, April 1993.

Industrial Relations Journal (Strathclyde)

Black, Boyd, Against the trend: trade union growth in Northern Ireland, Vol. 17, No. 1, 1986.

Black, Boyd, Collaboration or conflict? Strike activity in Northern Ireland,Vol. 18, No. 1, 1987.

Cradden, Terry, The Tories and employment law in Northern Ireland: seeing unions in a different light, Vol. 24, No. 1, March 1993.

International Journal of Human Resource Management (London)

Roche, William K. and Turner, Thomas, Testing alternative models of human resource policy effects on trade union recognition in the Republic of Ireland, 1994.

International Labour Review (Geneva)

McCarthy, Charles, Trade unions and economic planning in Ireland, July 1966.

International Review of Social History (Amsterdam)

McHugh, John, The Belfast labour dispute and riots of 1907, No. 22 (1), 1977.

Irish Historical Studies (Dublin)

Horn, P. L. R., The National Agricultural Labourers Union in Ireland, XVII, 1971-2.

Townshend, Charles, The Irish railway strike of 1920: industrial action and civil resistance in the struggle for independence, XXI, 1979.

Irish Jurist (Dublin)

McCartney, J. B., Strike law and the Constitution, Vol. 30, Part IV, 1964.

Heuston, R. F. V., Trade unions and the law, Vol. 4 (New Series), Summer 1969.

Gerry Whyte, Industrial relations and the Irish Constitution, Vol. XVI (New Series), Part 1, Summer 1981.

Von Prondzynski, Ferdinand, Trade disputes and the courts: the problem of the labour injunction, Vol. XVI (New Series), Part 2, Winter, 1981.

Kerr, Tony, Trade disputes, economic torts and the Constitution: the legacy of Talbot, Vol. XVI, Part 2, Winter, 1981.

Kerr, Tony, The problem of the labour injunction revisited, Vol. XVII, (New Series), 1983.

Journal of European Economic History (Rome)

McLernon, D. S., Trade union organisation in the South of Ireland in the 19th century, 10 (1), 1981.

Journal of the Irish Economic and Social History Society (Belfast and Dublin)

Murphy, M., The role of organised labour in the political and economic life of Cork city in the nineteenth century, 8, 1981.

O'Connor, Emmet, Active sabotage in industrial conflict, 1917-23, 12, 1985.

Journal of the Irish Society of Labour Law (Dublin)

Brannick, Teresa, and Kelly, Aidan, Unofficial strike action, No. 3, 1984.
Horan, Brid, Review of Mary Redmond, 'Redmond's Guide to Irish labour law'. Vol. 3, 1984.
Kerr, Tony, Industrial action: rights and immunities, Vol. 5, 1986.
Byrne, Gary, review of Tony Kerr and Gerry White, 'Irish Trade Union Law', Vol. 5, 1986.
McCarthy, Judge Niall, 'To do a great right, do a little wrong', (Reflections on decisions of the Irish Courts in respect of trade disputes), Vol. 6, 1987.
Costello, Judge Declan, Fair procedures, the Constitution and trade unions, Vol. 8, 1989.

Journal of the Statistical and Social Inquiry Society of Ireland (Dublin)

Mortished, R. J. P., Trade union organisation in Ireland, Vol. XV, 1925-26. (Paper read 7 January 1926).
Bleakley, David W., The Northern Ireland trade union movement, Vol. XX, 1953-4. (Paper read 14 May 1954).
Roberts, Ruaidhri, Trade union organisation in Ireland, Vol. XX, 1958-59. (Paper read 19 April 1959).

Labour History News (Irish Labour History Society, Dublin)

Morrissey, Hazel, Betty Sinclair (Secretary, Belfast Trades Council), Spring 1987.
Cody, Seamus, Dublin Trades Council and the 1913 lock-out, Summer 1987.
Callan, Charles, Peadar Macken (Dublin Metropolitan House Painters' Trade Union) 1878-1916, Autumn 1989.
Nevin, Donal The founding of the Irish Congress of Trade Unions, Autumn 1989.
Devine, Francis, John Swift 1896-1990, Summer 1990.
Collins, Peter, Mary Galway (Irish Textile Operatives Union), Summer 1991.
Smith, Brid, Cissy Cahalan (Irish Union of Distributive Workers and Clerks), Autumn 1992.
Deasy, Joe, Thomas Johnson, Autumn 1992.

Liberty Magazine/Liberty (ITGWU, Dublin)

Special issue commemorating ITGWU Golden Jubilee, 1959.
Souvenir issue commemorating the official opening of the new Liberty Hall, May 1965.
McMullen, William, Recollection of Liberty Hall, May 1965.
O'Shannon, Cathal, William O'Brien 1880-1968: An appreciation. November 1968.
Geraghty, Hugh, William P. Partridge 1874-1917, April 1974.
Beecher, Liam, Cork's role in ITGWU growth, October 1975.
Devine, Francis, Jim Larkin, January 1976.
Geraghty, Hugh, Have you heard of William Partridge?, April 1976.
Beecher, Liam, Cork Harbour strike of 1921, September-October 1976.
McMullen, William, Early days of ITGWU in Belfast, June and July 1977.
O'Dowd, John, Congress's early education policy, February 1981.
Sweeney, Jimmy, 1913 lock-out, December 1981.

McCamley, Bill, The third James [James Fearon of Newry], January 1982.
ITGWU Diamond Jubilee issue, June 1984.
Devlin, Paddy, Michael McKeown, June 1984.
Eighty years of the ITGWU, Special Supplement, December 1989.

Limerick Socialist (Limerick)
Kemmy, Jim, The Limerick Soviet, eleven parts, April 1972 to February 1973.

Management (Irish Management Institute, Dublin)
Larkin, James, Industrial relations: a trade union view, April 1966.
Hillery, Brian and Kelly, Aidan, Aspects of trade union membership, 1945-70, April 1974.
Nevin, Donal, The trade union role, May-June 1980.

Northern Ireland Legal Quarterly (Belfast)
Krislov, Joseph, The participants' view of the Appeal Board of the ICTU, Summer 1972.

Obair (Irish Labour History Society, Dublin)
Brosnahan, Sean, INTO: origin and development of the organisation, July 1975.
Devine, Francis, Women in the Irish trade unions, July 1975.
Heuston, C., The Thomas MacPartlin collection, July 1975.
Nevin, Donal, The birth of the Workers' Union of Ireland, May 1984.
Cody, Seamus, The remarkable P. T. Daly, January 1985.

Old Limerick Journal (Limerick)
Kemmy, Jim, The general strike in Limerick 1919, March 1980.
MacCarthy, M., The Broadford Soviet, September 1980.
Feeley, Pat, The Castlecomer Mine and Quarry Union, Spring, Summer, Autumn 1981.

Quorum (Marine, Port and General Workers' Union, Dublin)
Commemoration Issue: Jimmy Dunne, March 1972.

Kilkenny Standard (Kilkenny)
Francis Devine, Irish trade unions: a brief history, January 30, 6 and 13 February 1981.

Relay (Irish Post Office Engineering Union)
Fifty years of the Irish Post Office Engineering Union, April-June 1972.

Saothar (Journal of the Irish Labour History Society)
Saothar, 5 (1979) to 19 (1994)
O'Connell, Deirdre, A bibliography of Irish labour history, 1973 to 1993: Section 5 (Labour organisation) and Section 8 (Biography and autobiogrpahy). Addenda 1973-1984 in Saothar, 12 (1987).

Saothar 1 (1975)
MacGiolla Coille, Breandán, Dublin trades in procession.

Saothar 2 (1976)
Boyle, Emily, The linen strike of 1872.
Kemmy Jim, The Limerick Soviet.
Leckey, Joseph J., The railway servants' strike in Co. Cork 1898.
Doyle, Mel, Belfast and Tolpuddle.

Saothar 3 (1977)
Swift, John, The Bakers' records.
Rigney, Peter, Some records of the ITGWU in the National Library of
    Ireland.
Keogh, Dermot, Michael O'Lehane and the organisation of linen
    drapers' assistants.
Doyle, Mel, The Dublin guilds and the journeymen's clubs.

Saothar 4 (1978)
Taplin, Eric, James Larkin, Liverpool and the National Union of Dock
    Labourers: the apprenticeship of a revolutionary.
Patterson, Henry, James Larkin and the Belfast dockers' strike of 1907.
Keogh, Dermot, William Martin Murphy and the origins of the 1913
    lock-out.
Moran, Bill, 1913, Jim Larkin and the British labour movement.
O'Riordan, Manus, Larkin in America.
McCarthy, Charles, the impact of Larkinism on the Irish working class.
Nevin, Donal, Larkin bibliography.
Devine, Francis, Review of Emmet Larkin 'James Larkin, 1876-1947,
    Irish Labour Leader'.

Saothar 5 (1979)
McMullan, Gordon, The Irish bank 'strike' 1919.
Brown, Kenneth D., Review of Charles McCarthy, 'Trade unions in
    Ireland 1894-1960'.
Cody, Seamus, May Day in Dublin 1890 to the present.
Gorman, John, Review of Belinda Loftus, 'Marching Banners'.

Saothar 6 (1980)
Fitzpatrick, David, Strikes in Ireland 1914-21.
Hannigan, Ken, Labour records in the Public Record Office of Ireland.
Sweeney, Jimmy, The Dublin lock-out 1913: the response of British
    labour.
O'Connor, Emmet, Agrarian unrest and the labour movement in
    County Waterford 1917-23.

Saothar 7 (1981)
Callan, Charles, The Regular Operative House Painters' Trade Union.
Hannigan, Ken, British-based unions in Ireland: building workers and
    the split in Congress.
Morgan, Austen, review of J. Anthony Gaughan, 'Thomas Johnson 1872-
    1963'.
Smethurst, John B. and Devine, Francis, Trade union badges.
Parkhill, Trevor, Labour records in the Public Record Office in Northern
    Ireland.

Daly, Mary E., Women in the Irish workforce from pre-industrial to modern times.

Saothar 8 (1982)
Deighan, Joe, Betty Sinclair 1908-1981.
Lyne, Gerard J., Labour history sources in the National Library of Ireland.

Saothar 9 (1983)
Geraghty, Hugh and Rigney, Peter, The engineers' strike in Inchicore railway works 1902.
Owens, Rosemary, Organised labour and the suffrage movement 1876-1922.
O'Connor Lysaght, D. R., The rake's progress of a syndicalist: the political career of William O'Brien.
O'Connor, Emmet, Reviews of Dermot Keogh, 'The rise of the working class: the Dublin trade union movement and labour leadership, 1890-1914' and C. Desmond Greaves, 'The Irish Transport and General Workers' Union: the formative years'.
Brown, Kenneth, Labour and the strikes of 1913: their place in British history.
Donnelly, Brian, Records of the Irish Graphical Society.

Saothar 10 (1984)
Donnelly, Edna, The struggle for Whitleyism in the Northern Ireland Civil Service.
Coolahan, John, The ASTI and the secondary teachers' strike of 1920.
Cox, Hugh, Review of Sean Redmond, 'The Irish Municipal Employees' Union 1883-1983'.

Saothar 11 (1986)
Bradley, Daniel G., Speeding the plough: the formation of the Federation of Rural Workers 1944-1948.
Cradden, Terry, Review of John Gray, 'City in revolt: James Larkin and the Belfast dock strike of 1907'.
Murphy, John A., Review of John Coolahan, 'The ASTI and post-primary education in Ireland 1909-1984'.
Devine, Francis, Trade union records in the Registry of Friendly Societies, Dublin.
Kiernan, Eugene, Drogheda and the British general strike 1926.

Saothar 12 (1987)
Mapstone, Richard H., Trade union and Government relations: a case study of influence on the Stormont government (Ulster Teachers' Union).
Conneely, Martin, Review of Seamus Cody, John O'Dowd, and Peter Rigney, 'The Parliament of Labour: 100 years of the Dublin Council of Trade Unions'.
Kenny, Bob, The growth of the Irish Transport and General Workers' Union: a geographer's view.
Finaly, Andrew, Trade union records in the Northern Ireland Registry of Friendly Societies.
O'Leary, Eoin, The INTO and the marriage bar for women national teachers 1933-58.

Saothar 13 (1988)
Hazelkorn, Ellen, The social and political views of Louie Bennett 1870-1956.
Ward-Perkins, Sarah, Trade union journals in the National Library of Ireland.

Saothar 14 (1989)
Boyle, John W., Review of Fergus D'Arcy and Ken Hannigan (editors), 'Workers in Union'.
Bedarida, Francois, Review of Emmet O'Connor, 'Syndicalism in Ireland 1917-23'.
King, Carla, Review of Mary Jones, 'These obstreperous lassies: a history of the Irish Women Workers' Union'.
Bergin, Paddy, Reviews of Daniel G. Bradley, 'Farm labourers' Irish struggle 1900-1976' and Patrick Murphy, 'The Federation of Rural Workers 1946-1979'.
Flynn, Mary E., Ten year retrospective bibliography of Irish labour history 1963-1972 – Section 5 (Labour organisation) and Section 8 (Biography and autobiography).
Lammey, David, More labour records in the Public Record Office of Northern Ireland.

Saothar 15 (1990)
Devine, Francis, 'A dangerous agitator': John Swift 1896-1990.
Quinn, Jim, Labouring on the margins: trade union activity in Enniskillen 1917-1923.
Foster, John, Review of John W. Boyle, 'The Irish labour movement in the nineteenth century'.
Wallace, Joe, Review of Matt Merrigan, 'Eagle or cuckoo? the story of the ATGWU in Ireland'.
Hywel, Francis, Review of Emmet O'Connor, 'A labour history of Waterford'.
Cunningham, John F. A glimpse of the Galway Workers' and General Labourers' Union, 1913.

Saothar 16 (1991)
Byrom-O'Brien, Gerard, Review of John P. Swift, 'John Swift: an Irish dissident'.
Cullen, Paul, Review of Gary Sweeney, 'In public service: a history of the Public Service Executive Union 1890-1990'.
Barr, Andy, Reminiscence of a Communist trade unionist.
Ryan, Nicholas M., Minute book of the County Dublin Stone-cutters' Society of Stepaside and its locality 1889-1892.
McCaffrey, Patricia, Jacob's women workers during the 1913 lock-out.
Flynn, Mary E., A retrospective bibliography of Irish labour history, 1960-72. Section 5 (Labour organisation) and Section 8 (Biography and autobiography).
McAteer, Shane, The 'new unionism' in Derry 1889-92.

Saothar 17 (1992)
Quinn, Oisin, Labour law and the labour historian.
Finlay, Andrew, Politics, sectarianism and the 'failure' of trade unionism in Northern Ireland: the case of garment workers in

Derry 1945-68.

O'Connor, Emmet, Review essay of Ken Coates and Tony Topham, The history of the Transport and General Workers' Union Vol. 1, Parts 1 and 2.

Saothar 18 (1993)

Henry, Brian, Industrial violence, combinations and the law in late eighteenth century Dublin.

Hynes, Tina, A polite struggle: the Dublin seamstresses' campaign 1869-1872

Howell, David, Review of Emmet O'Connor, A Labour history of Ireland 1824-1960

Anderson, Brian, Reviews of Tony Foley, A most formidable union: the history of DATA and TASS; and Brian Graham, The history of Tass in Ireland: chronicle of a union in action.

Casey, Anne, Review of Nicholas Rossiter, Wexford May 1917: people of steel.

O'Dowd, John, Reviews of Ross M. Connolly, By common council and common action: an outline history of the Bray and District Council of Trade Unions 1917-1922; and Ross M. Connolly, The Labour Movement in County Wicklow.

Newsinger, John, 'The devil it was who sent Larkin to Ireland': The Liberator, Larkinism and the Dublin lock-out of 1913.

Saothar 19 (1994)

Crean, Thomas Neilan, Labour and politics in Kerry during the First World War.

McCabe, Anton, 'The stormy petrel of the Transport Union': Peadar O'Donnell, trade unionist, 1917-1920.

O'Riordan, Manus, James Larkin Junior and the forging of a thinking intelligent movement.

Silvester, Nic, The Cathal O'Shannon Papers in the Irish Labour History Society Archive.

Devine, Francis, Labour records in the Public Record Office of Northern Ireland: some recent deposits; Trade union records in the Registry of Friendly Societies, Dublin and the National Archives.

Wallace, Joe, Waterford 1947: Year of the two Congresses.

Terry Cradden, Reminiscence: Billy Blease from McClure Street to the House of Lords.

Richard Mapstone, Reviews of Terry Cradden, Trade unionism, socialism and partition: the labour movement in Northern Ireland; and Paddy Devlin, Straight left: an autobiography.

Maurice Manning, Review of Thomas J. Morrissey, A man called Hughes: the life and times of Seamus Hughes 1881-1943.

Catriona Crowe, Some sources in the National Archives for women's history. [Includes ICTU records].

Tomás MacSiomóin, Review of Éamon Ó Ciosáin, An t-Éireannach 1934-37. Paipear Soisialach Gaeltachta.

Studies (Dublin)

Mitchell, Arthur, Thomas Johnson 1872-1963: a pioneer labour leader, 18, 1969.

Mitchell, Arthur, William O'Brien 1881-1968 and the Irish labour movement, 20, 1971.

Morrissey, Thomas J., The 1913 lock-out: letters for the Archbishop, 75 (297), 1986.

Trade Union Information (Irish TUC/ICTU, Dublin)
Trade union membership surveys, March, April 1953, July 1961, February-March, July, August 1967, December 1968, June 1971, January, February 1972, October-December 1974, November-December 1975, Spring 1978, Summer 1980, Winter 1980-81.
Survey of trade union officials, September 1968.
ICTU Submission to Commission on the Status of Women, December 1970, January, February 1971.
Check-off system, April-May 1973.
Report on National Minimum Wage, Summer 1974.
Trade union finance, February-March 1954, September 1962, January 1968, December 1972, January-March 1974, January-March, November-December 1975, Autumn 1977.
Bibliography on industrial relations: trade union organisation, industrial relations, pay and incomes policy, industrial democracy, labour law, Spring 1978.
Labour law – Statutory Instruments 1876-1978, Summer 1978.

Pamphlets

Association of Higher Civil Servants Annual Report 1993. [Includes history of AHCS.] Dublin: AHCS, 1993.
Belfast and District Trades Union Council. Souvenir Programme: Irish TUC annual conference. Belfast, 1949.
Cody, Seamus, May Day in Dublin 1890-1986. Dublin Council of Trade Unions, 1986.
Connolly, R.M., Outline history of the Bray and District Council of Trade Unions 1917-1992. Bray Council of Trade Unions, 1992.
Connolly, Ross, The Labour movement in County Wicklow. Bray: Bray Council of Trade Unions, 1992.
Cooke, J., Technical education and the foundation of the Dublin United Trades Council, 1886. Teachers' Union of Ireland, 1987.
Devine, Francis, Irish Women Workers' Union 1911-1984. Report on SIPTU Women's Consultative Conference. Dublin: SIPTU, 1992.
Getgood, Robert, Development of Irish trade unionism (Address to 50th annual meeting of Irish TUC, Drogheda 1944). Belfast, 1945.
Greaves, C. Desmond, James Connolly and trade unionism. Dublin, ITGWU, 1978.
Larkin, James, A common loyalty – a bridge to unity (Address to 55th annual meeting of Irish TUC, Belfast, 1949). Dublin, 1949.
Lee, D., *et al.* Revolt of the bottom dogs: history of the trade union movement in Limerick city and county, 1916-1921. Limerick: Labour History Research Group, 1989.
McCamley, Bill, The role of the rank and file in the 1935 Dublin tram and bus strike. Dublin: Labour History Workshop, 1981.
McCamley, Bill, The third James: the story of Irish labour pioneer, James Fearon. Dublin: Dublin History Workshop, 1984.
McCamley, Bill, The rise of the National Busworkers' Union. Dublin: Labour History Workshop, 1988.
MacDonnell, J.M., The story of Irish labour. Cork: Cork Workers' Club,

1974. (Reprint of 1921 edition).

McKee, Ann, Belfast Trades Council: the first one hundred years (1881-1981). Belfast, 1983.

Morrissey, Hazel, Betty Sinclair: A woman's fight for socialism. Belfast: ATGWU, 1983.

O'Connor, Lysaght, D. R., The story of the Limerick soviet. Limerick: People's Democracy, 1979.

O'Hare, Fergus, The divine gospel of discontent: the story of the Belfast dockers' and carters' strike 1907. Belfast, 1982.

O'Shannon, Cathal, The planting of the seed: an account of the founding of the ITGWU and the role it played up to the Rising in 1916. Dublin: ITGWU, 1966.

Rossiter, Nicholas, Wexford May 1917: People of steel. Wexford Council of Trade Unions, 1992.

Ryan, Bob (editor), Irish Bank Officials' Association: 70 years a-growing, 1918-1988. Dublin: IBOA, 1988.

Sinclair, Betty, A short history of the Belfast Trades Council 1881-1951. Belfast: Belfast Council of Trade Unions, 1951.

Waterford Council of Trade Unions. ICTU Souvenir Programme. Waterford, 1984.

Workers' Union of Ireland. Silver Jubilee Souvenir. Dublin, 1949.

Main Publications of ICTU

1959:   Defend Democracy – Defend PR
1963:   Guide to Safety at Work
1964:   Trade Union Structure: Report of Conference, October 1964
1972:   Memorandum on Congress Structure, Organisation and Finance
1973:   Looking at the European Community
1974:   Industrial Democracy. Report on Summer Course, July 1974
1975:   Restructuring the Irish Trade Union Movement. Report on Seminar, November 1975
1976:   Economic and Social Planning. Report of Summer Course, July 1976
1977:   Industrial Development and Job Creation. Report of Summer Course, July 1977
1980:   World Economic and Social Development: Trade Union Perspectives. Report of Summer Course, July 1980
1982:   Job Evaluation.
        Productivity Agreements
1984:   Confronting the Jobs Crisis
        Policy on Job Sharing
        Positive Action for Equal Opportunities at Work
        Third World Development: Issues for Trade Unionists
1985:   Worker Co-operatives
        Sexual Harassment
        Health and Safety Aspects of VDUs
        Women, Work and Health
1986:   Public Enterprise – Everybody's Business
        Equal Rights for Part-Time Workers
        A Plan to Work
        Using Job Evaluation to Eliminate Sex Discrimination at Work
1987:   Equality Review
        Lesbian and Gay Rights: Guidelines for Negotiators
        A Programme for Progress: Equality Report
        Understanding Trade Unions – Yesterday and Today
1988:   Trade Unions and Change
        Poverty, Unemployment and the Future of Work
        Low Pay
        A Development Plan for Dublin (with Dublin Council of Trade Unions)
1989:   Sharing the Benefits of Economic Recovery
        Public Enterprise and Economic Development. A Policy Statement on Privatisation
        A New Environment for Health and Safety at Work. Safety Health and Welfare at Work Act 1989
        Women's Participation in Trade Unions
        Third World Awareness
        Technology and Work
        Low Pay and a Legal Minimum Wage
1990:   Learning Together: Report of Conference on Joint Research between Trade Unions and Third-level Education and Research Institutes, October 1990
        Forging Links – Trading Places: You and Your Union's Role in Global Solidarity (Joint ICTU/Trocaire publication)

Industrial Relations Act 1990. A User's Guide
Submission to Second Commission on the Status of Women
Code of Practice for the Commission of Art for Public Places
1991: Economic Review
1992: Structural Funds: Opportunity for Jobs and Growth
Irish Political Economy. The Case for Consensus
A Budget for Jobs and Fairness
1993: New Forms of Work Organisation: Options for Trade Unions
    Mainstreaming Equality: Third Equality Programme 1993-98
    Working Women and Europe
    Construction Today
1994: The Intelligent Island. Developing Science, Technology and
    Information
    Network News
    The Change Project. The Changing World of Work

Northern Ireland Committee

1961: Facing the Issues
1969: Programme for Peace and Progress in Northern Ireland
1971: Programme for Peace, Employment, Reconstruction
1973: Political Policy in Northern Ireland
1974: Trade Union Policies for Peace and Prosperity in Northern
    Ireland
    Workers' Participation: A Basis for Discussion
1983: The Trade Union Alternative
1985: Reform of Social Security
    Into the 1990s
1986: A Charter for Equal Opportunity
    Peace, Work, Progress: A Statement of Principles
1987: Equality of Opportunity in Northern Ireland: A Statement of
    Trade Union Policy

Other Publications

Other publications of the ICTU include the annual (now biennial) reports; reports of the proceedings of the annual (now biennial) conferences; *Trade Union Information* (April 1960 to Winter 1980-81); various Bulletins including Third World Bulletin, Economic Bulletin, Information Bulletin; Congress Newsletter; Statistical Indicators, etc.

Trade Union Records and Archives

Cork Archives Institute, Christchurch, South Main Street, Cork.

Irish Labour History Museum and Archive, Beggar's Bush, Haddington Road, Dublin 4. [From *Saothar* 5 (1979), an annual account of all accessions has been included in the journal].

Limerick Civic Museum, John Square, Limerick.

Mid West Regional Archive, The Granary, Limerick.

Modern Records Centre, University of Warwick Library, Coventry CV4 7AL. (Contains important records, including annual reports, of trade unions and Trades Councils in Ireland).

Municipal Library, Galway.

Municipal Library, Waterford.

National Archives, Bishop Street, Dublin 2. (Includes records of Irish TUC and ICTU)

National Library of Ireland, Kildare Street, Dublin 2 (Includes Records of Irish Transport and General Workers' Union; Minute Books of Dublin Trades Council; William O'Brien Papers; Thomas Kennedy Papers; Thomas Johnson Papers; Trade union journals).

Northern Ireland Registry of Friendly Societies, 64 Chicester Street, Belfast.

Public Record Office of Northern Ireland, 66 Balmoral Avenue, Belfast. (Includes Minute Books of Belfast Trades Council).

Registry of Friendly Societies, Ship Street Gate, Dublin Castle, Dublin 2

University College Dublin, Archives Department, Belfield, Dublin 4. [Includes much of the archive material of the Irish Labour History Society].

Abbreviations

AEEU: Amalgamated Engineering and Electrical Trade Union
ASPD: Amalgamated Society of Painters and Decorators
ASTI: Association of Secondary Teachers Ireland
ASTMS: Association of Scientific, Technical, Managerial Staffs
ASW: Amalgamated Society of Woodworkers
ATGWU: Amalgamated Transport and General Workers' Union

CIU: Congress of Irish Unions
COHSE: Confederation of Health Service Employees
CPSSU: Civil and Public Services Staff Union
CSCA: Civil Service Clerical Association

DTPS: Dublin Typographical Provident Society

EETPU: Electrical Electronic Telecommunications Plumbing Union

FWUI: Federated Workers' Union of Ireland

GMB: General Municipal and Boilermakers

IBOA: Irish Bank Officials' Association
ICTU: Irish Congress of Trade Unions
IDAA: Irish Drapers' Assistants' Association
IDATU: Irish Distributive and Administrative Trade Union
IMPACT: Irish Municipal Public and Civil Service Union
INO: Irish Nurses' Organisation
INTO: Irish National Teachers' Organisation
INU: Irish Nurses Union
ITGWU: Irish Transport and General Workers' Union
ITUC: Irish Trade Union Congress
IUDWC: Irish Union of Distributive Workers and Clerks
IWWU: Irish Women Workers' Union

LGPSU: Local Government and Public Services Union

MSF: Manufacturing Science Finance Union

NICSA: Northern Ireland Civil Service Alliance
NIPSA: Northern Ireland Public Service Alliance
NUPE: National Union of Public Employees
NUR: National Union of Railwaymen
NUTGW: National Union of Tailors and Garment Workers

POWU: Post Office Workers' Union

RCA: Railway Clerks' Association

SIPTU: Services Industrial Professional Technical Union

TASS: AUEW (Technical and Supervisory Section)
TEEU: Technical Engineering and Electrical Union
TUI: Teachers' Union of Ireland

WUI: Workers' Union of Ireland

473

*Mercier Press is the oldest independent Irish
publishing house and has published books in the
fields of history, literature, folklore, music, art,
humour, drama, politics, current affairs, law
and religion. It was founded in 1944 by John
and Mary Feehan.*

*In the building up of a country
few needs are as great as that of a publishing
house which would make the people proud of
their past, and proud of themselves as a people
capable of inspiring and supporting a world of
books which was their very own. Mercier Press
has tried to be that publishing house. On the
occasion of our fiftieth anniversary we thank
the many writers and readers who have
supported us and contributed to our success.*

*We face our second half-century
with confidence.*